Shojo Beat

From Me to You

Vol. 13

Story & Art by
Karuho Shiina

Volume 13

Contents

Story Thus Far

Sawako Kuronuma has always been a loner. Though not by choice, this optimistic 16-year-old girl can't seem to make any friends. Stuck with the unfortunate nickname "Sadako" after the haunting movie character, rumors about her summoning spirits have been greatly exaggerated. With her shy personality and scary looks, most of her classmates will barely talk to her, much less look into her eyes for more than three seconds lest they be cursed. Thanks to Kazehaya, who always treats her nicely, Sawako makes her first friends at school, Ayane and Chizu.

Finally, Sawako and Kazehaya begin dating and hold hands on their first date. They unexpectedly run into Sawako's mother, who invites Kazehaya over for dinner. Sawako's father grudgingly accepts Kazehaya as his precious daughter's boyfriend. Sawako and Kazehaya become an official couple with her parents' blessing. ♥

Sawako tells Ayane and Chizu about Kazehaya and her parents. She finds out that there were some misunderstandings between the two girls in the beginning of their friendship...

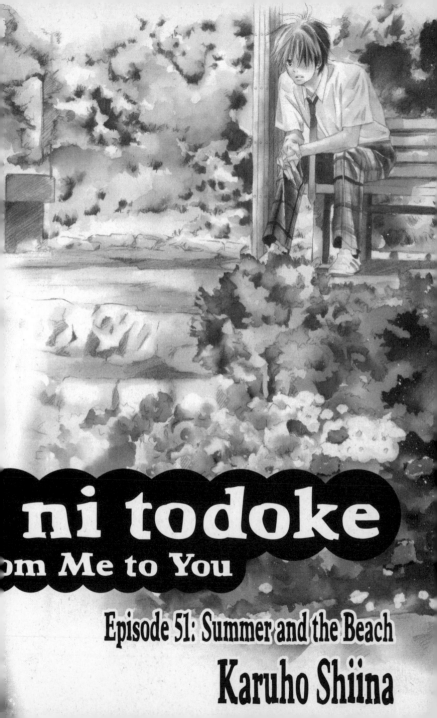

ni todoke
om Me to You

Episode 51: Summer and the Beach
Karuho Shiina

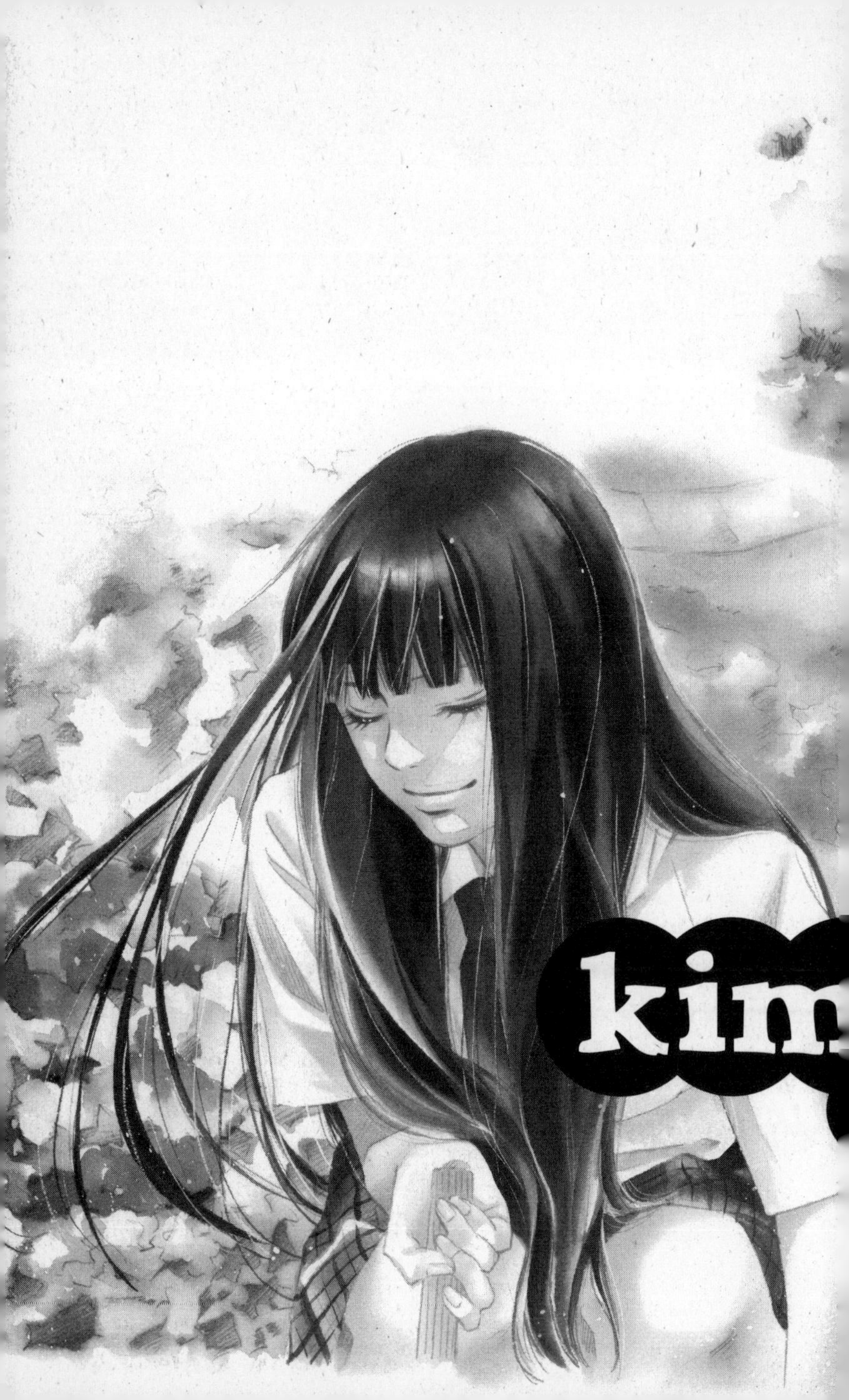
kim

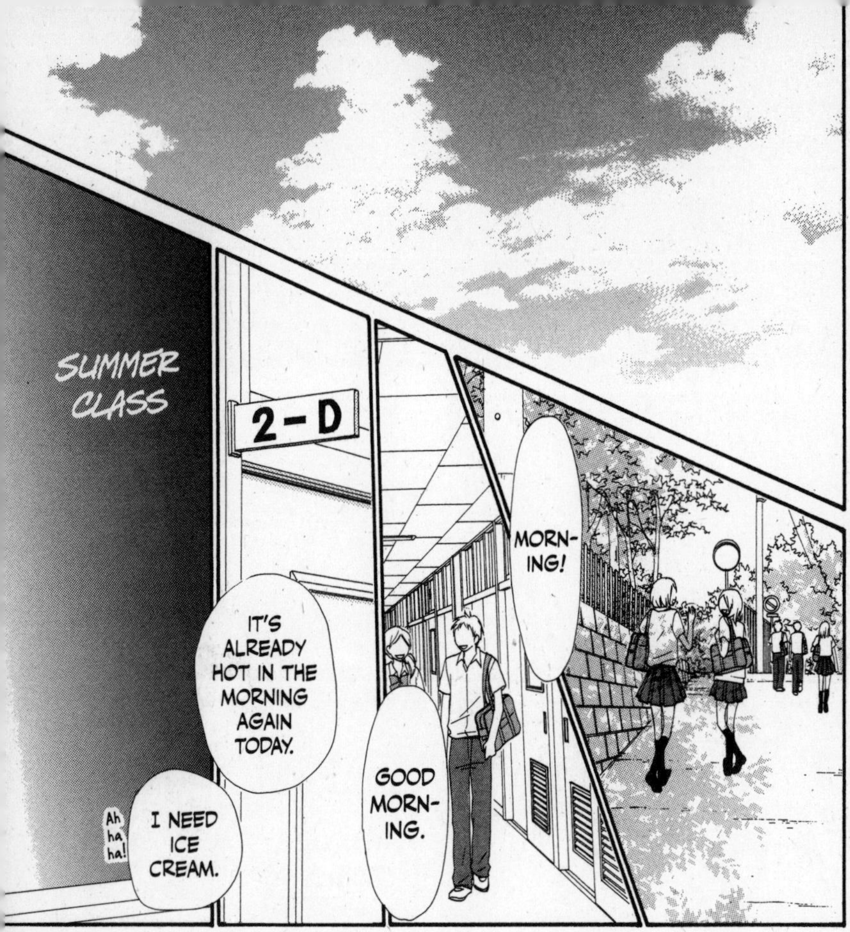
MORNING!
GOOD MORNING.
2-D
IT'S ALREADY HOT IN THE MORNING AGAIN TODAY.
I NEED ICE CREAM.
Ah ha ha!
SUMMER CLASS

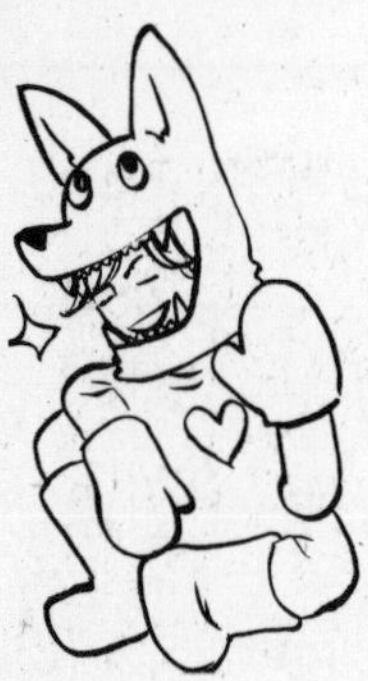

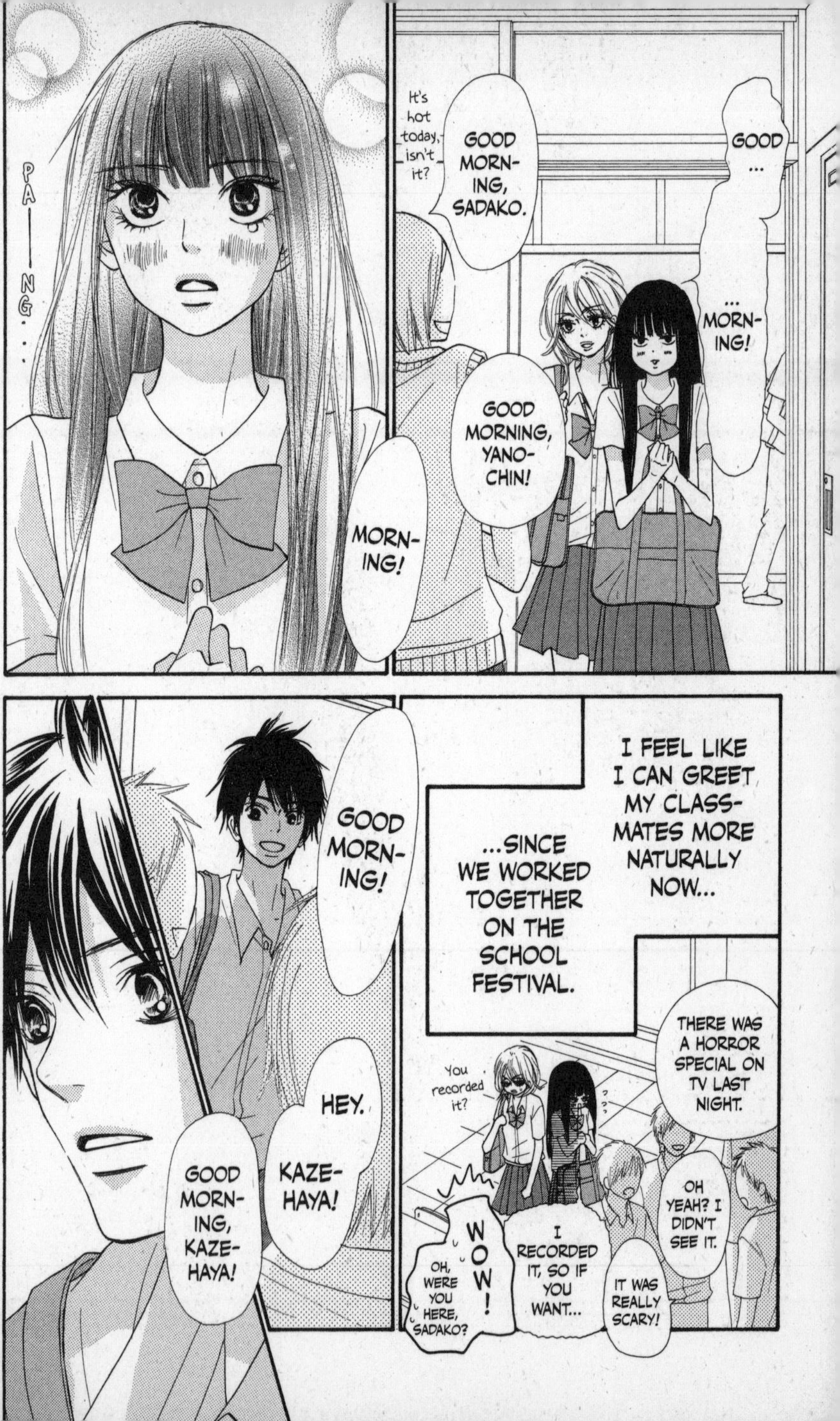
GOOD ...
... MORNING!
GOOD MORNING, SADAKO.
It's hot today, isn't it?
GOOD MORNING, YANO-CHIN!
MORNING!
PA—NG...
I FEEL LIKE I CAN GREET MY CLASSMATES MORE NATURALLY NOW...
...SINCE WE WORKED TOGETHER ON THE SCHOOL FESTIVAL.
THERE WAS A HORROR SPECIAL ON TV LAST NIGHT.
OH YEAH? I DIDN'T SEE IT.
You recorded it?
IT WAS REALLY SCARY!
I RECORDED IT, SO IF YOU WANT...
WOW!
OH, WERE YOU HERE, SADAKO?
GOOD MORNING!
HEY.
KAZEHAYA!
GOOD MORNING, KAZEHAYA!

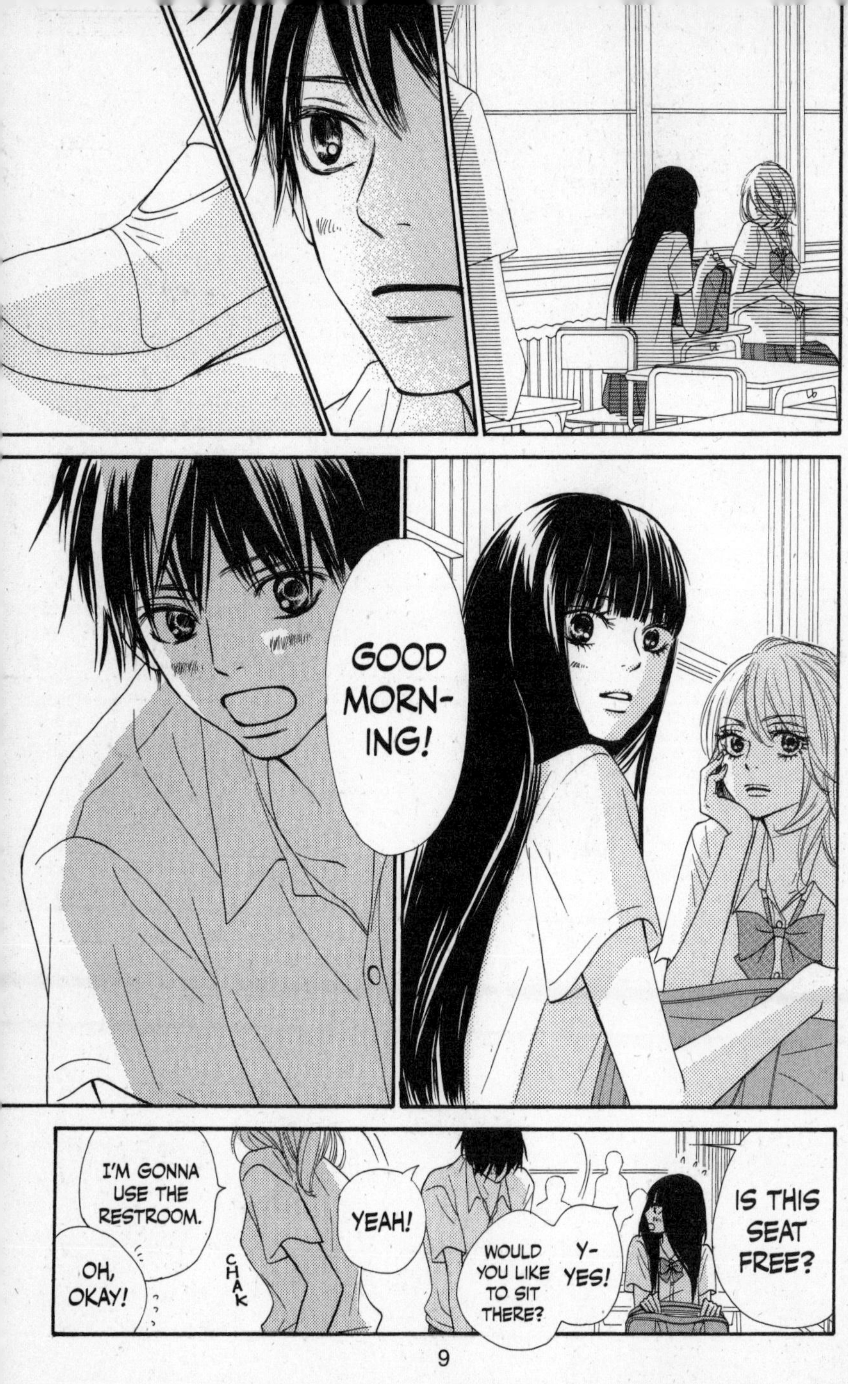

GOOD MORNING!
IS THIS SEAT FREE?
Y- YES!
WOULD YOU LIKE TO SIT THERE?
YEAH!
CHAK
I'M GONNA USE THE RESTROOM.
OH, OKAY!

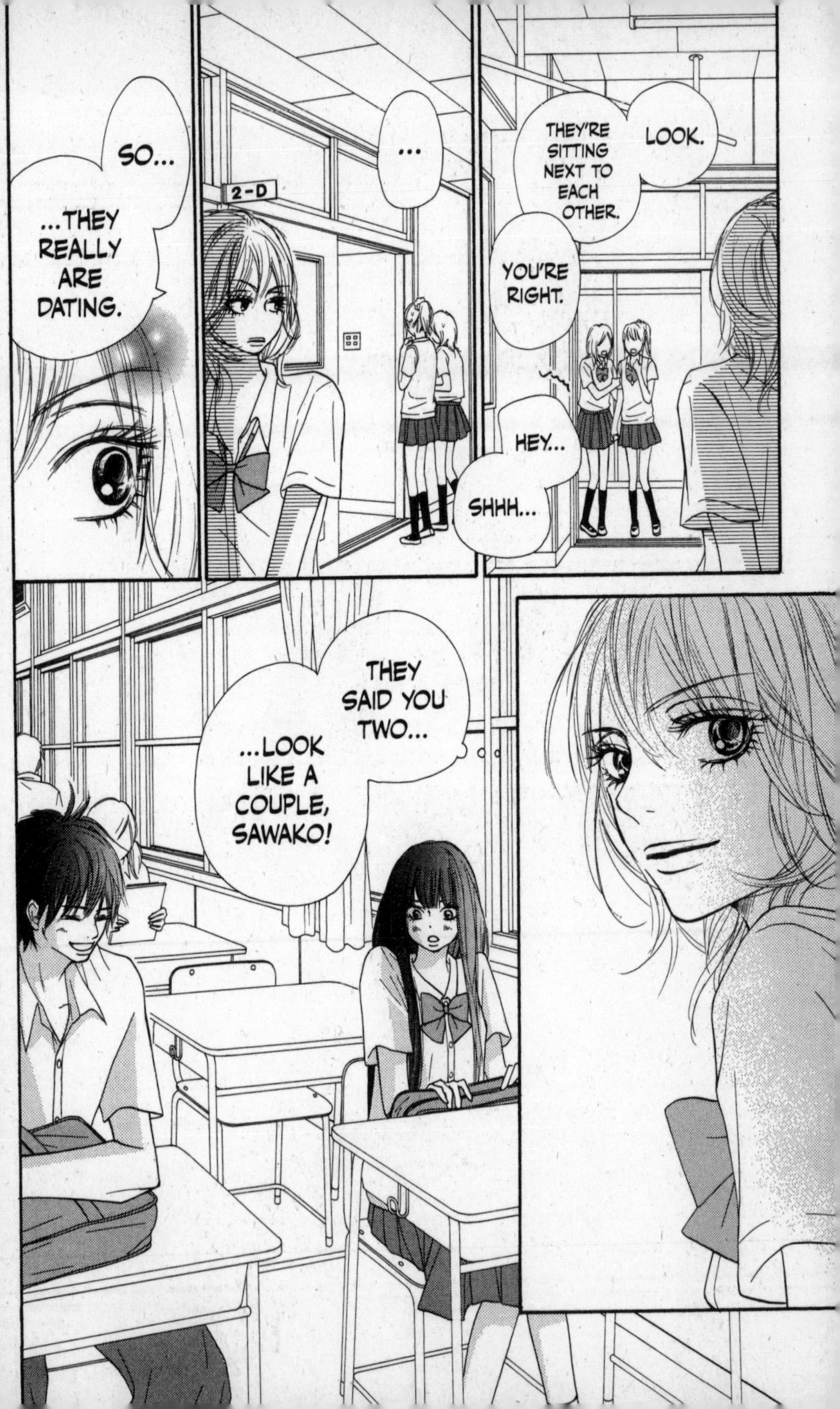
LOOK.
THEY'RE SITTING NEXT TO EACH OTHER.
YOU'RE RIGHT.
HEY...
SHHH...
...
SO...
...THEY REALLY ARE DATING.
THEY SAID YOU TWO...
...LOOK LIKE A COUPLE, SAWAKO!

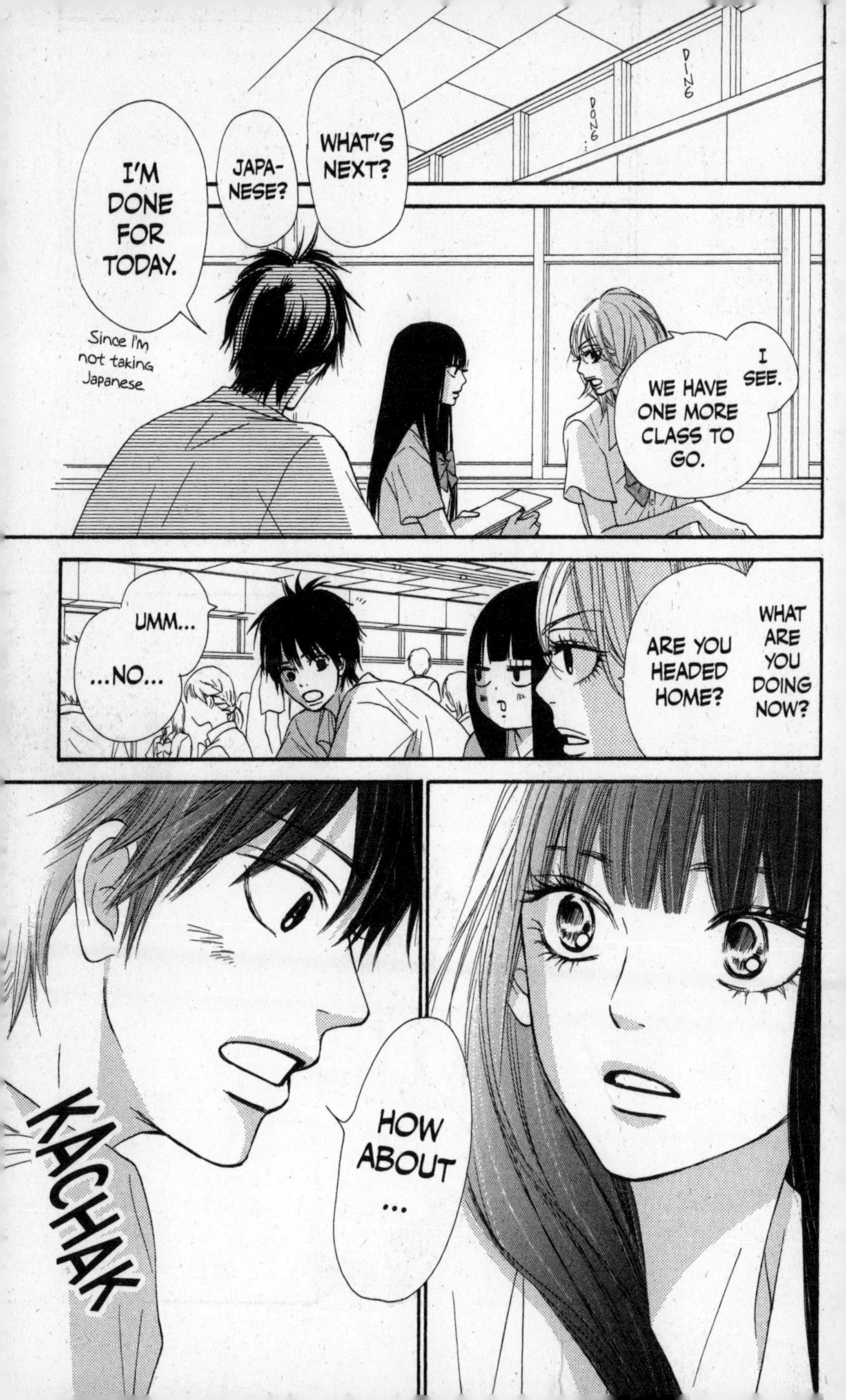
DING
DONG...
WHAT'S NEXT?
JAPA-NESE?
I'M DONE FOR TODAY.
Since I'm not taking Japanese.
I SEE.
WE HAVE ONE MORE CLASS TO GO.
WHAT ARE YOU DOING NOW?
ARE YOU HEADED HOME?
UMM...
...NO...
HOW ABOUT ...
KACHAK

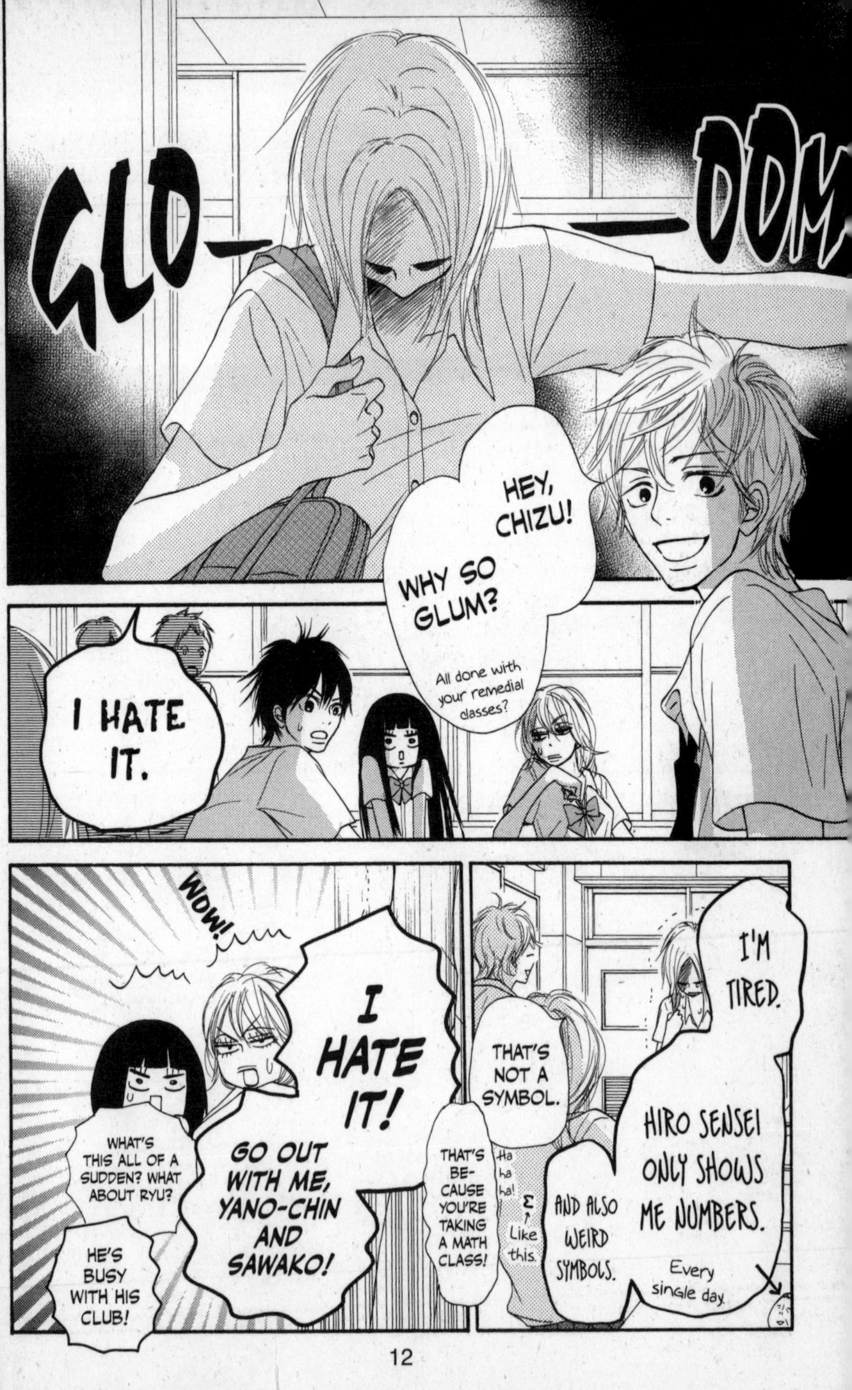
GLO——OOM
HEY, CHIZU! WHY SO GLUM?
All done with your remedial classes?
I HATE IT.
I'M TIRED.
HIRO SENSEI ONLY SHOWS ME NUMBERS.
Every single day.
AND ALSO WEIRD SYMBOLS.
Σ Like this.
Ha ha ha!
THAT'S NOT A SYMBOL.
THAT'S BE-CAUSE YOU'RE TAKING A MATH CLASS!
WOW!
I HATE IT!
GO OUT WITH ME, YANO-CHIN AND SAWAKO!
WHAT'S THIS ALL OF A SUDDEN? WHAT ABOUT RYU?
HE'S BUSY WITH HIS CLUB!

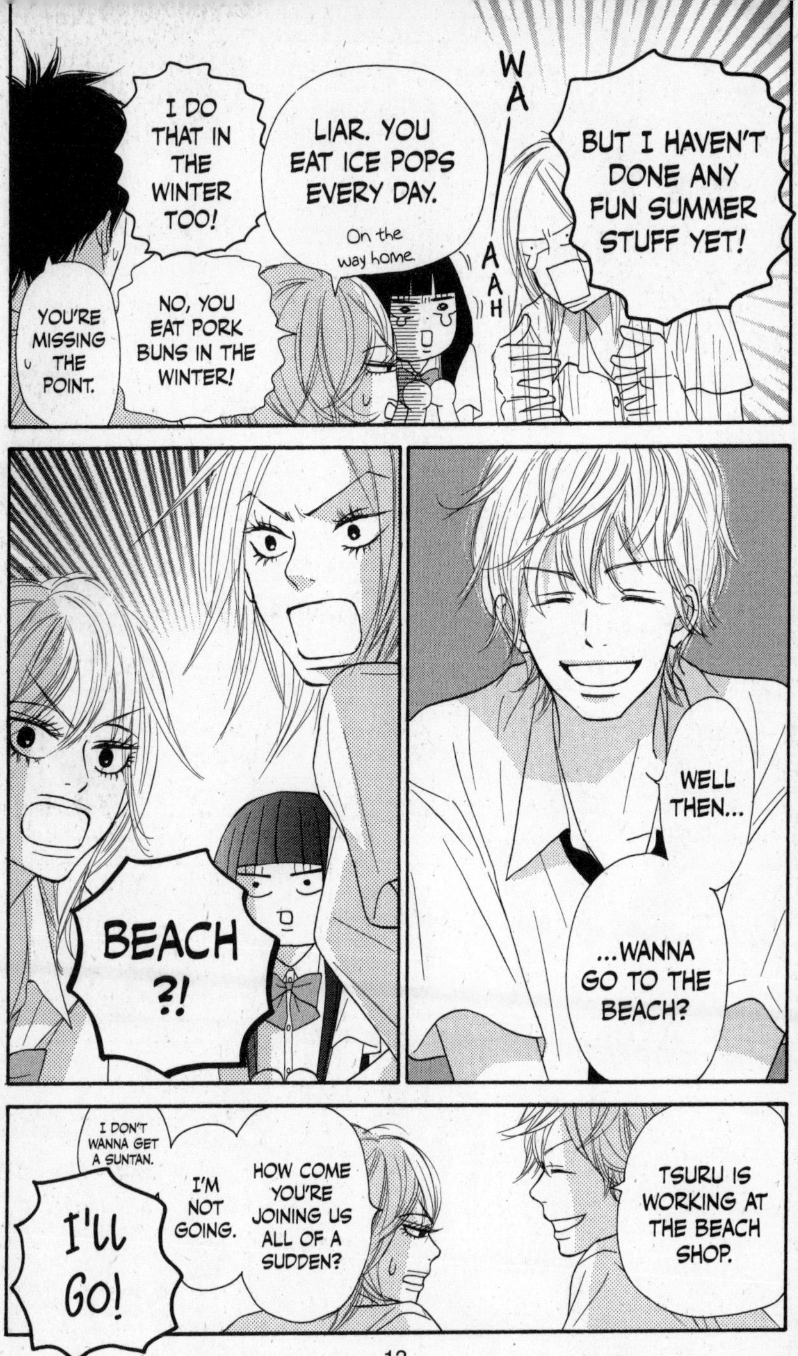
WAAAH
BUT I HAVEN'T DONE ANY FUN SUMMER STUFF YET!
LIAR. YOU EAT ICE POPS EVERY DAY.
On the way home.
I DO THAT IN THE WINTER TOO!
NO, YOU EAT PORK BUNS IN THE WINTER!
YOU'RE MISSING THE POINT.
WELL THEN...
...WANNA GO TO THE BEACH?
BEACH ?!
TSURU IS WORKING AT THE BEACH SHOP.
HOW COME YOU'RE JOINING US ALL OF A SUDDEN?
I'M NOT GOING.
I DON'T WANNA GET A SUNTAN.
I'LL GO!

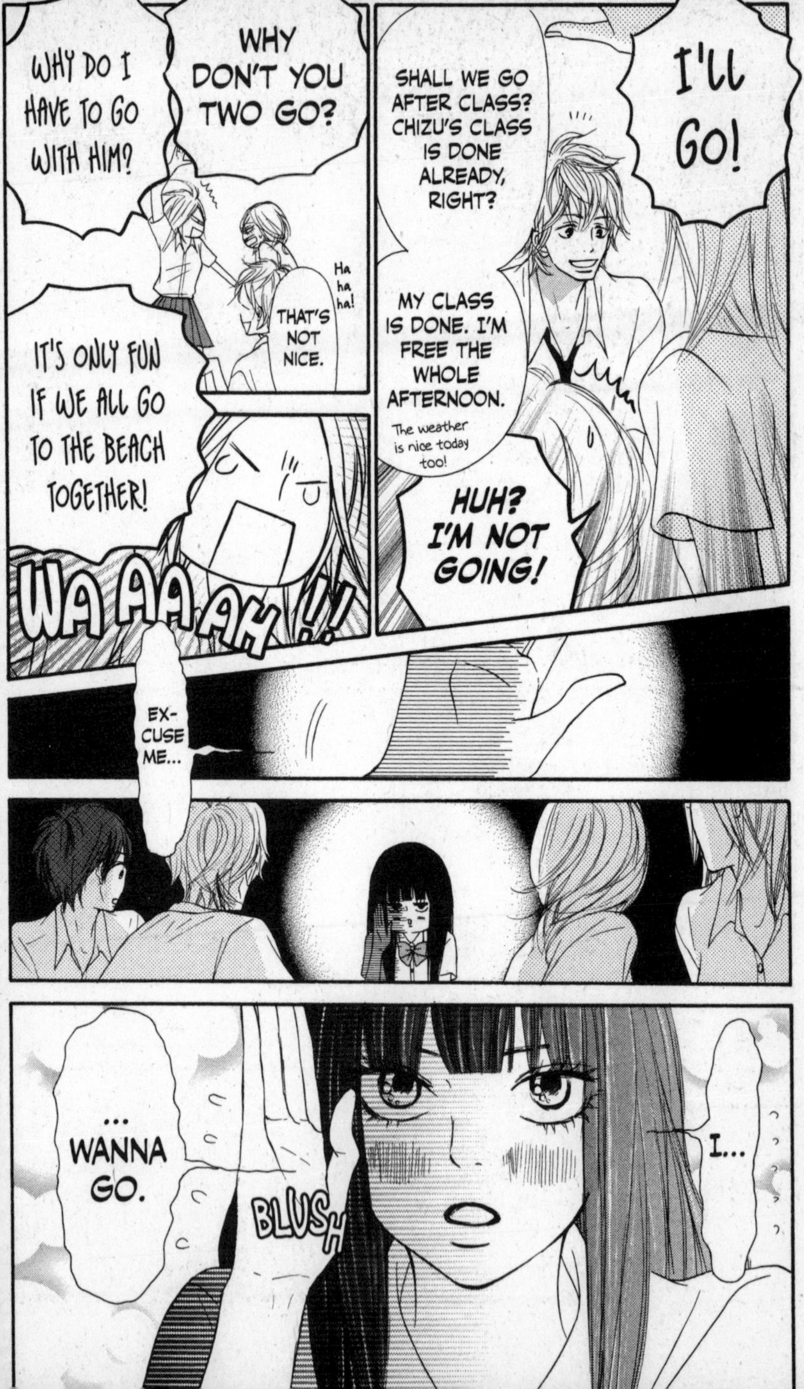
I'LL GO!
SHALL WE GO AFTER CLASS? CHIZU'S CLASS IS DONE ALREADY, RIGHT?
MY CLASS IS DONE. I'M FREE THE WHOLE AFTERNOON.
The weather is nice today too!
HUH? I'M NOT GOING!
WHY DON'T YOU TWO GO?
WHY DO I HAVE TO GO WITH HIM?
Ha ha ha!
THAT'S NOT NICE.
IT'S ONLY FUN IF WE ALL GO TO THE BEACH TOGETHER!
WA AA AH !!
EX-CUSE ME...
I...
... WANNA GO.
BLUSH

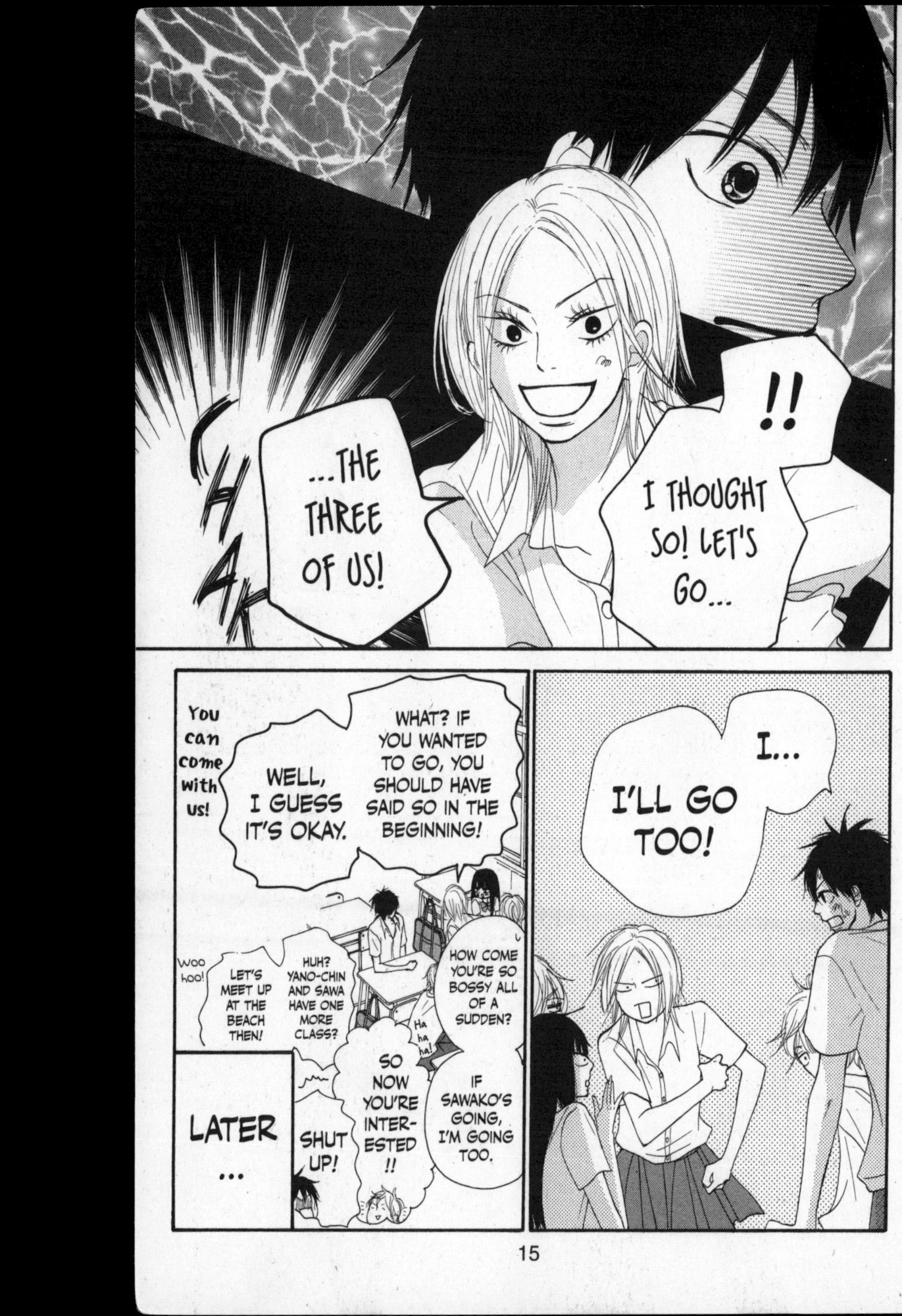
!!
I THOUGHT SO! LET'S GO...
...THE THREE OF US!
CHAK
I...
I'LL GO TOO!
WHAT? IF YOU WANTED TO GO, YOU SHOULD HAVE SAID SO IN THE BEGINNING!
WELL, I GUESS IT'S OKAY.
You can come with us!
HOW COME YOU'RE SO BOSSY ALL OF A SUDDEN?
HUH? YANO-CHIN AND SAWA HAVE ONE MORE CLASS?
LET'S MEET UP AT THE BEACH THEN!
Woo hoo!
Ha ha ha!
IF SAWAKO'S GOING, I'M GOING TOO.
SO NOW YOU'RE INTERESTED!!
SHUT UP!
LATER ...

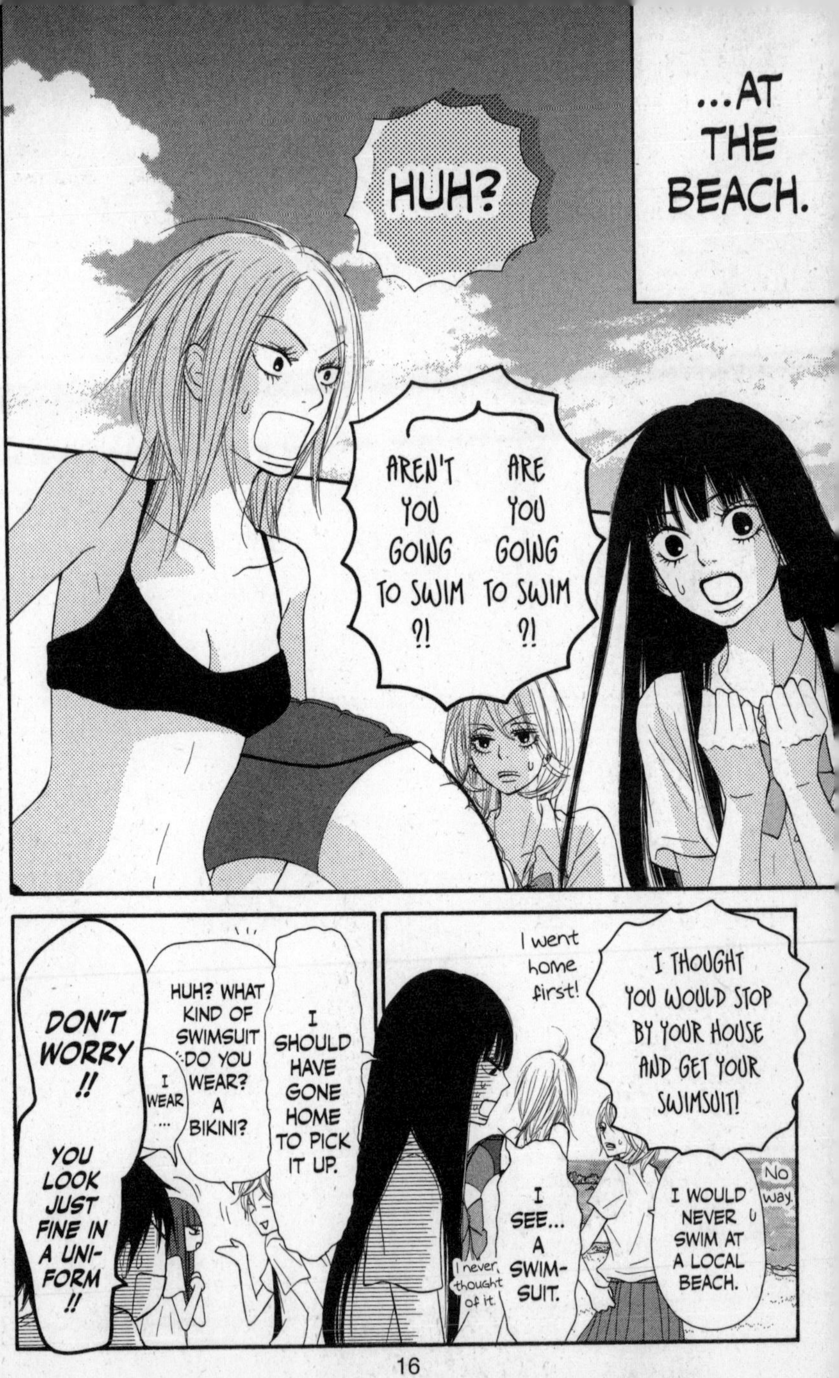
...AT THE BEACH.
HUH?
AREN'T YOU GOING TO SWIM ?! ARE YOU GOING TO SWIM ?!
I THOUGHT YOU WOULD STOP BY YOUR HOUSE AND GET YOUR SWIMSUIT!
I went home first!
No way.
I WOULD NEVER SWIM AT A LOCAL BEACH.
I SEE... A SWIM-SUIT.
I never thought of it.
I SHOULD HAVE GONE HOME TO PICK IT UP.
HUH? WHAT KIND OF SWIMSUIT DO YOU WEAR? A BIKINI?
I WEAR ...
DON'T WORRY !!
YOU LOOK JUST FINE IN A UNI-FORM !!

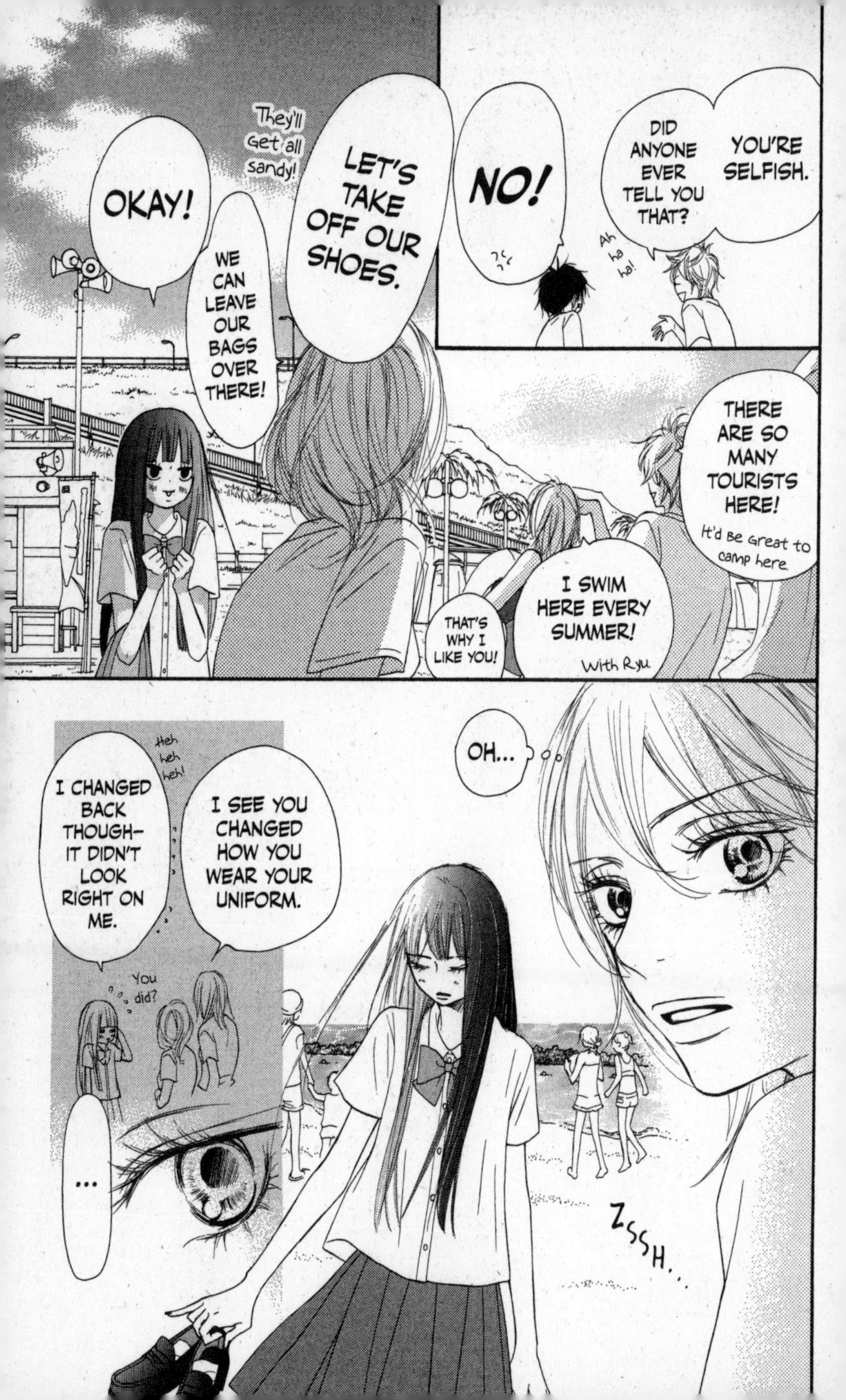
YOU'RE SELFISH.
DID ANYONE EVER TELL YOU THAT?
Ah ha ha!
NO!
THERE ARE SO MANY TOURISTS HERE!
It'd be great to camp here.
I SWIM HERE EVERY SUMMER!
With Ryu
THAT'S WHY I LIKE YOU!
LET'S TAKE OFF OUR SHOES.
They'll get all sandy!
OKAY!
WE CAN LEAVE OUR BAGS OVER THERE!
OH...
ZSSH...
I SEE YOU CHANGED HOW YOU WEAR YOUR UNIFORM.
Heh heh heh!
I CHANGED BACK THOUGH— IT DIDN'T LOOK RIGHT ON ME.
You did?
...

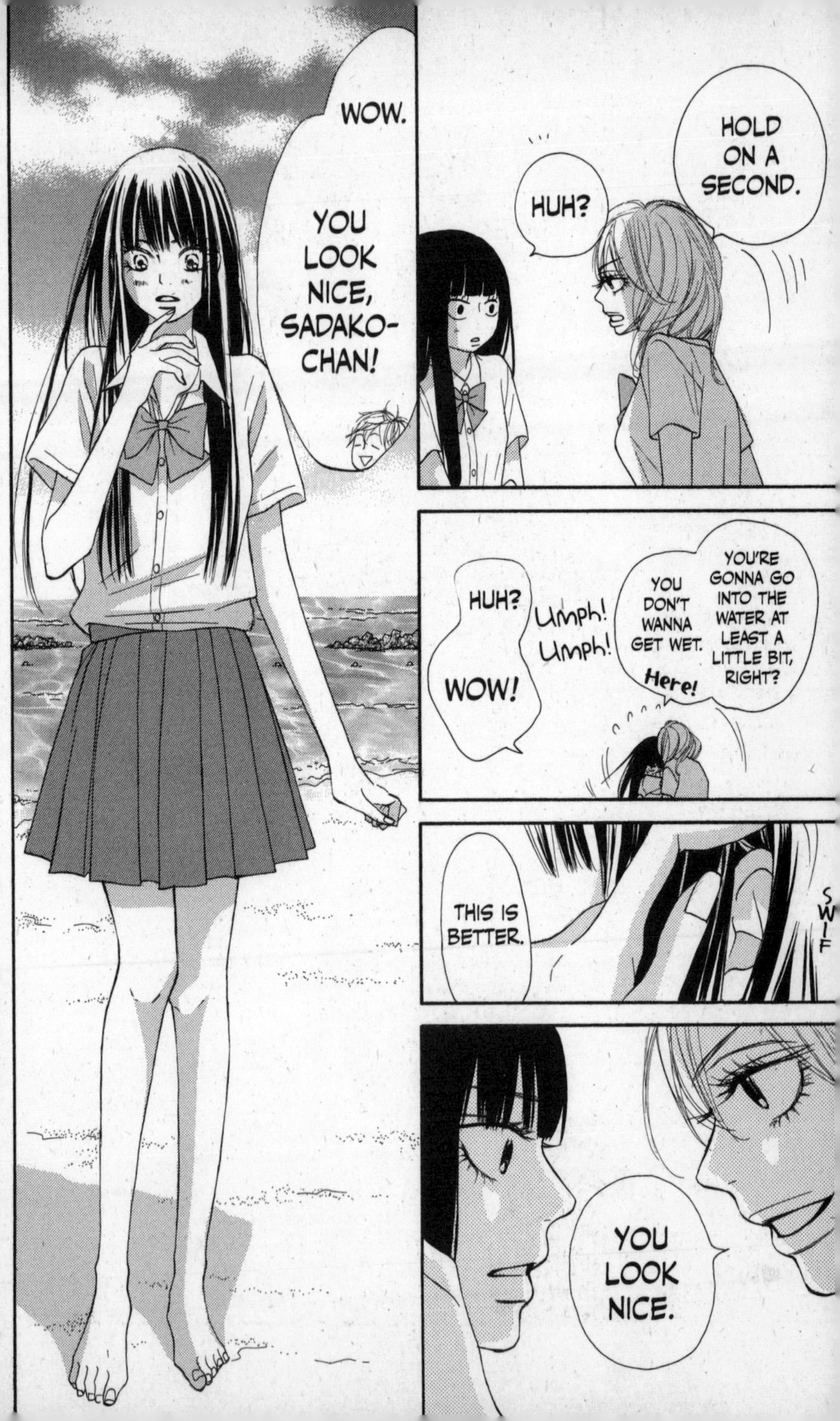
HOLD ON A SECOND.
HUH?
YOU'RE GONNA GO INTO THE WATER AT LEAST A LITTLE BIT, RIGHT?
YOU DON'T WANNA GET WET.
Here!
Umph! Umph!
HUH?
WOW!
SWIF
THIS IS BETTER.
YOU LOOK NICE.
WOW.
YOU LOOK NICE, SADAKO-CHAN!

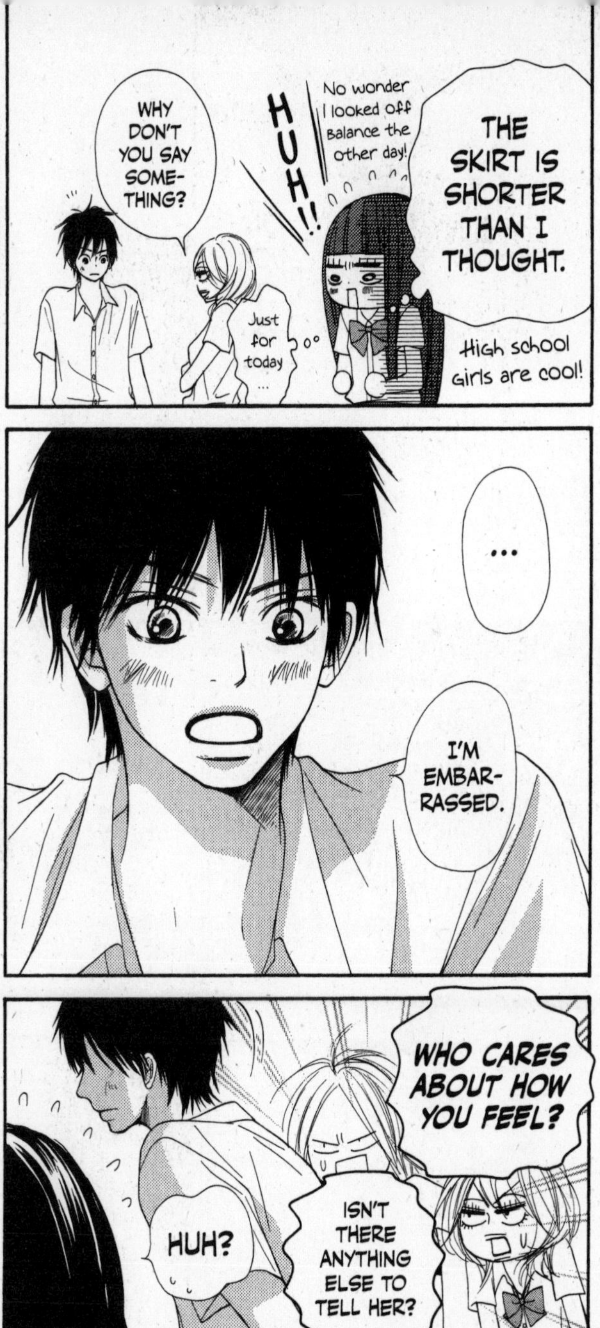

THE SKIRT IS SHORTER THAN I THOUGHT.
No wonder I looked off balance the other day!
HUH!!
WHY DON'T YOU SAY SOME-THING?
High school girls are cool!
Just for today ...
...
I'M EMBAR-RASSED.
WHO CARES ABOUT HOW YOU FEEL?
ISN'T THERE ANYTHING ELSE TO TELL HER?
HUH?

KARUPIN on JAPAN 1

Hi, how are you? I'm Shiina. This is volume 13. There are six sidebars in this volume. I usually only have four, but there are five episodes and I made the mistake of making two sidebars for one episode, so there are a total of six in this volume.

I'm forgetful these days. I forget things just by changing the position of my neck. Every day is a battle. I have to write down necessary stuff right away. Seriously.

If I remember correctly, volume 12 came out while the movie of *Kimi ni* was showing in theaters. Between volumes 12 and 13, there was the movie, and the second season of the TV anime series started. Lots of fun stuff has happened. I'm so happy! ♡

Since I have six sidebars, I can spread out my comments.

Continued in sidebar 2 →

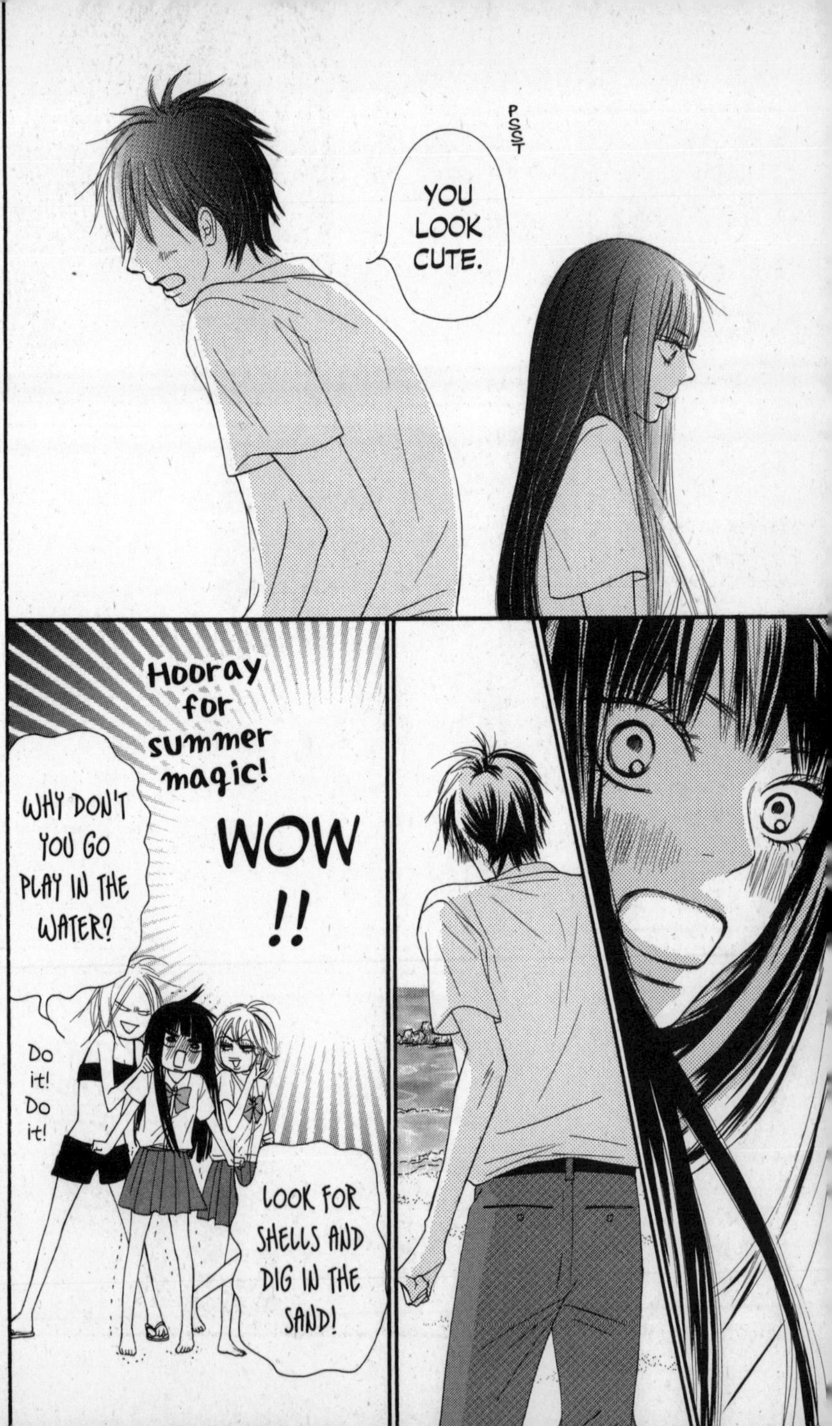
PSST
YOU LOOK CUTE.
Hooray for summer magic!
WOW!!
WHY DON'T YOU GO PLAY IN THE WATER?
Do it! Do it!
LOOK FOR SHELLS AND DIG IN THE SAND!

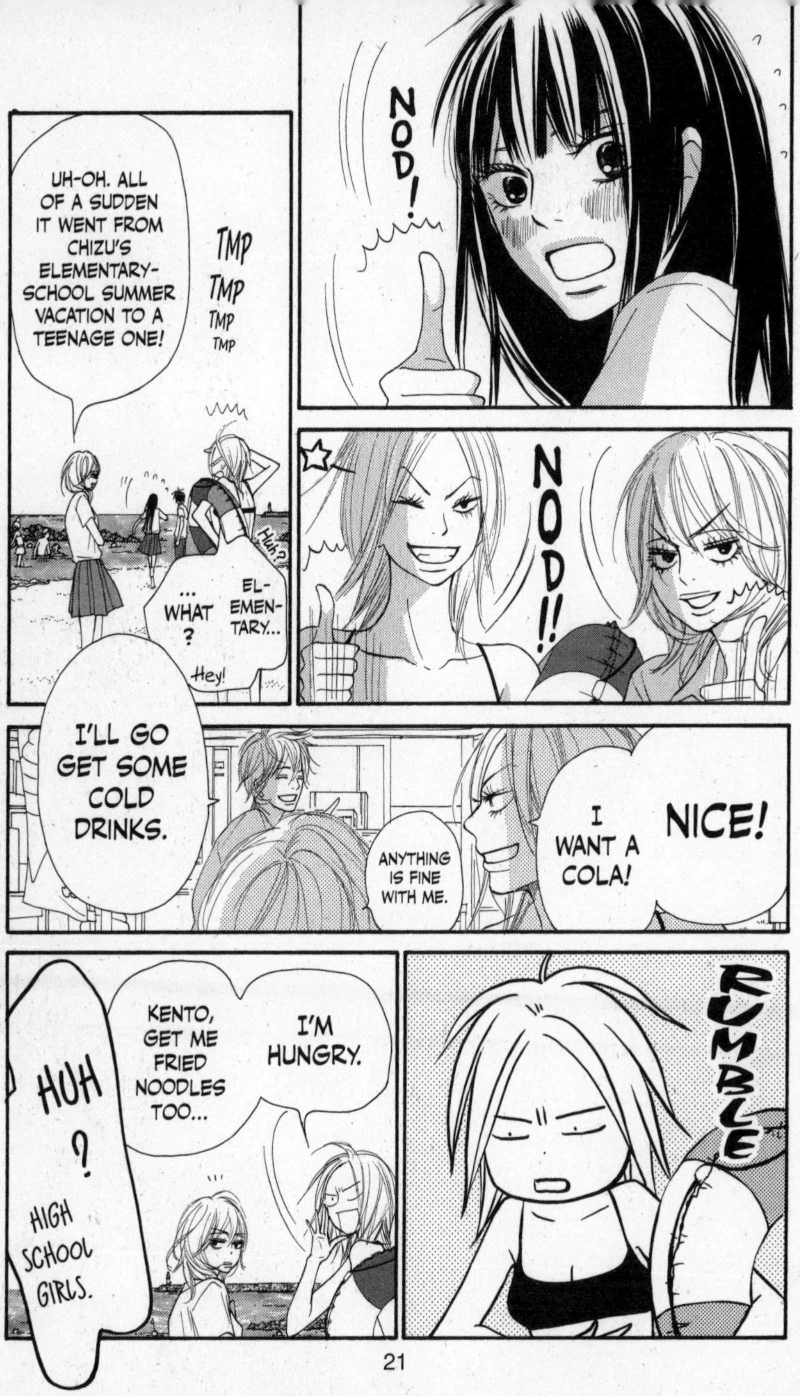
NOD!
NOD!!
UH-OH. ALL OF A SUDDEN IT WENT FROM CHIZU'S ELEMENTARY-SCHOOL SUMMER VACATION TO A TEENAGE ONE!
TMP TMP TMP TMP
Huh?
EL-EMENTARY...
... WHAT?
Hey!
NICE!
I WANT A COLA!
ANYTHING IS FINE WITH ME.
I'LL GO GET SOME COLD DRINKS.
RUMBLE
I'M HUNGRY.
KENTO, GET ME FRIED NOODLES TOO...
HUH?
HIGH SCHOOL GIRLS.

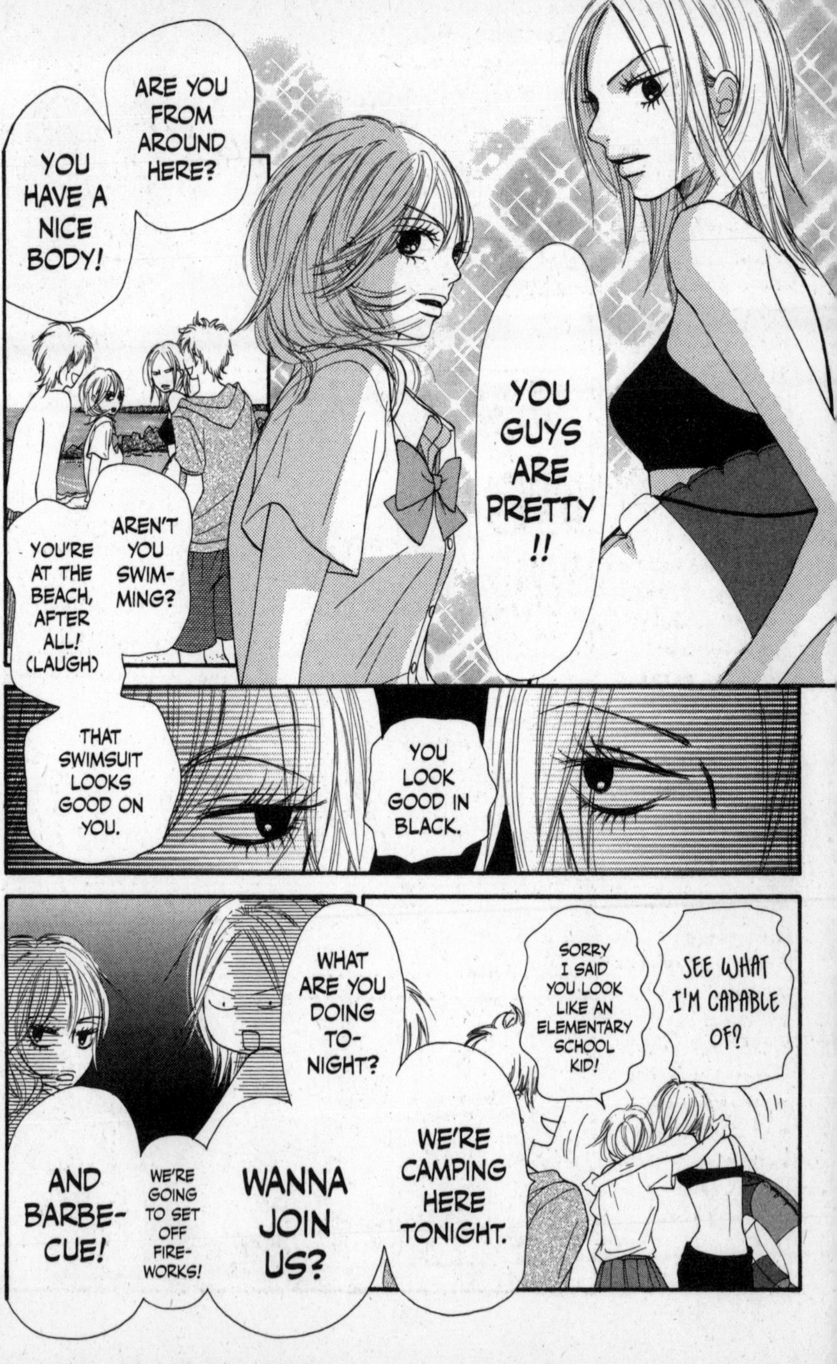
YOU GUYS ARE PRETTY!!
ARE YOU FROM AROUND HERE?
YOU HAVE A NICE BODY!
AREN'T YOU SWIMMING?
YOU'RE AT THE BEACH, AFTER ALL! (LAUGH)
YOU LOOK GOOD IN BLACK.
THAT SWIMSUIT LOOKS GOOD ON YOU.
SEE WHAT I'M CAPABLE OF?
SORRY I SAID YOU LOOK LIKE AN ELEMENTARY SCHOOL KID!
WHAT ARE YOU DOING TONIGHT?
WE'RE CAMPING HERE TONIGHT.
WANNA JOIN US?
WE'RE GOING TO SET OFF FIREWORKS!
AND BARBECUE!

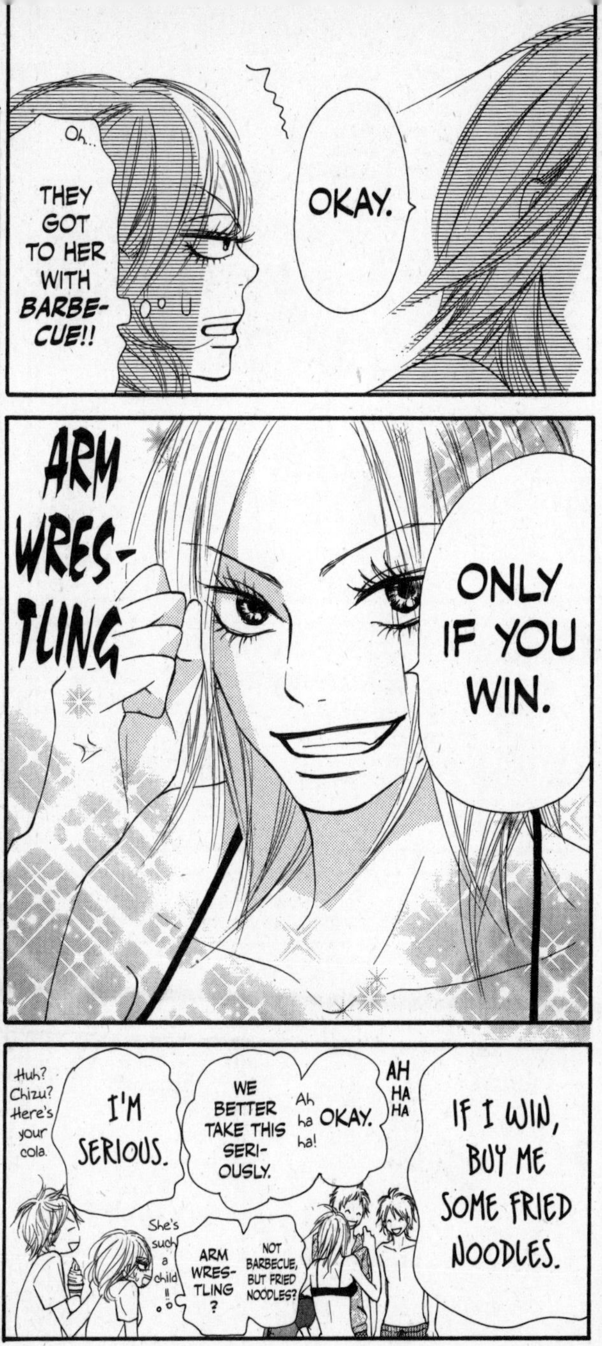
OKAY.
Oh...
THEY GOT TO HER WITH BARBECUE!!
ONLY IF YOU WIN.
ARM WRES-TLING
IF I WIN, BUY ME SOME FRIED NOODLES.
AH HA HA
OKAY.
Ah ha ha!
WE BETTER TAKE THIS SERI-OUSLY.
I'M SERIOUS.
Huh? Chizu? Here's your cola.
NOT BARBECUE, BUT FRIED NOODLES?
ARM WRES-TLING?
She's such a child!!

KARUPIN on JAPAN 2

I was so glad to be able to meet the staff in charge of promoting the movie, Tabe Mikako-chan (who plays Sawako), and Miura Haruma-kun (who plays Kazehaya) at the prerelease event for the movie in Sapporo. They were cute and cool! I'll be their fan and support their work from afar forever...! I had a chance to watch them while they attended a local afternoon show in Hokkaido. Ms. Hoshizawa, a professional chef, walked by right in front of me... Sorry for talking about such local stuff.

At the premier, girls were screaming at Haruma-kun and boys were sending out love-shouts to Mikako-chan. The fans were pretty excited to see the stars right in front of them. I was watching from a corner, but my tension was pretty high as well!

Continued in sidebar 3 ➜

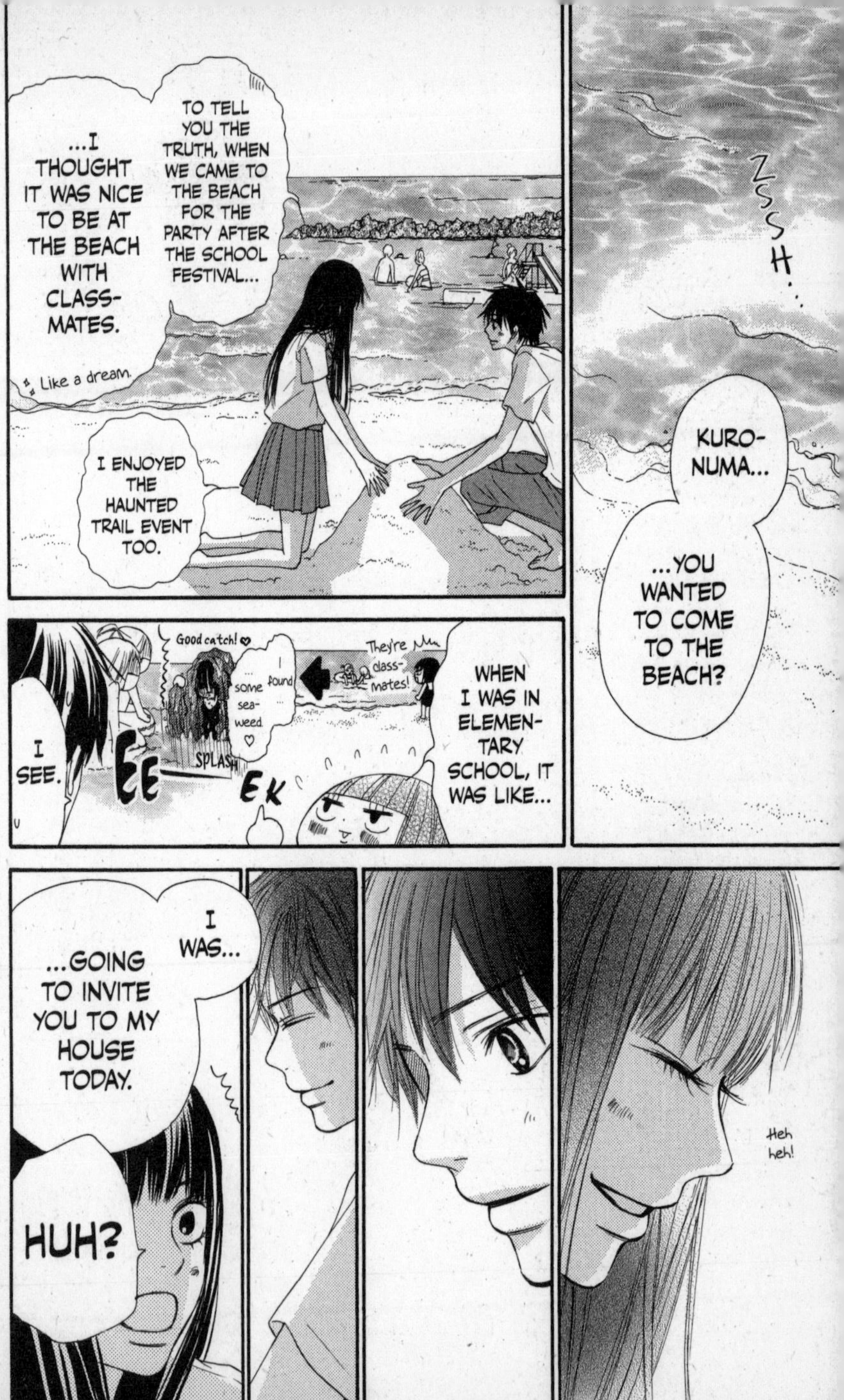
ZSSH...
KURONUMA...
...YOU WANTED TO COME TO THE BEACH?
TO TELL YOU THE TRUTH, WHEN WE CAME TO THE BEACH FOR THE PARTY AFTER THE SCHOOL FESTIVAL...
...I THOUGHT IT WAS NICE TO BE AT THE BEACH WITH CLASSMATES.
Like a dream.
I ENJOYED THE HAUNTED TRAIL EVENT TOO.
WHEN I WAS IN ELEMENTARY SCHOOL, IT WAS LIKE...
They're classmates!
I found... some seaweed.
Good catch!
EEK
SPLASH
I SEE.
Heh heh!
I WAS...
...GOING TO INVITE YOU TO MY HOUSE TODAY.
HUH?

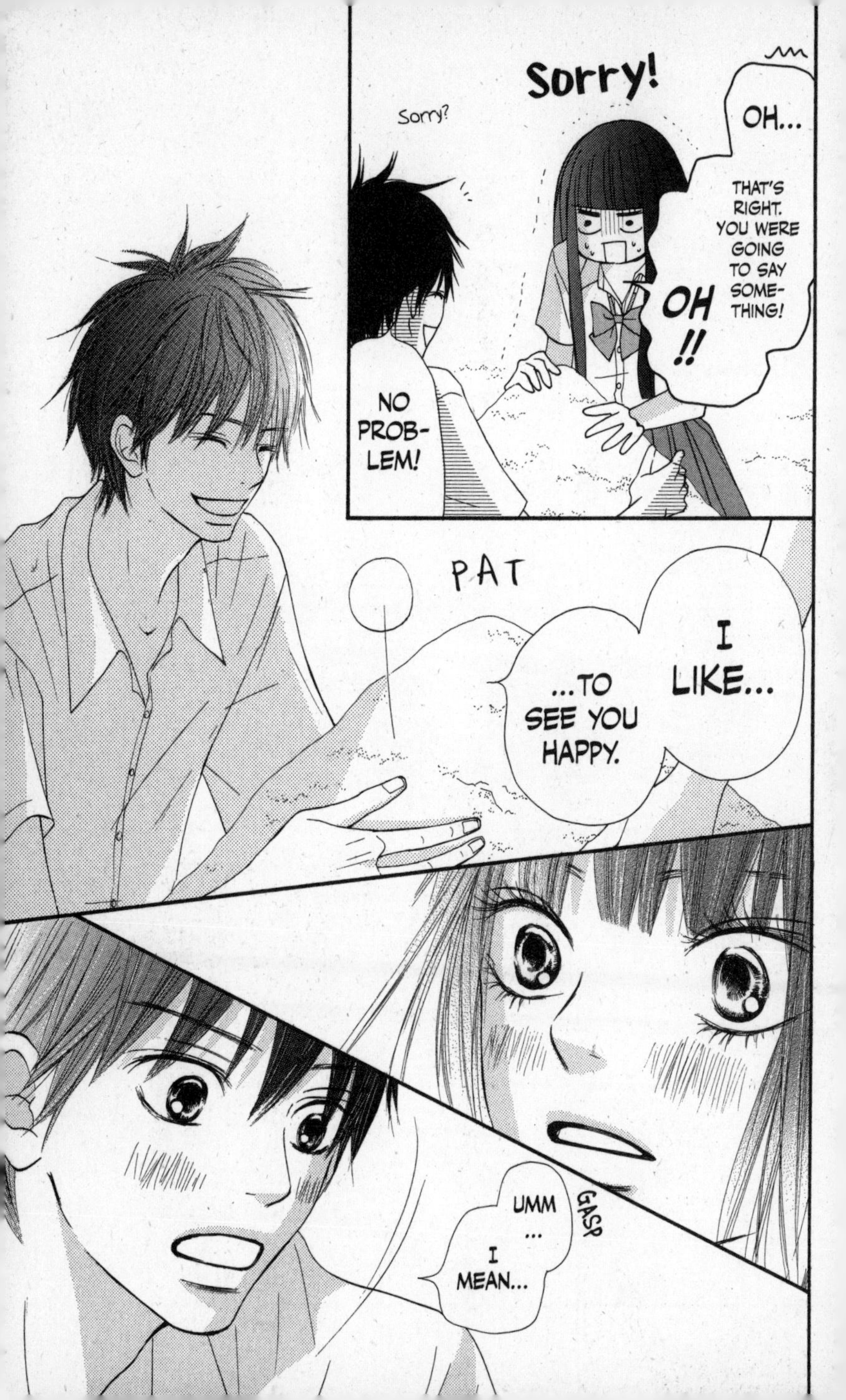
OH...
THAT'S RIGHT. YOU WERE GOING TO SAY SOMETHING!
Sorry!
OH!!
Sorry?
NO PROBLEM!
I LIKE...
PAT
...TO SEE YOU HAPPY.
GASP
UMM... I MEAN...

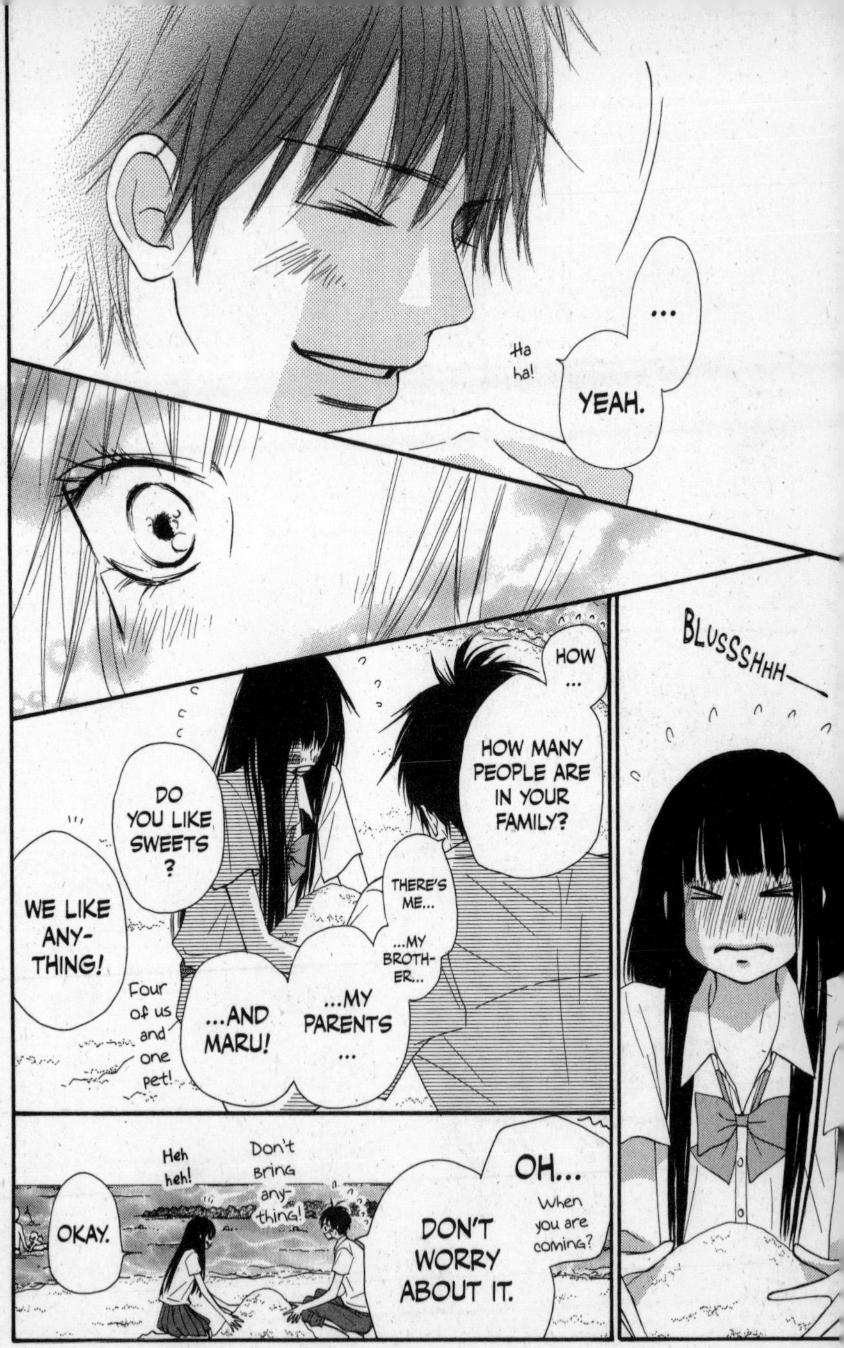
...
Ha ha!
YEAH.
BLUSSSHHH—
HOW ...
HOW MANY PEOPLE ARE IN YOUR FAMILY?
THERE'S ME...
...MY BROTHER...
...MY PARENTS ...
...AND MARU!
Four of us and one pet!
DO YOU LIKE SWEETS ?
WE LIKE ANYTHING!
OH...
When you are coming?
DON'T WORRY ABOUT IT.
Don't bring anything!
Heh heh!
OKAY.

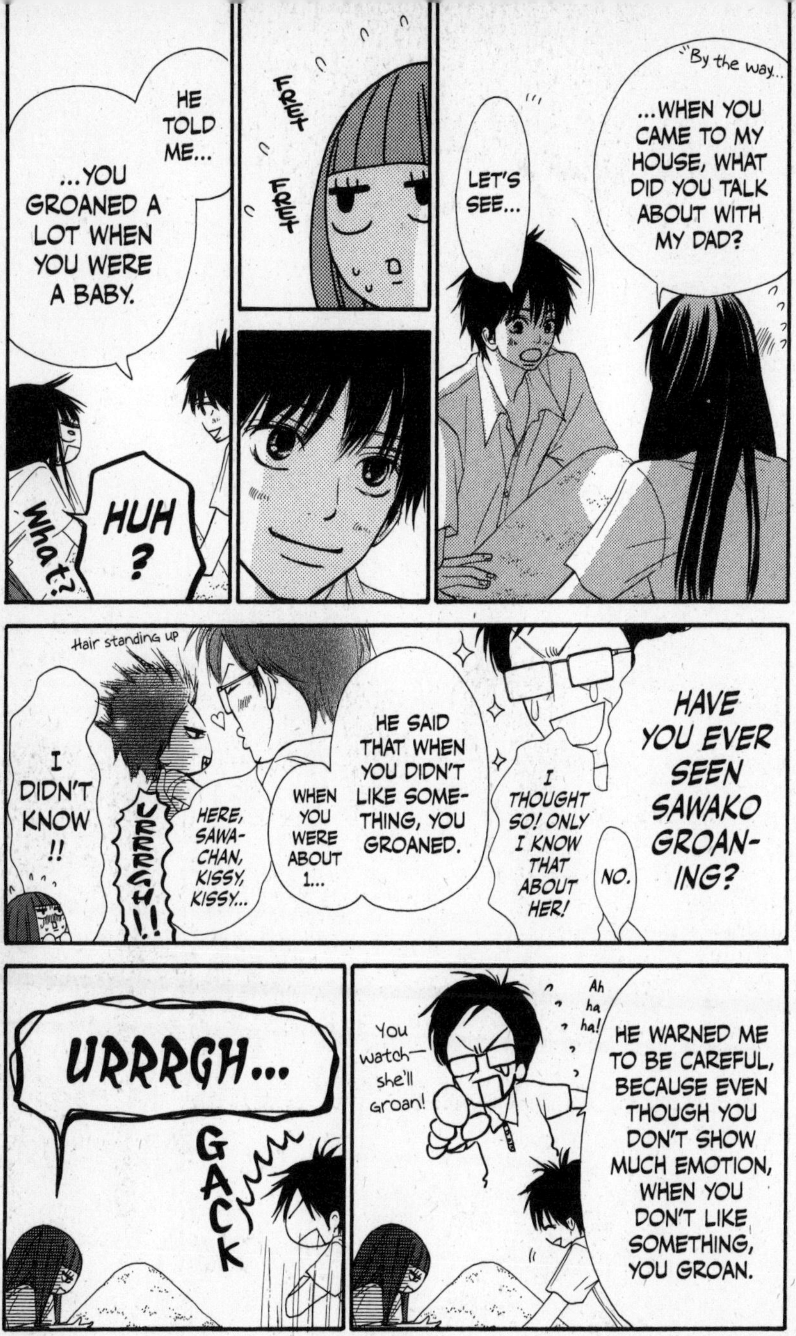
By the way...
...WHEN YOU CAME TO MY HOUSE, WHAT DID YOU TALK ABOUT WITH MY DAD?
LET'S SEE...
FRET FRET
HE TOLD ME...
...YOU GROANED A LOT WHEN YOU WERE A BABY.
HUH?
What?
HAVE YOU EVER SEEN SAWAKO GROAN-ING?
NO.
I THOUGHT SO! ONLY I KNOW THAT ABOUT HER!
HE SAID THAT WHEN YOU DIDN'T LIKE SOME-THING, YOU GROANED.
WHEN YOU WERE ABOUT 1...
HERE, SAWA-CHAN, KISSY, KISSY...
URRRGH!!
Hair standing up
I DIDN'T KNOW!!
HE WARNED ME TO BE CAREFUL, BECAUSE EVEN THOUGH YOU DON'T SHOW MUCH EMOTION, WHEN YOU DON'T LIKE SOMETHING, YOU GROAN.
Ah ha ha!
You watch—she'll Groan!
URRRGH...
GACK

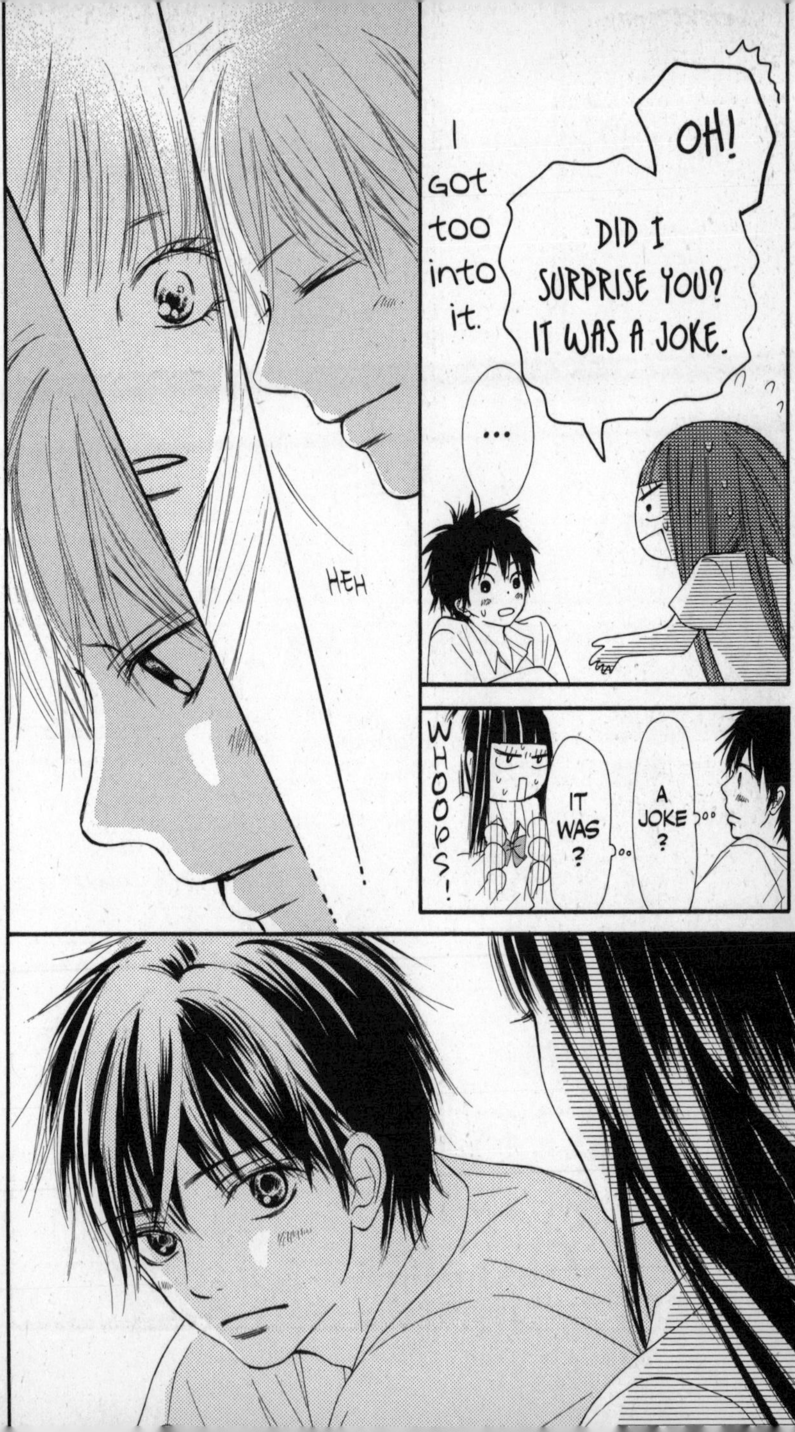
OH!
DID I SURPRISE YOU? IT WAS A JOKE.
I got too into it.
...
A JOKE..?
IT WAS?..
WHOOPS!
HEH

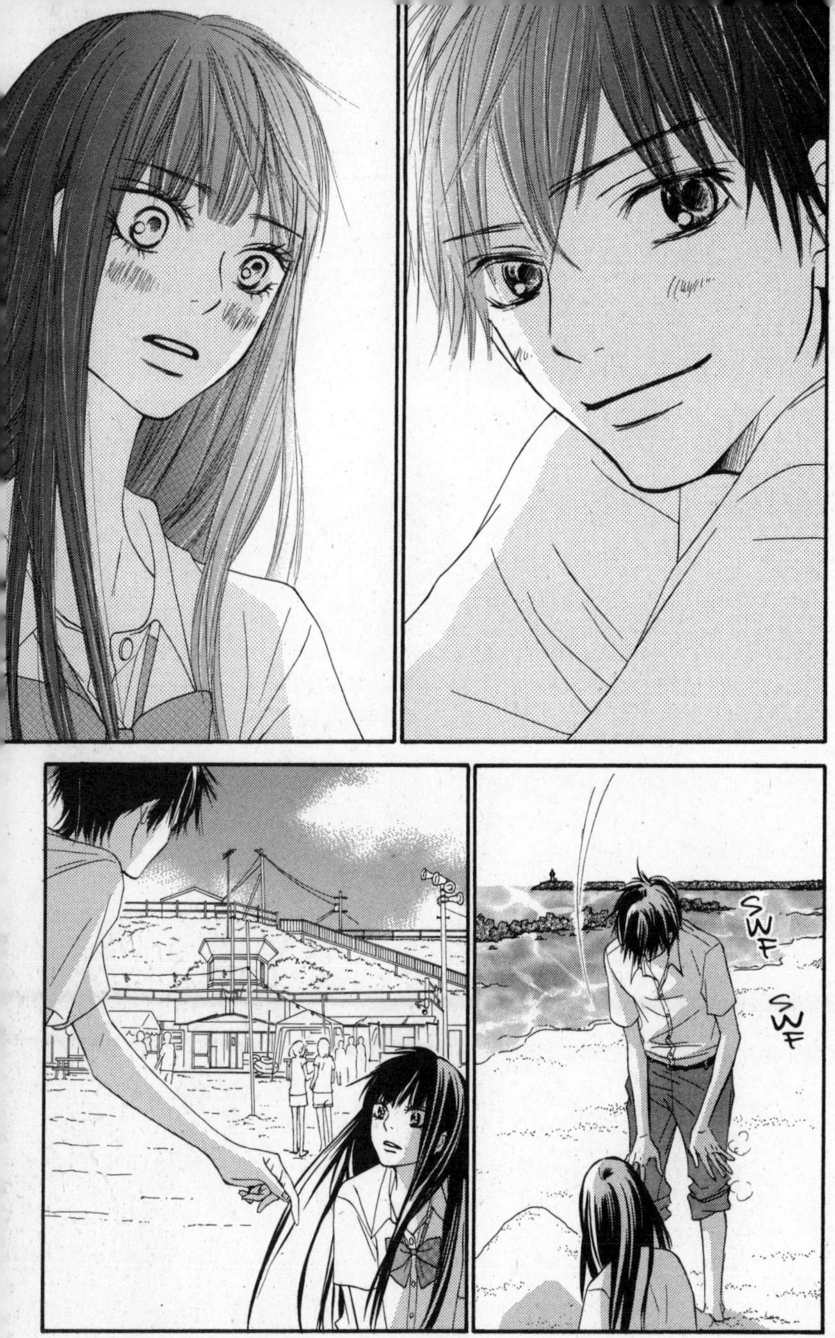
SWF
SWF

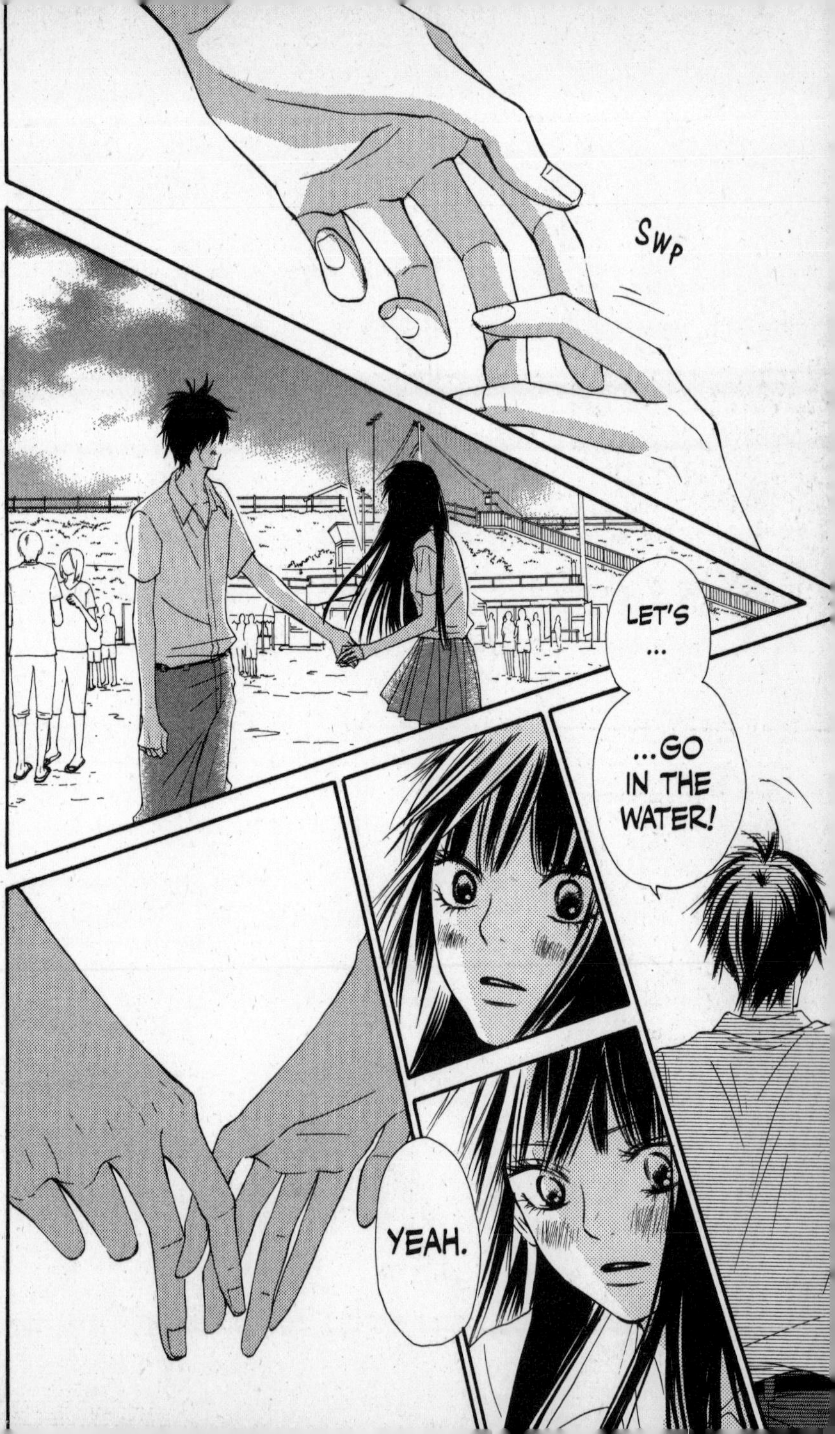
SWP
LET'S ...
...GO IN THE WATER!
YEAH.

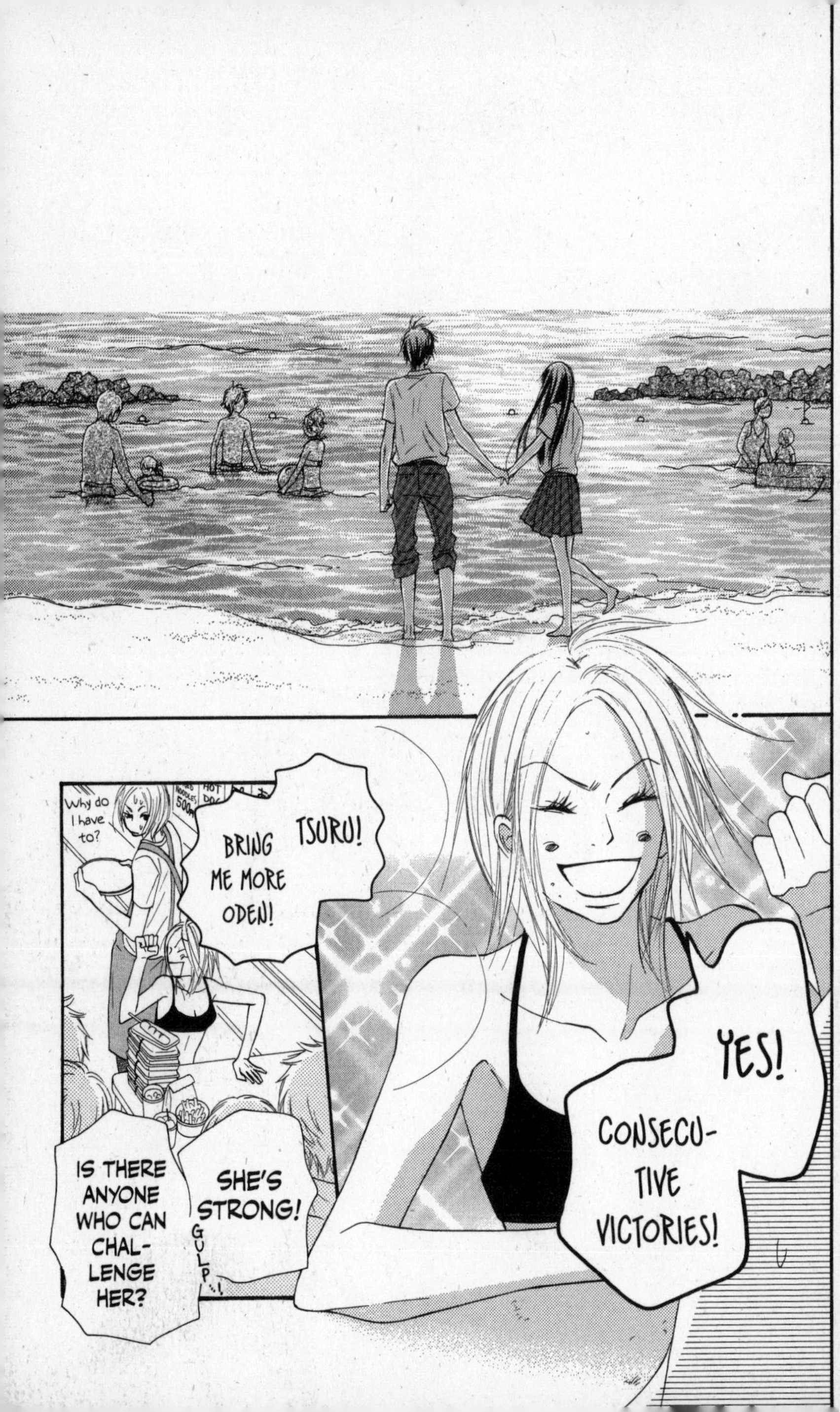
YES!
CONSECUTIVE VICTORIES!
TSURU!
BRING ME MORE ODEN!
Why do I have to?
SHE'S STRONG!
GULP..!
IS THERE ANYONE WHO CAN CHALLENGE HER?

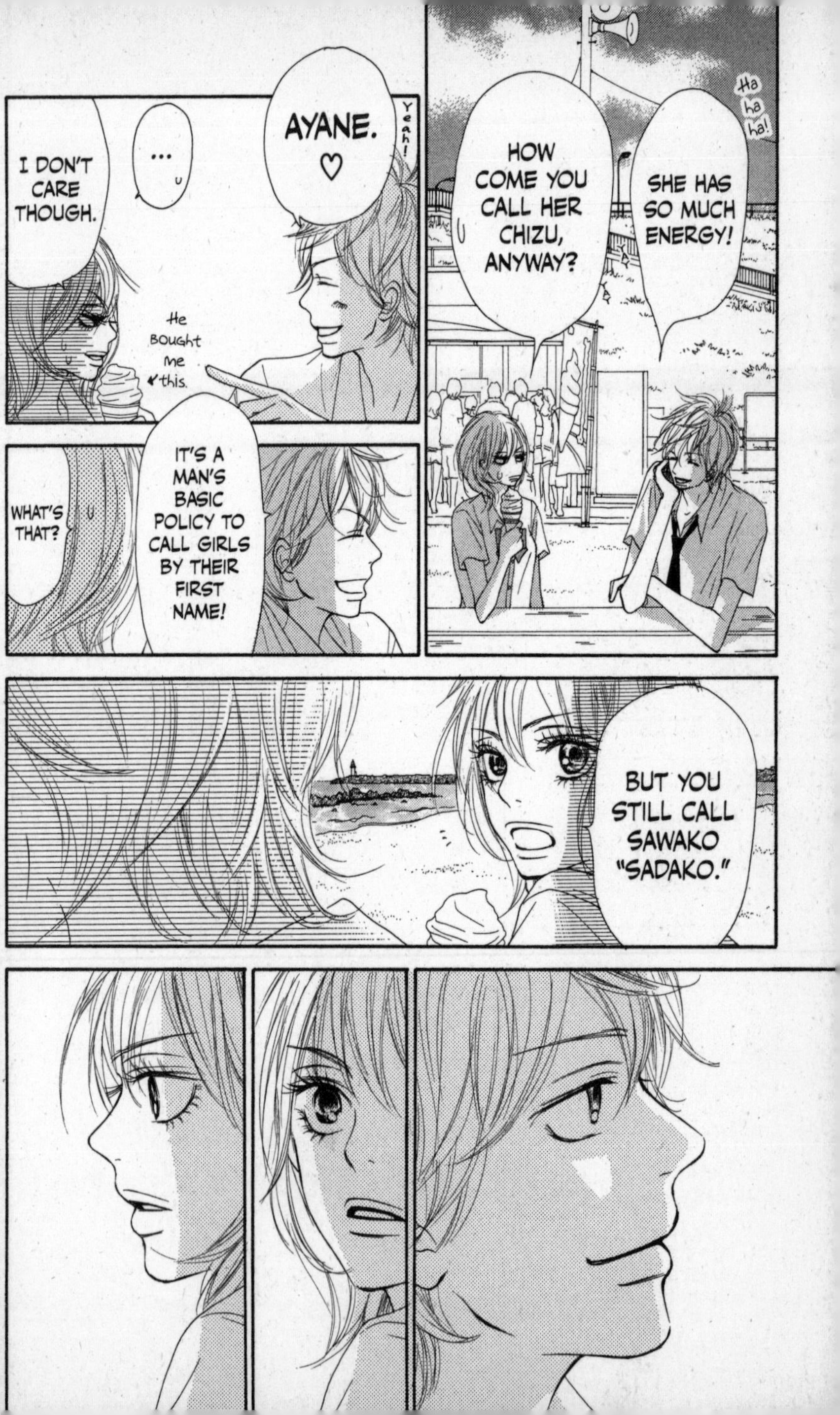
Ha ha ha!
SHE HAS SO MUCH ENERGY!
HOW COME YOU CALL HER CHIZU, ANYWAY?
Yeah!
AYANE. ♡
He bought me this.
...
I DON'T CARE THOUGH.
IT'S A MAN'S BASIC POLICY TO CALL GIRLS BY THEIR FIRST NAME!
WHAT'S THAT?
BUT YOU STILL CALL SAWAKO "SADAKO."

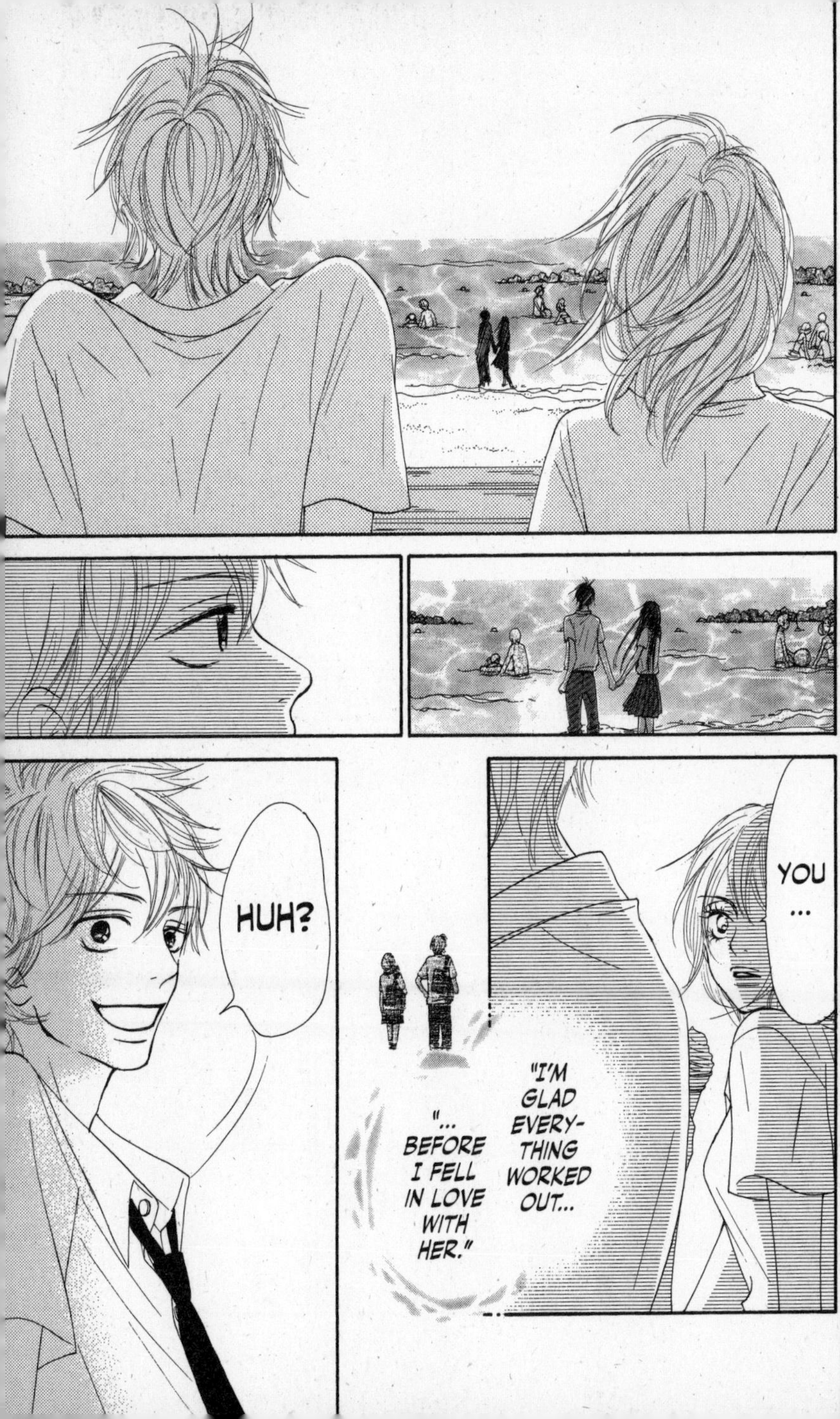
YOU ...
"I'M GLAD EVERY-THING WORKED OUT...
"... BEFORE I FELL IN LOVE WITH HER."
HUH?

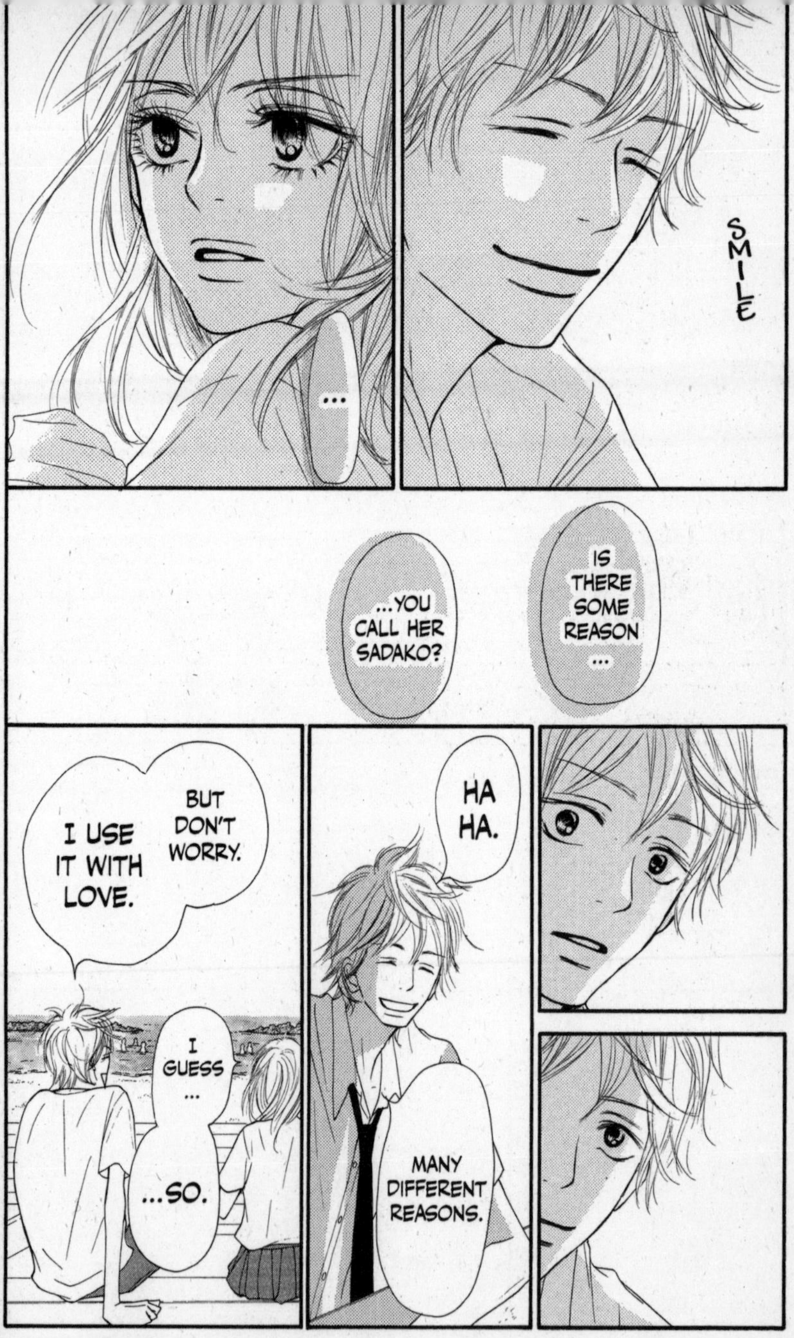
SMILE
...
IS THERE SOME REASON ...
...YOU CALL HER SADAKO?
HA HA.
MANY DIFFERENT REASONS.
BUT DON'T WORRY.
I USE IT WITH LOVE.
I GUESS ...
...SO.

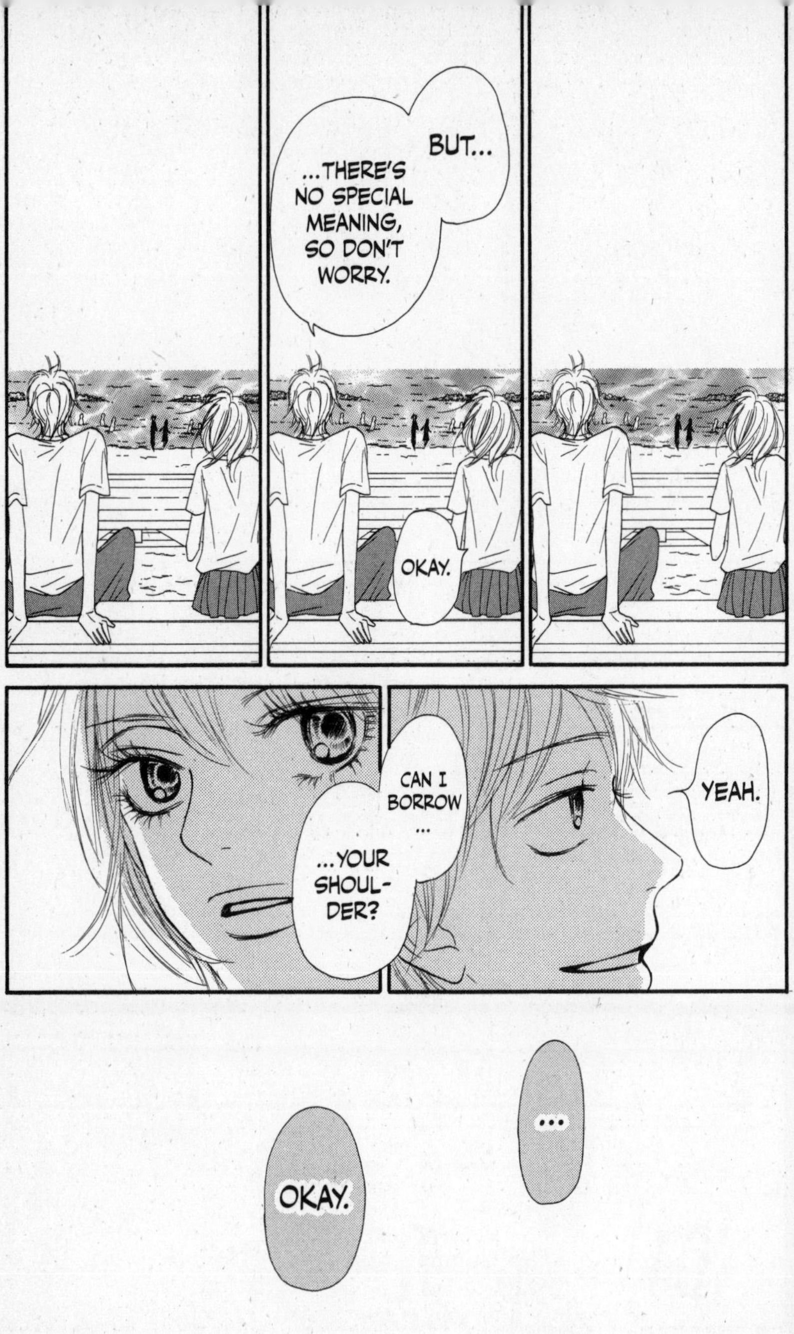
BUT...
...THERE'S NO SPECIAL MEANING, SO DON'T WORRY.
OKAY.
CAN I BORROW ...
...YOUR SHOUL-DER?
YEAH.
...
OKAY.

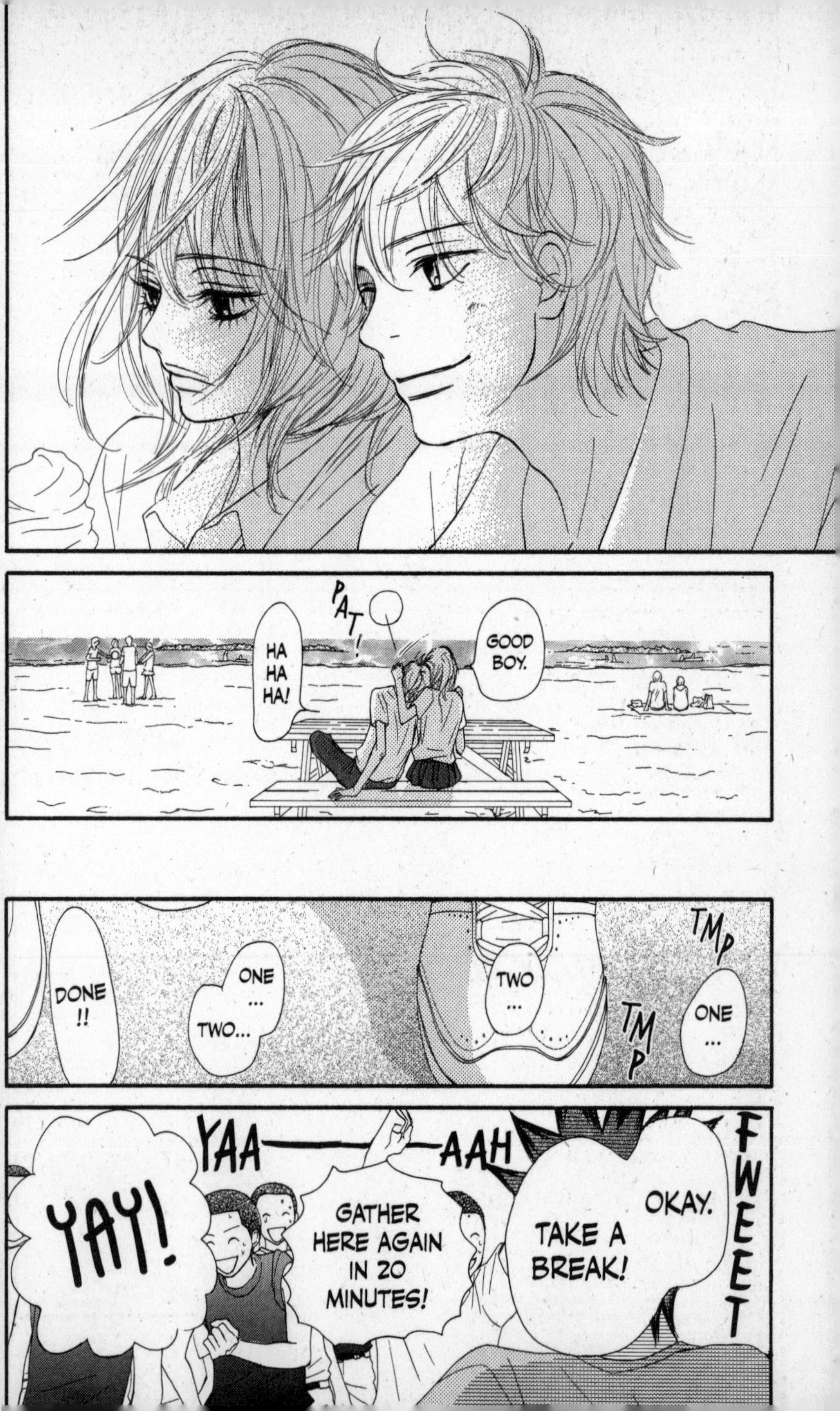
GOOD BOY.
PAT!
HA HA HA!
TMP
ONE ...
TMP
TWO ...
ONE ... TWO...
DONE !!
FWEET
OKAY.
TAKE A BREAK!
YAA———AAH
GATHER HERE AGAIN IN 20 MINUTES!
YAY!

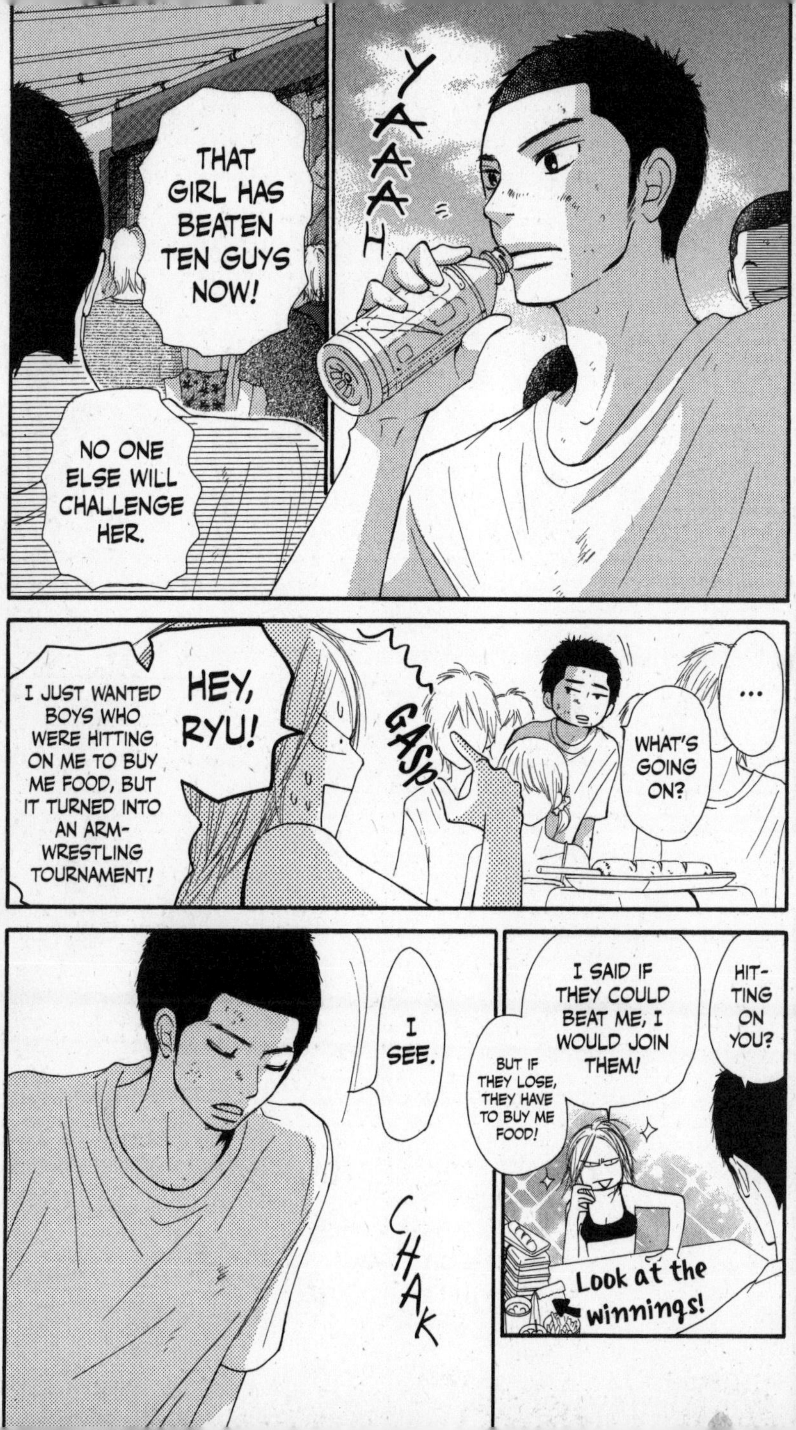
YAAAAH
THAT GIRL HAS BEATEN TEN GUYS NOW!
NO ONE ELSE WILL CHALLENGE HER.
...
WHAT'S GOING ON?
GASP
HEY, RYU!
I JUST WANTED BOYS WHO WERE HITTING ON ME TO BUY ME FOOD, BUT IT TURNED INTO AN ARM-WRESTLING TOURNAMENT!
HIT-TING ON YOU?
I SAID IF THEY COULD BEAT ME, I WOULD JOIN THEM!
BUT IF THEY LOSE, THEY HAVE TO BUY ME FOOD!
Look at the winnings!
I SEE.
CHAK

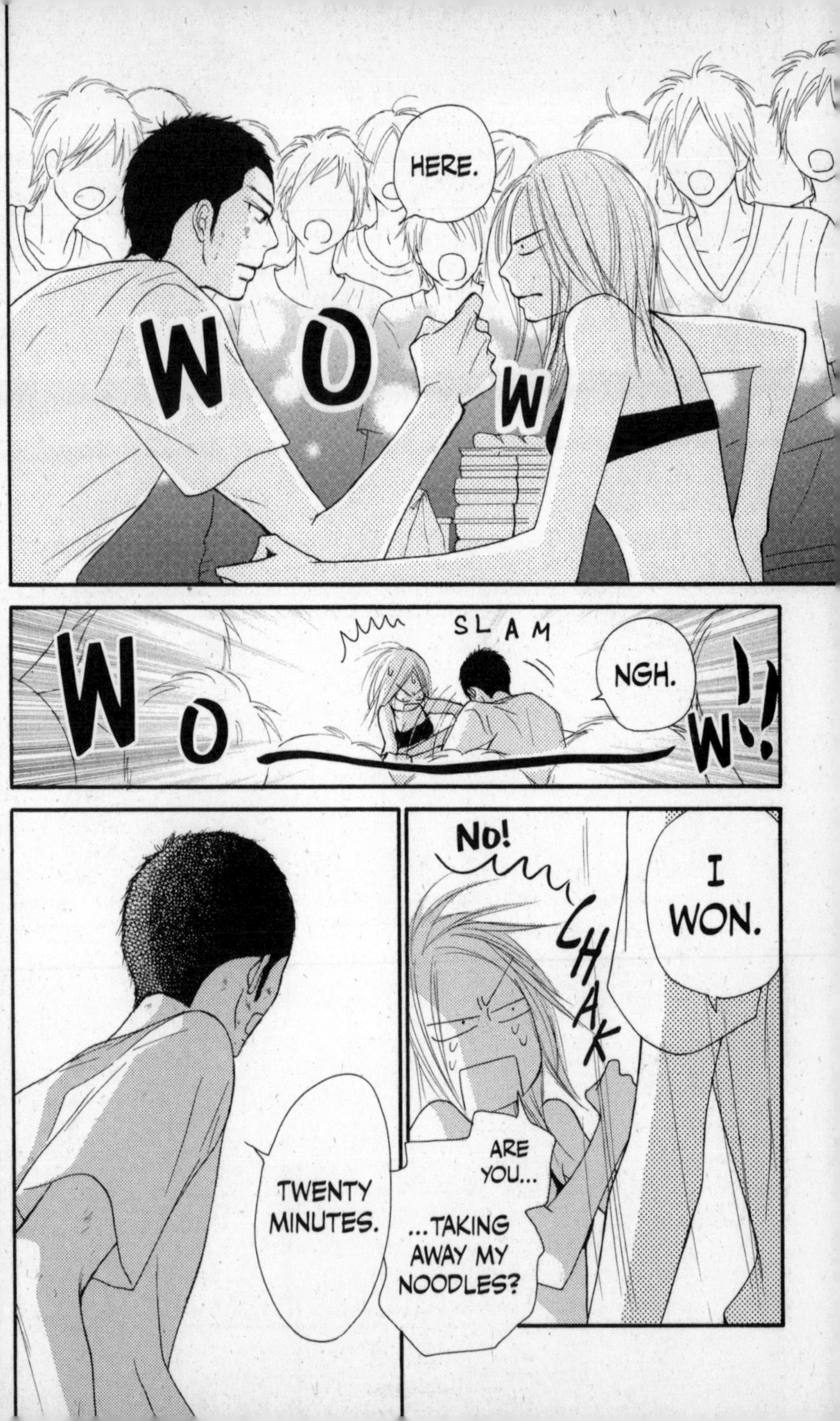
HERE.
WOW
NGH.
SLAM
WOW!!
I WON.
No!
CHAK
ARE YOU...
...TAKING AWAY MY NOODLES?
TWENTY MINUTES.

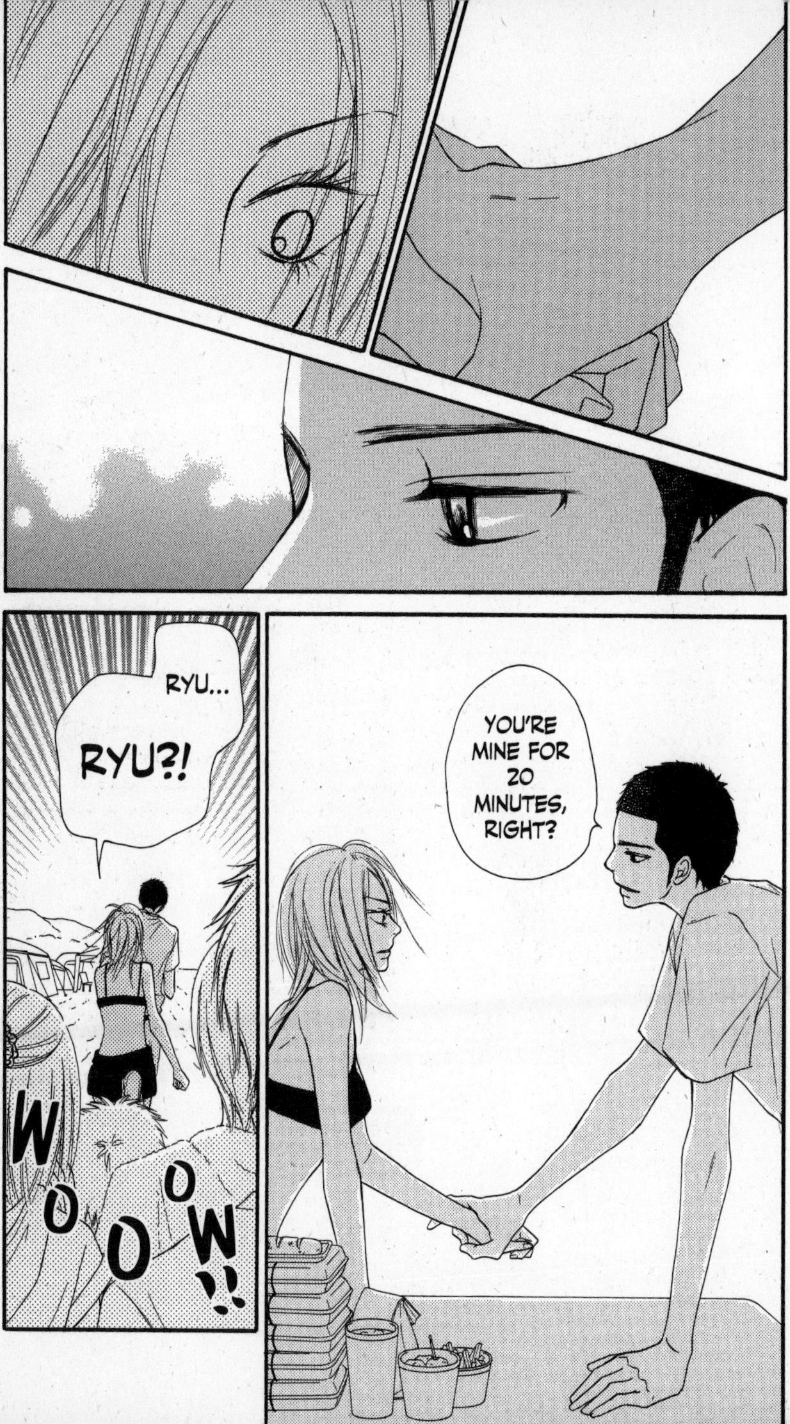
YOU'RE MINE FOR 20 MINUTES, RIGHT?
RYU... RYU?!
WOOOW!!

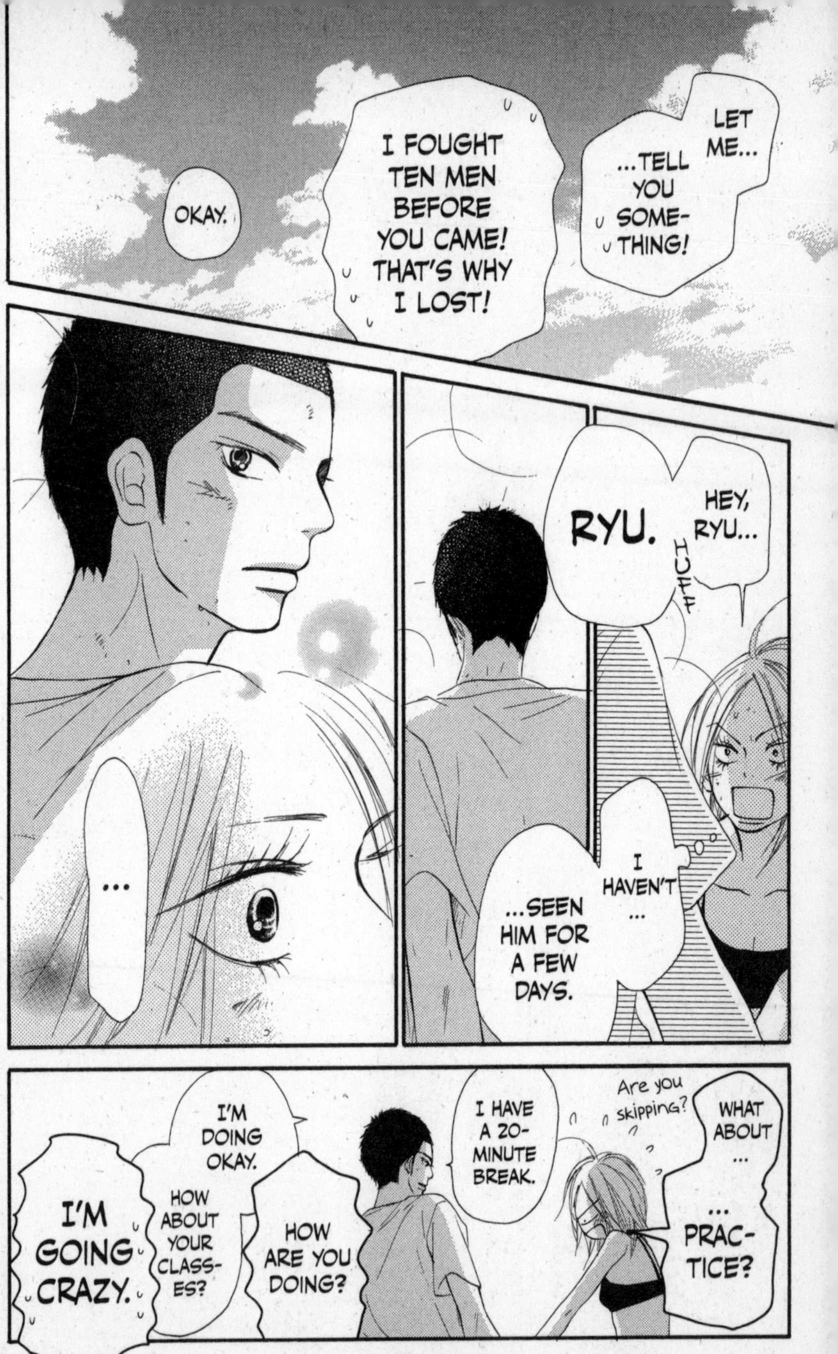
LET ME...
...TELL YOU SOMETHING!
I FOUGHT TEN MEN BEFORE YOU CAME! THAT'S WHY I LOST!
OKAY.
HEY, RYU...
RYU.
HUFF
I HAVEN'T ...
...SEEN HIM FOR A FEW DAYS.
...
WHAT ABOUT ...
... PRAC-TICE?
Are you skipping?
I HAVE A 20-MINUTE BREAK.
I'M DOING OKAY.
HOW ARE YOU DOING?
HOW ABOUT YOUR CLASS-ES?
I'M GOING CRAZY.

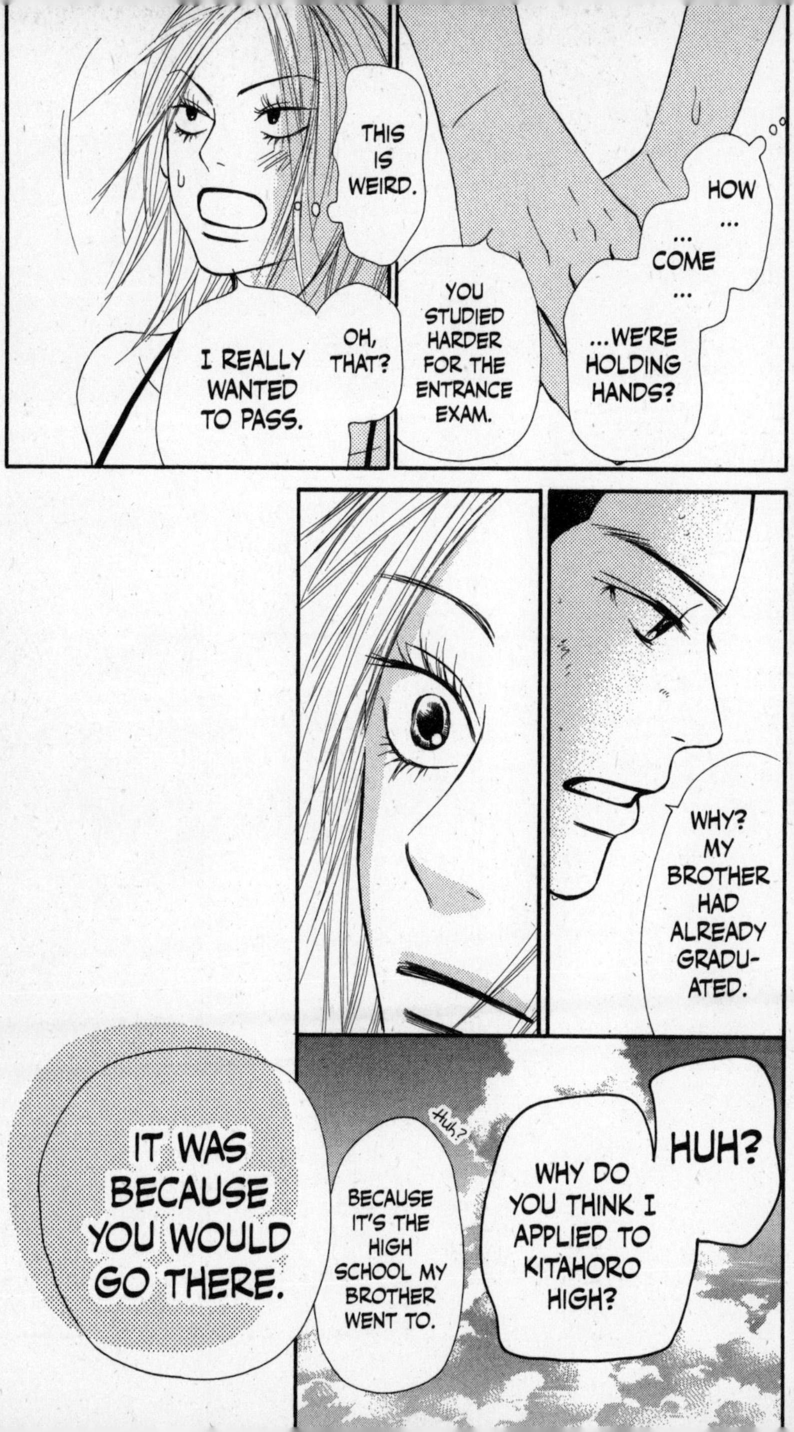
HOW ... ...COME ... ...WE'RE HOLDING HANDS?
YOU STUDIED HARDER FOR THE ENTRANCE EXAM.
THIS IS WEIRD.
OH, THAT?
I REALLY WANTED TO PASS.
WHY? MY BROTHER HAD ALREADY GRADUATED.
HUH?
WHY DO YOU THINK I APPLIED TO KITAHORO HIGH?
HUH?
BECAUSE IT'S THE HIGH SCHOOL MY BROTHER WENT TO.
IT WAS BECAUSE YOU WOULD GO THERE.

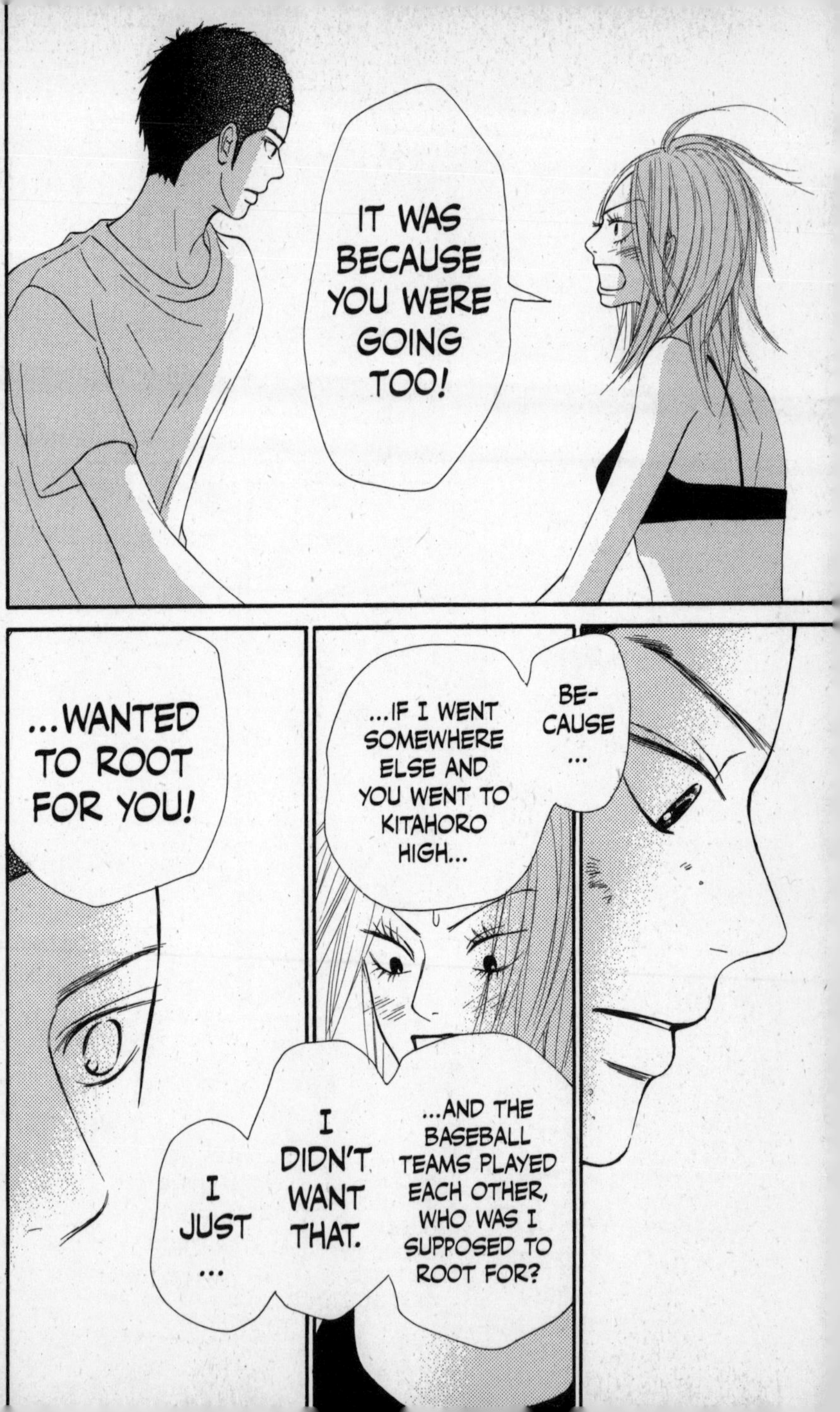
IT WAS BECAUSE YOU WERE GOING TOO!
BE-CAUSE...
...IF I WENT SOMEWHERE ELSE AND YOU WENT TO KITAHORO HIGH...
...AND THE BASEBALL TEAMS PLAYED EACH OTHER, WHO WAS I SUPPOSED TO ROOT FOR?
I DIDN'T WANT THAT.
I JUST...
...WANTED TO ROOT FOR YOU!

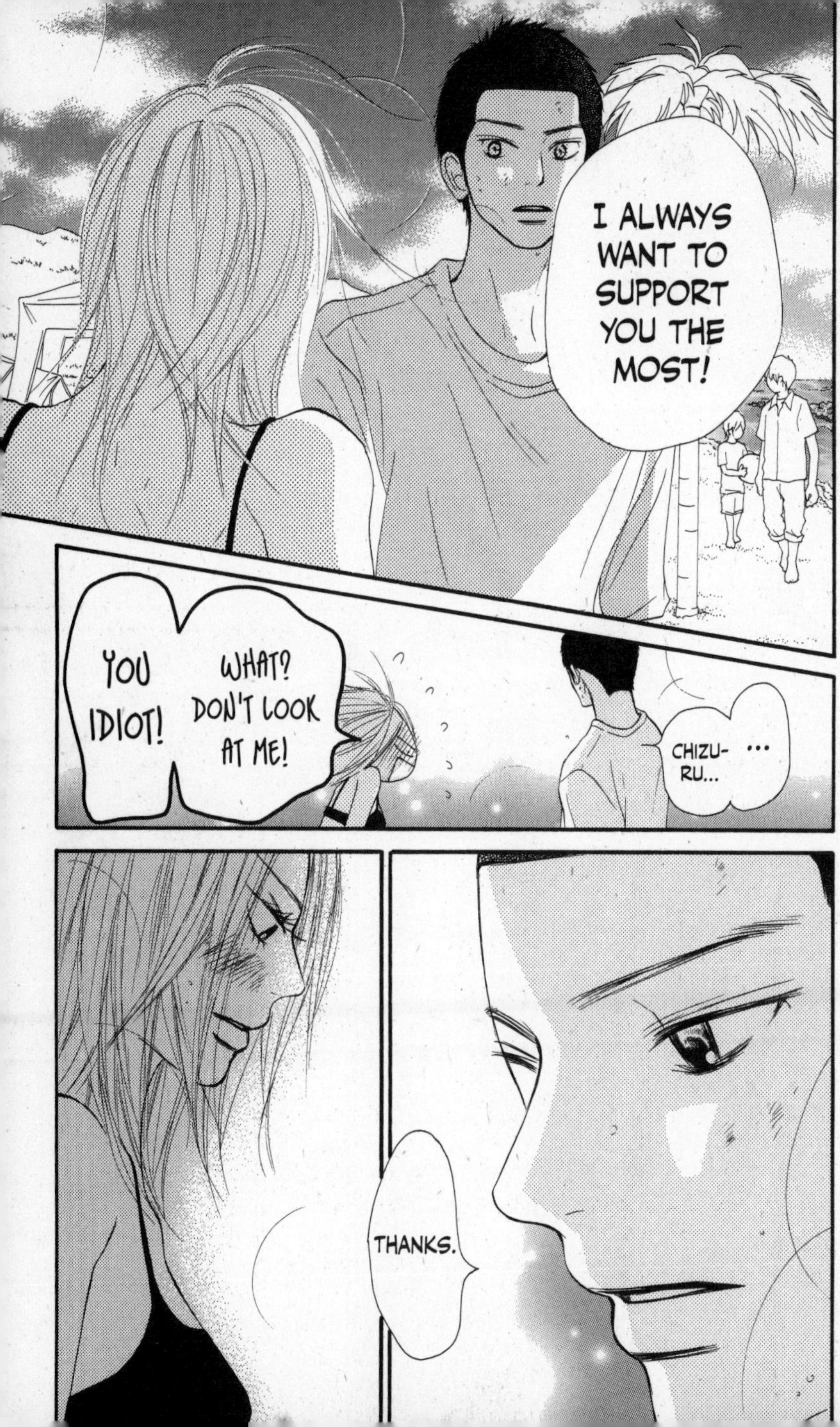
I ALWAYS WANT TO SUPPORT YOU THE MOST!
CHIZU-RU... ...
WHAT? DON'T LOOK AT ME!
YOU IDIOT!
THANKS.

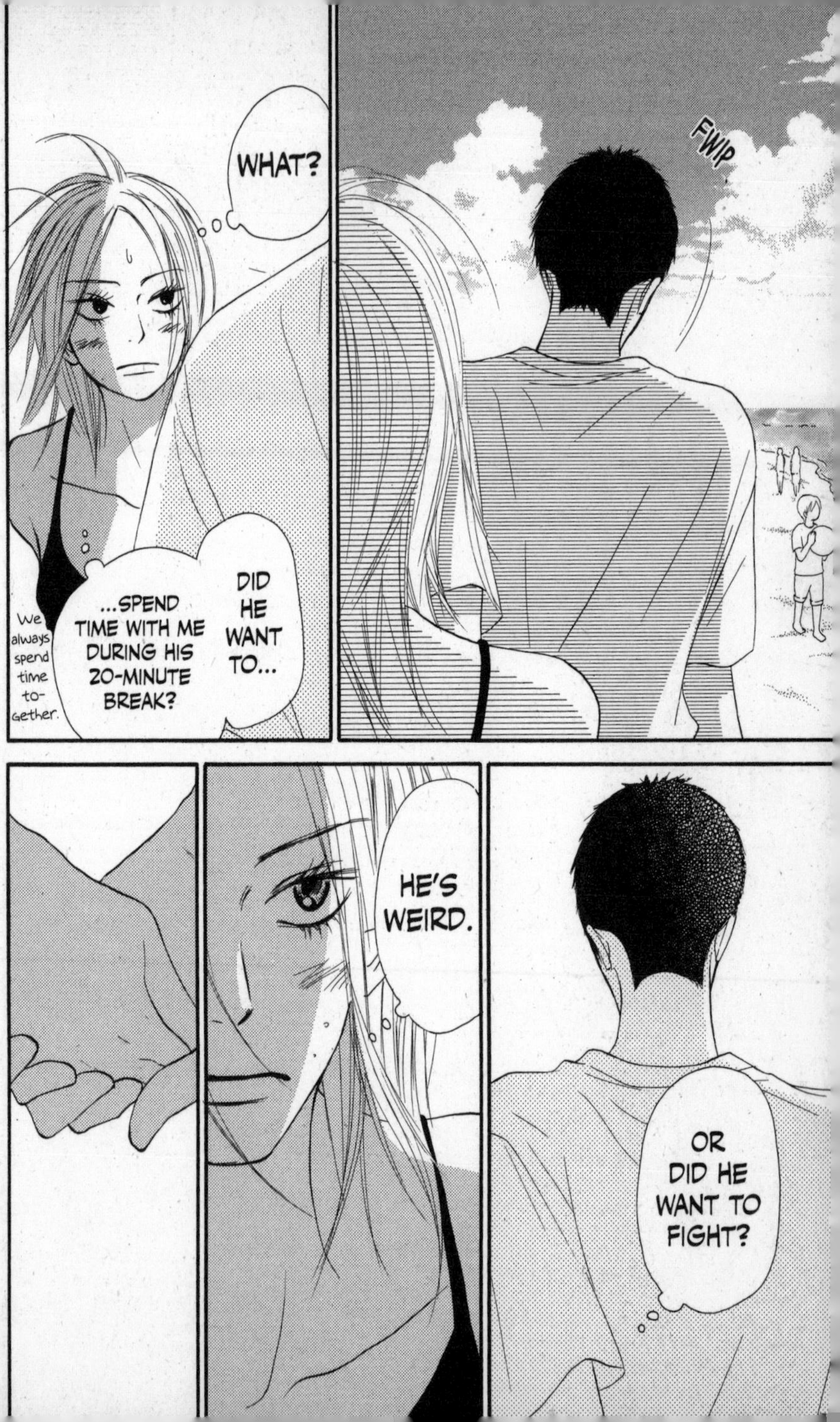
FWIP
WHAT?
DID HE WANT TO...
...SPEND TIME WITH ME DURING HIS 20-MINUTE BREAK?
We always spend time to-gether.
OR DID HE WANT TO FIGHT?
HE'S WEIRD.

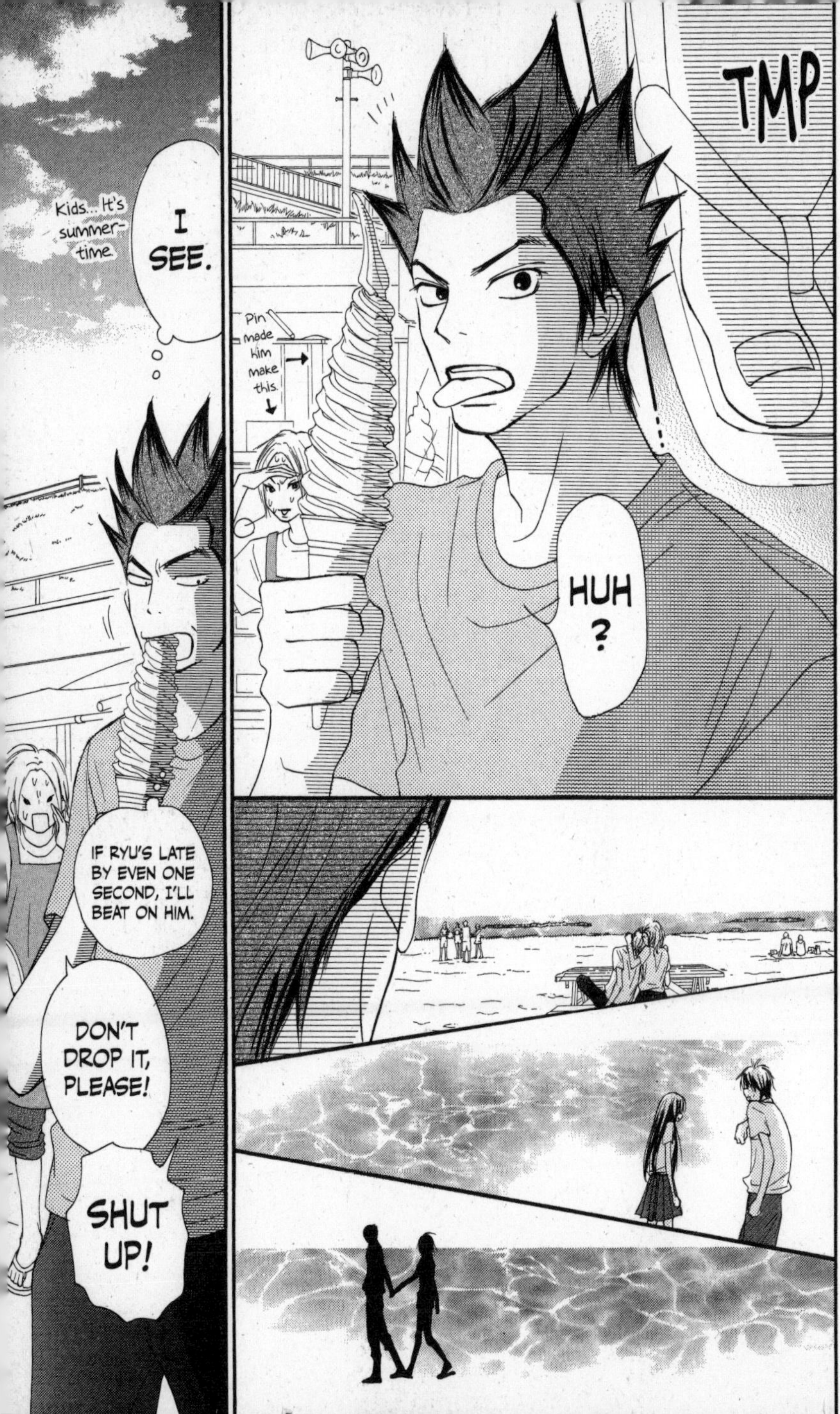
TMP
HUH?
Pin made him make this.
I SEE.
Kids... It's summertime.
IF RYU'S LATE BY EVEN ONE SECOND, I'LL BEAT ON HIM.
DON'T DROP IT, PLEASE!
SHUT UP!

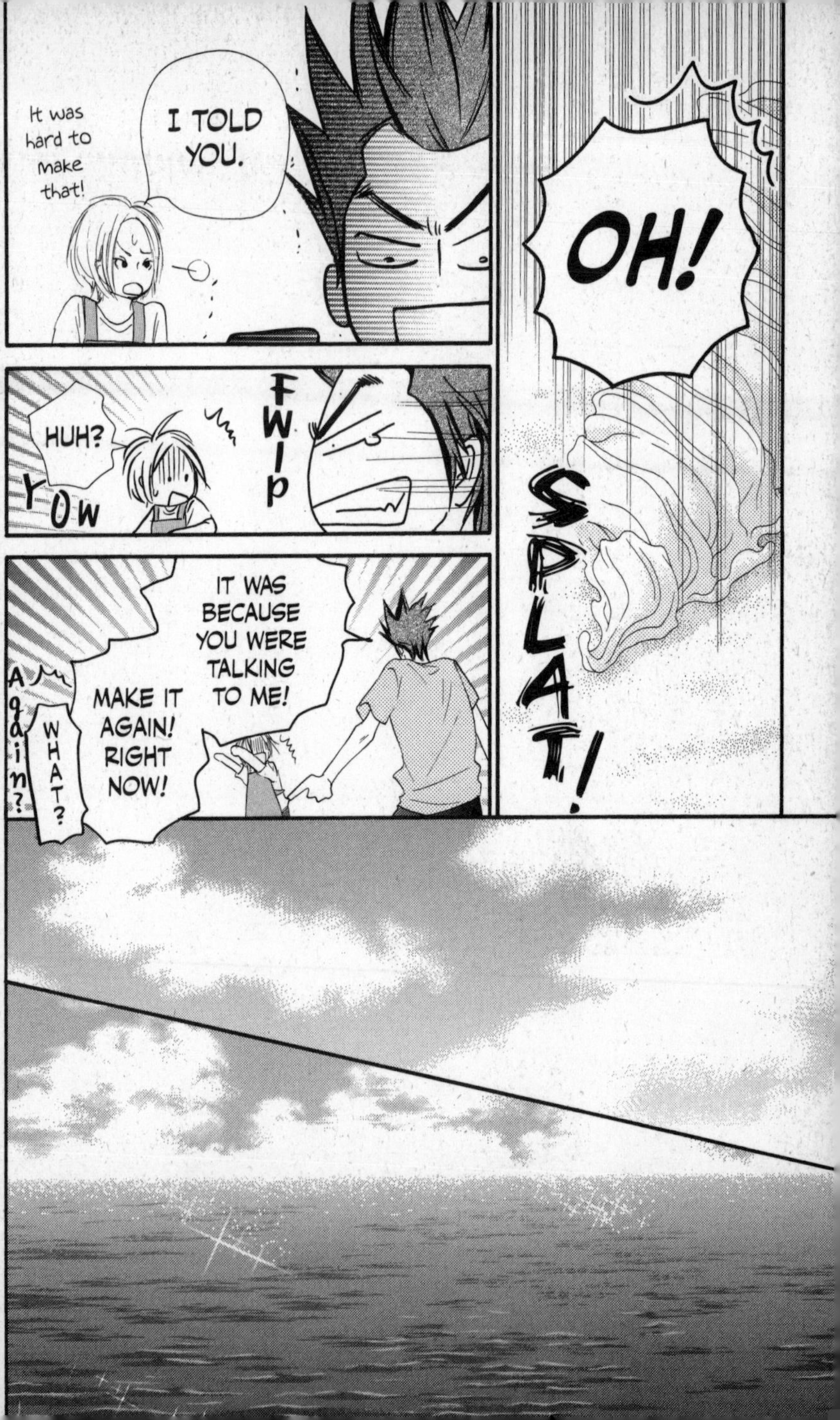
OH!
SPLAT!
I TOLD YOU.
It was hard to make that!
FWIp
HUH?
YOW
IT WAS BECAUSE YOU WERE TALKING TO ME!
MAKE IT AGAIN! RIGHT NOW!
WHAT?
Again?

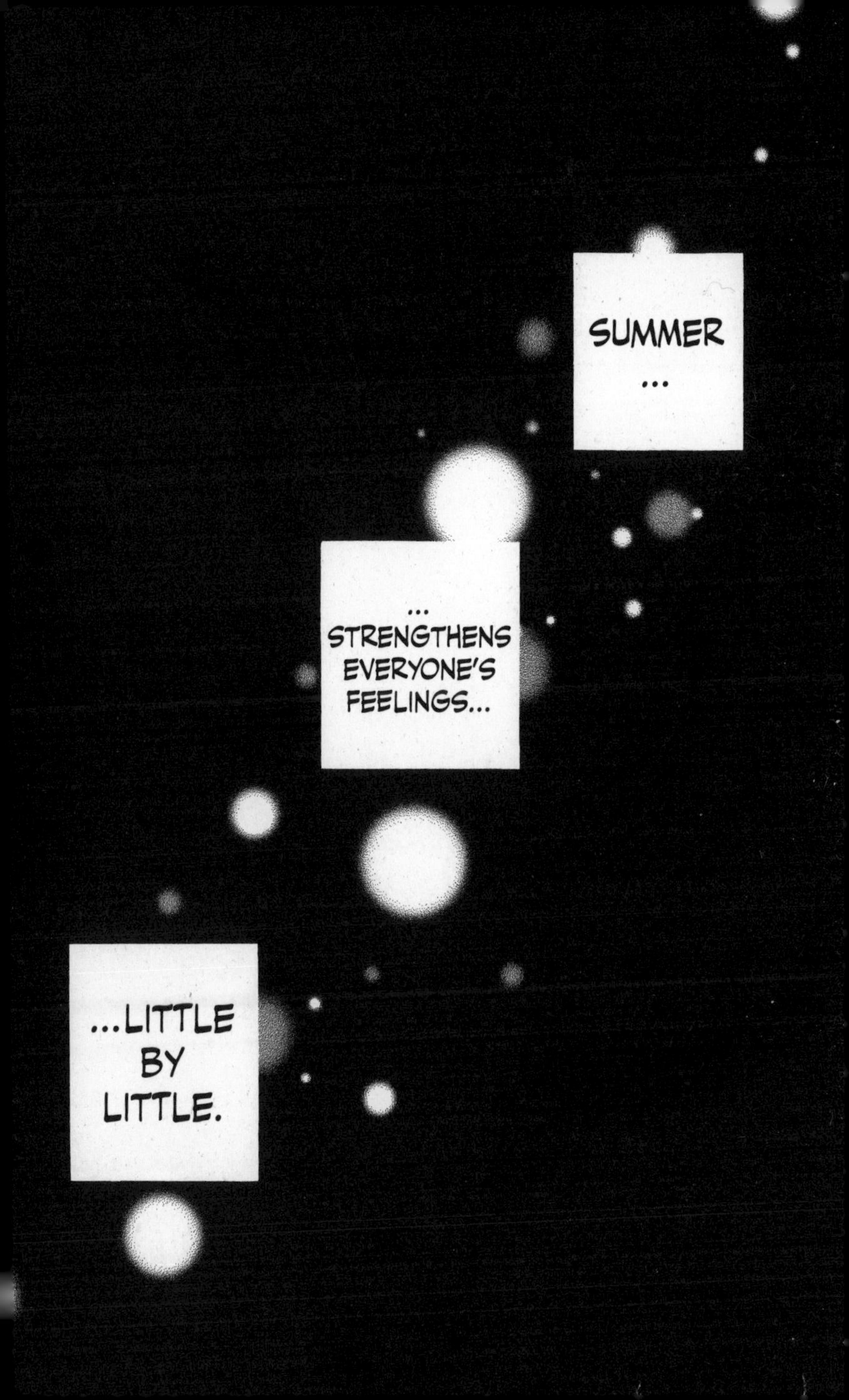
SUMMER ...
... STRENGTHENS EVERYONE'S FEELINGS...
...LITTLE BY LITTLE.

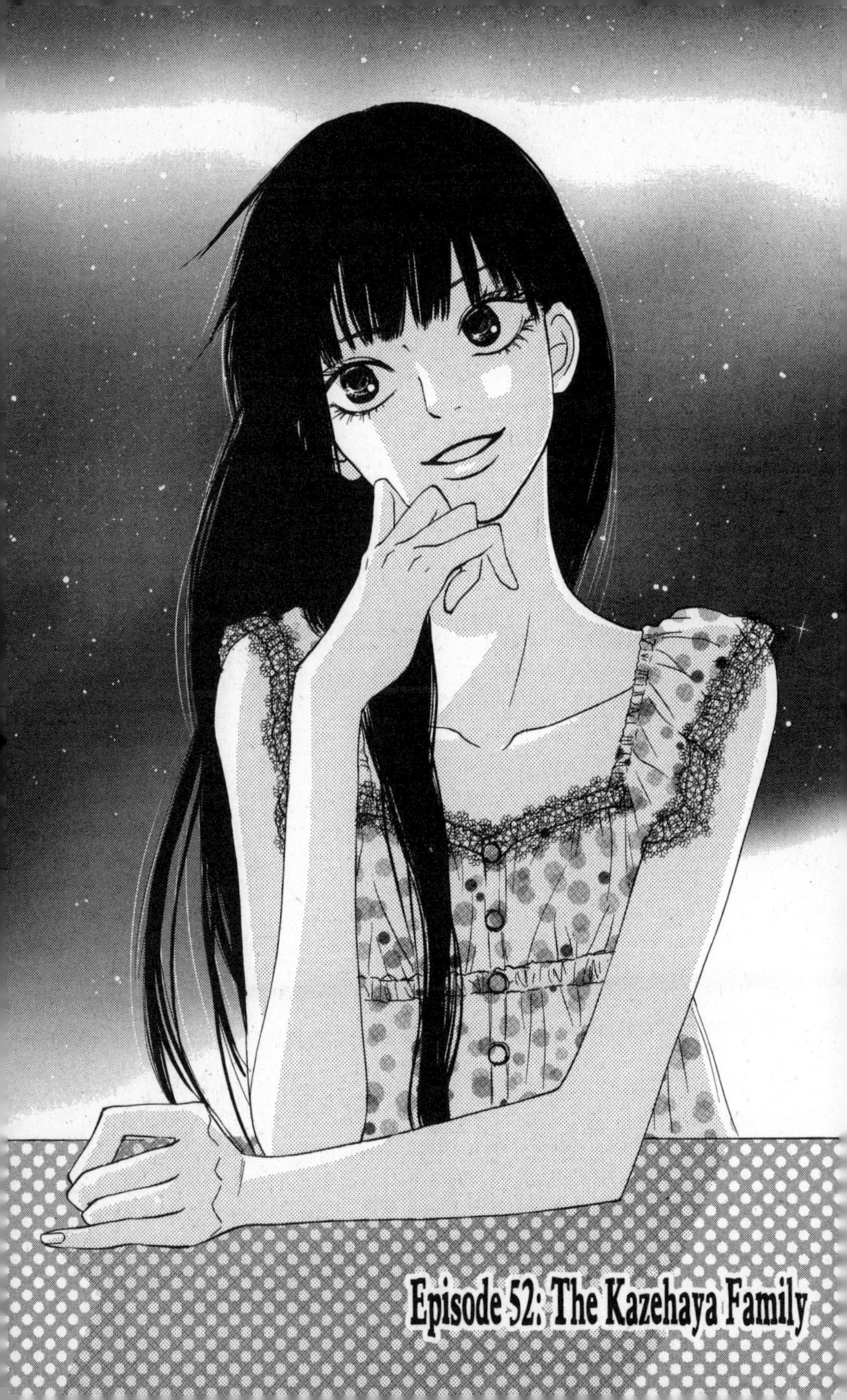
Episode 52: The Kazehaya Family

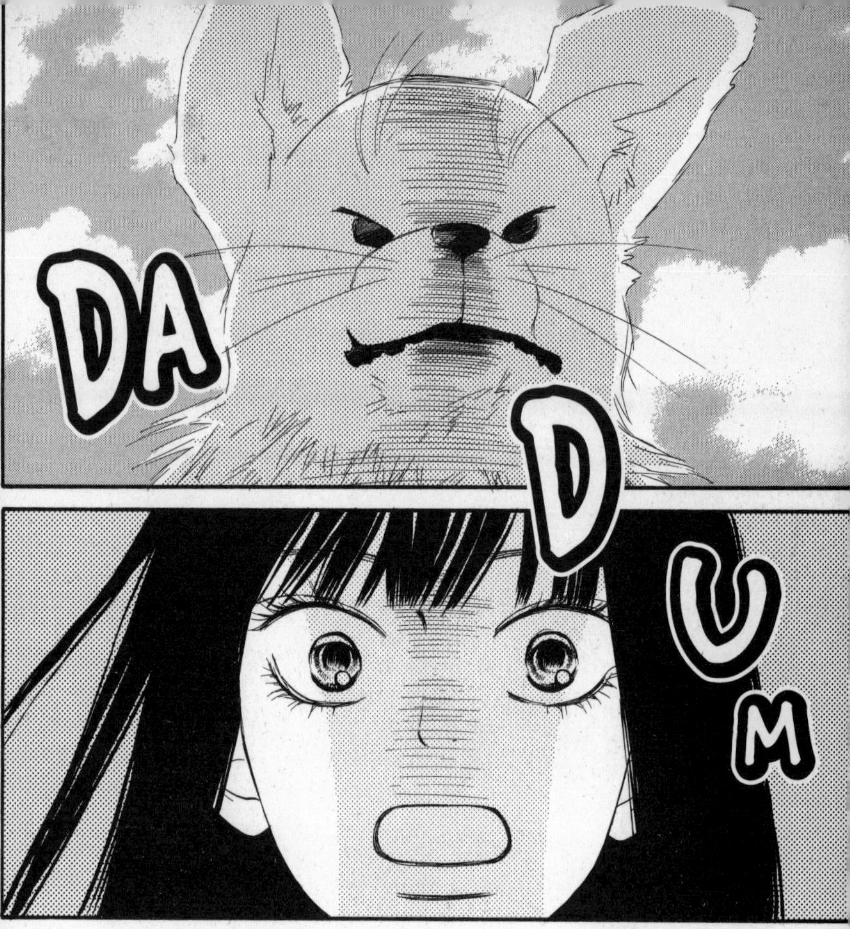
DA
DUM
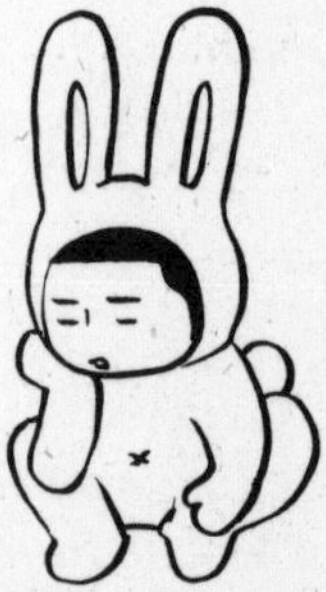

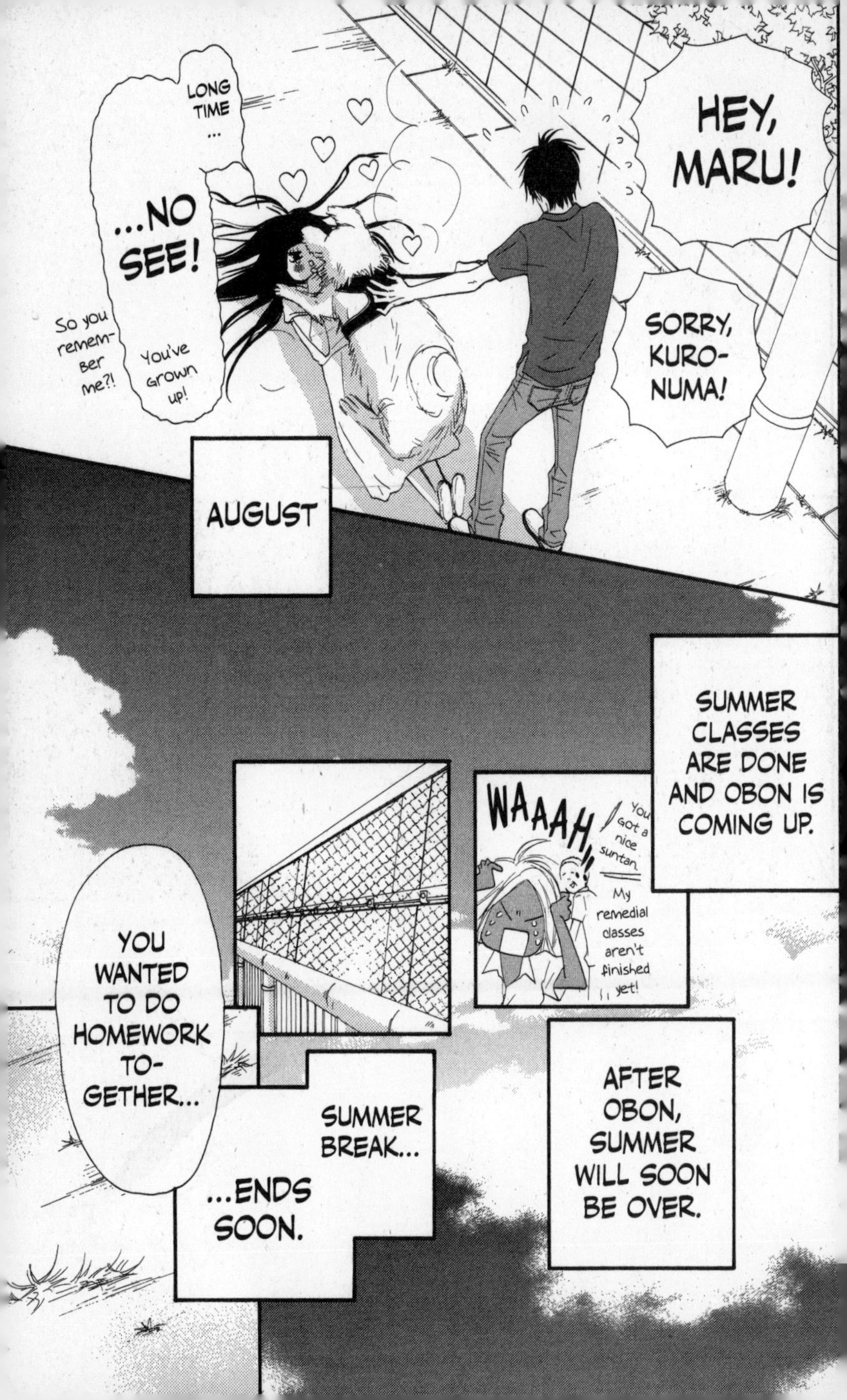
HEY, MARU!
SORRY, KURO-NUMA!
LONG TIME ...
...NO SEE!
You've grown up!
So you remem-ber me?!
AUGUST
SUMMER CLASSES ARE DONE AND OBON IS COMING UP.
WAAAH
You got a nice suntan.
My remedial classes aren't finished yet!
YOU WANTED TO DO HOMEWORK TO-GETHER...
AFTER OBON, SUMMER WILL SOON BE OVER.
SUMMER BREAK...
...ENDS SOON.

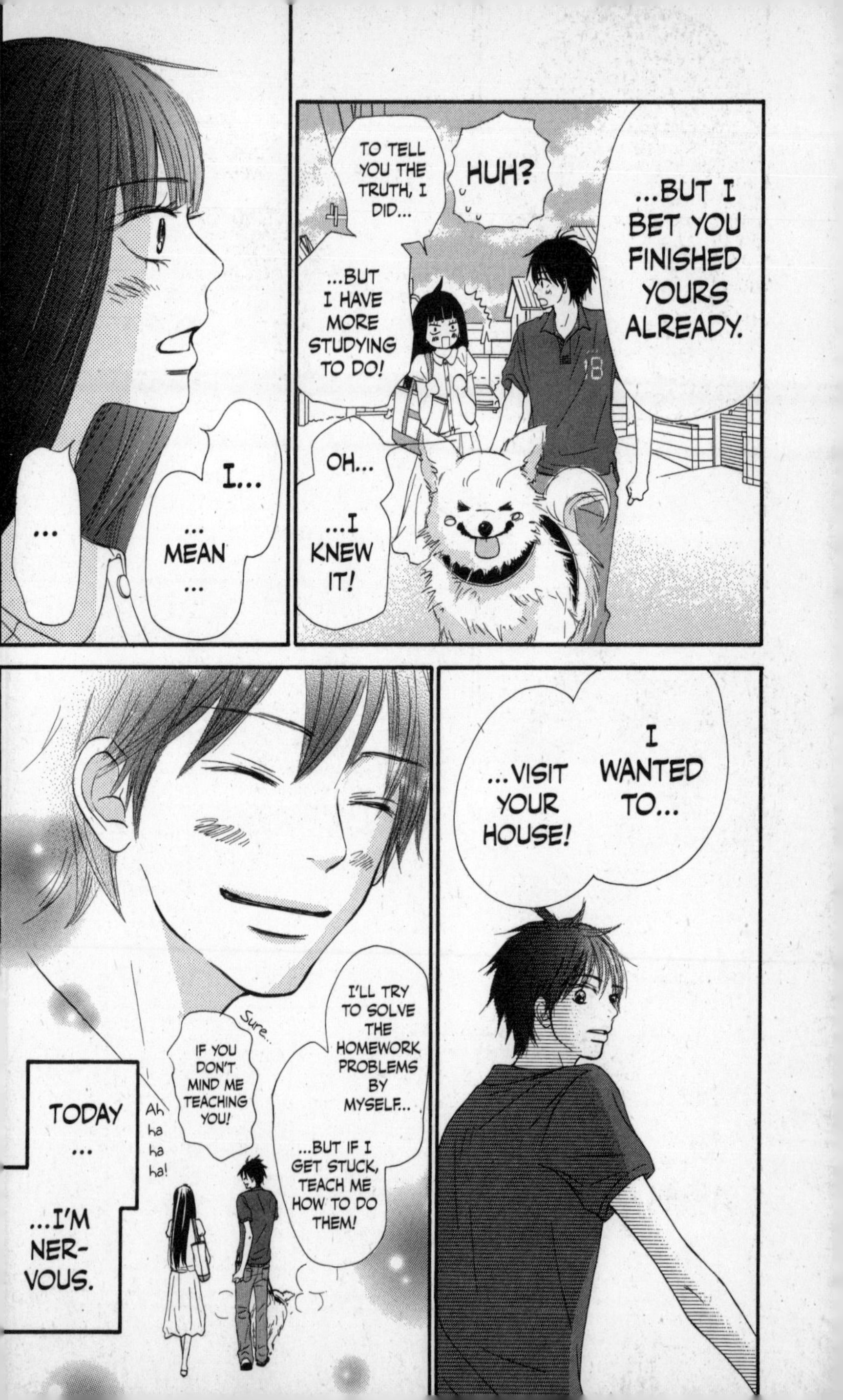
...BUT I BET YOU FINISHED YOURS ALREADY.
HUH?
TO TELL YOU THE TRUTH, I DID...
...BUT I HAVE MORE STUDYING TO DO!
OH...
...I KNEW IT!
I...
...MEAN...
...
I WANTED TO...
...VISIT YOUR HOUSE!
I'LL TRY TO SOLVE THE HOMEWORK PROBLEMS BY MYSELF...
...BUT IF I GET STUCK, TEACH ME HOW TO DO THEM!
Sure...
IF YOU DON'T MIND ME TEACHING YOU!
Ah ha ha ha!
TODAY...
...I'M NER-VOUS.

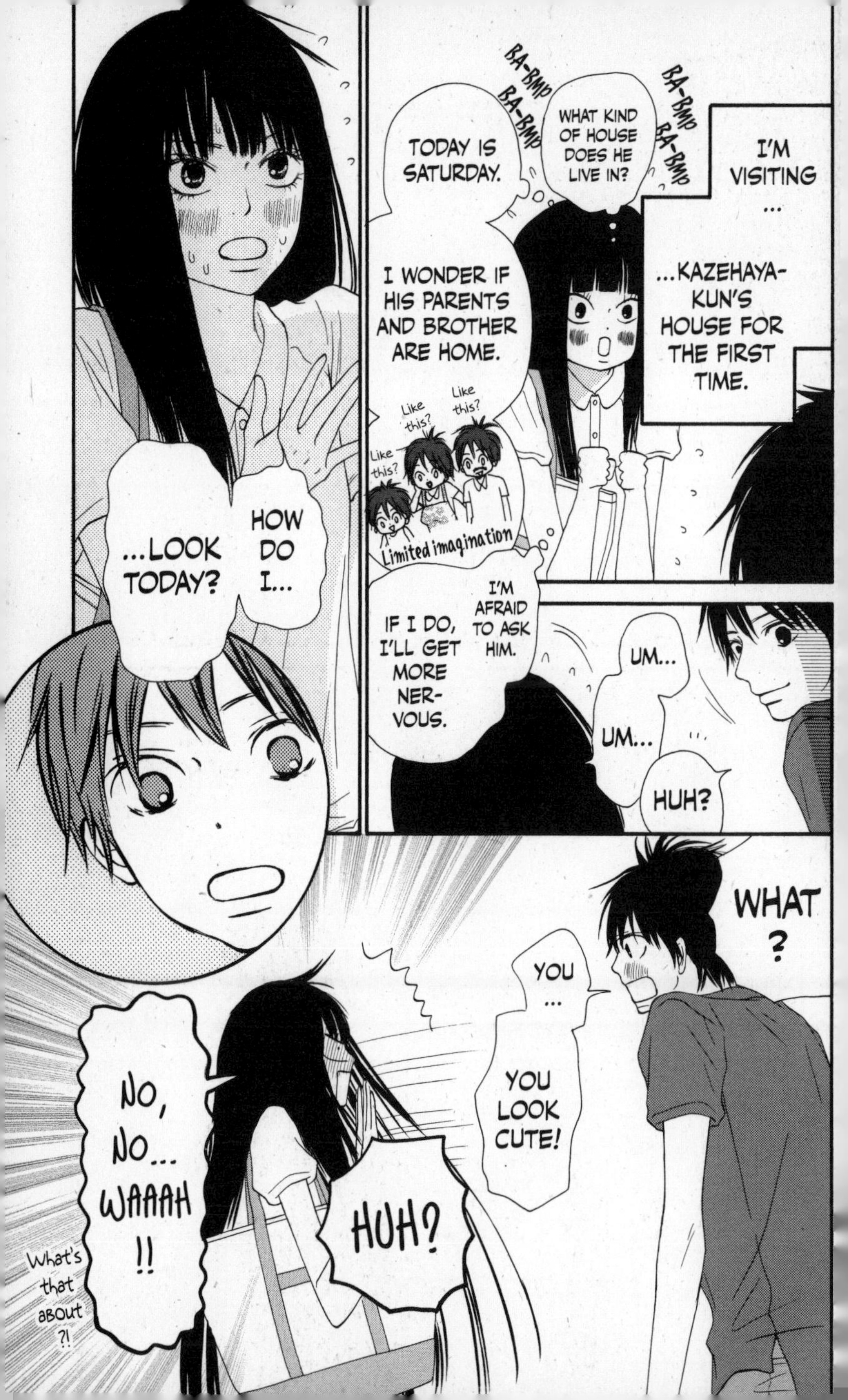
I'M VISITING ...
...KAZEHAYA-KUN'S HOUSE FOR THE FIRST TIME.
BA-BMP BA-BMP
WHAT KIND OF HOUSE DOES HE LIVE IN?
BA-BMP BA-BMP
TODAY IS SATURDAY.
I WONDER IF HIS PARENTS AND BROTHER ARE HOME.
Like this?
Like this?
Like this?
Limited imagination
I'M AFRAID TO ASK HIM.
IF I DO, I'LL GET MORE NERVOUS.
UM...
UM...
HUH?
HOW DO I...
...LOOK TODAY?
WHAT?
YOU ...
YOU LOOK CUTE!
HUH?
NO, NO... WAAAH!!
What's that about?!

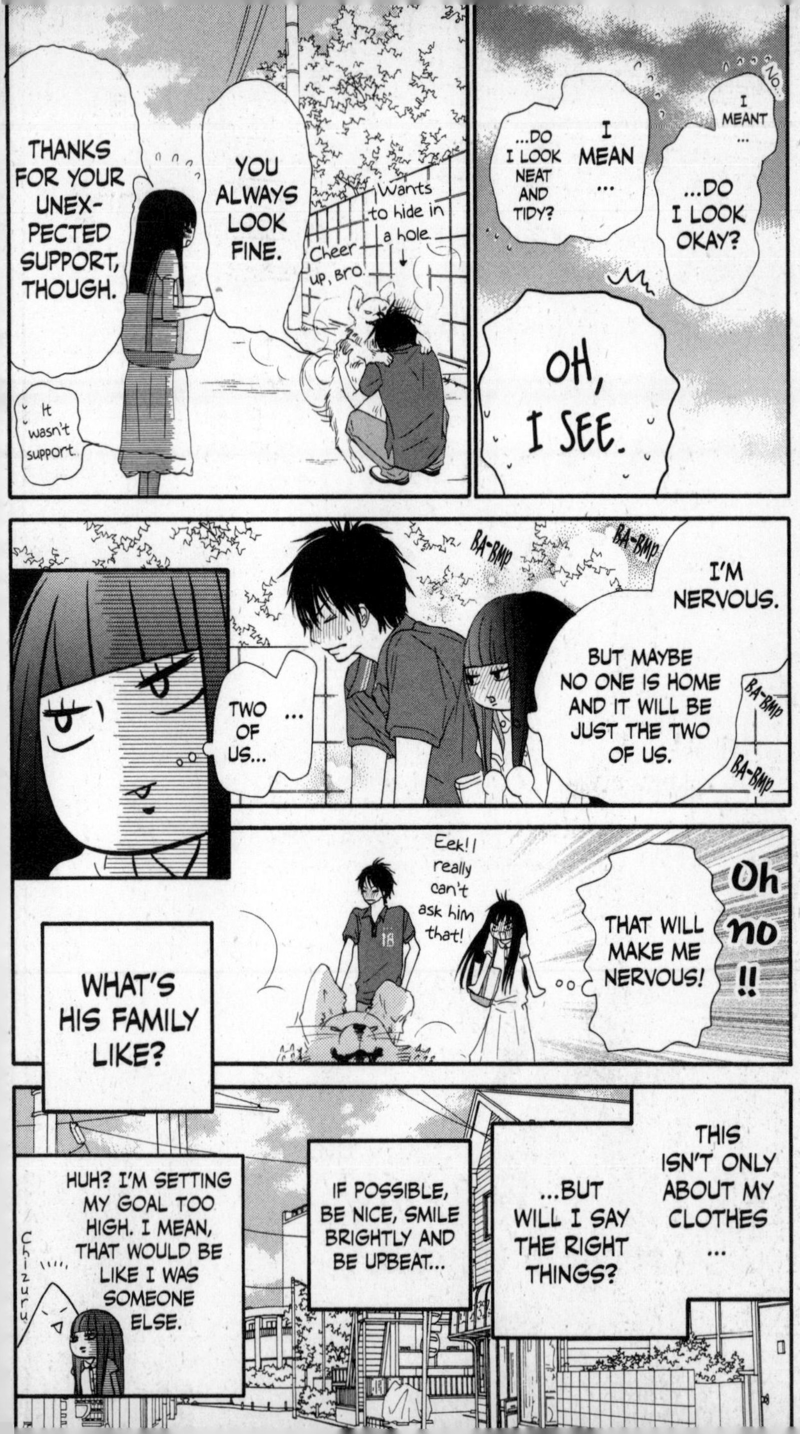
No...
I MEANT ...
...DO I LOOK OKAY?
I MEAN ...
...DO I LOOK NEAT AND TIDY?
OH, I SEE.
YOU ALWAYS LOOK FINE.
Wants to hide in a hole.
Cheer up, bro.
THANKS FOR YOUR UNEX-PECTED SUPPORT, THOUGH.
It wasn't support.
BA-BMP
BA-BMP
I'M NERVOUS.
BUT MAYBE NO ONE IS HOME AND IT WILL BE JUST THE TWO OF US.
BA-BMP
BA-BMP
Oh no!!
THAT WILL MAKE ME NERVOUS!
Eek!! I really can't ask him that!
TWO OF US... ...
WHAT'S HIS FAMILY LIKE?
THIS ISN'T ONLY ABOUT MY CLOTHES ...
...BUT WILL I SAY THE RIGHT THINGS?
IF POSSIBLE, BE NICE, SMILE BRIGHTLY AND BE UPBEAT...
HUH? I'M SETTING MY GOAL TOO HIGH. I MEAN, THAT WOULD BE LIKE I WAS SOMEONE ELSE.
Chizuru

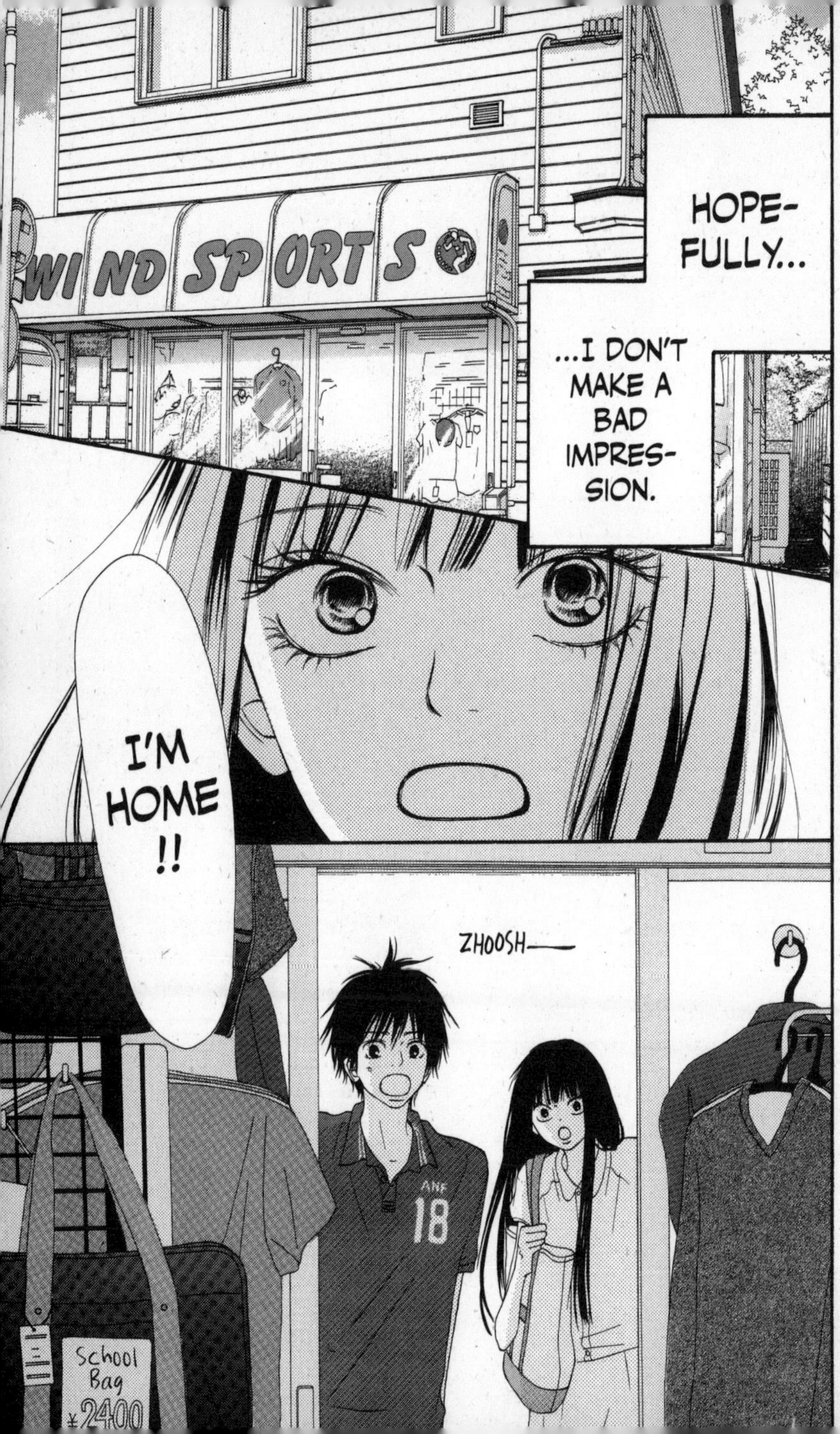
HOPE-FULLY...
...I DON'T MAKE A BAD IMPRESSION.
WIND SPORTS
I'M HOME!!
ZHOOSH—
School Bag ¥2400

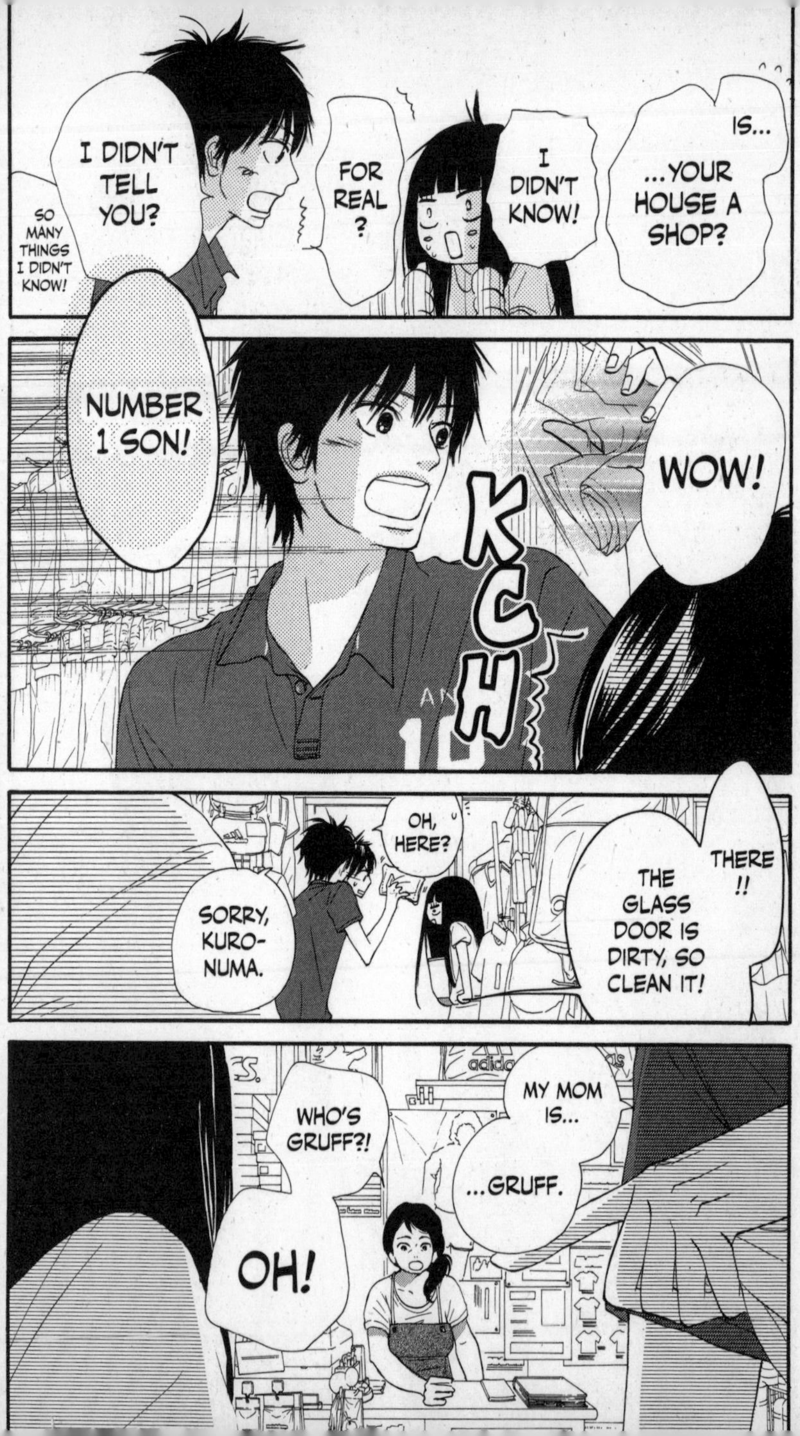
IS... ...YOUR HOUSE A SHOP?
I DIDN'T KNOW!
FOR REAL?
I DIDN'T TELL YOU?
SO MANY THINGS I DIDN'T KNOW!
WOW!
KCH
NUMBER 1 SON!
THERE!! THE GLASS DOOR IS DIRTY, SO CLEAN IT!
OH, HERE?
SORRY, KURO-NUMA.
MY MOM IS... ...GRUFF.
WHO'S GRUFF?!
OH!

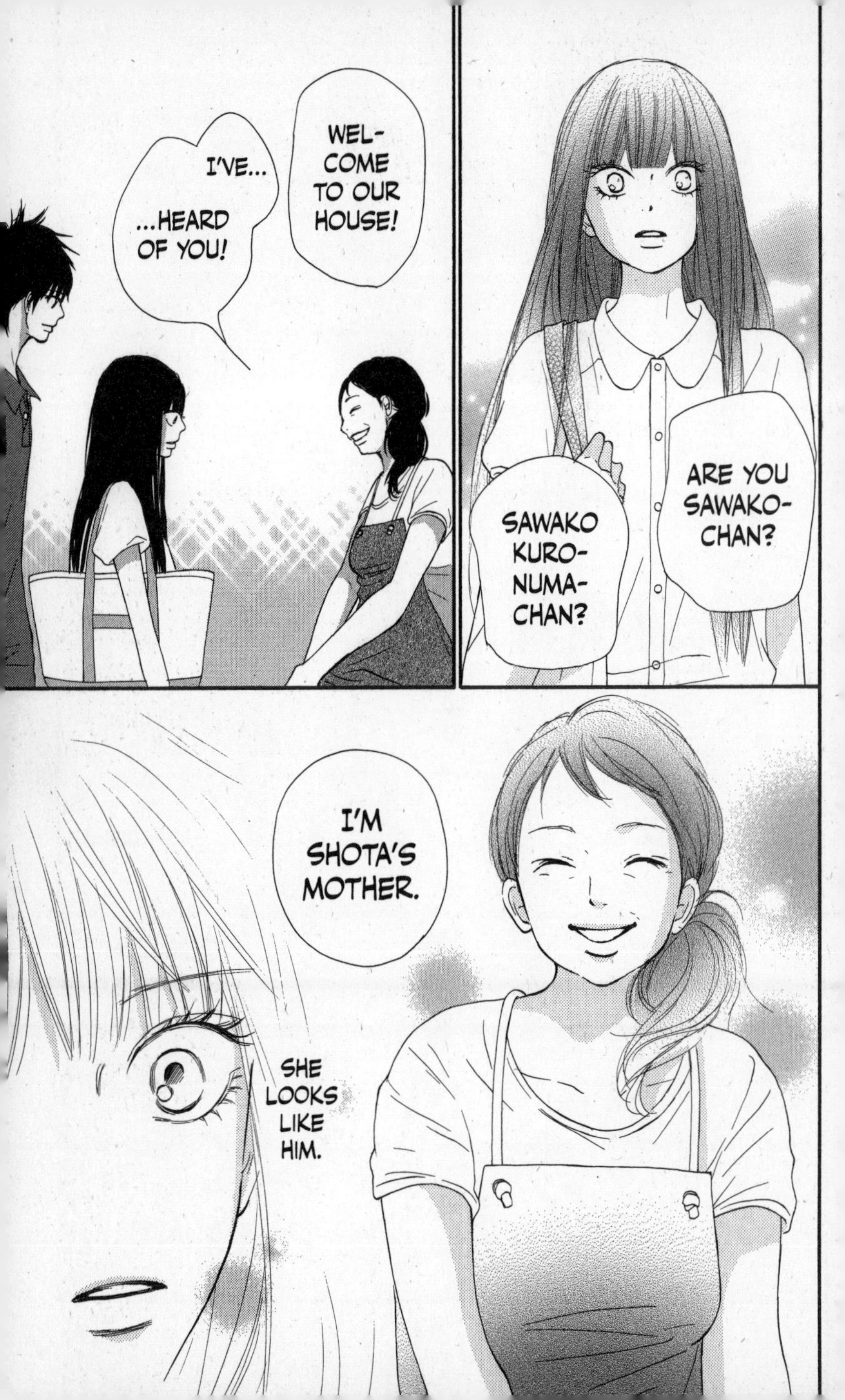
ARE YOU SAWAKO-CHAN?
SAWAKO KURO-NUMA-CHAN?
WEL-COME TO OUR HOUSE!
I'VE...
...HEARD OF YOU!
I'M SHOTA'S MOTHER.
SHE LOOKS LIKE HIM.

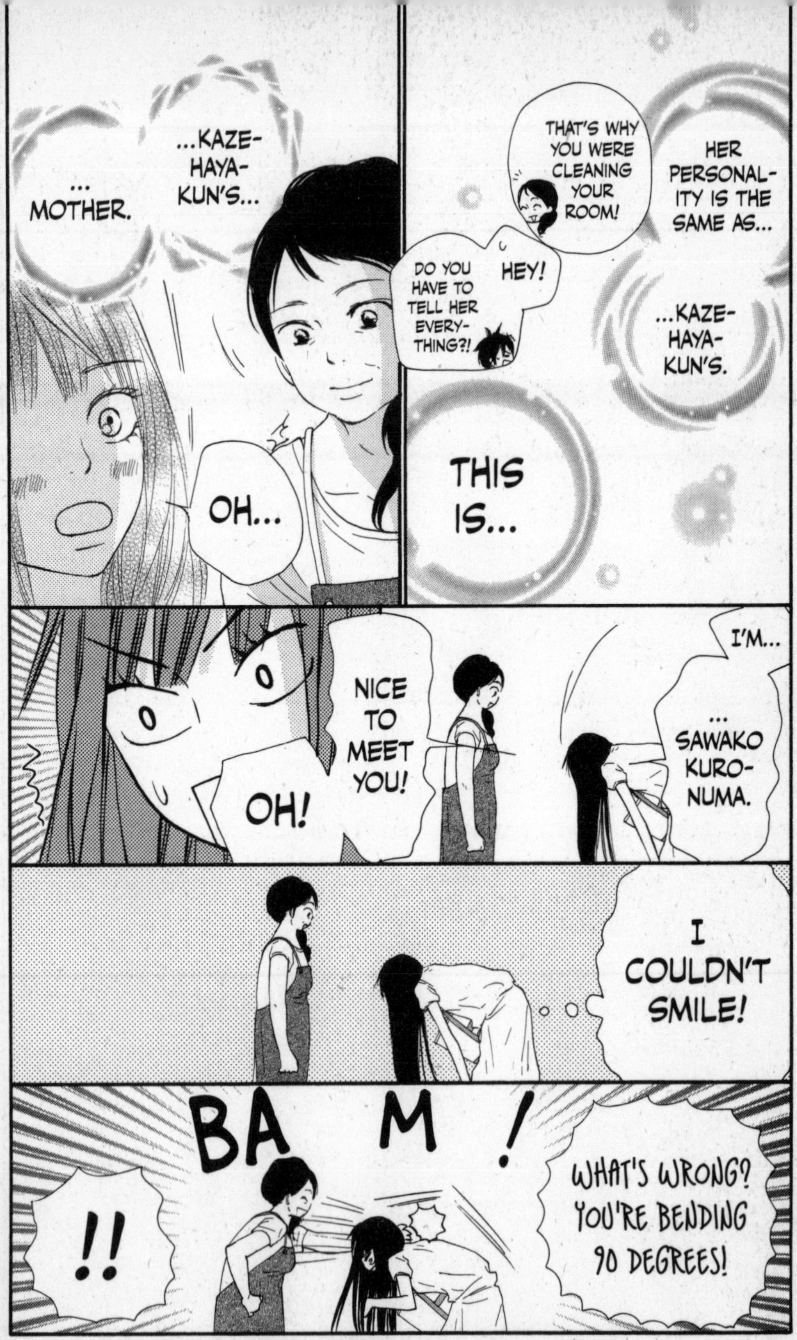
HER PERSONALITY IS THE SAME AS...
THAT'S WHY YOU WERE CLEANING YOUR ROOM!
HEY!
DO YOU HAVE TO TELL HER EVERYTHING?!
...KAZEHAYA-KUN'S.
THIS IS...
...KAZEHAYA-KUN'S...
... MOTHER.
OH...
I'M...
... SAWAKO KURONUMA.
NICE TO MEET YOU!
OH!
I COULDN'T SMILE!
WHAT'S WRONG? YOU'RE BENDING 90 DEGREES!
BAM!
!!

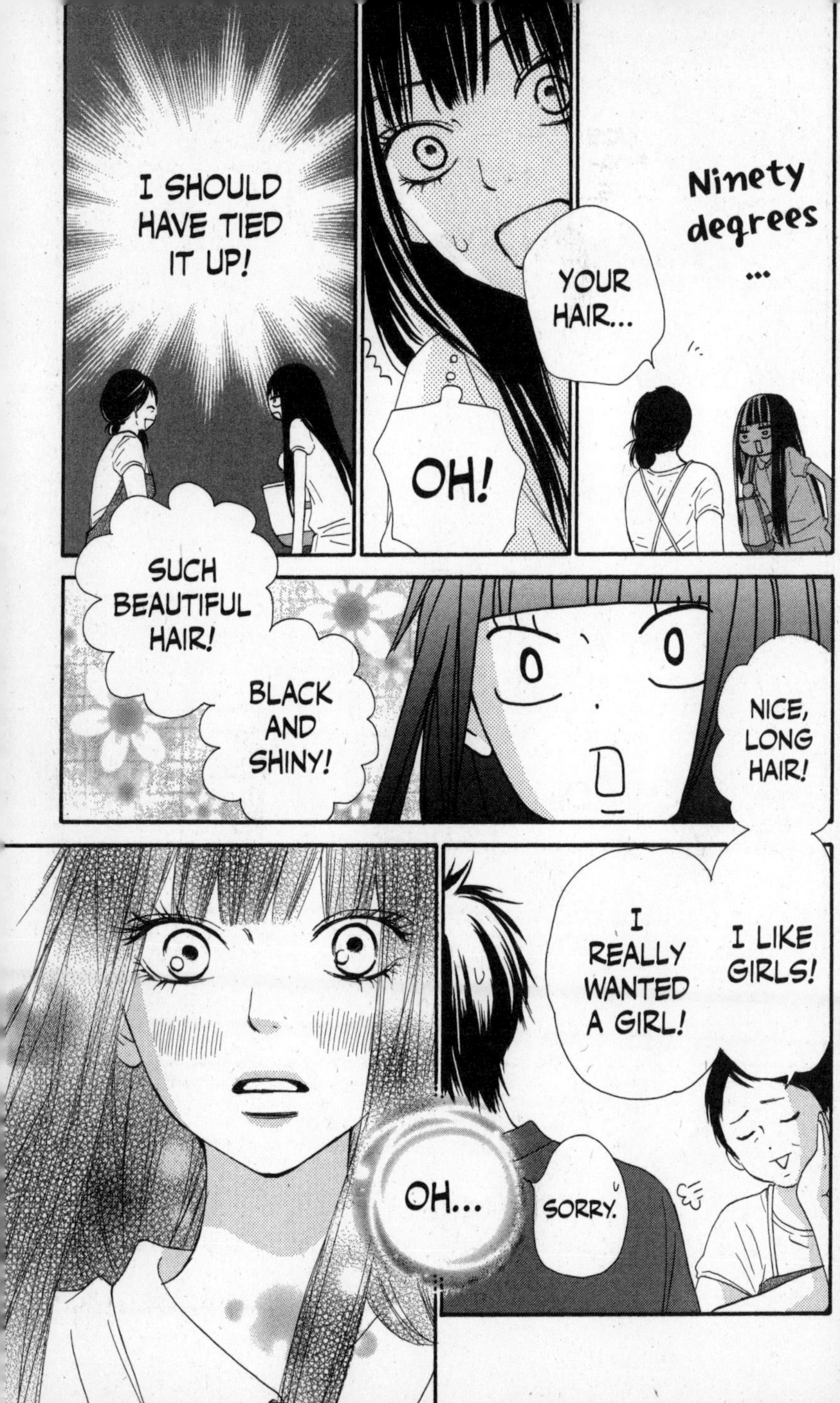
Ninety degrees ...
YOUR HAIR...
OH!
I SHOULD HAVE TIED IT UP!
NICE, LONG HAIR!
BLACK AND SHINY!
SUCH BEAUTIFUL HAIR!
I LIKE GIRLS!
I REALLY WANTED A GIRL!
SORRY.
OH...

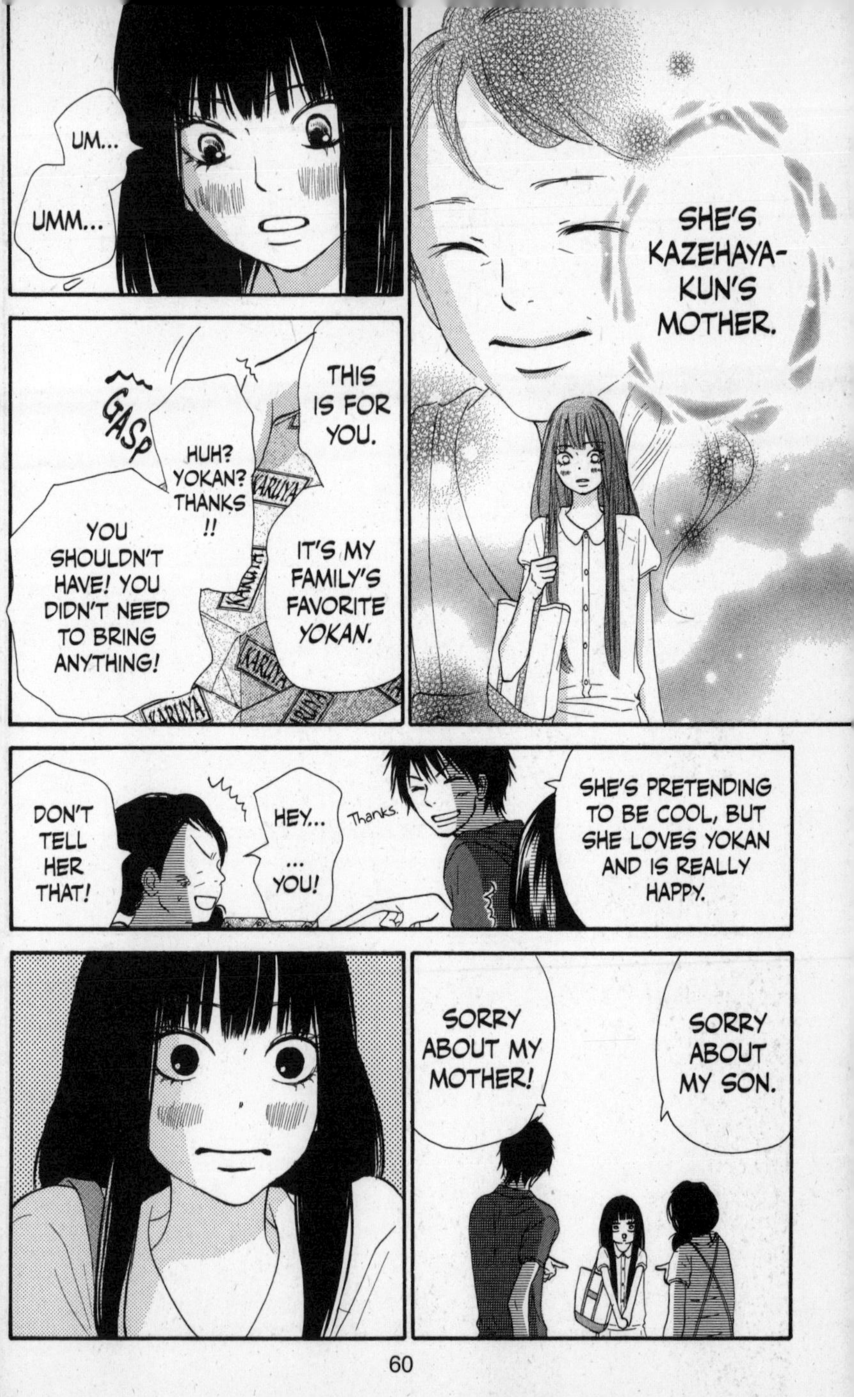
SHE'S KAZEHAYA-KUN'S MOTHER.
UM...
UMM...
THIS IS FOR YOU.
GASP
HUH? YOKAN? THANKS !!
IT'S MY FAMILY'S FAVORITE YOKAN.
YOU SHOULDN'T HAVE! YOU DIDN'T NEED TO BRING ANYTHING!
SHE'S PRETENDING TO BE COOL, BUT SHE LOVES YOKAN AND IS REALLY HAPPY.
Thanks.
HEY... ...YOU!
DON'T TELL HER THAT!
SORRY ABOUT MY SON.
SORRY ABOUT MY MOTHER!

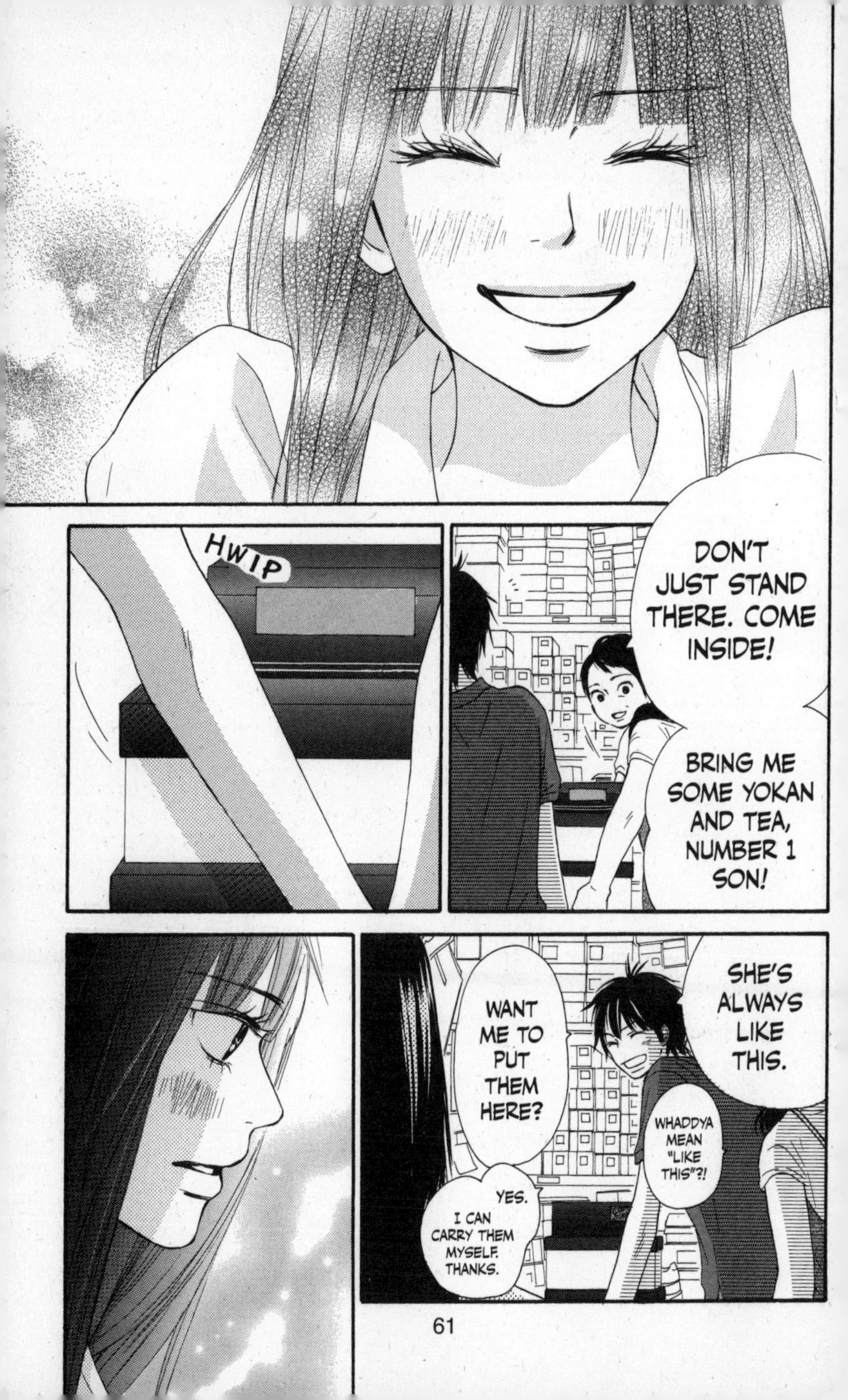
DON'T JUST STAND THERE. COME INSIDE!
BRING ME SOME YOKAN AND TEA, NUMBER 1 SON!
HWIP
SHE'S ALWAYS LIKE THIS.
WHADDYA MEAN "LIKE THIS"?!
WANT ME TO PUT THEM HERE?
YES. I CAN CARRY THEM MYSELF. THANKS.

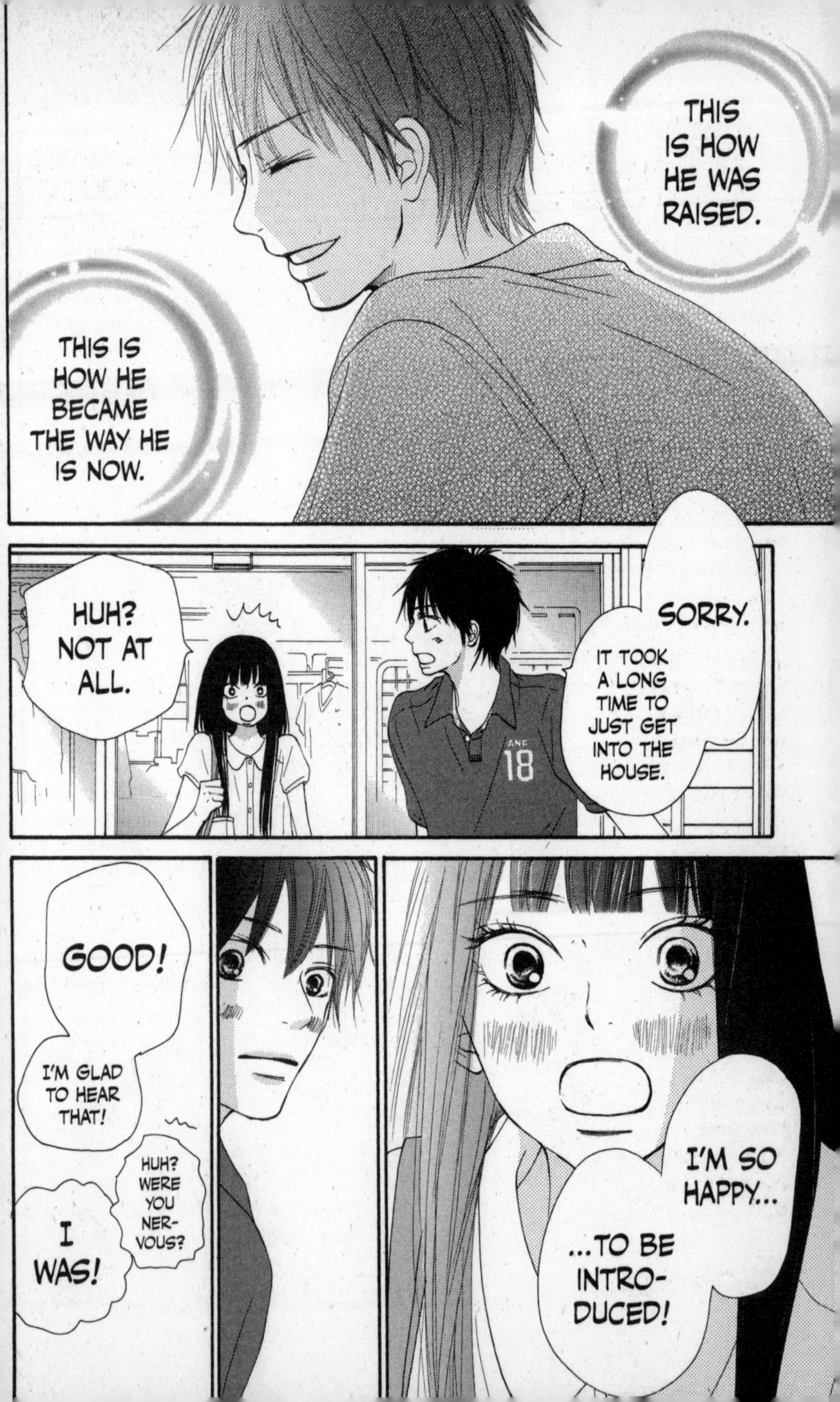
THIS IS HOW HE WAS RAISED.
THIS IS HOW HE BECAME THE WAY HE IS NOW.
SORRY.
IT TOOK A LONG TIME TO JUST GET INTO THE HOUSE.
HUH? NOT AT ALL.
I'M SO HAPPY...
...TO BE INTRODUCED!
GOOD!
I'M GLAD TO HEAR THAT!
HUH? WERE YOU NERVOUS?
I WAS!

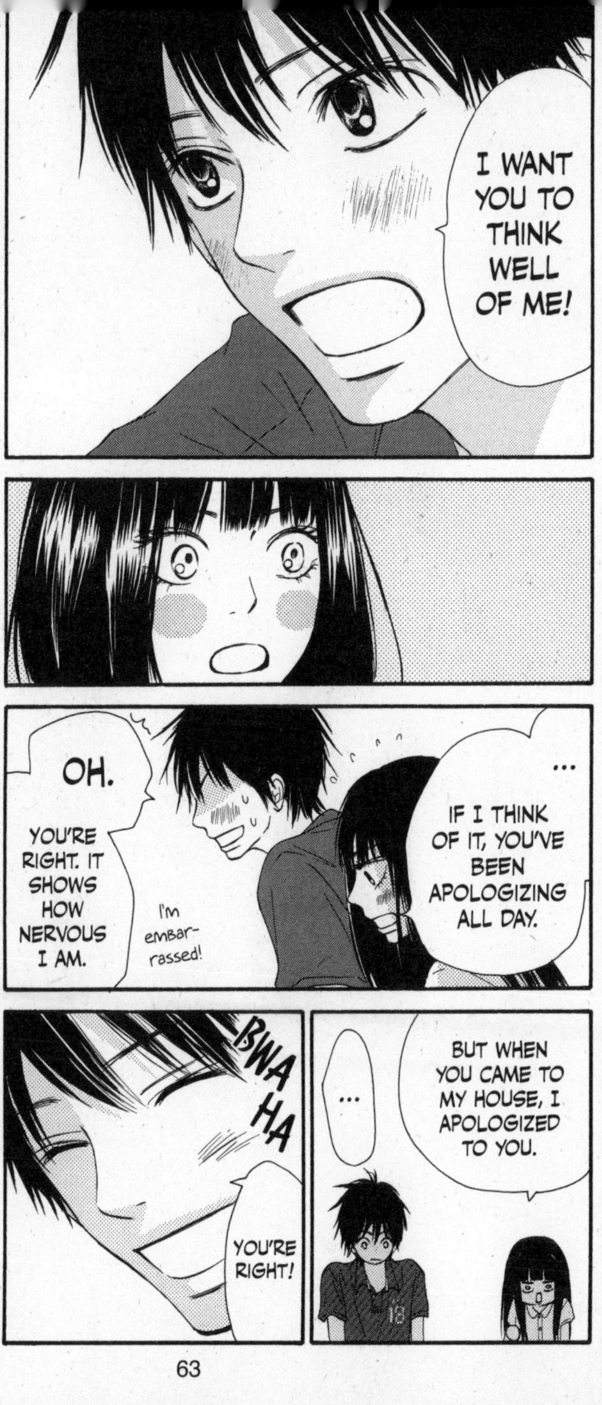
I WANT YOU TO THINK WELL OF ME!
...
IF I THINK OF IT, YOU'VE BEEN APOLOGIZING ALL DAY.
OH.
YOU'RE RIGHT. IT SHOWS HOW NERVOUS I AM.
I'm embar-rassed!
BUT WHEN YOU CAME TO MY HOUSE, I APOLOGIZED TO YOU.
...
BWA HA HA
YOU'RE RIGHT!

KARUPIN on JAPAN 3

There were lots of high school girls at the movie premiere. They were cute. I wonder if anyone went to the event who's reading this volume right now? Did you enjoy it? I sure did!

Also, by the time this volume comes out, the second season of the TV anime series will have reached its climax.

During the first season, I never thought that I would see episodes from volumes 8 to 10 on TV (I was writing the beginning of volume 10 at that time), so I'm simply overwhelmed. I would've never thought they could make such a wonderful anime. I'm very thankful that they did, though!

Season Two will be a tough time for Sawako and Kazehaya in their relationship... (I'm exaggerating a little, but...)

Continued in sidebar 4

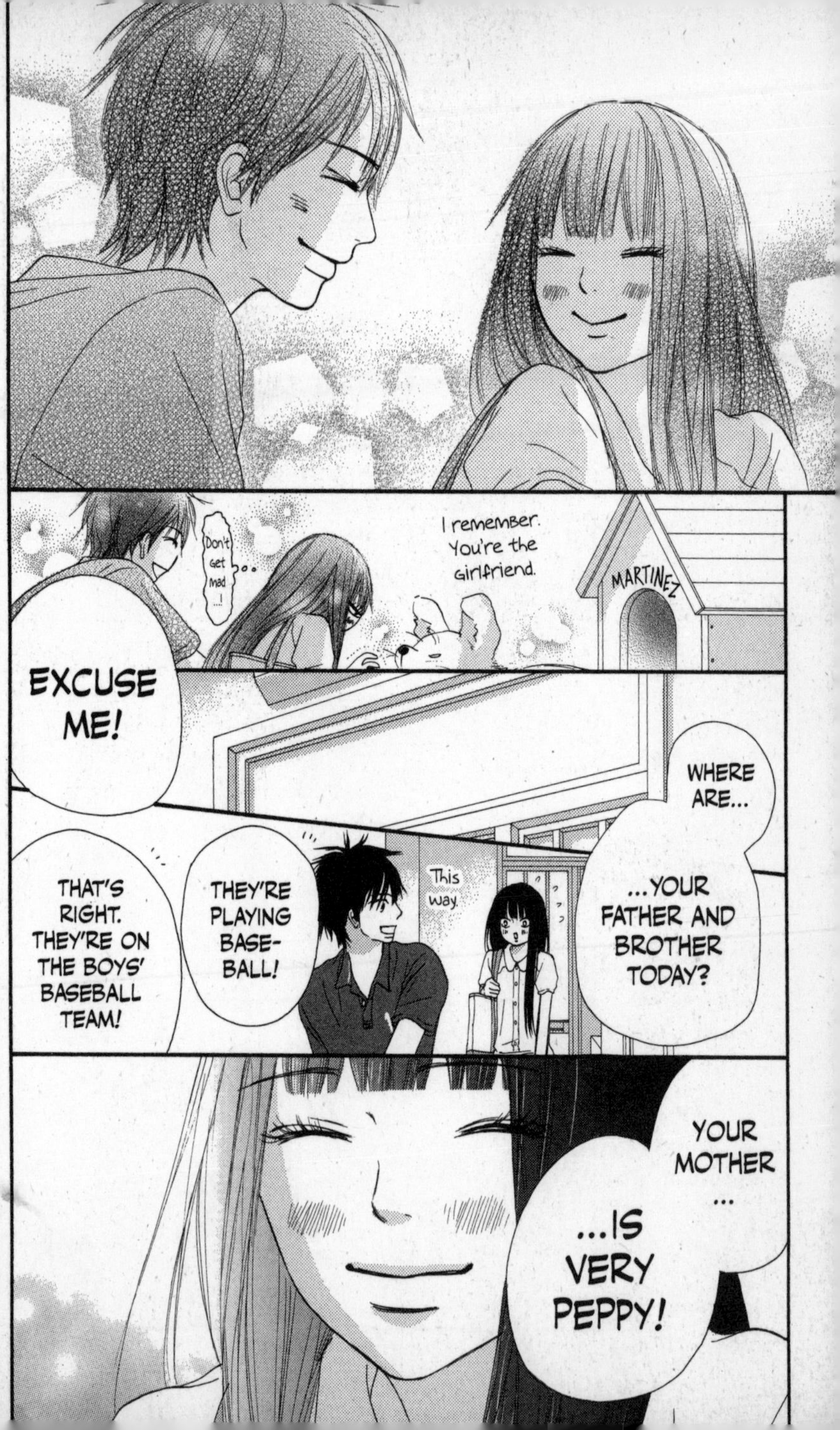
MARTINEZ
I remember. You're the Girlfriend.
Don't get mad ...!
EXCUSE ME!
WHERE ARE...
...YOUR FATHER AND BROTHER TODAY?
This way.
THEY'RE PLAYING BASE-BALL!
THAT'S RIGHT. THEY'RE ON THE BOYS' BASEBALL TEAM!
YOUR MOTHER ...
...IS VERY PEPPY!

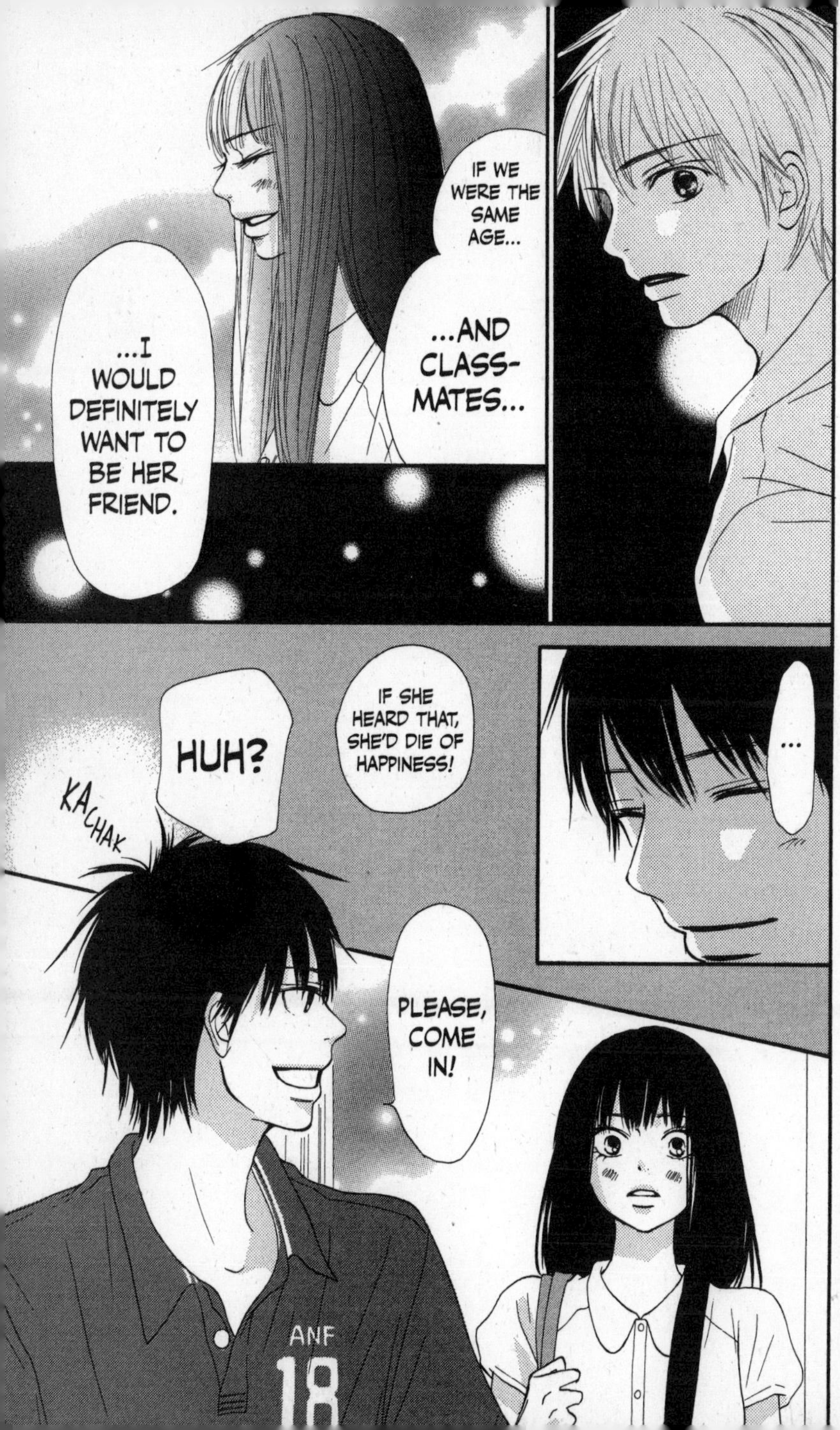
IF WE WERE THE SAME AGE...
...AND CLASSMATES...
...I WOULD DEFINITELY WANT TO BE HER FRIEND.
...
IF SHE HEARD THAT, SHE'D DIE OF HAPPINESS!
HUH?
KACHAK
PLEASE, COME IN!
ANF
18

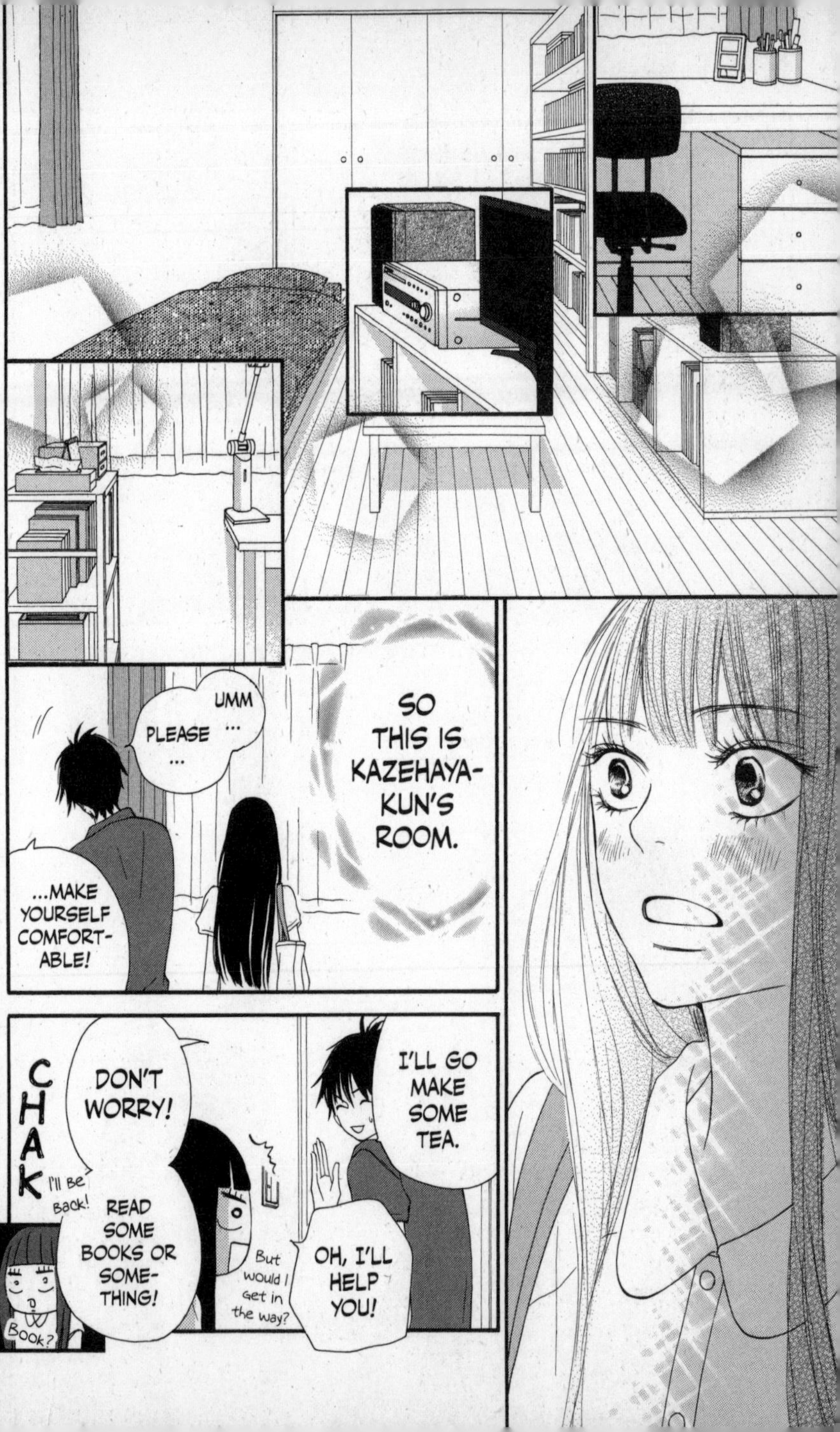
SO THIS IS KAZEHAYA-KUN'S ROOM.
UMM... PLEASE...
...MAKE YOURSELF COMFORT-ABLE!
I'LL GO MAKE SOME TEA.
OH, I'LL HELP YOU!
But would I get in the way?
DON'T WORRY!
READ SOME BOOKS OR SOME-THING!
CHAK
I'll Be Back!
Book?

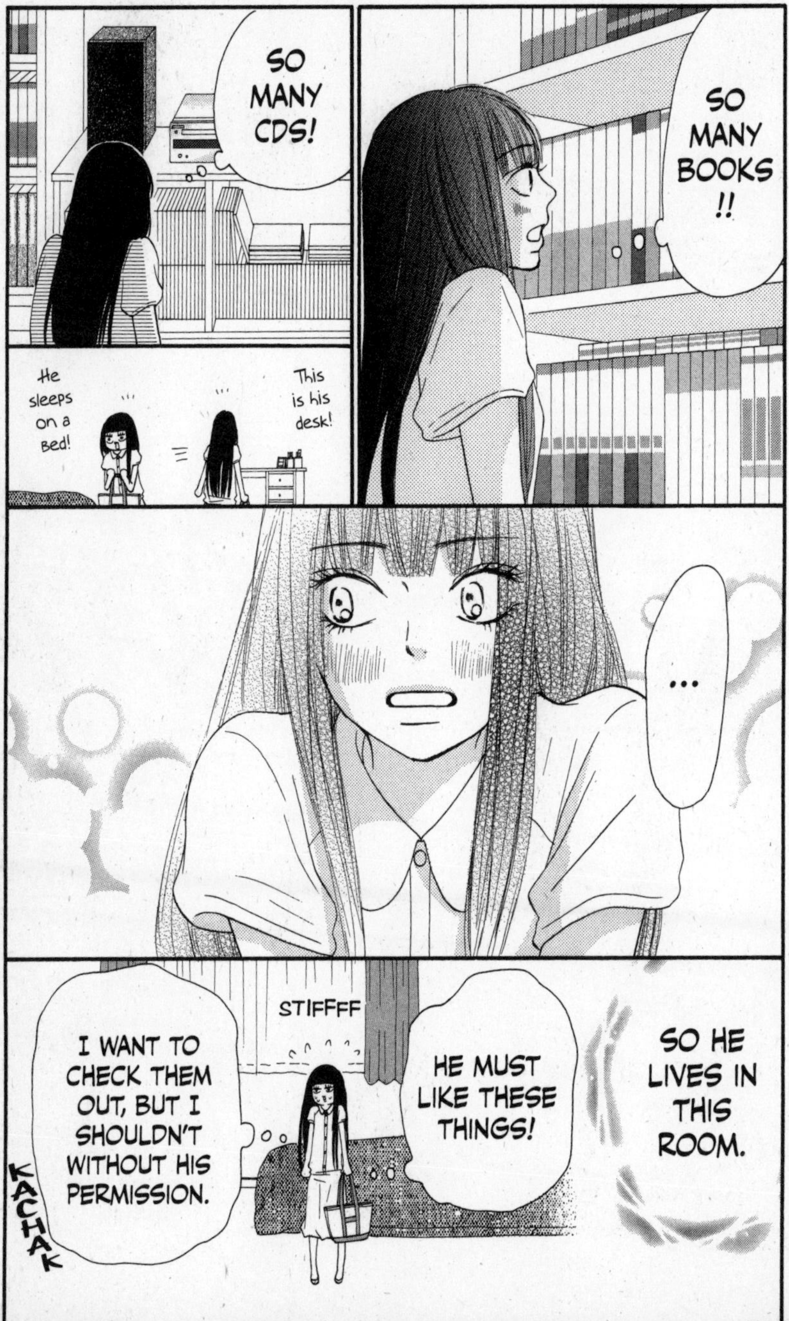
SO MANY BOOKS!!
SO MANY CDS!
This is his desk!
He sleeps on a bed!
...
SO HE LIVES IN THIS ROOM.
HE MUST LIKE THESE THINGS!
STIFFFF
I WANT TO CHECK THEM OUT, BUT I SHOULDN'T WITHOUT HIS PERMISSION.
KACHAK

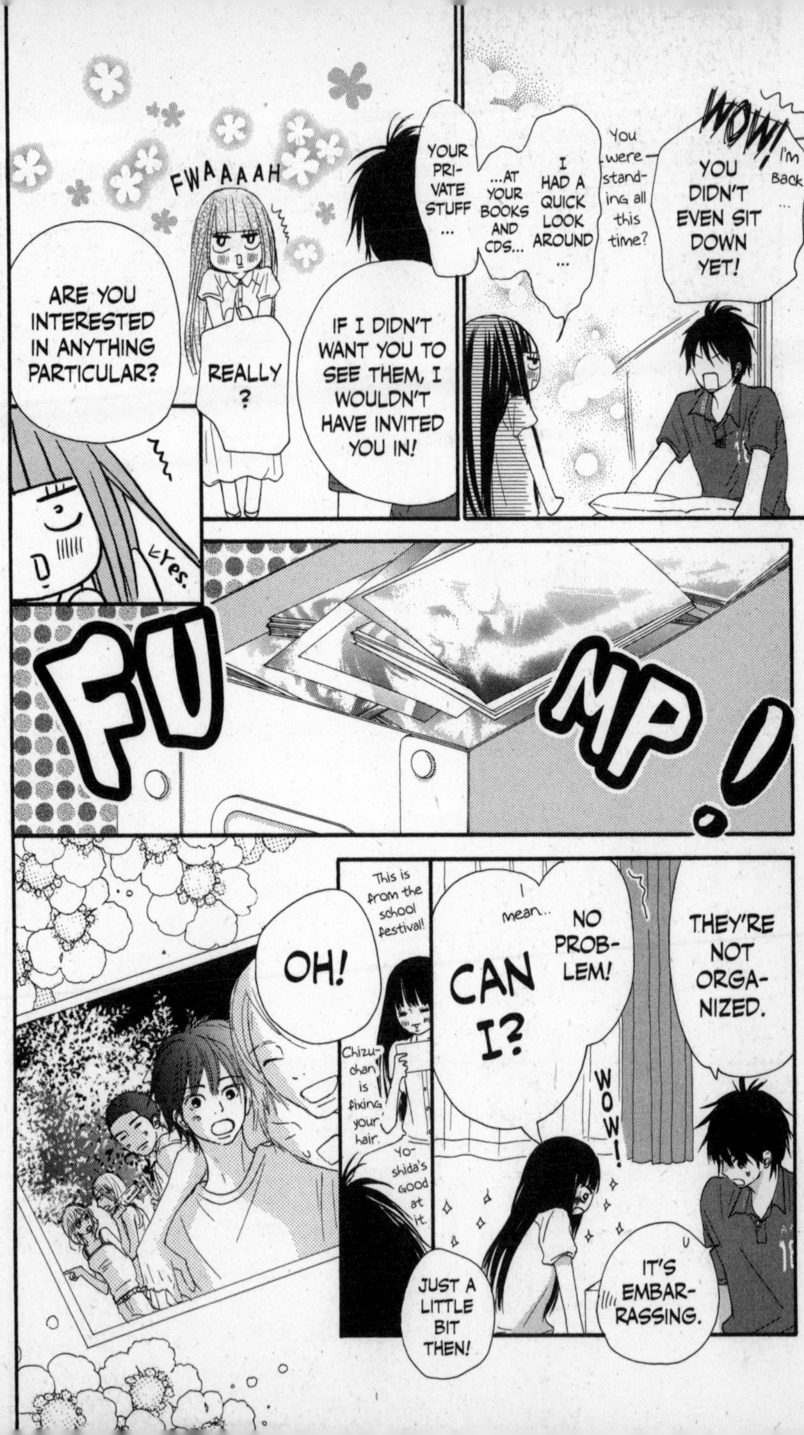
WOW!
I'm Back...
YOU DIDN'T EVEN SIT DOWN YET!
You were standing all this time?
I HAD A QUICK LOOK AROUND...
...AT YOUR BOOKS AND CDS...
YOUR PRIVATE STUFF...
IF I DIDN'T WANT YOU TO SEE THEM, I WOULDN'T HAVE INVITED YOU IN!
FWAAAAAH
REALLY?
ARE YOU INTERESTED IN ANYTHING PARTICULAR?
←Yes.
FUMP!
THEY'RE NOT ORGANIZED.
IT'S EMBARRASSING.
NO PROBLEM!
I mean...
CAN I?
WOW!
JUST A LITTLE BIT THEN!
This is from the school festival!
Chizu-chan is fixing your hair.
Yoshida's Good at it.
OH!

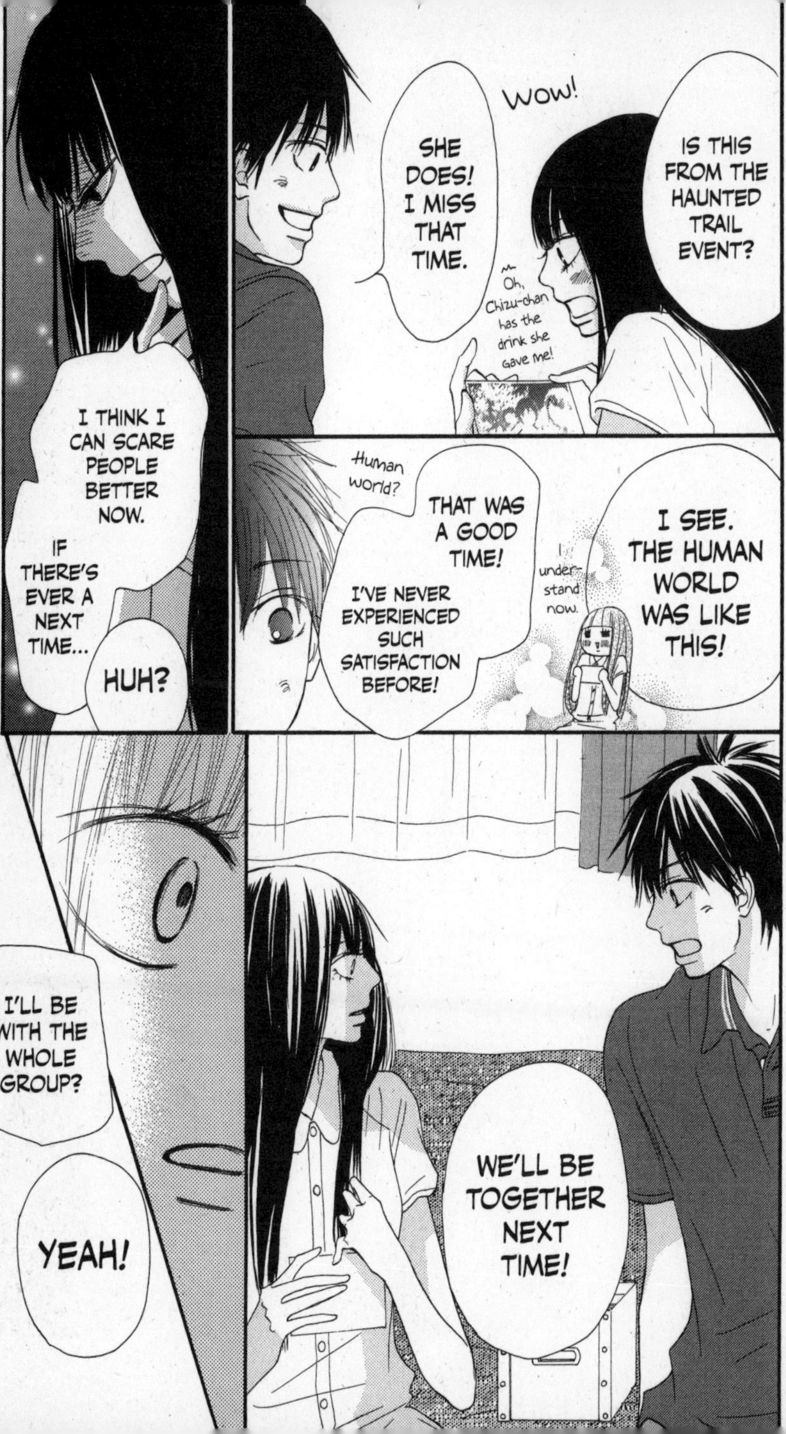
IS THIS FROM THE HAUNTED TRAIL EVENT?
WOW!
Oh, Chizu-chan has the drink she gave me!
SHE DOES! I MISS THAT TIME.
I SEE. THE HUMAN WORLD WAS LIKE THIS!
I understand now.
THAT WAS A GOOD TIME!
Human world?
I'VE NEVER EXPERIENCED SUCH SATISFACTION BEFORE!
I THINK I CAN SCARE PEOPLE BETTER NOW.
IF THERE'S EVER A NEXT TIME...
HUH?
WE'LL BE TOGETHER NEXT TIME!
I'LL BE WITH THE WHOLE GROUP?
YEAH!

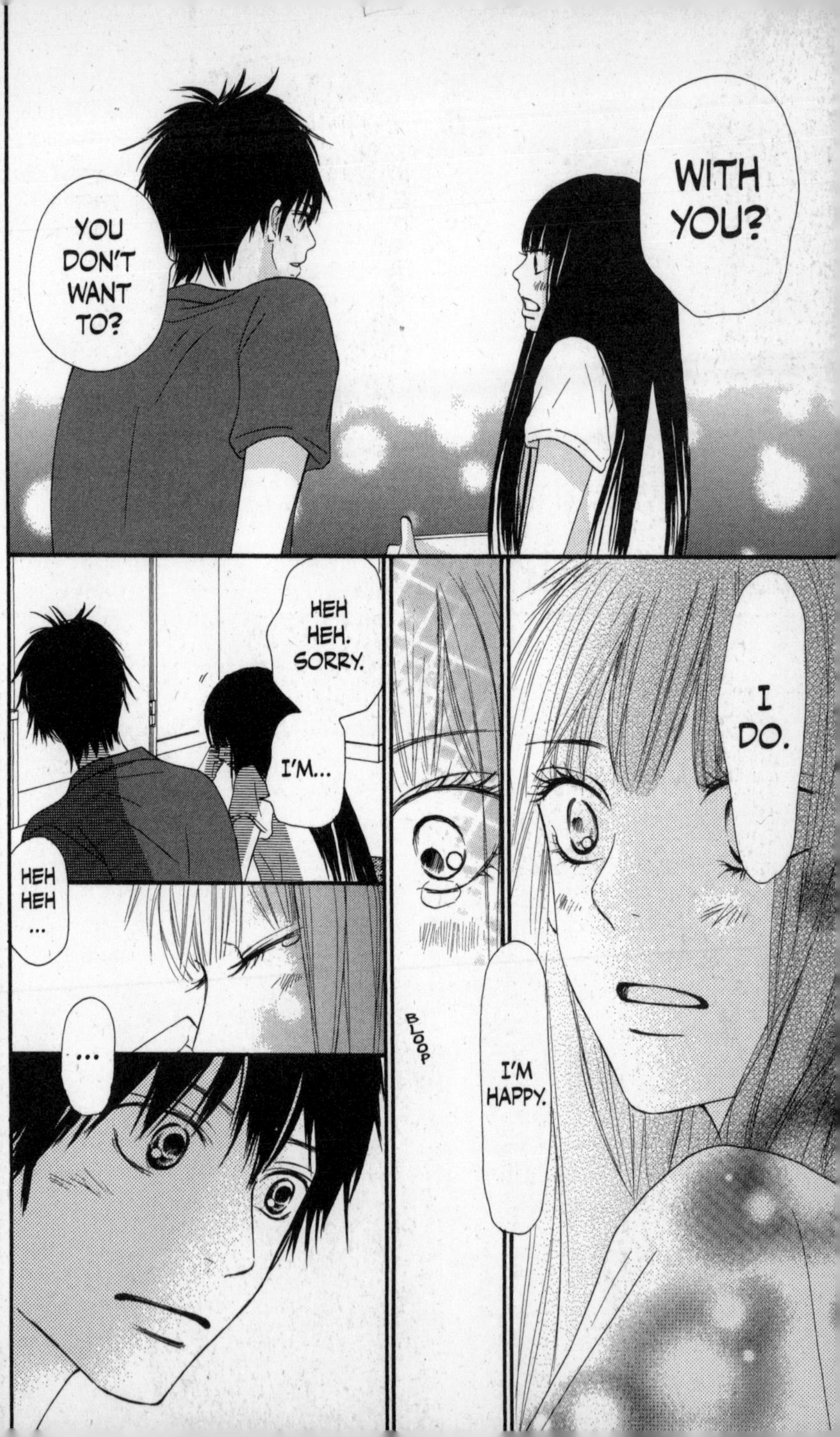
WITH YOU?
YOU DON'T WANT TO?
I DO.
I'M HAPPY.
BLOOP
HEH HEH. SORRY.
I'M...
HEH HEH ...
...

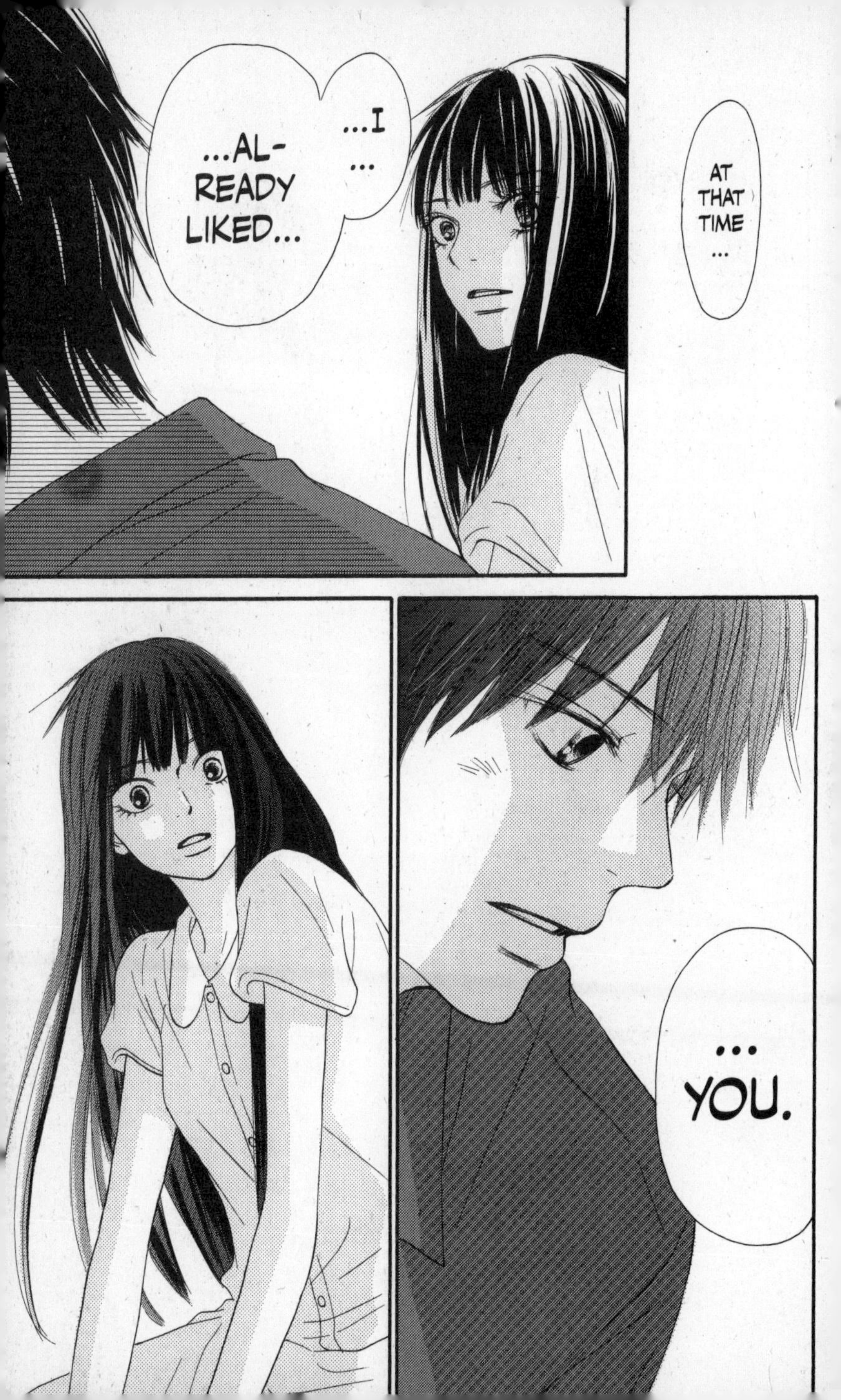
AT THAT TIME ...
...I ...
...AL-READY LIKED...
... YOU.

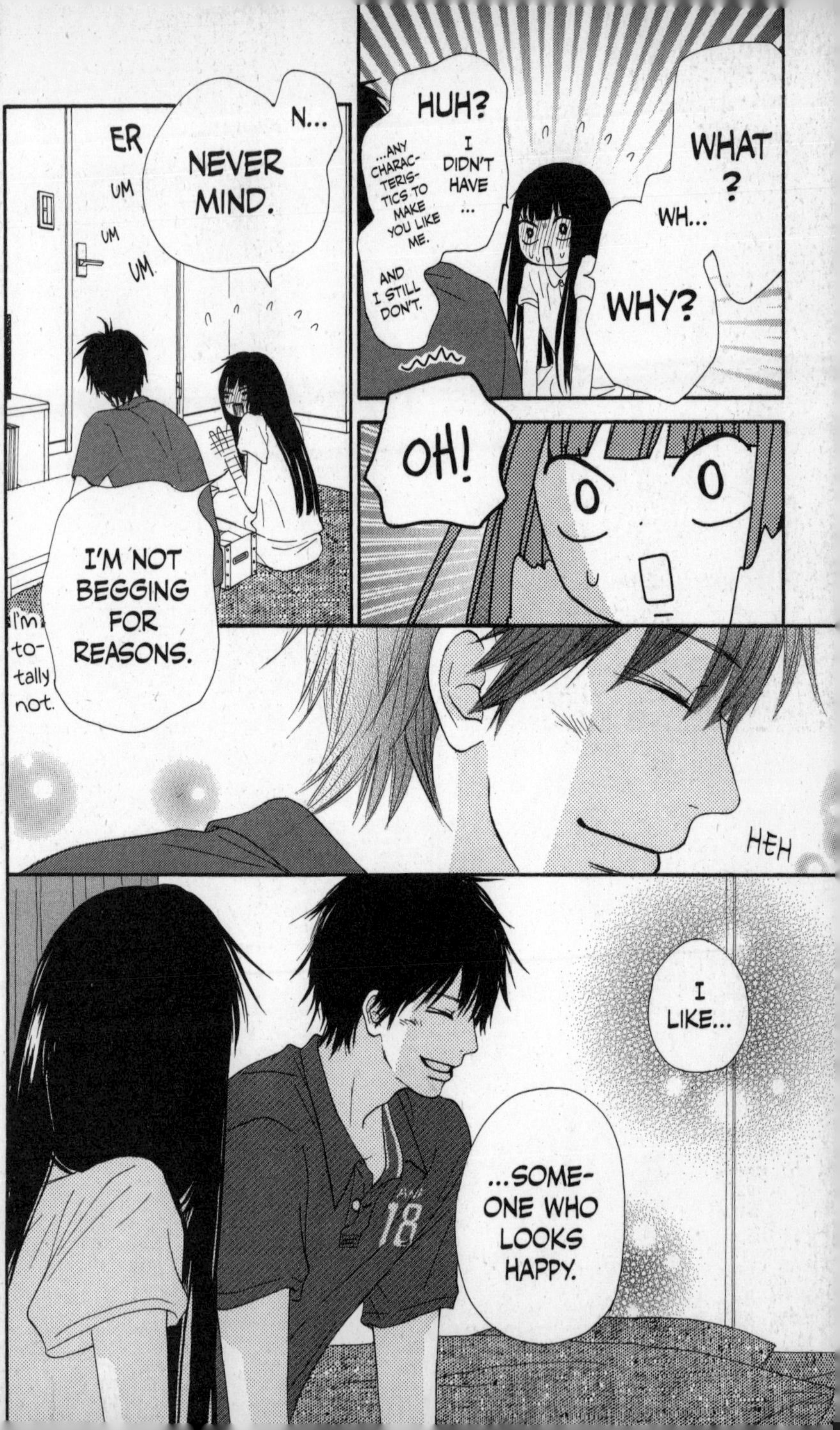

HUH?
WHAT?
WH...
WHY?
I DIDN'T HAVE...
...ANY CHARAC-TERIS-TICS TO MAKE YOU LIKE ME.
AND I STILL DON'T.
OH!
N...
NEVER MIND.
ER
UM
UM
UM.
I'M NOT BEGGING FOR REASONS.
I'm to-tally not.
HEH
I LIKE...
...SOME-ONE WHO LOOKS HAPPY.

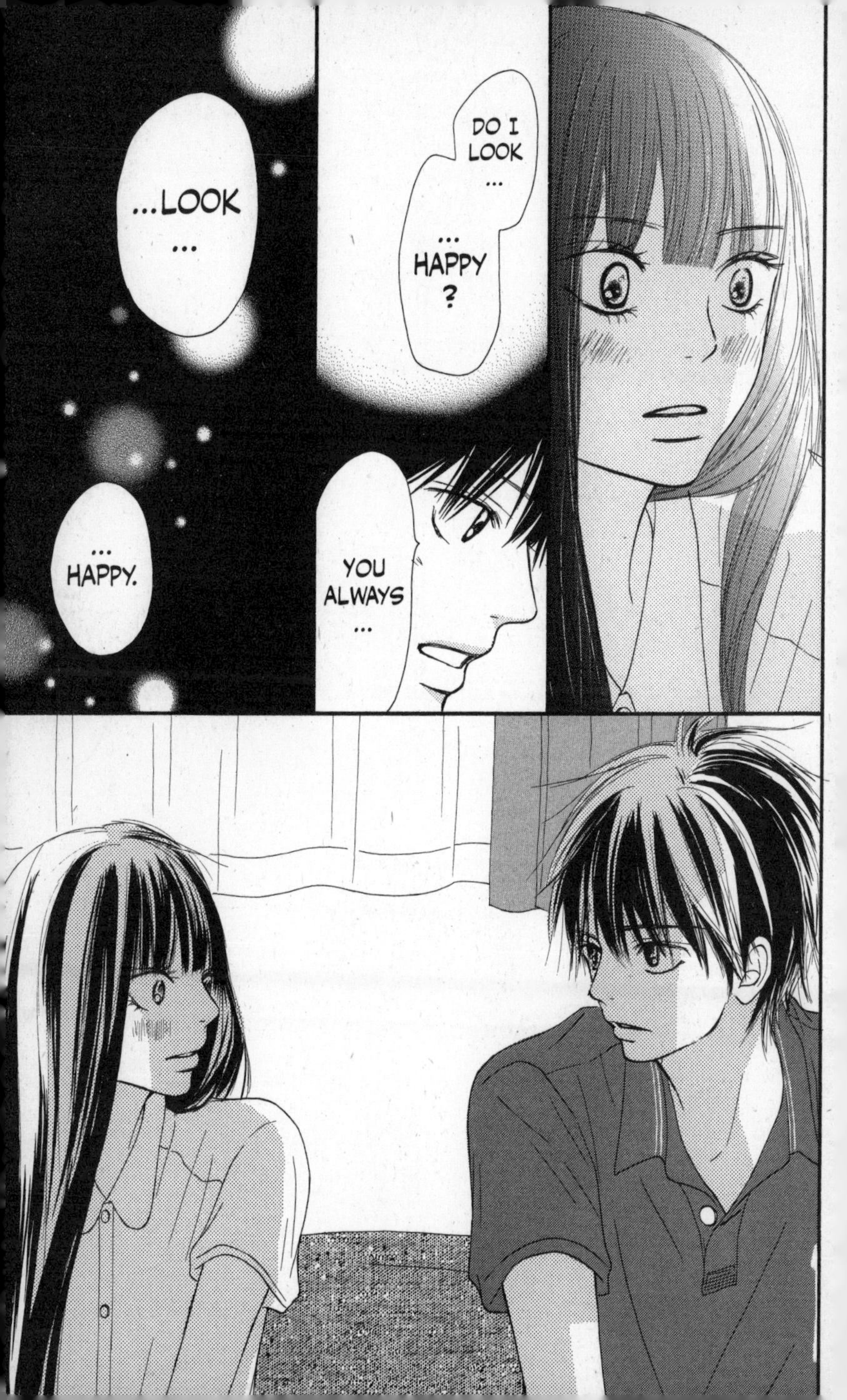
DO I LOOK ... ... HAPPY ?
YOU ALWAYS ...
...LOOK ...
... HAPPY.

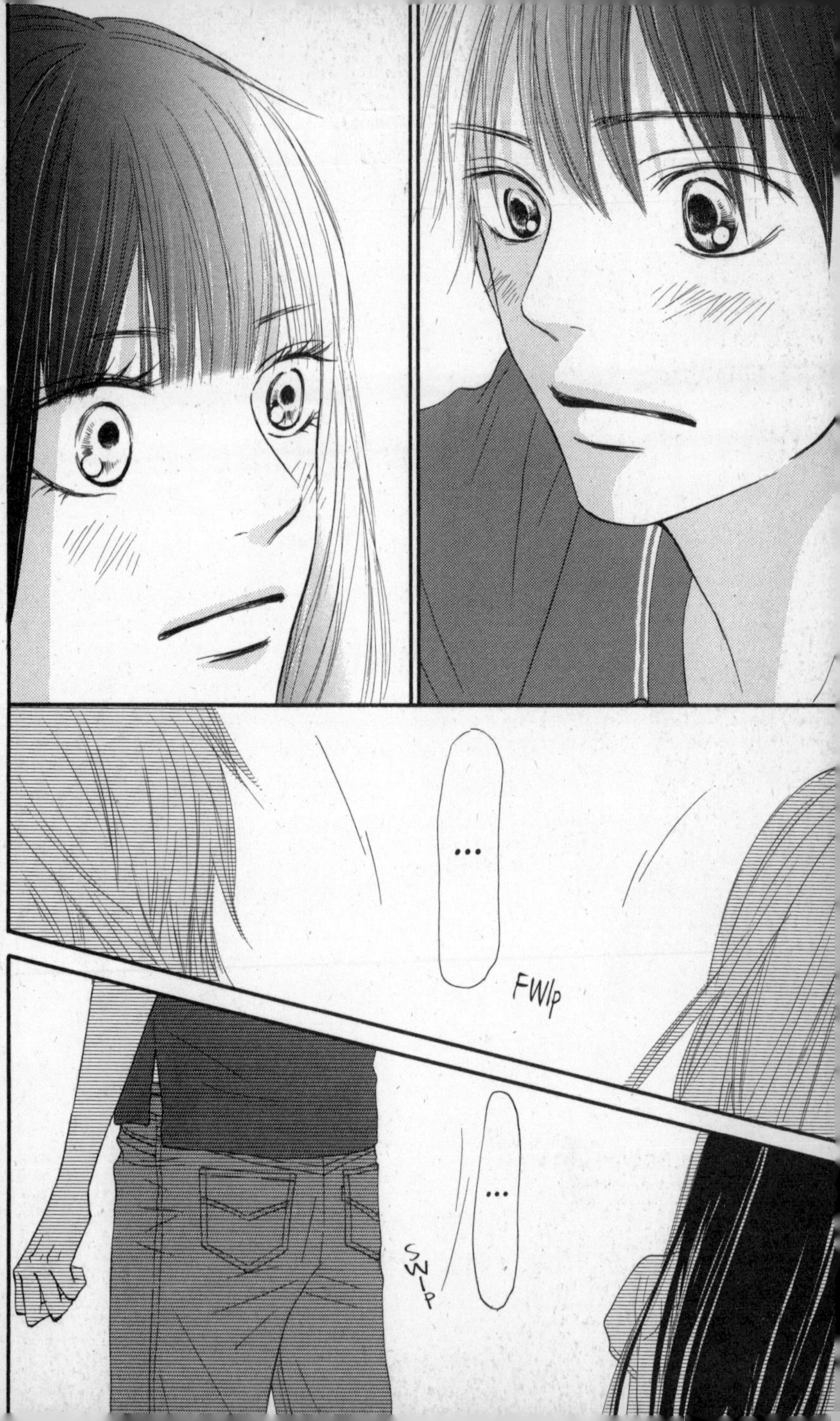
...
FWIP
...
SWIP

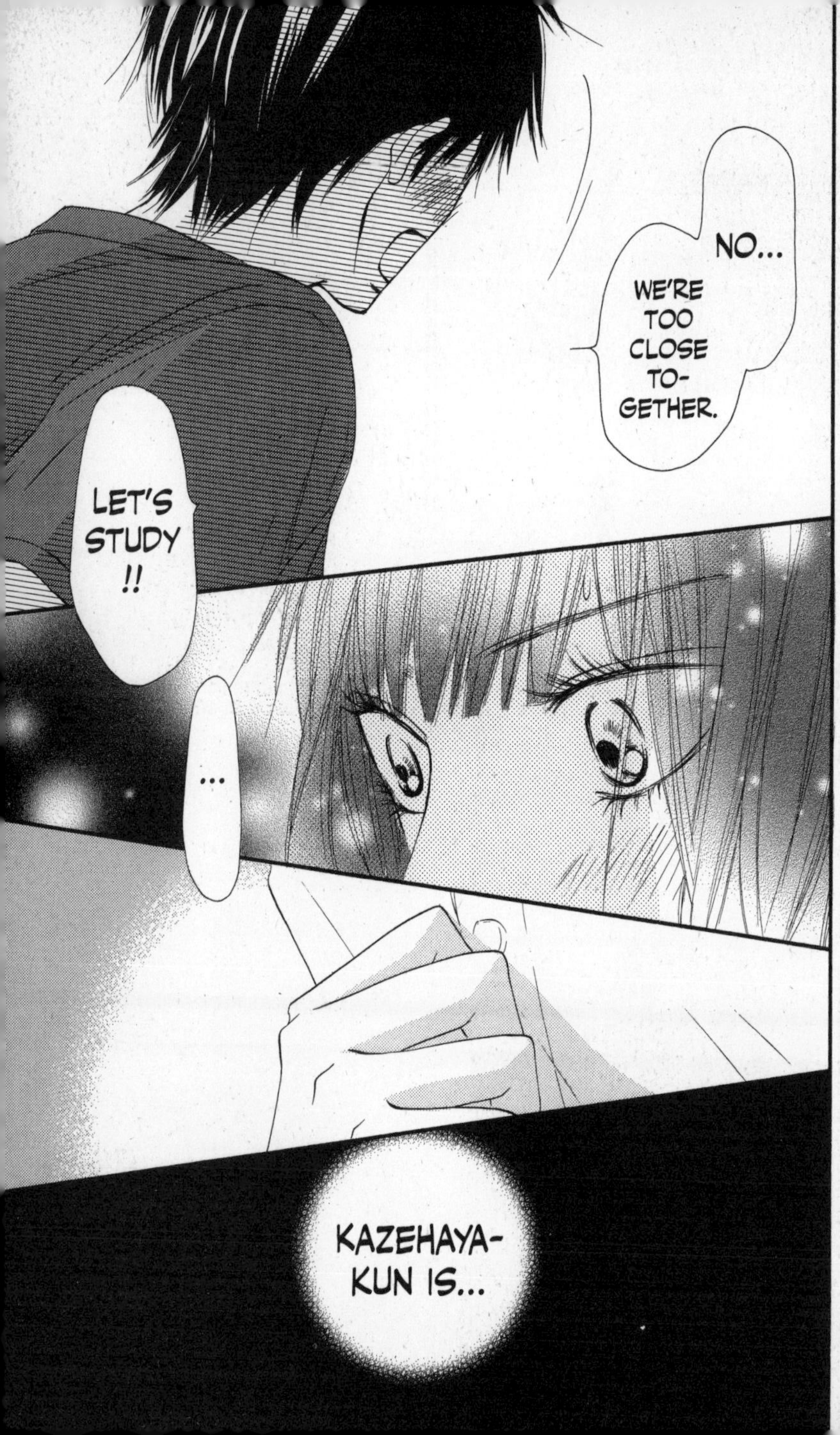
NO... WE'RE TOO CLOSE TO-GETHER.
LET'S STUDY !!
...
KAZEHAYA-KUN IS...

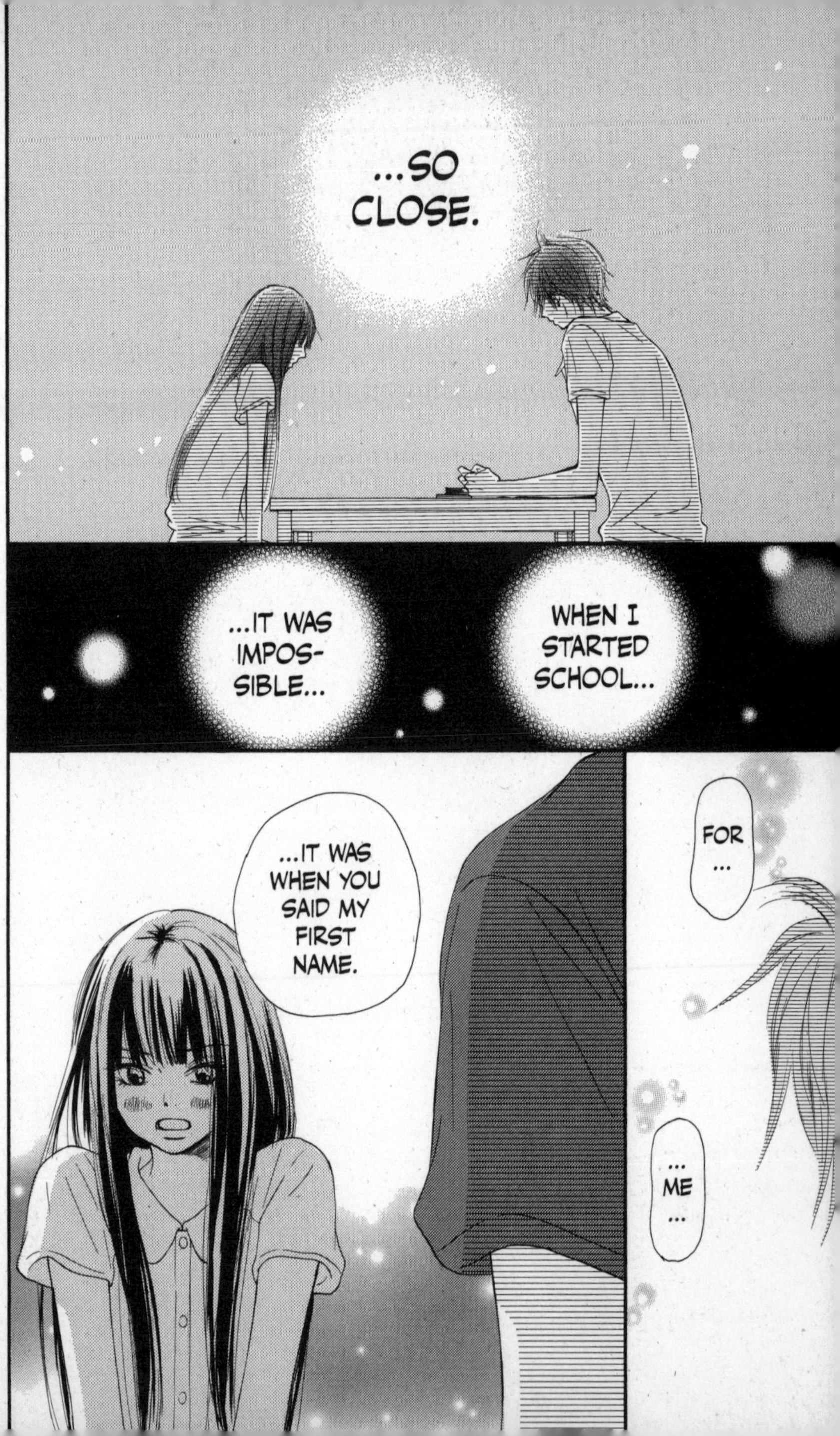
...SO CLOSE.
WHEN I STARTED SCHOOL...
...IT WAS IMPOS-SIBLE...
FOR ...
... ME ...
...IT WAS WHEN YOU SAID MY FIRST NAME.

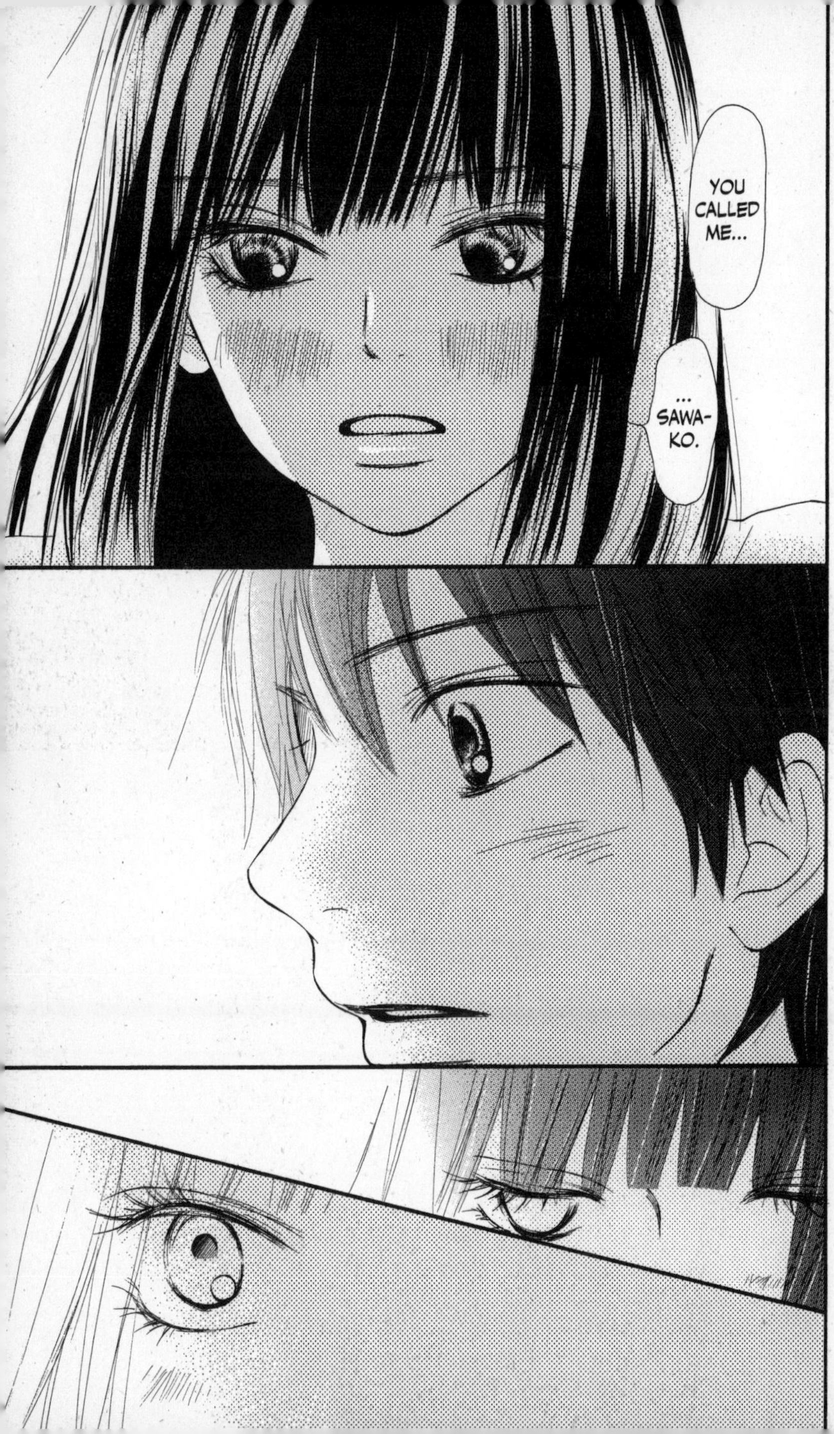
YOU CALLED ME...
...SAWA-KO.

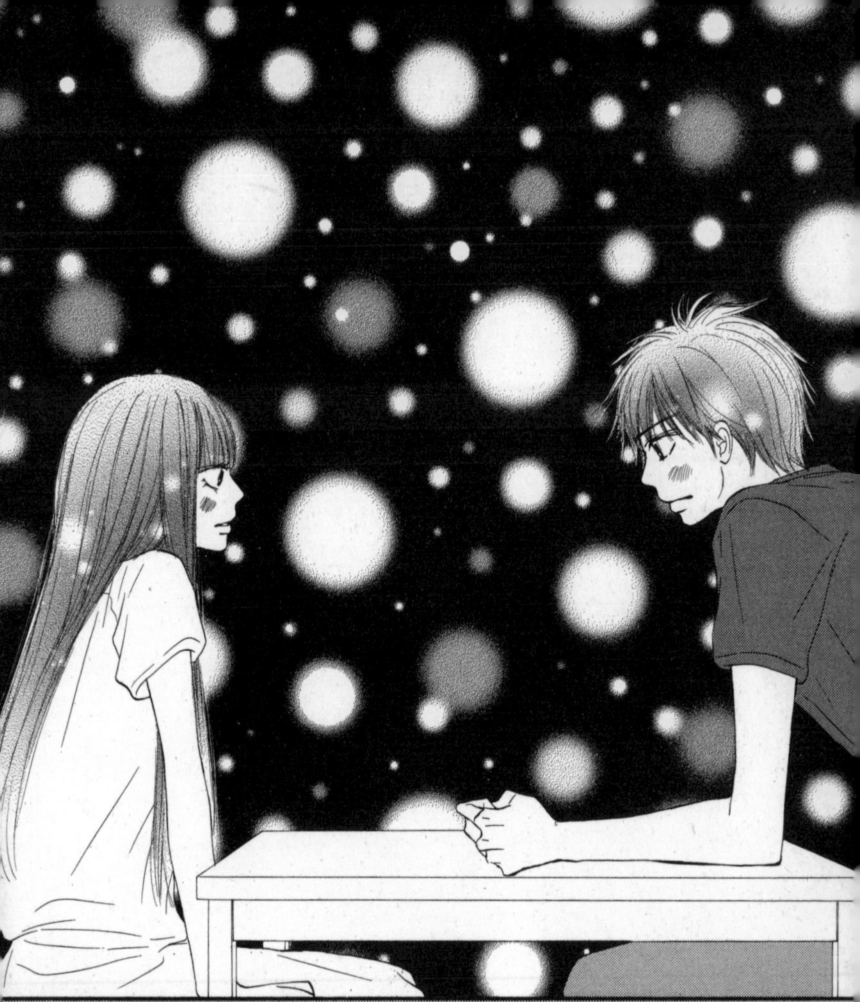

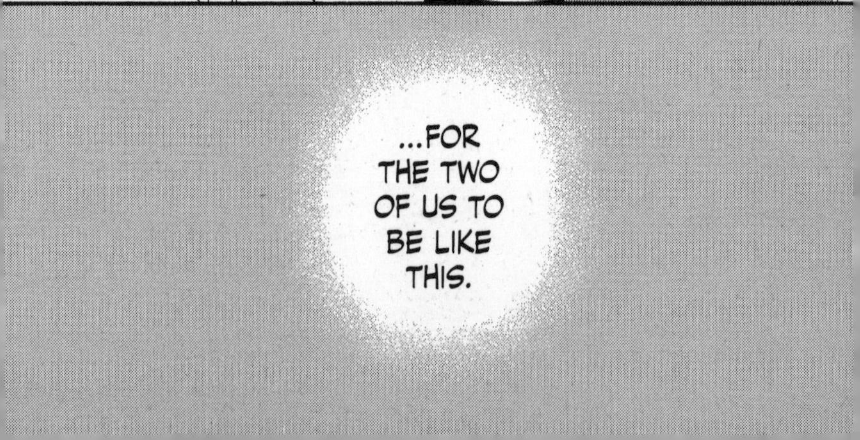
...FOR THE TWO OF US TO BE LIKE THIS.

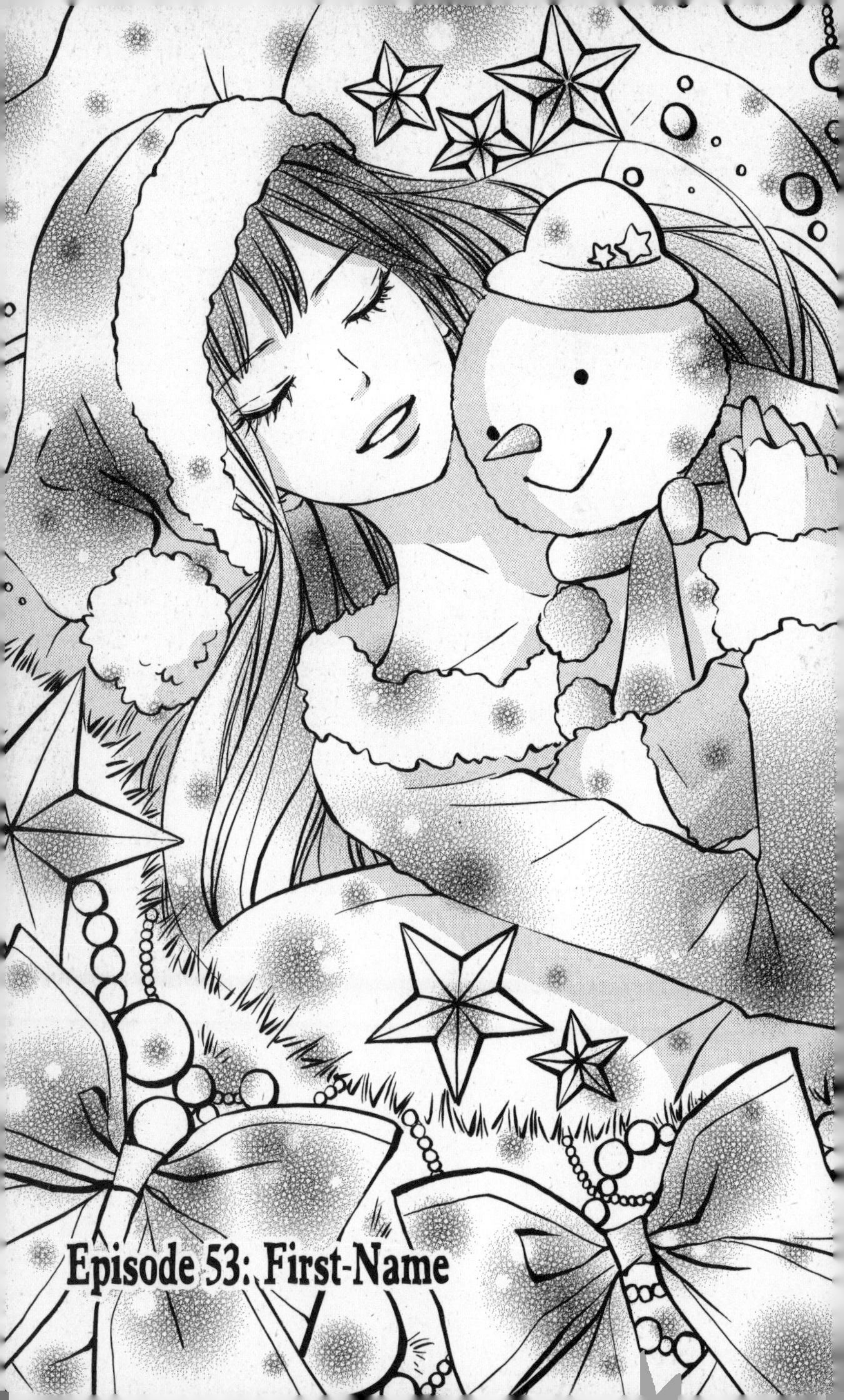
Episode 53: First-Name

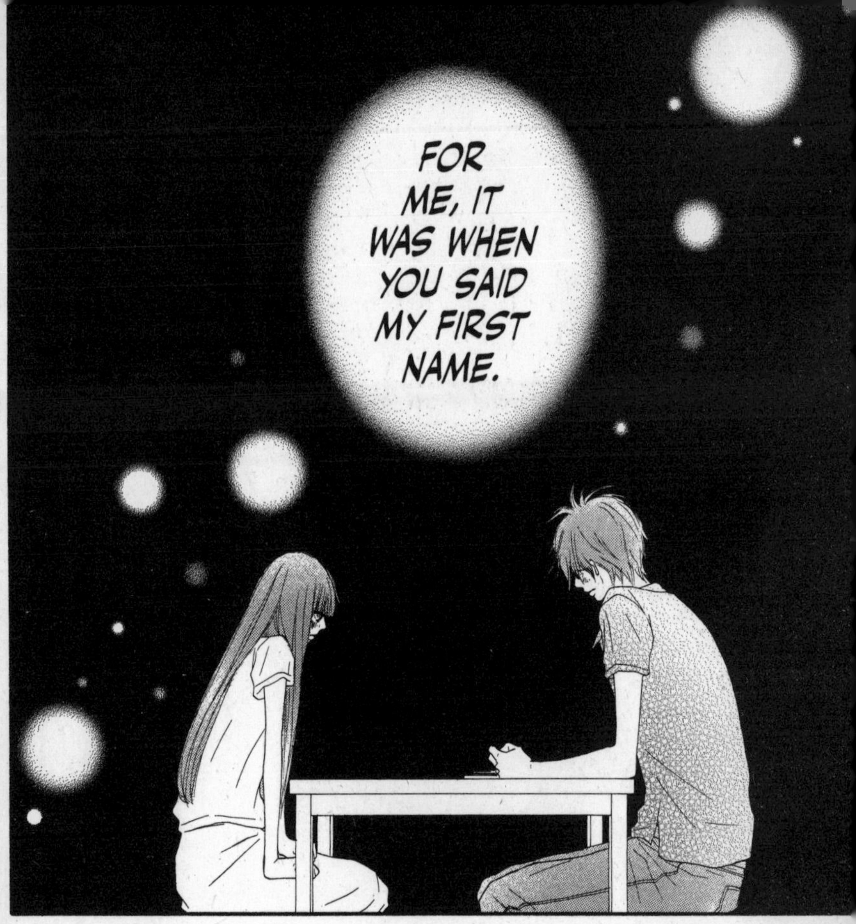
FOR ME, IT WAS WHEN YOU SAID MY FIRST NAME.

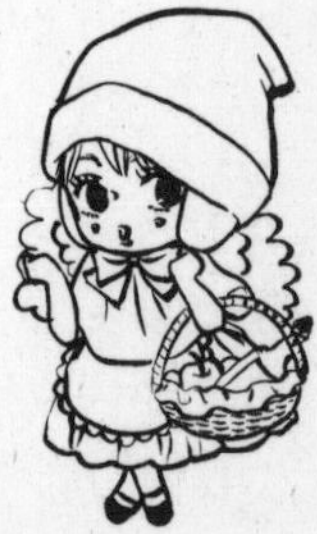

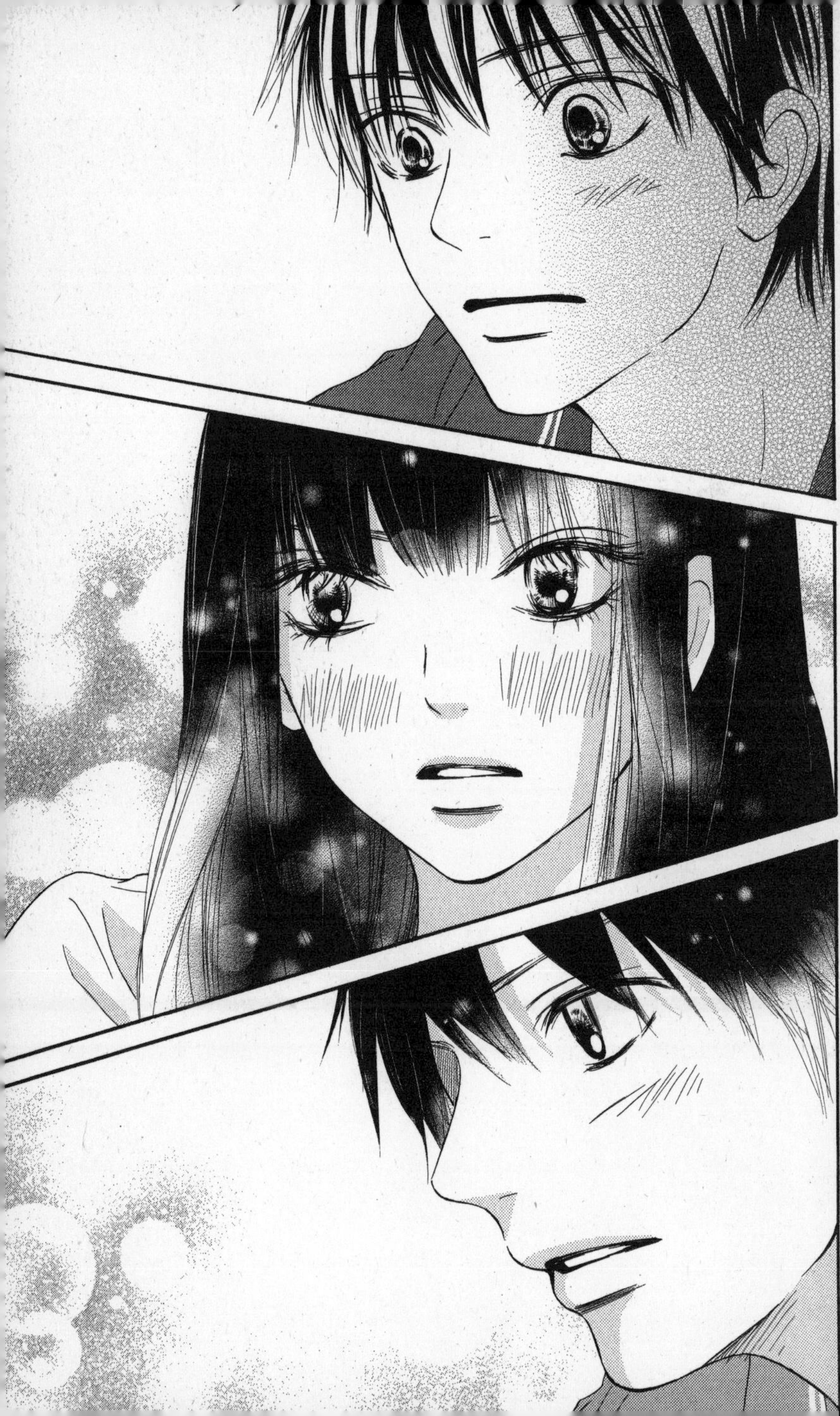

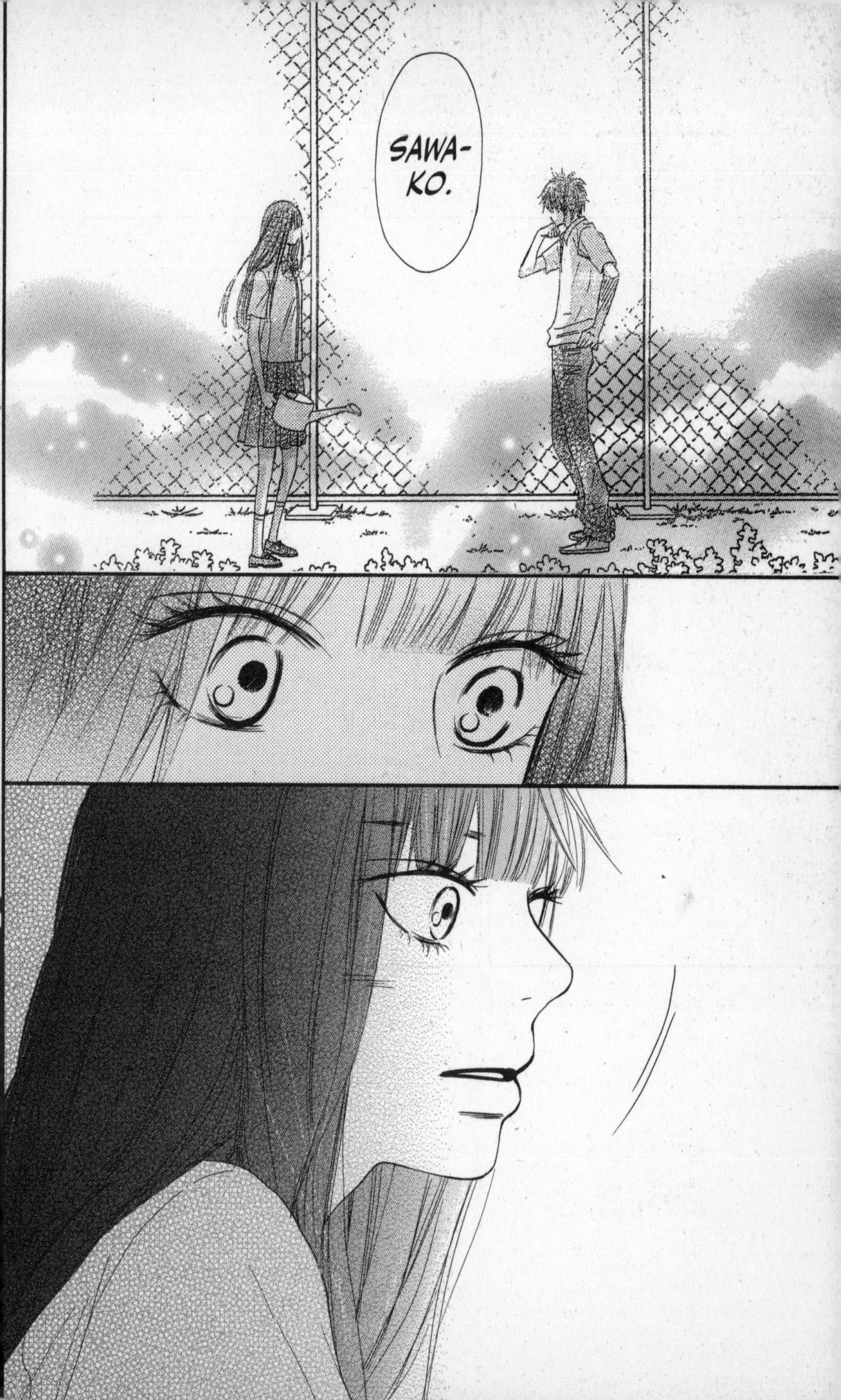
SAWA-
KO.

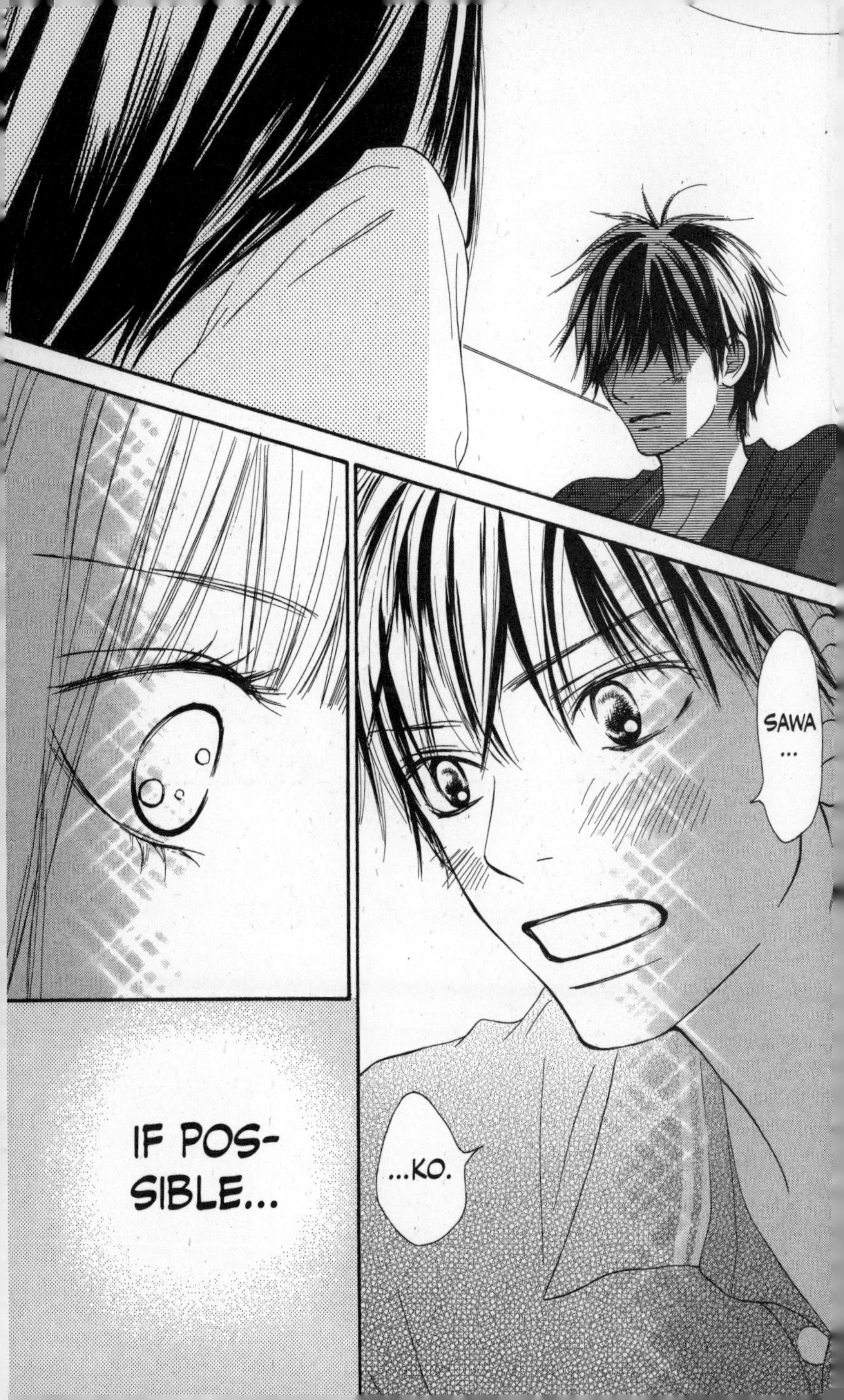
SAWA ...
...KO.
IF POS-
SIBLE...

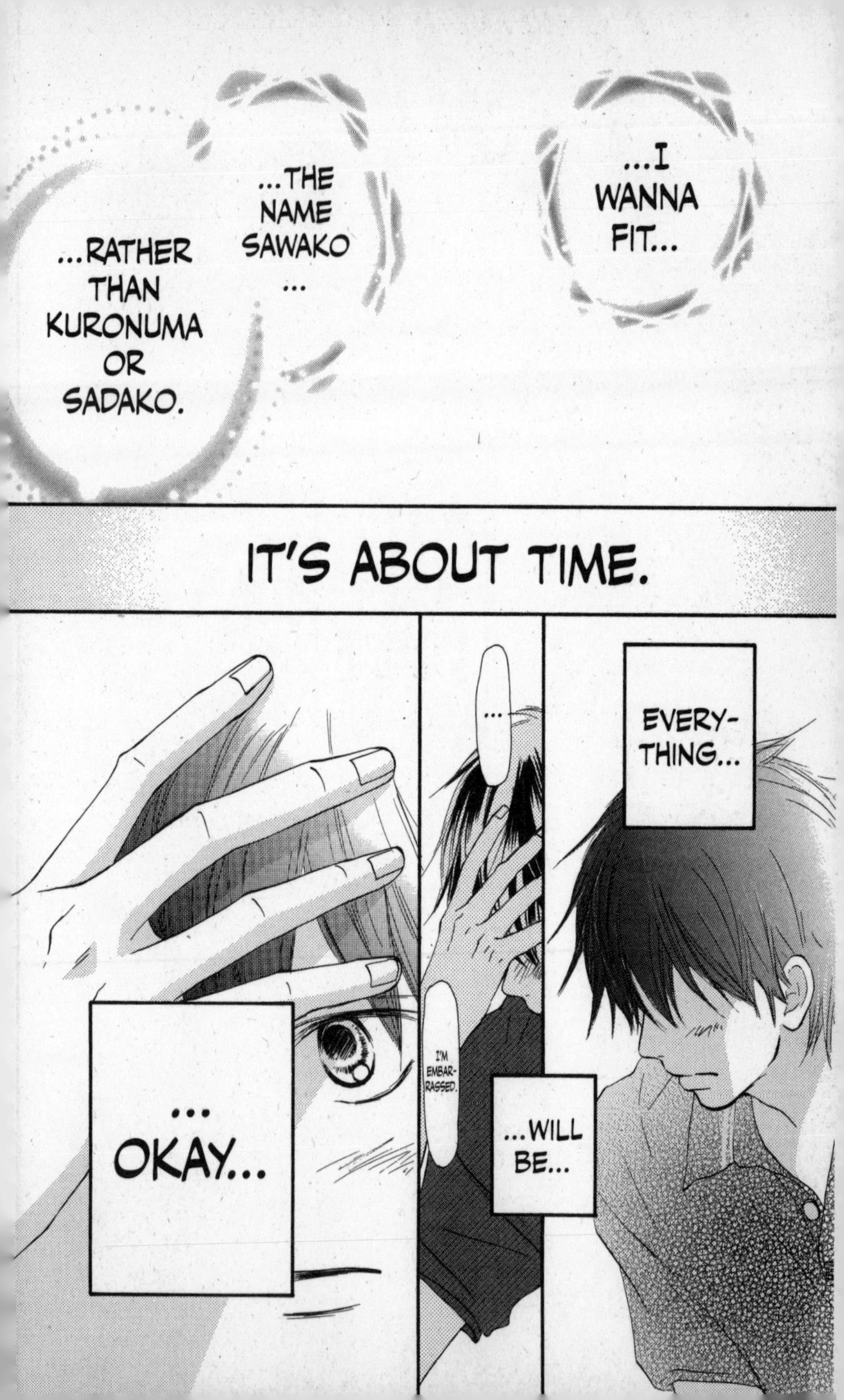
...I WANNA FIT...
...THE NAME SAWAKO ...
...RATHER THAN KURONUMA OR SADAKO.
IT'S ABOUT TIME.
EVERY-THING...
...WILL BE...
...
I'M EMBAR-RASSED.
... OKAY...

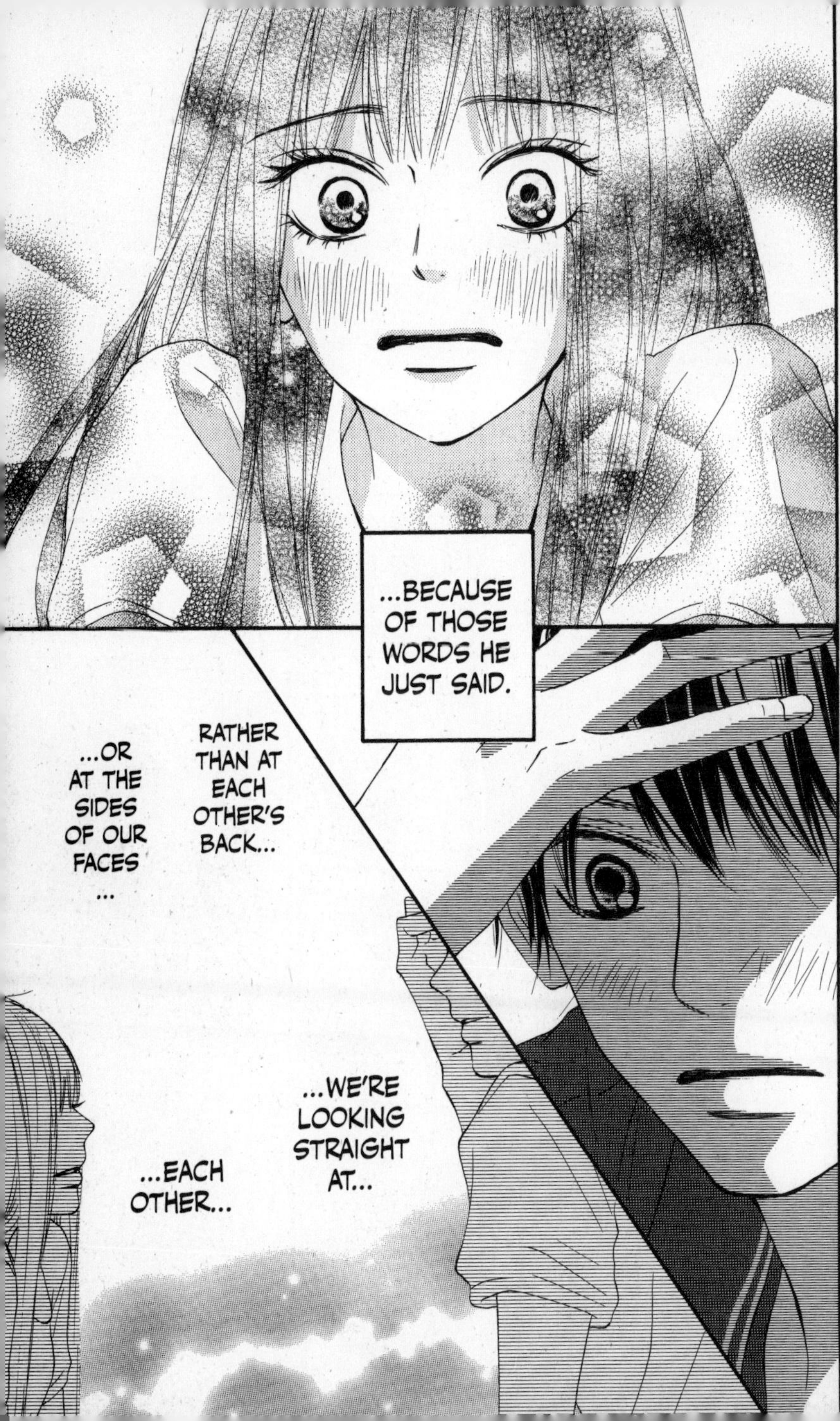
...BECAUSE OF THOSE WORDS HE JUST SAID.
RATHER THAN AT EACH OTHER'S BACK...
...OR AT THE SIDES OF OUR FACES ...
...WE'RE LOOKING STRAIGHT AT...
...EACH OTHER...

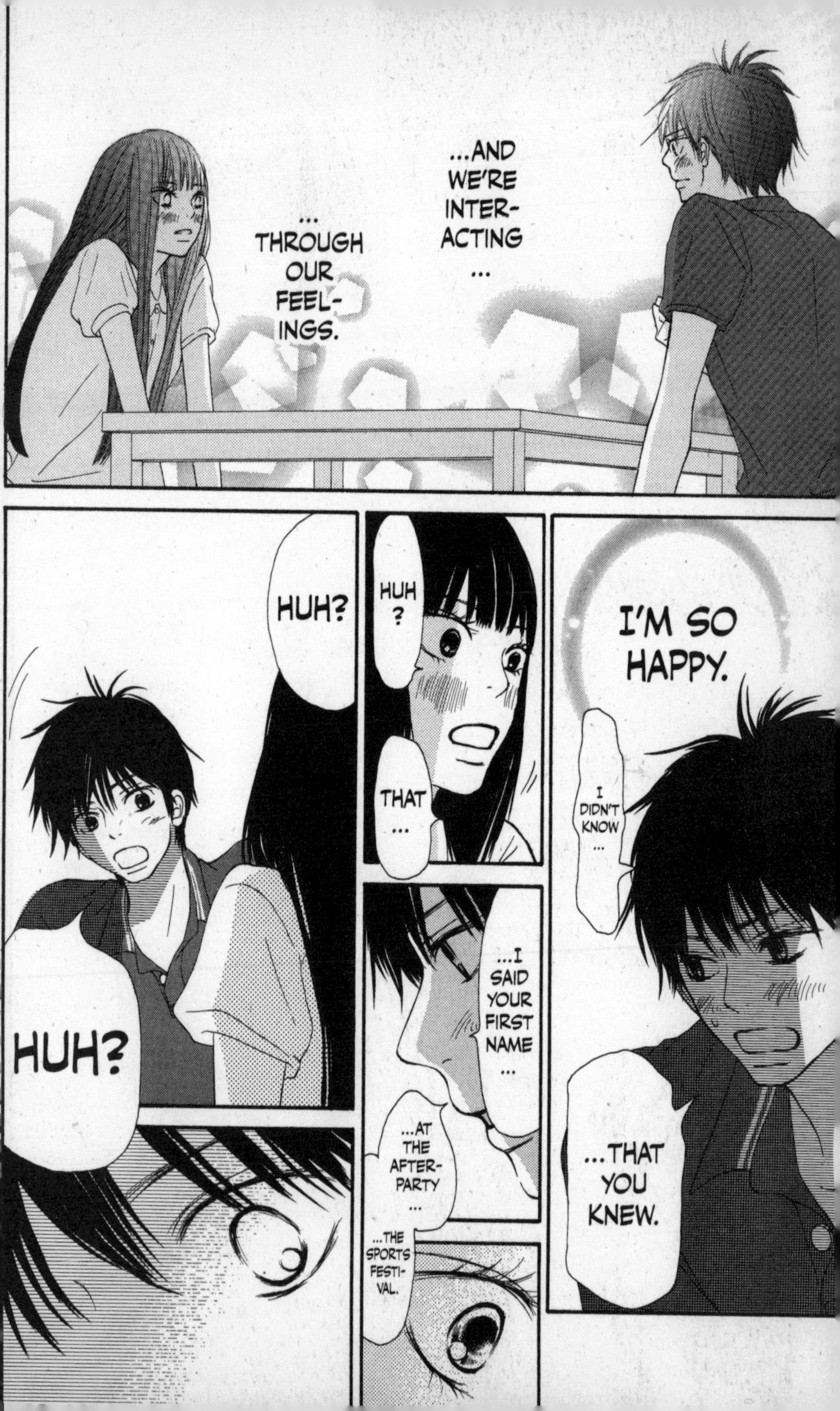
...AND WE'RE INTER-ACTING...
...THROUGH OUR FEEL-INGS.
I'M SO HAPPY.
I DIDN'T KNOW...
...THAT YOU KNEW.
HUH?
THAT...
...I SAID YOUR FIRST NAME...
...AT THE AFTER-PARTY...
...THE SPORTS FESTI-VAL.
HUH?
HUH?

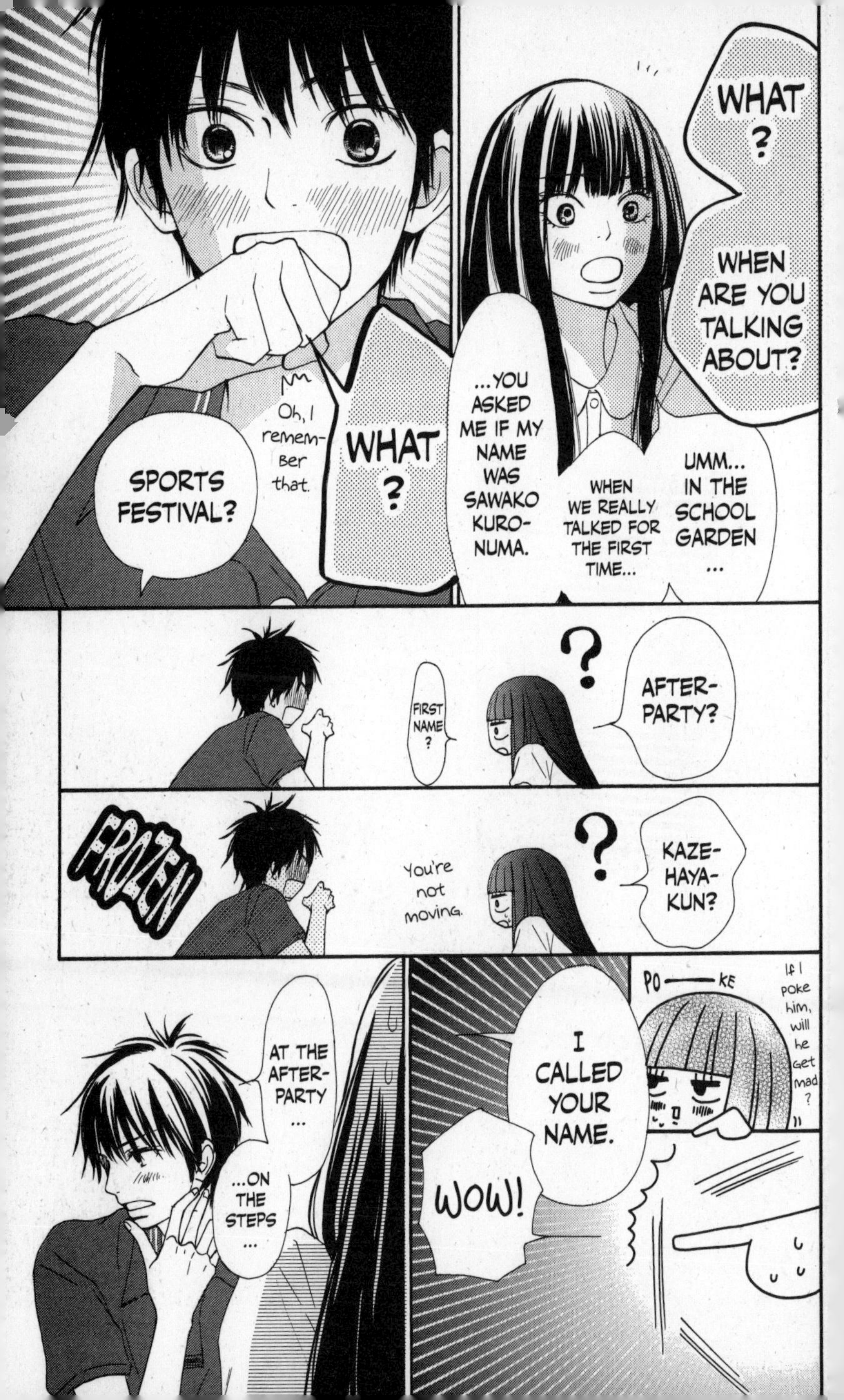
WHAT?
WHEN ARE YOU TALKING ABOUT?
UMM... IN THE SCHOOL GARDEN...
WHEN WE REALLY TALKED FOR THE FIRST TIME...
...YOU ASKED ME IF MY NAME WAS SAWAKO KURONUMA.
WHAT?
Oh, I remember that.
SPORTS FESTIVAL?
AFTER-PARTY?
FIRST NAME?
KAZE-HAYA-KUN?
You're not moving.
FROZEN
PO——KE
If I poke him, will he get mad?
I CALLED YOUR NAME.
WOW!
AT THE AFTER-PARTY...
...ON THE STEPS...

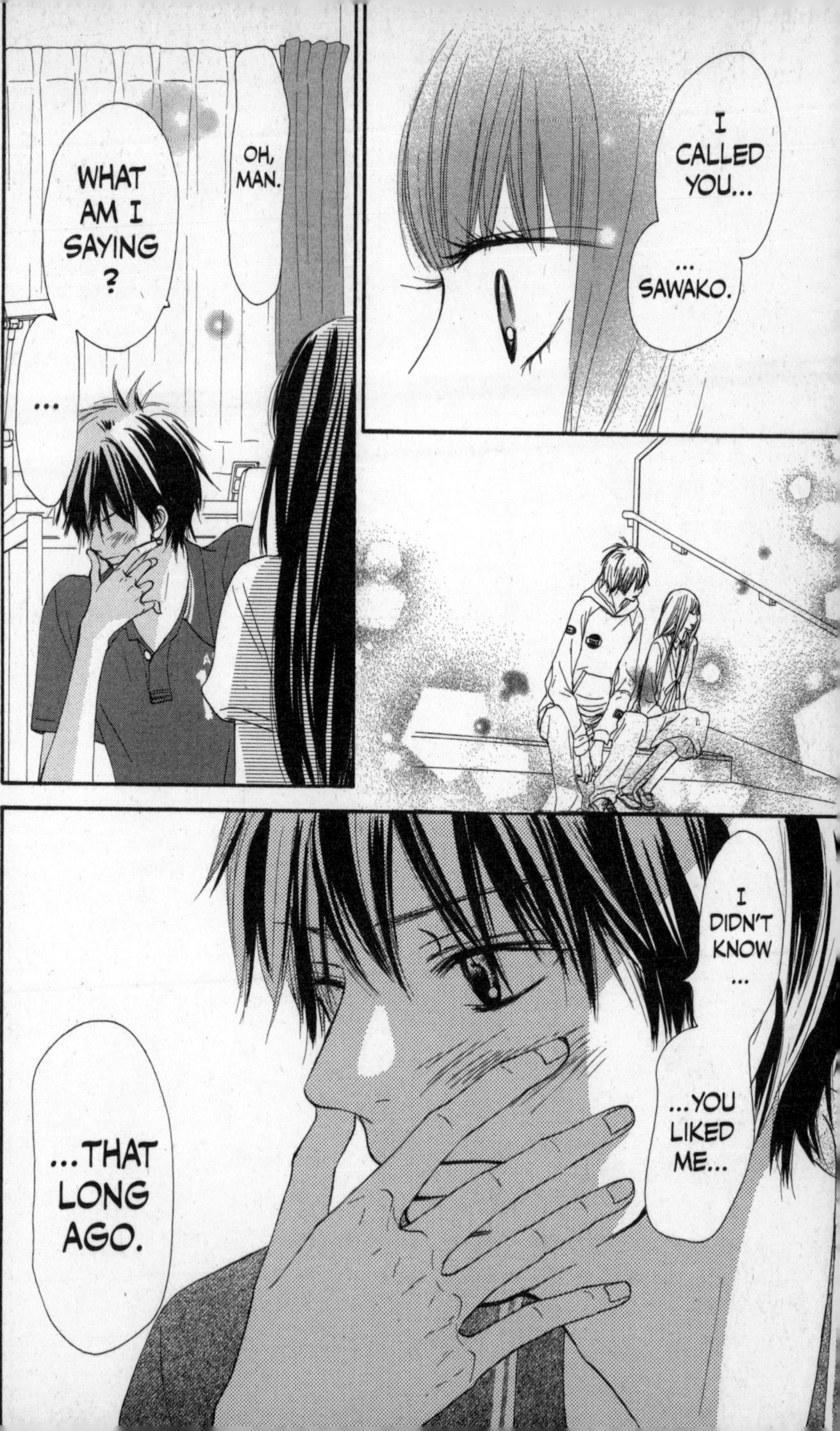
I CALLED YOU...
...SAWAKO.
OH, MAN.
WHAT AM I SAYING?
...
I DIDN'T KNOW...
...YOU LIKED ME...
...THAT LONG AGO.

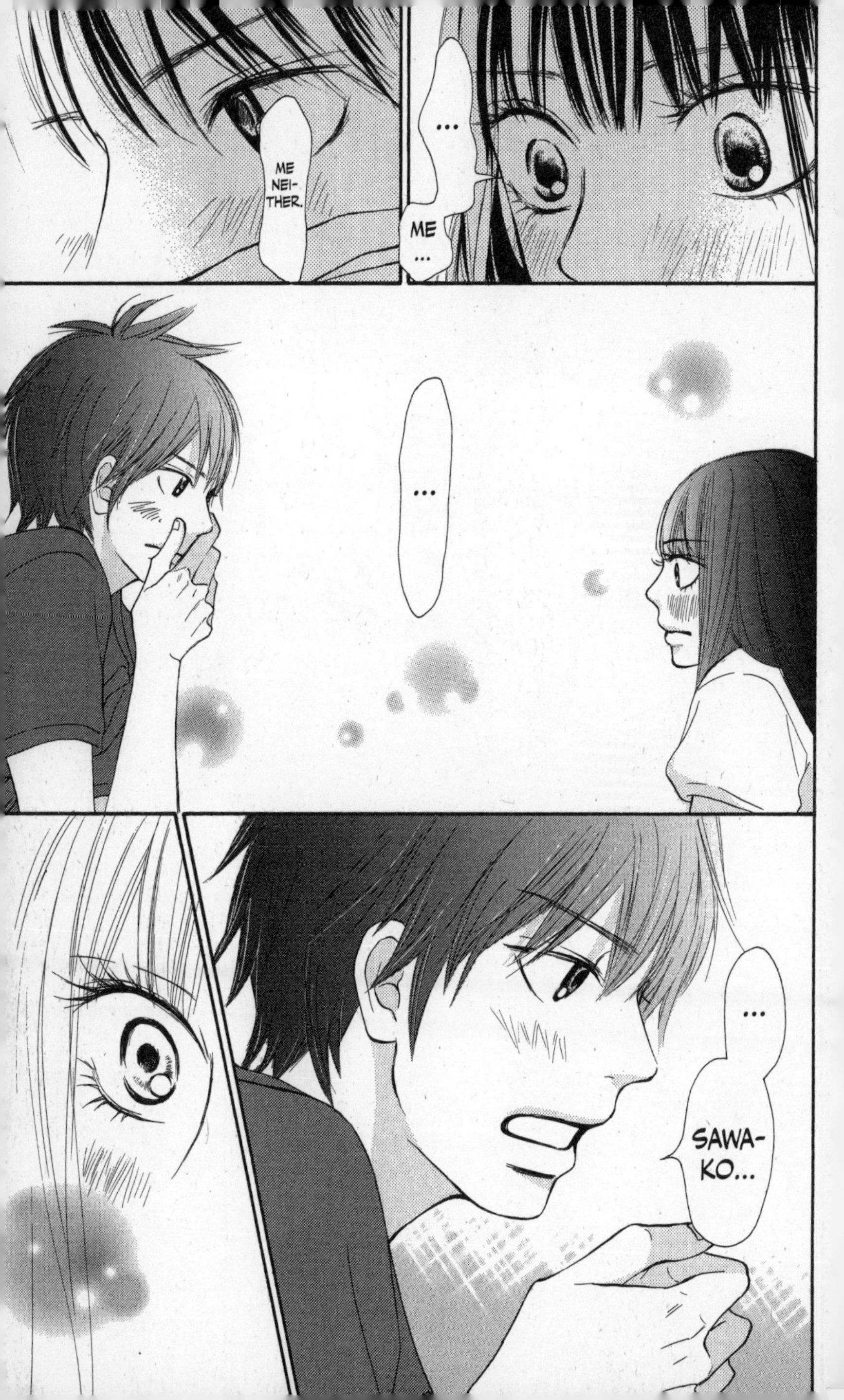
...
ME ...
ME NEI-THER.
...
...
SAWA-KO...

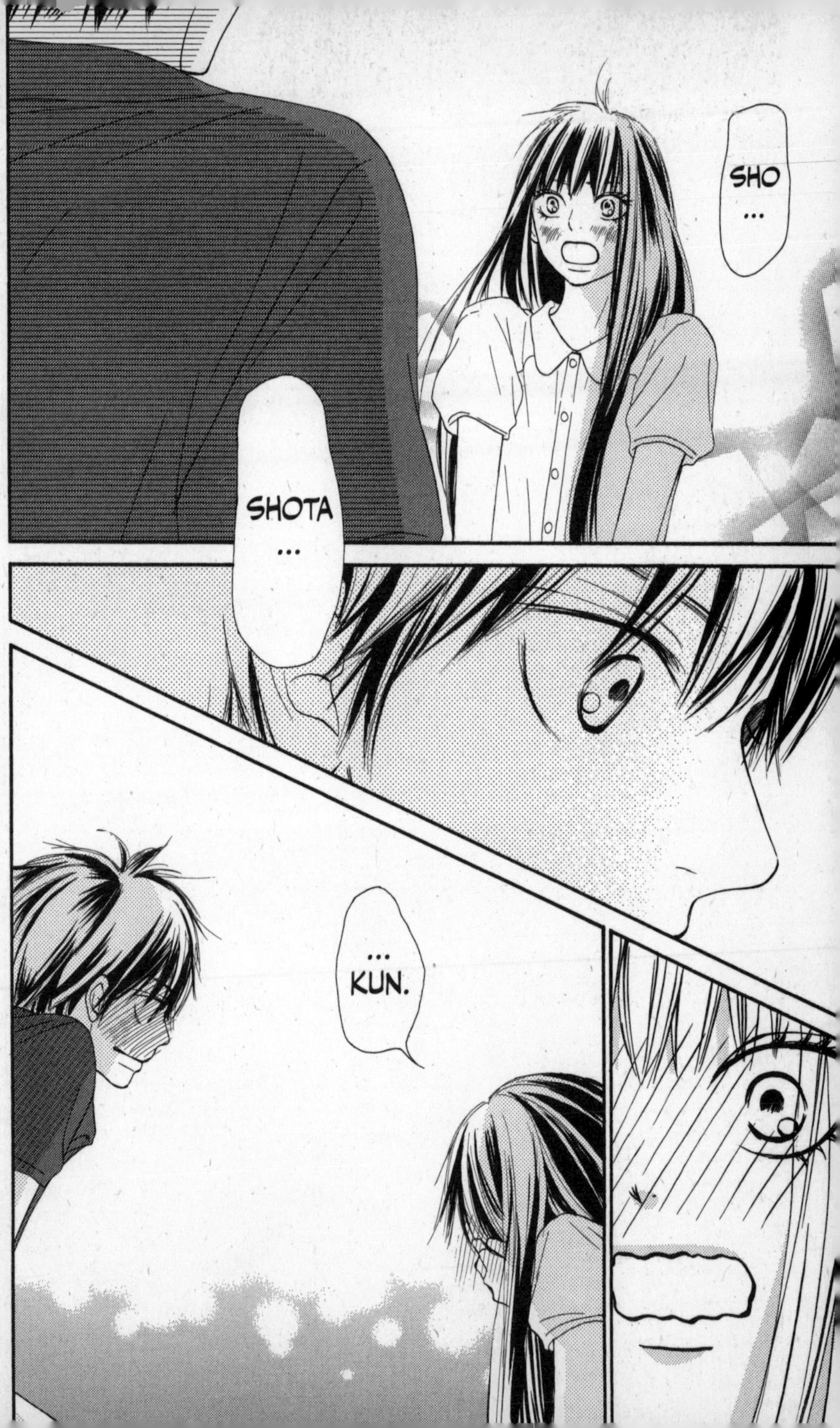
SHO ...
SHOTA ...
... KUN.

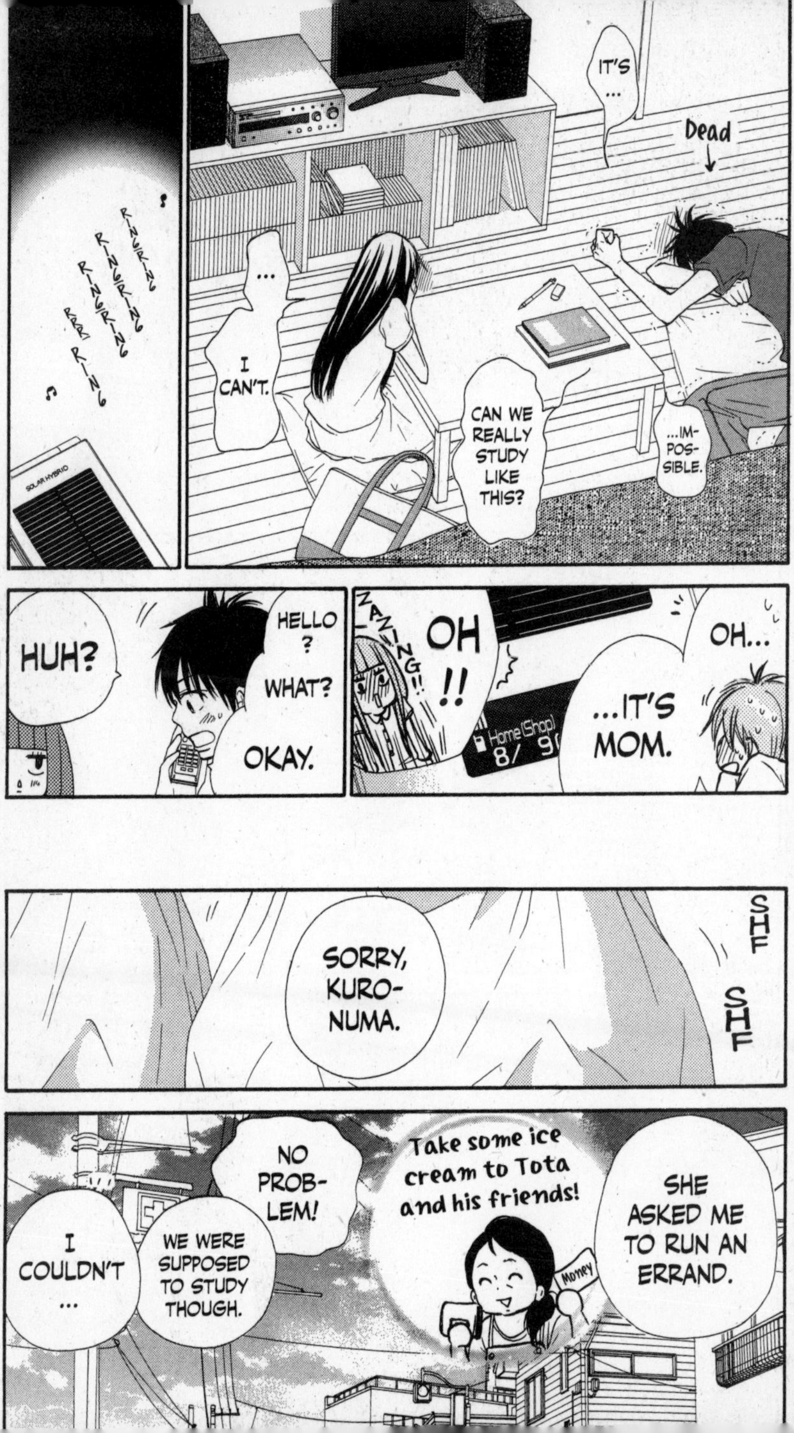
IT'S ...
Dead
...IMPOSSIBLE.
CAN WE REALLY STUDY LIKE THIS?
...
I CAN'T.
RINGRING
RINGRING
RINGRING
RRRI RING
SOLAR HYBRID
OH...
...IT'S MOM.
OH !!
ZAZING!!
Home (Shop)
HELLO? WHAT?
OKAY.
HUH?
SHF
SHF
SORRY, KURONUMA.
SHE ASKED ME TO RUN AN ERRAND.
Take some ice cream to Tota and his friends!
Money
NO PROBLEM!
WE WERE SUPPOSED TO STUDY THOUGH.
I COULDN'T ...

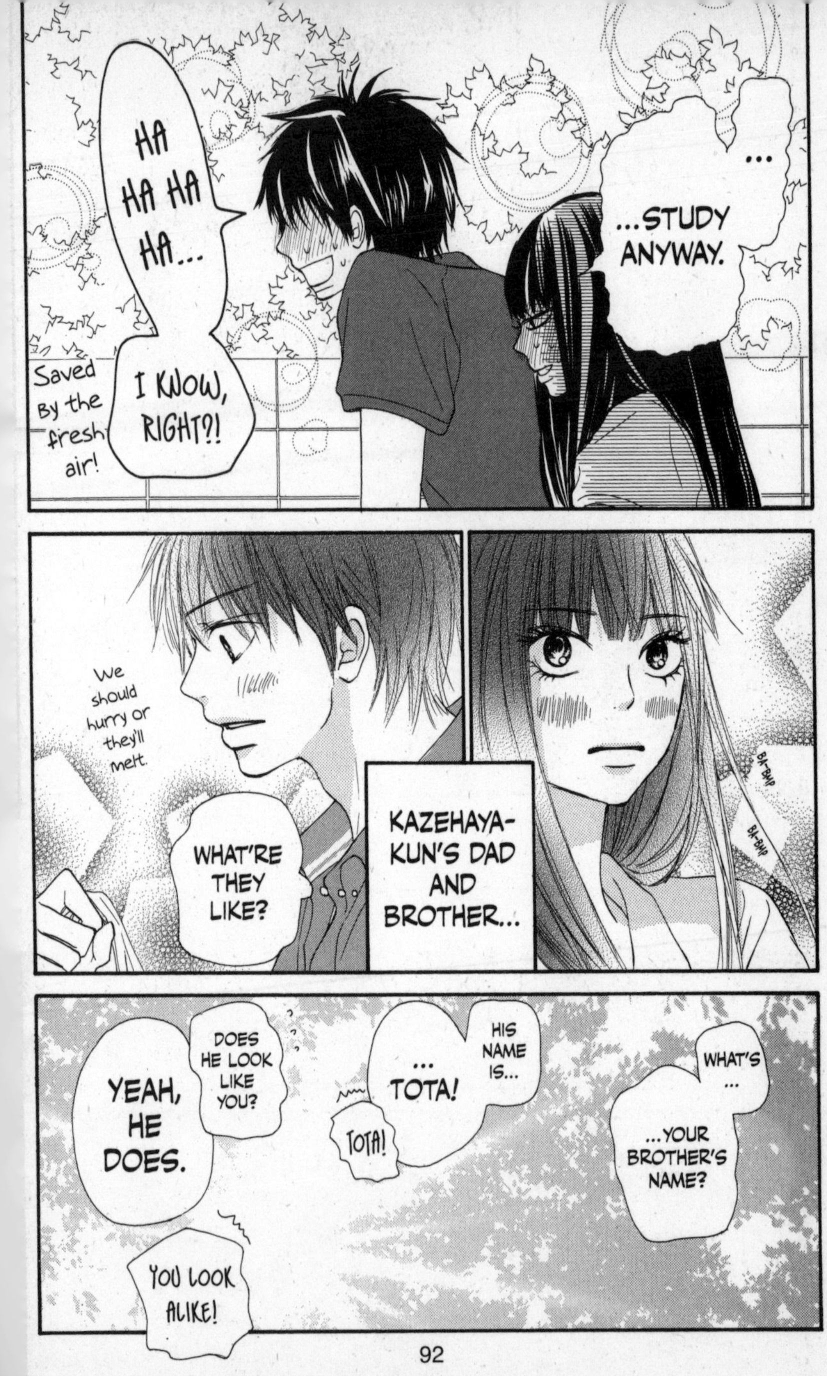
...
...STUDY ANYWAY.
HA HA HA HA...
I KNOW, RIGHT?!
Saved by the fresh air!
BA-BMP
BA-BMP
KAZEHAYA-KUN'S DAD AND BROTHER...
WHAT'RE THEY LIKE?
We should hurry or they'll melt.
WHAT'S ...
...YOUR BROTHER'S NAME?
HIS NAME IS...
... TOTA!
TOTA!
DOES HE LOOK LIKE YOU?
YEAH, HE DOES.
YOU LOOK ALIKE!

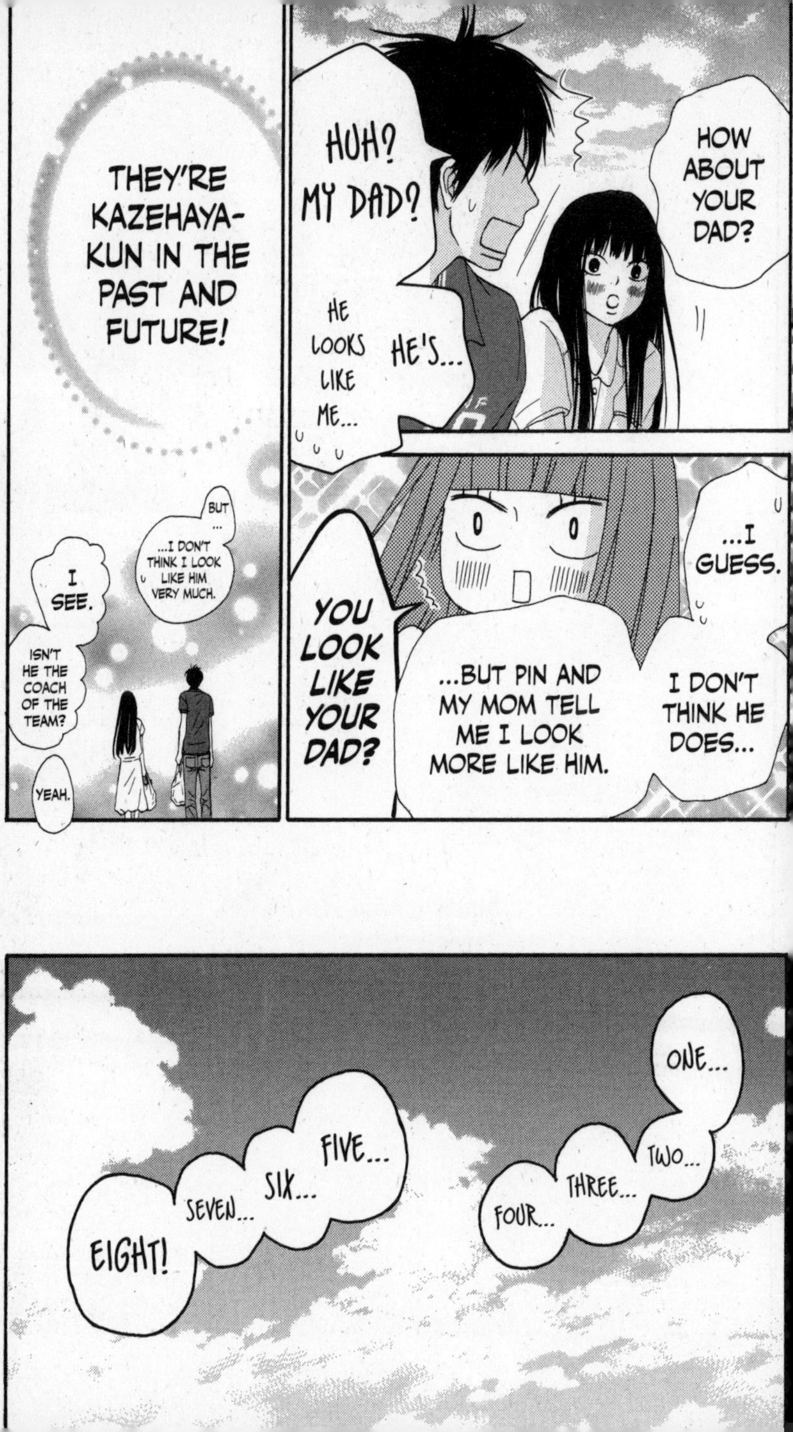

HOW ABOUT YOUR DAD?
HUH? MY DAD?
HE'S...
HE LOOKS LIKE ME...
...I GUESS.
YOU LOOK LIKE YOUR DAD?
I DON'T THINK HE DOES...
...BUT PIN AND MY MOM TELL ME I LOOK MORE LIKE HIM.
THEY'RE KAZEHAYA-KUN IN THE PAST AND FUTURE!
BUT...
...I DON'T THINK I LOOK LIKE HIM VERY MUCH.
I SEE.
ISN'T HE THE COACH OF THE TEAM?
YEAH.
ONE...
TWO...
THREE...
FOUR...
FIVE...
SIX...
SEVEN...
EIGHT!

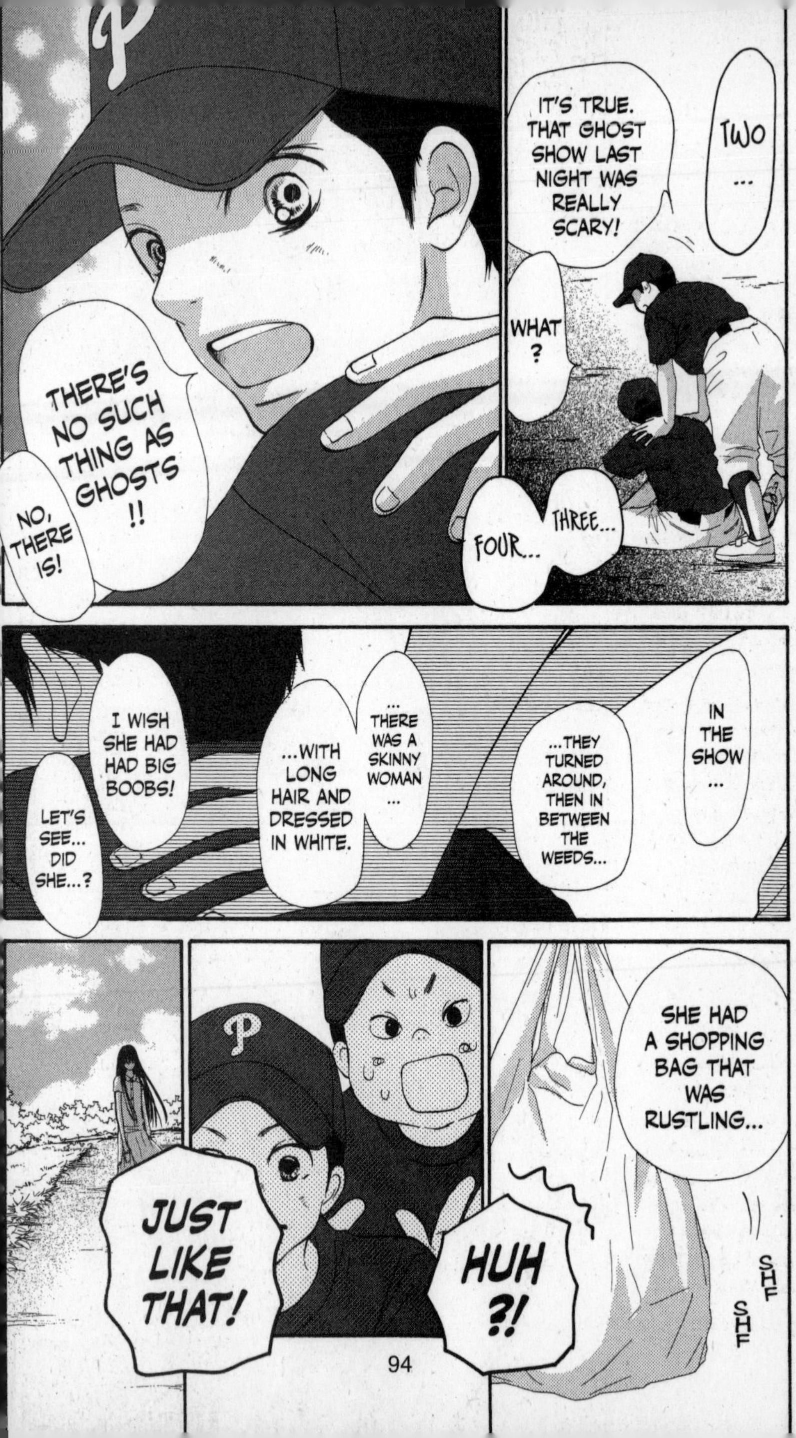
TWO...
IT'S TRUE. THAT GHOST SHOW LAST NIGHT WAS REALLY SCARY!
WHAT?
THREE...
FOUR...
THERE'S NO SUCH THING AS GHOSTS!!
NO, THERE IS!
IN THE SHOW...
...THEY TURNED AROUND, THEN IN BETWEEN THE WEEDS...
...THERE WAS A SKINNY WOMAN...
...WITH LONG HAIR AND DRESSED IN WHITE.
I WISH SHE HAD HAD BIG BOOBS!
LET'S SEE... DID SHE...?
SHE HAD A SHOPPING BAG THAT WAS RUSTLING...
SHF SHF
HUH?!
JUST LIKE THAT!

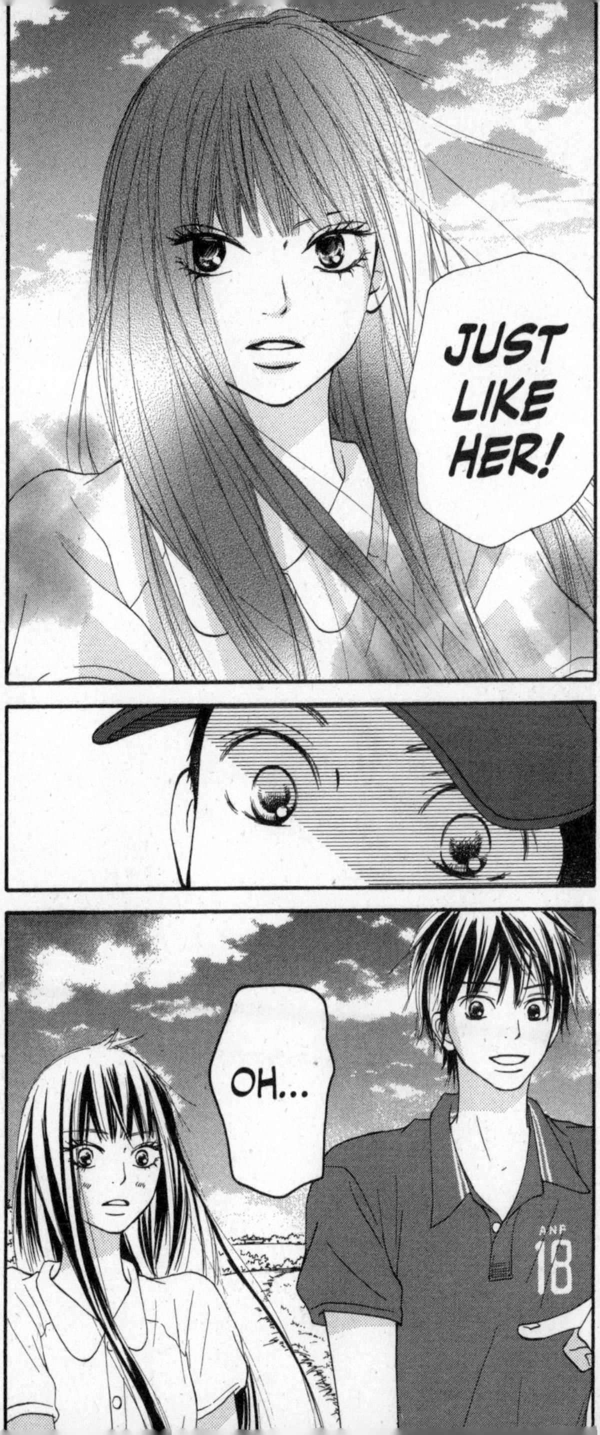
JUST LIKE HER!
OH...

KARUPIN on JAPAN 4

...so some people might feel frustrated, but it really is portrayed wonderfully. Those of you who watched the first season, please keep watching! People who live in rural areas and can't watch it on TV, please wait for the DVD. The direction, illustration and voice acting generate some serious tension in the anime!

Right now, I'm looking for the release of the movie DVD! I use Blu-ray at home. ♥
I reserved some extras to give out to people! Heh heh heh...

I can't wait to see it again. I'm so happy. I heard that there are many extra scenes! I have some scenes I want to see, especially Renbutsu-chan's part! Heh heh heh...

I'm also looking forward to seeing the making of the movie. It's been a while since the movie was in theaters, so I'm thankful I can enjoy it again. Thank you!

Continued in sidebar 5 →

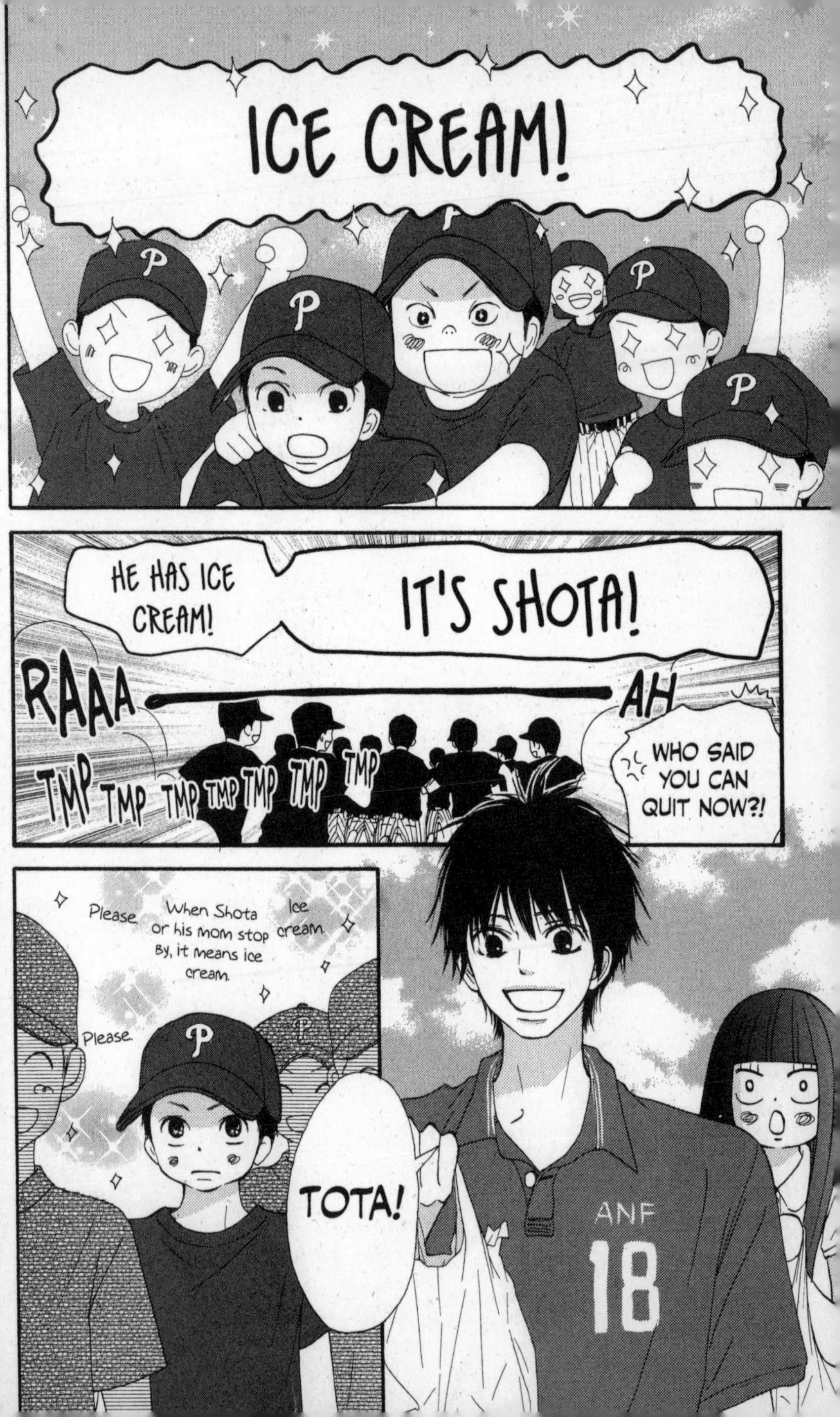
ICE CREAM!
IT'S SHOTA!
HE HAS ICE CREAM!
WHO SAID YOU CAN QUIT NOW?!
RAAA————AH
TMP TMP TMP TMP TMP TMP TMP
TOTA!
Ice cream.
When Shota or his mom stop by, it means ice cream.
Please.
Please.

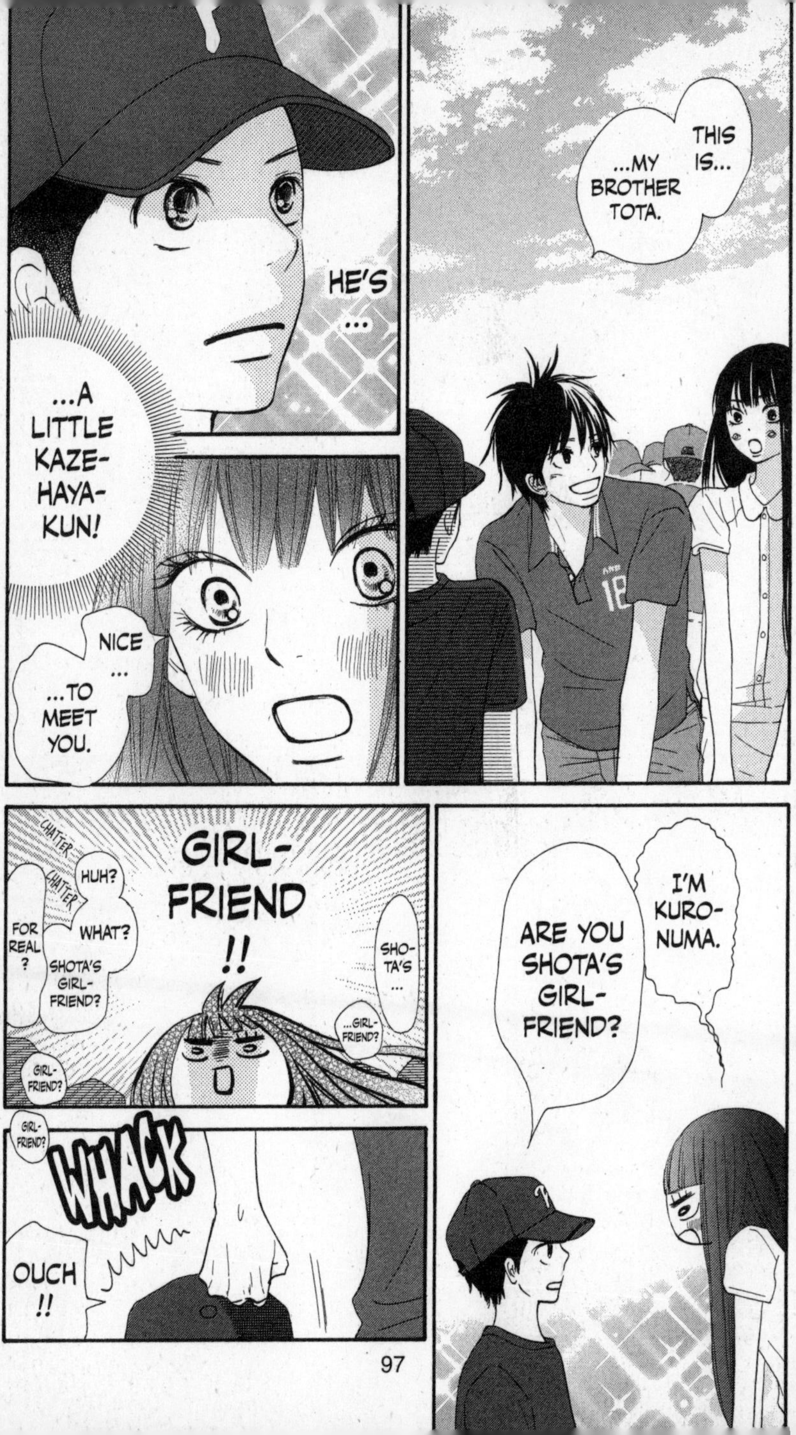
THIS IS... ...MY BROTHER TOTA.
HE'S ...
...A LITTLE KAZE-HAYA-KUN!
NICE ... ...TO MEET YOU.
I'M KURO-NUMA.
ARE YOU SHOTA'S GIRL-FRIEND?
SHO-TA'S ...
...GIRL-FRIEND?
GIRL-FRIEND !!
CHATTER CHATTER
HUH?
WHAT?
SHOTA'S GIRL-FRIEND?
FOR REAL ?
GIRL-FRIEND?
GIRL-FRIEND?
WHACK
OUCH !!

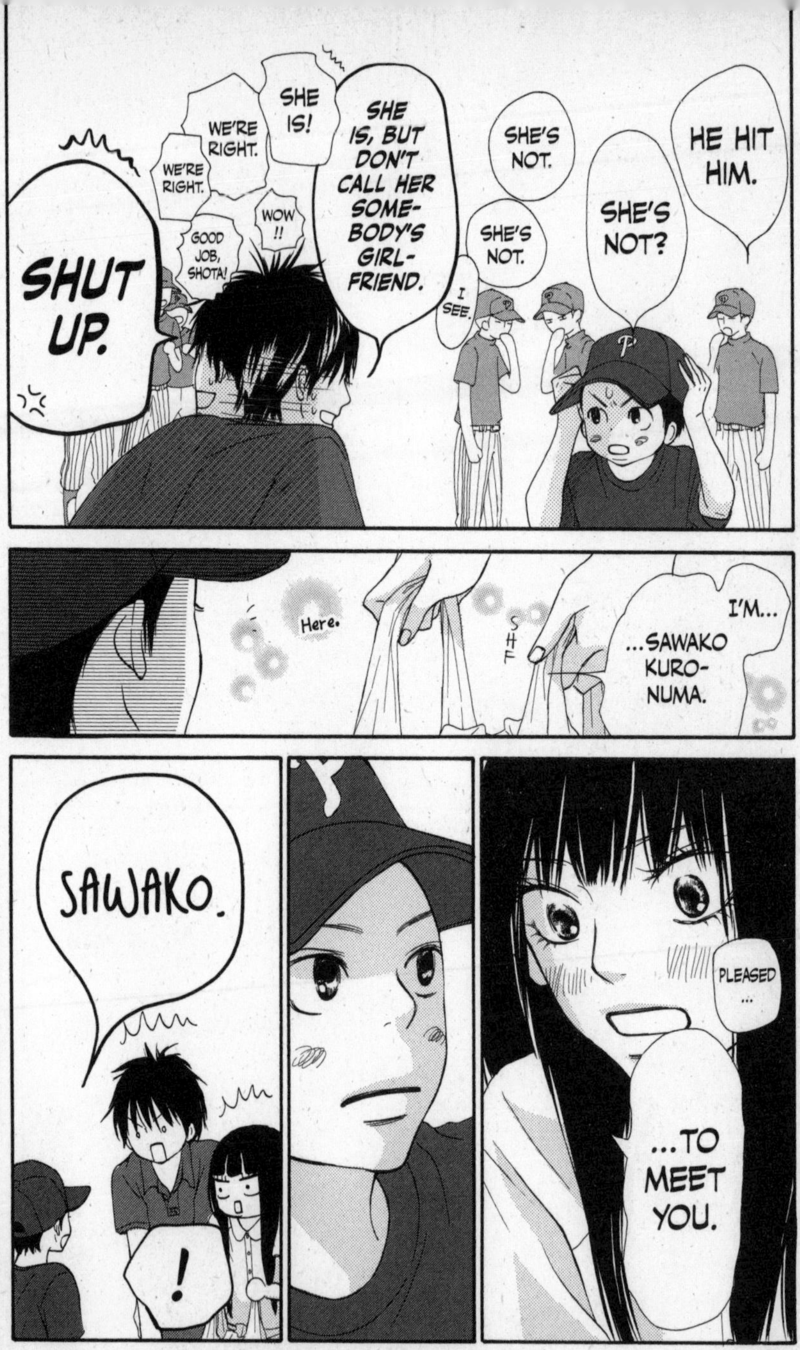
HE HIT HIM.
SHE'S NOT?
SHE'S NOT.
SHE'S NOT.
I SEE.
SHE IS, BUT DON'T CALL HER SOMEBODY'S GIRL-FRIEND.
SHE IS!
WE'RE RIGHT.
WE'RE RIGHT.
WOW!!
GOOD JOB, SHOTA!
SHUT UP.
I'M...
...SAWAKO KURO-NUMA.
SHF
Here.
PLEASED...
...TO MEET YOU.
SAWAKO.
!

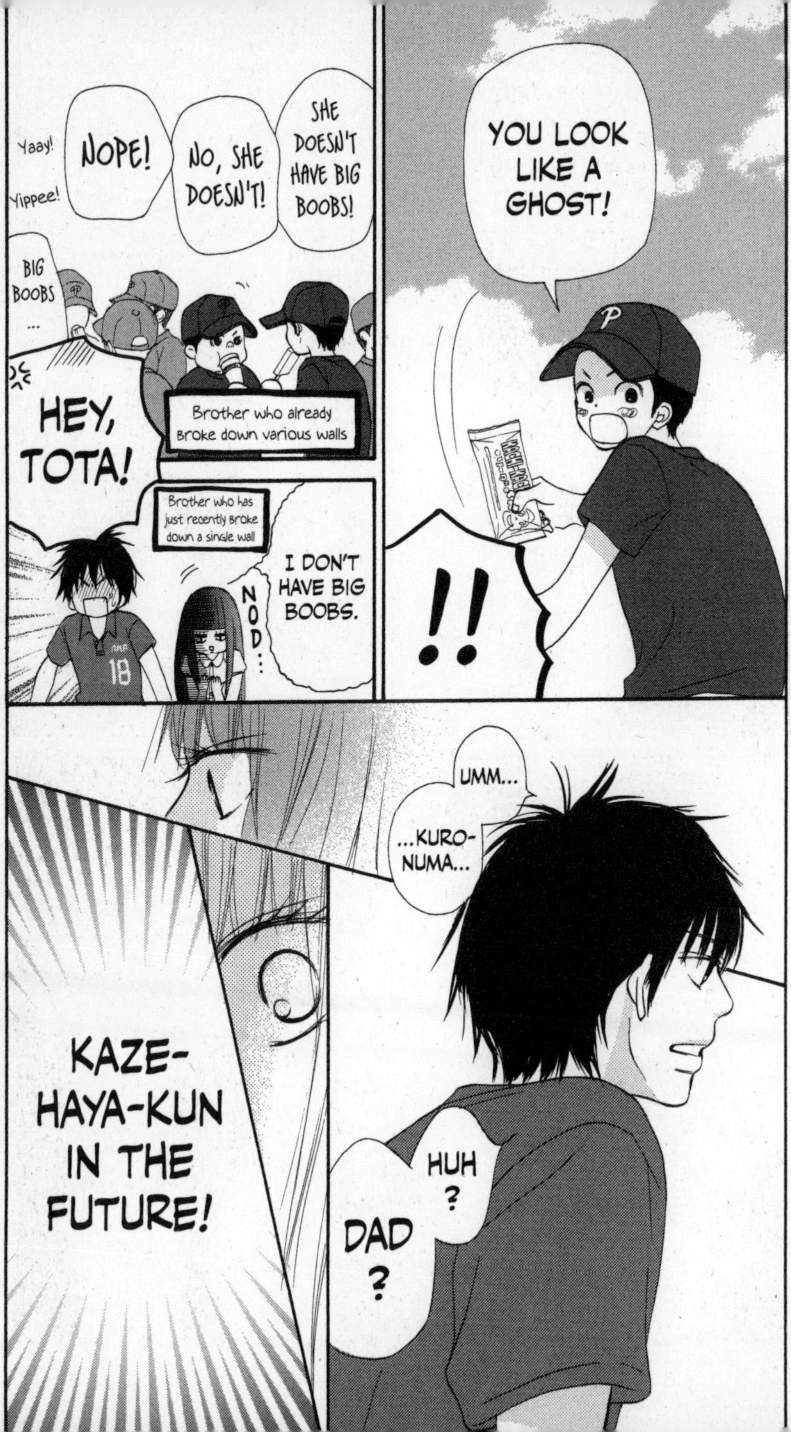
YOU LOOK LIKE A GHOST!
!!
SHE DOESN'T HAVE BIG BOOBS!
NO, SHE DOESN'T!
NOPE!
Yaay!
Yippee!
BIG BOOBS ...
Brother who already broke down various walls
HEY, TOTA!
Brother who has just recently broke down a single wall
I DON'T HAVE BIG BOOBS.
NOD...
UMM...
...KURO-NUMA...
HUH?
DAD?
KAZE-HAYA-KUN IN THE FUTURE!

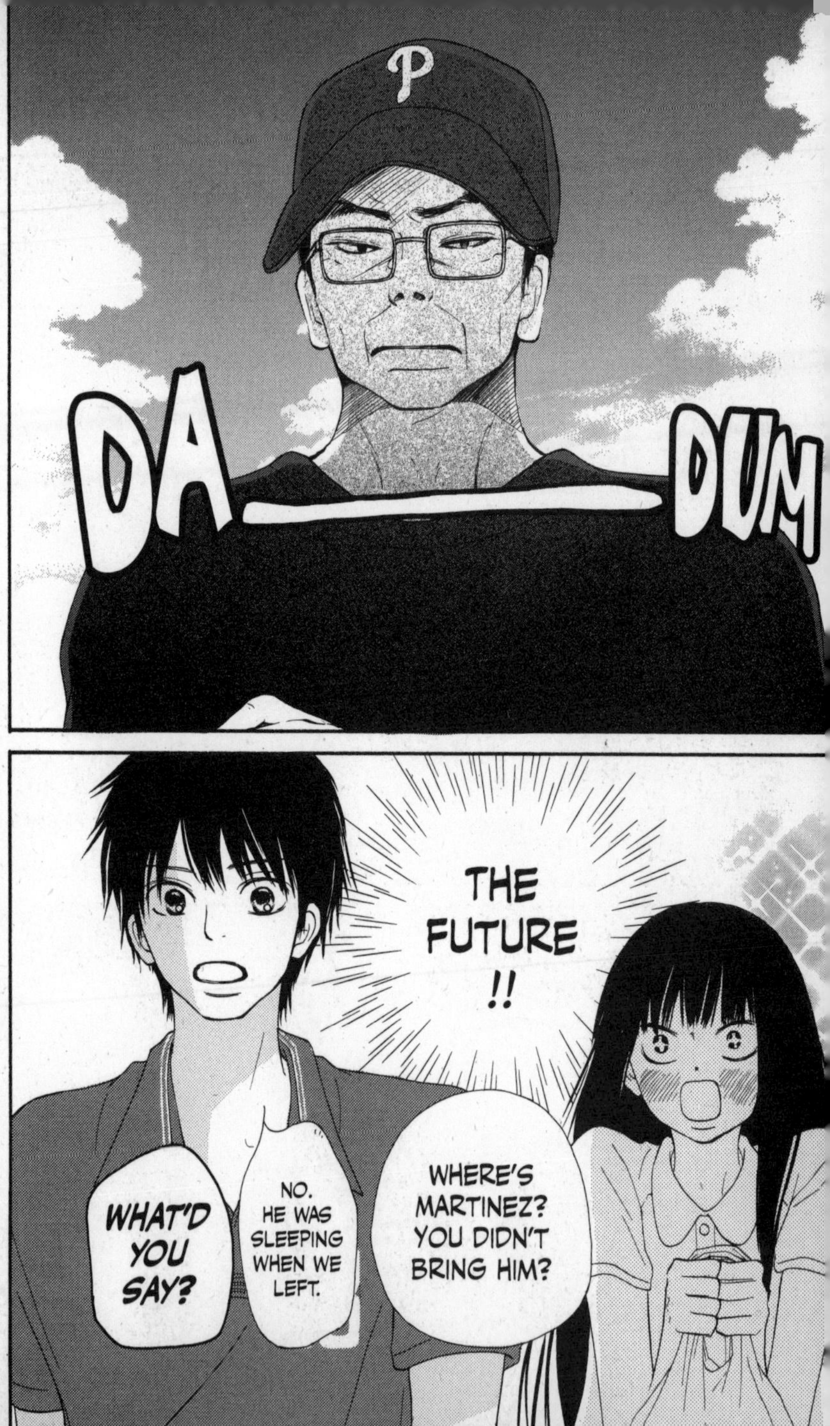
DA—DUM
THE FUTURE !!
WHERE'S MARTINEZ? YOU DIDN'T BRING HIM?
NO. HE WAS SLEEPING WHEN WE LEFT.
WHAT'D YOU SAY?

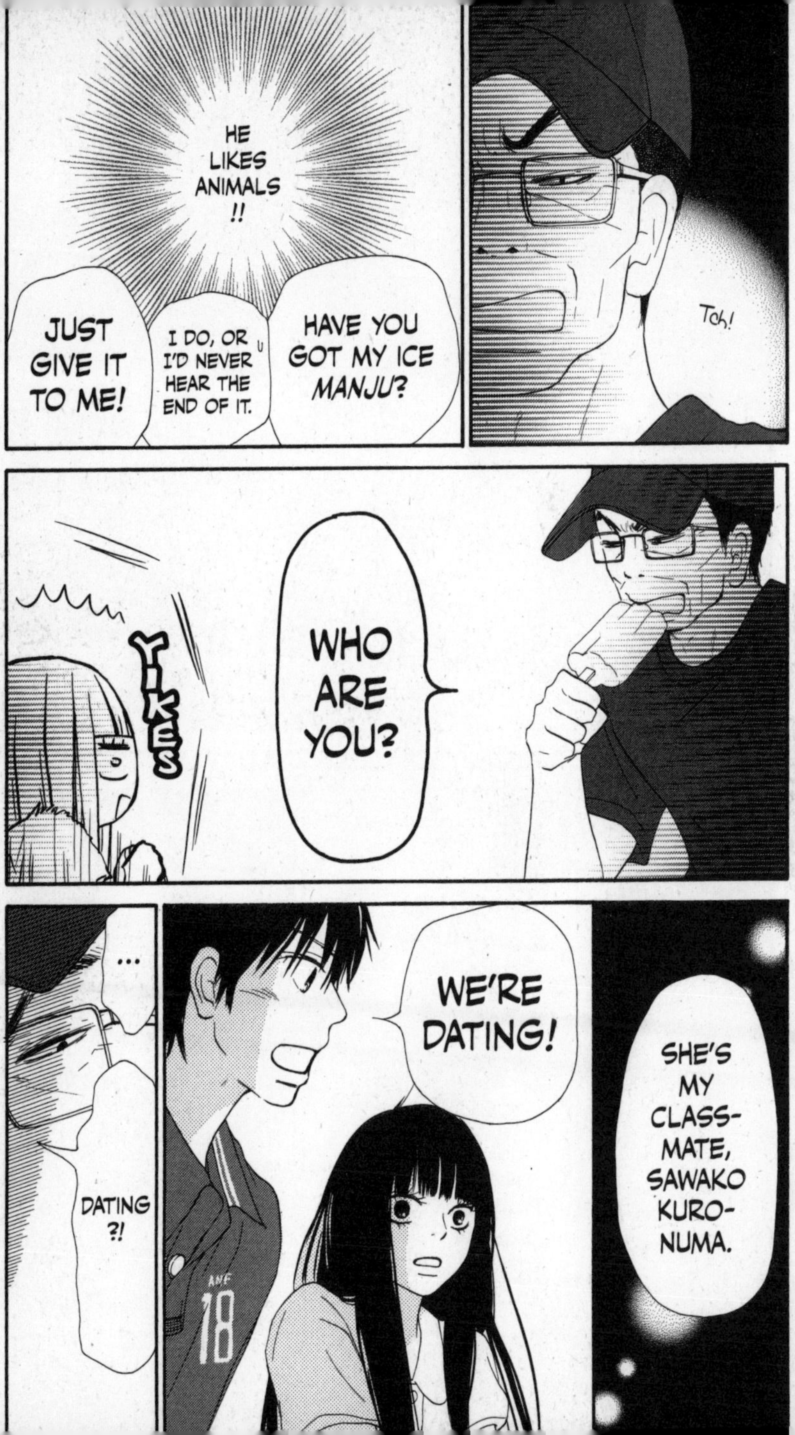
Tch!
HE LIKES ANIMALS !!
HAVE YOU GOT MY ICE *MANJU*?
I DO, OR I'D NEVER HEAR THE END OF IT.
JUST GIVE IT TO ME!
WHO ARE YOU?
YIKES
SHE'S MY CLASSMATE, SAWAKO KURONUMA.
WE'RE DATING!
...
DATING ?!

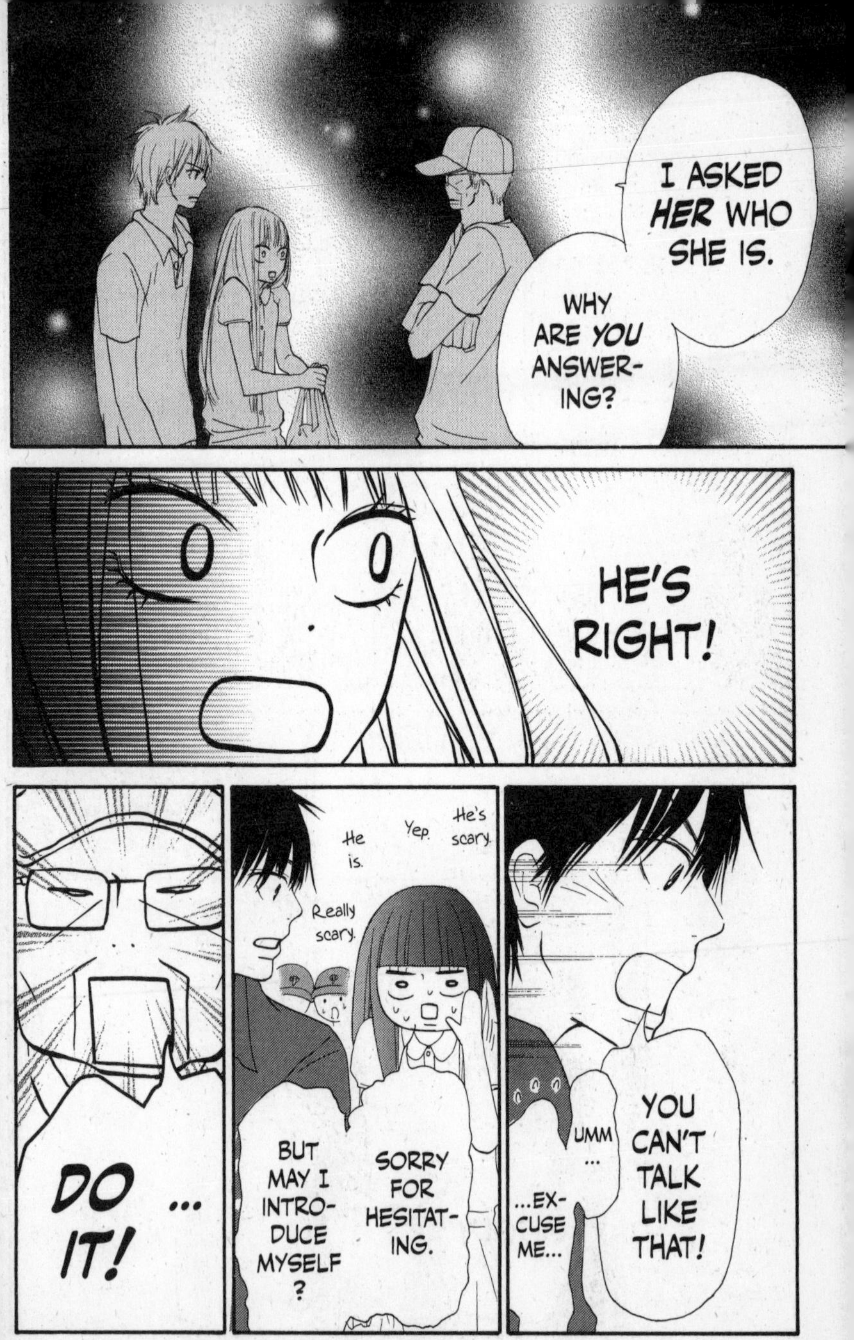
I ASKED HER WHO SHE IS.
WHY ARE YOU ANSWER-ING?
HE'S RIGHT!
YOU CAN'T TALK LIKE THAT!
UMM...
...EX-CUSE ME...
He's scary.
Yep.
He is.
Really scary.
SORRY FOR HESITAT-ING.
BUT MAY I INTRO-DUCE MYSELF?
DO...
IT!

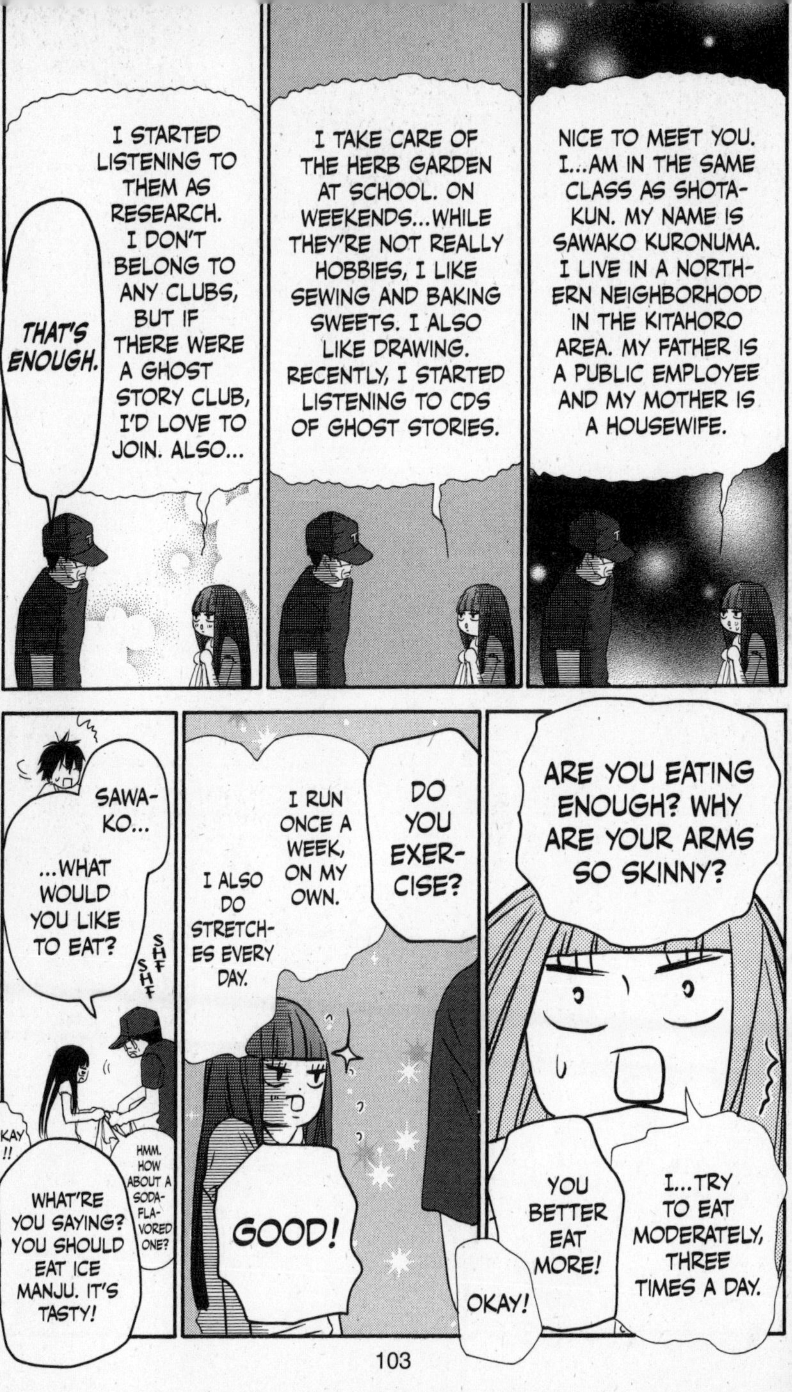
NICE TO MEET YOU. I...AM IN THE SAME CLASS AS SHOTA-KUN. MY NAME IS SAWAKO KURONUMA. I LIVE IN A NORTH-ERN NEIGHBORHOOD IN THE KITAHORO AREA. MY FATHER IS A PUBLIC EMPLOYEE AND MY MOTHER IS A HOUSEWIFE.
I TAKE CARE OF THE HERB GARDEN AT SCHOOL. ON WEEKENDS...WHILE THEY'RE NOT REALLY HOBBIES, I LIKE SEWING AND BAKING SWEETS. I ALSO LIKE DRAWING. RECENTLY, I STARTED LISTENING TO CDS OF GHOST STORIES.
I STARTED LISTENING TO THEM AS RESEARCH. I DON'T BELONG TO ANY CLUBS, BUT IF THERE WERE A GHOST STORY CLUB, I'D LOVE TO JOIN. ALSO...
THAT'S ENOUGH.
ARE YOU EATING ENOUGH? WHY ARE YOUR ARMS SO SKINNY?
I...TRY TO EAT MODERATELY, THREE TIMES A DAY.
YOU BETTER EAT MORE!
OKAY!
DO YOU EXERCISE?
I RUN ONCE A WEEK, ON MY OWN.
I ALSO DO STRETCH-ES EVERY DAY.
GOOD!
SAWA-KO...
...WHAT WOULD YOU LIKE TO EAT?
SHF SHF
HMM. HOW ABOUT A SODA-FLA-VORED ONE?
OKAY!!
WHAT'RE YOU SAYING? YOU SHOULD EAT ICE MANJU. IT'S TASTY!

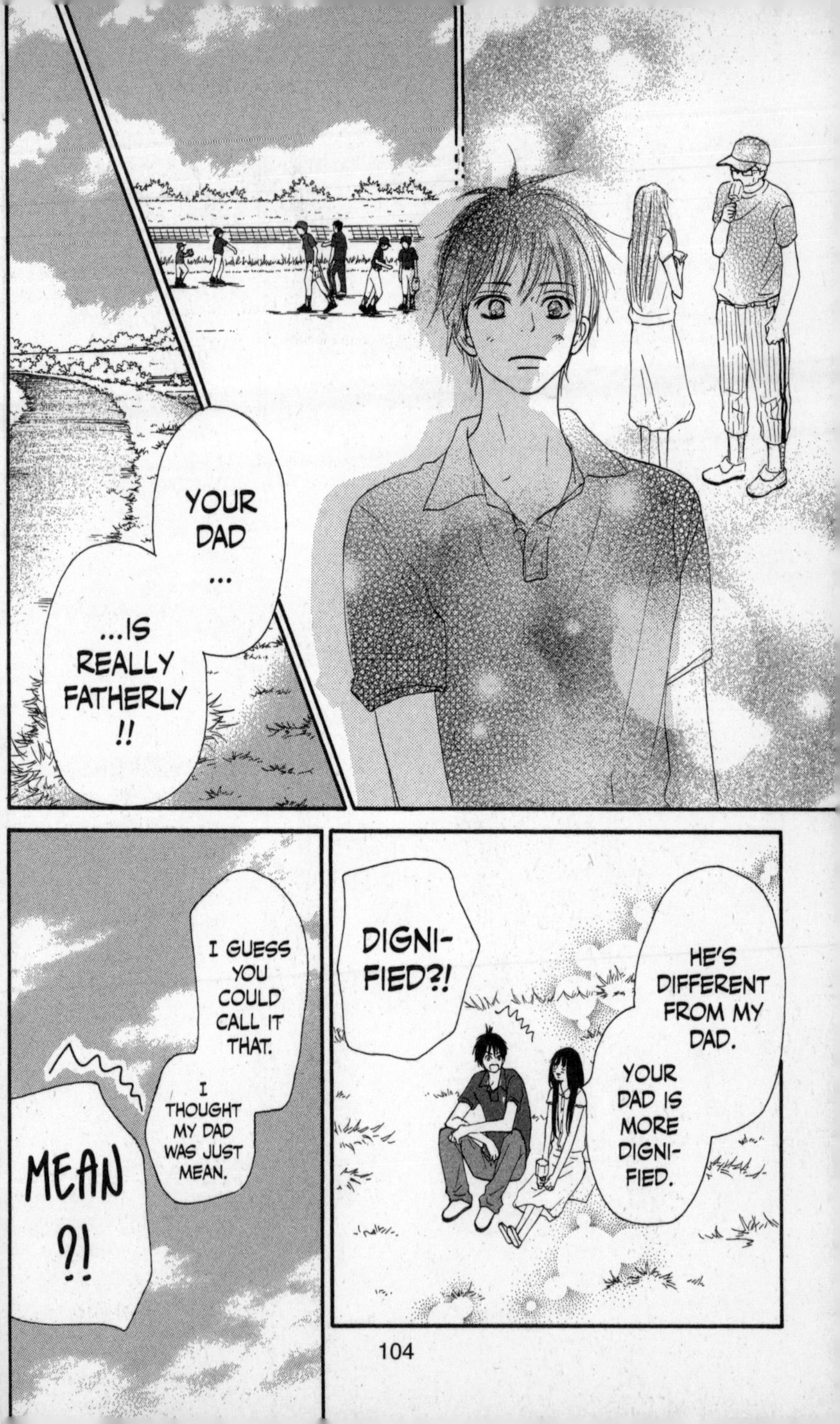
YOUR DAD ...
...IS REALLY FATHERLY !!
HE'S DIFFERENT FROM MY DAD.
YOUR DAD IS MORE DIGNI- FIED.
DIGNI- FIED?!
I GUESS YOU COULD CALL IT THAT.
I THOUGHT MY DAD WAS JUST MEAN.
MEAN ?!

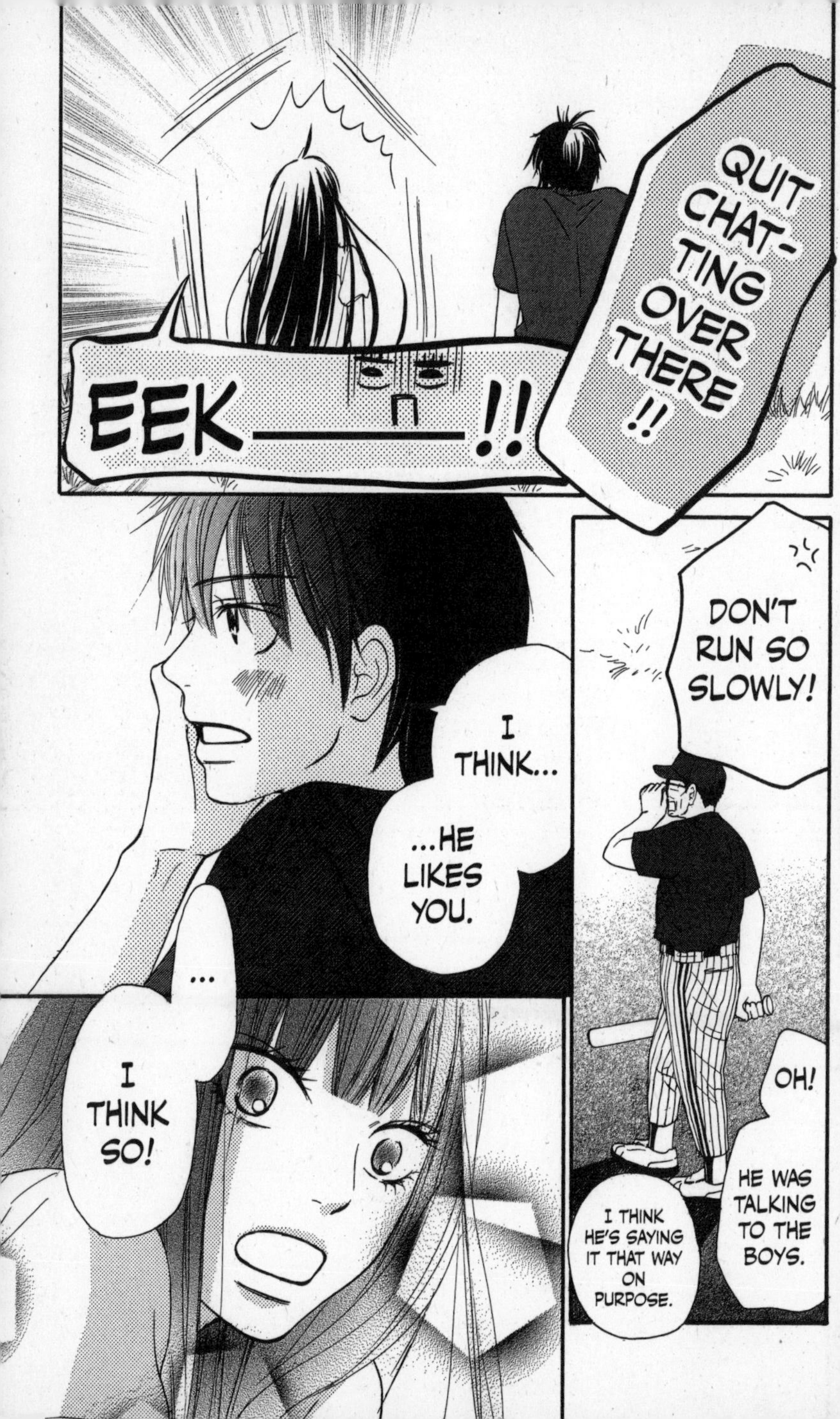
QUIT CHAT-TING OVER THERE!!
EEK___!!
DON'T RUN SO SLOWLY!
OH!
HE WAS TALKING TO THE BOYS.
I THINK HE'S SAYING IT THAT WAY ON PURPOSE.
I THINK...
...HE LIKES YOU.
...
I THINK SO!

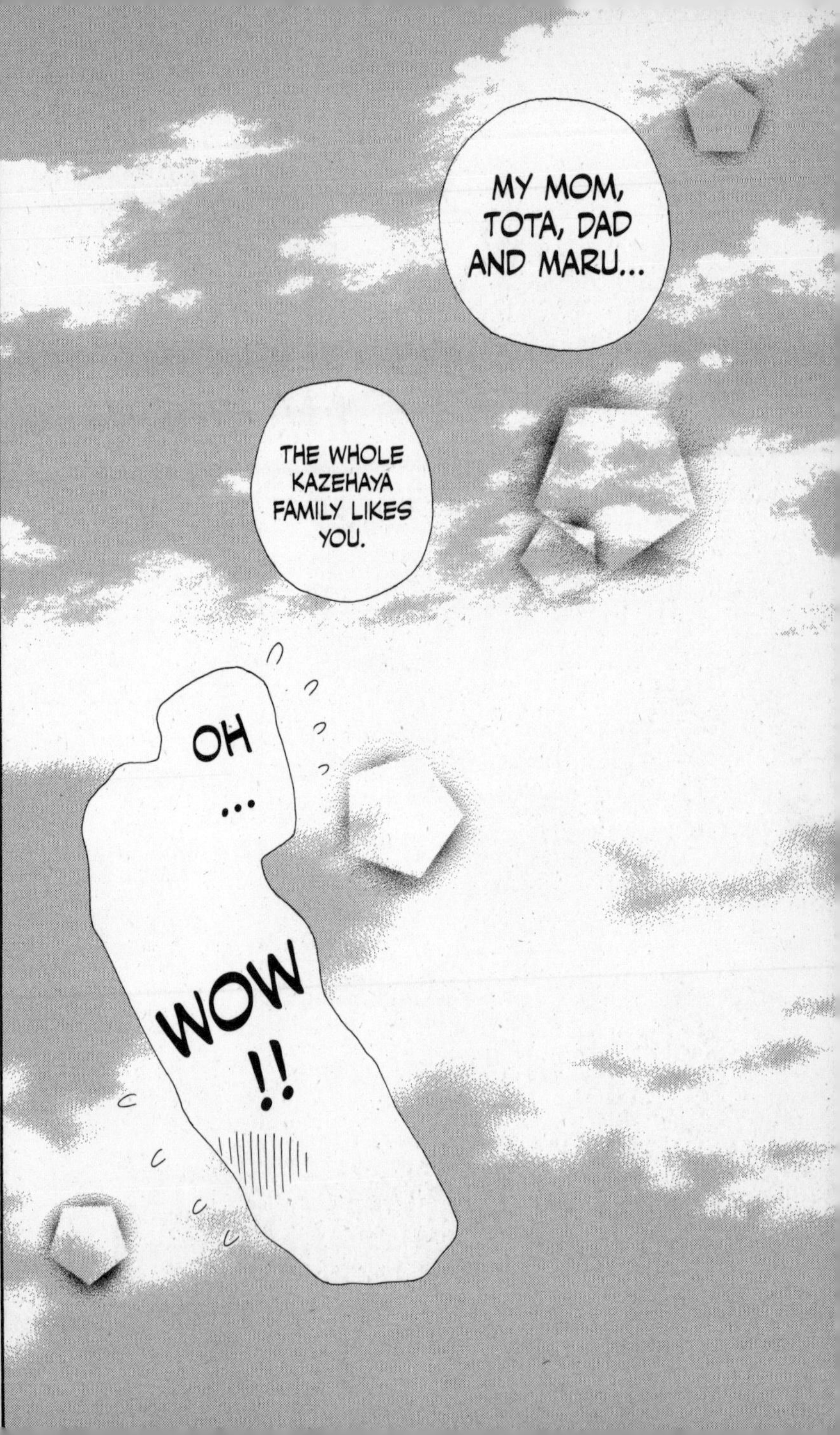
MY MOM, TOTA, DAD AND MARU...
THE WHOLE KAZEHAYA FAMILY LIKES YOU.
OH ... WOW !!

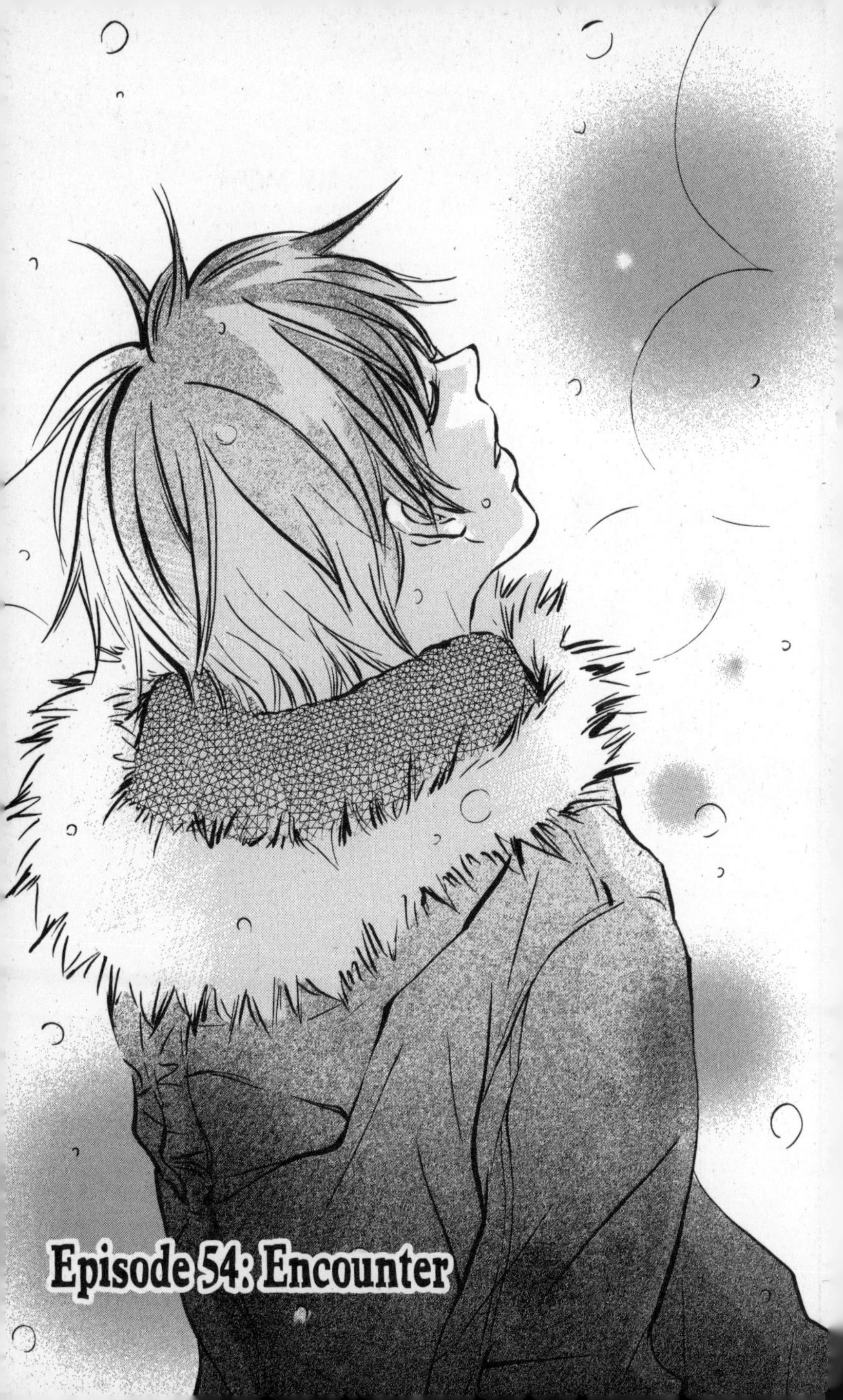
Episode 54: Encounter

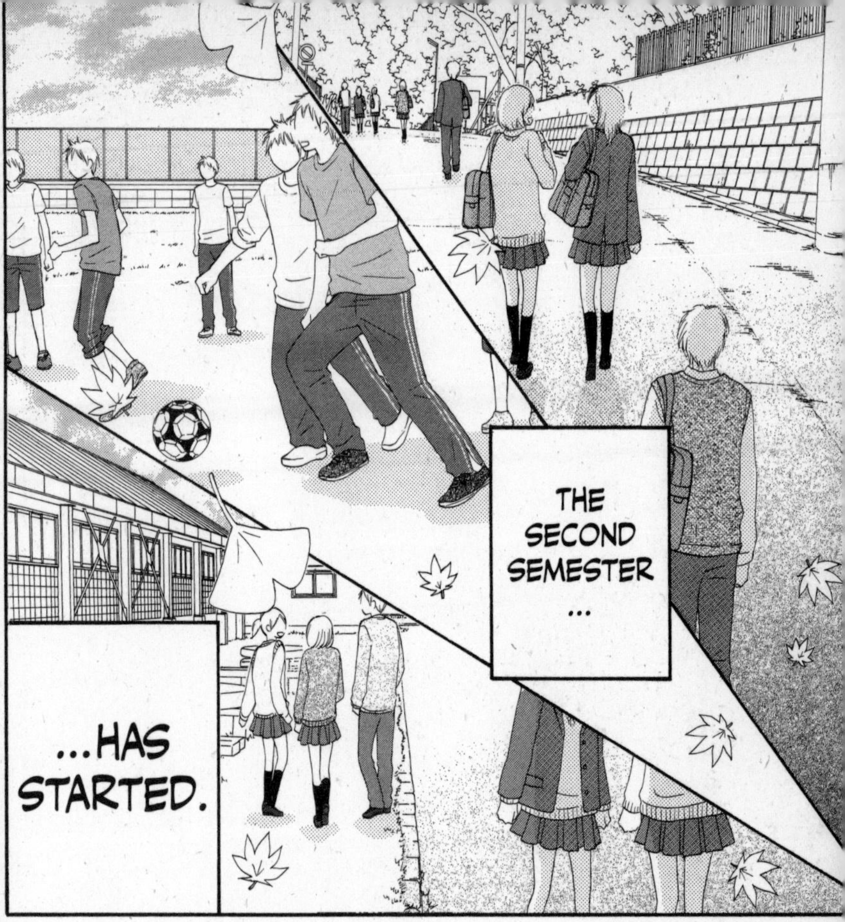
THE SECOND SEMESTER ...
...HAS STARTED.
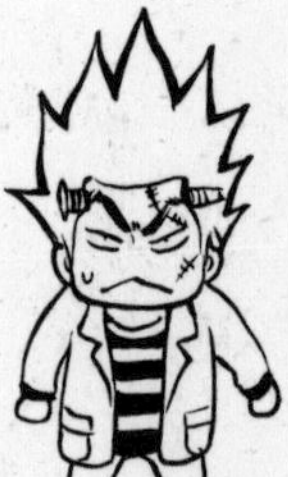

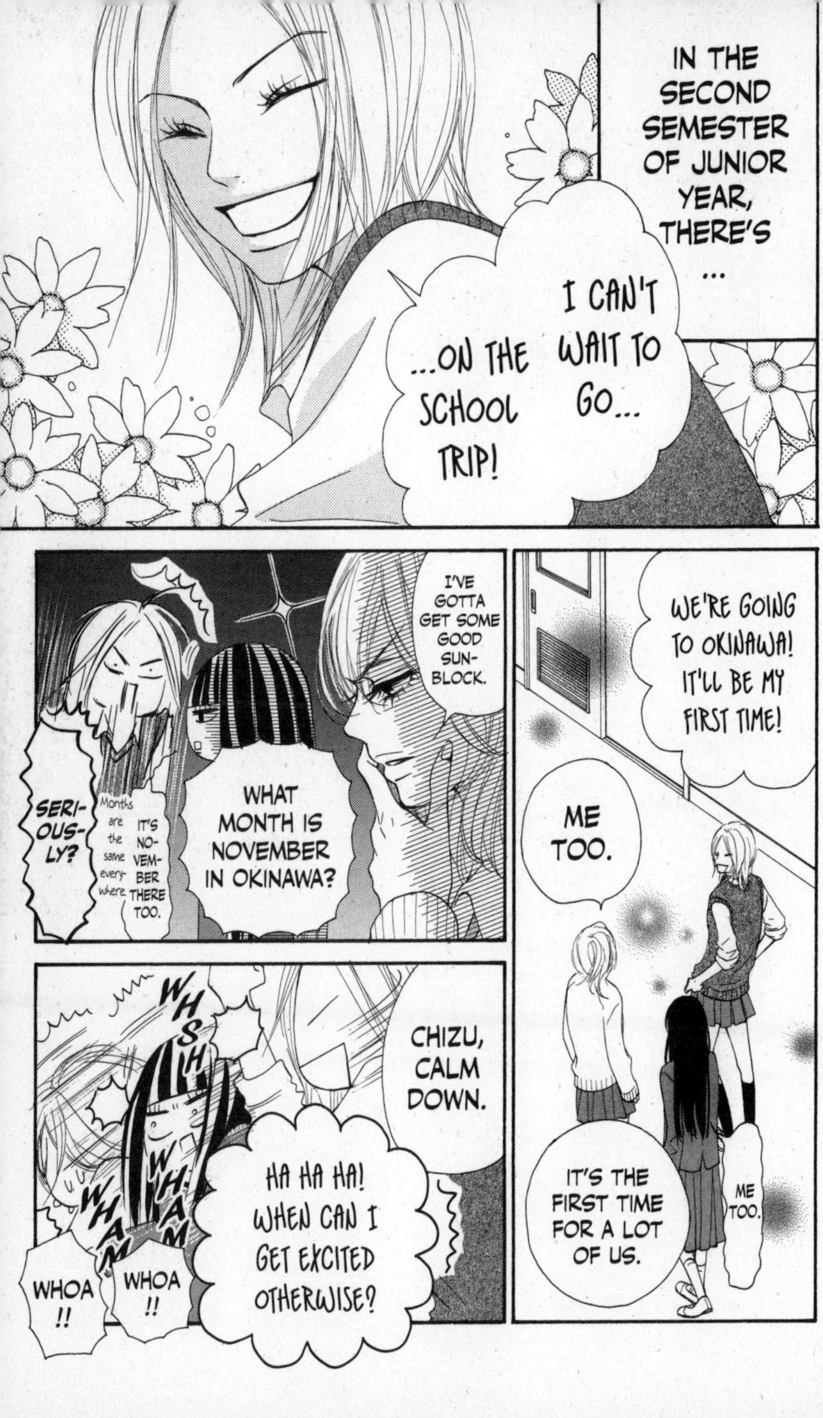
IN THE SECOND SEMESTER OF JUNIOR YEAR, THERE'S ...
I CAN'T WAIT TO GO...
...ON THE SCHOOL TRIP!
WE'RE GOING TO OKINAWA! IT'LL BE MY FIRST TIME!
ME TOO.
IT'S THE FIRST TIME FOR A LOT OF US.
ME TOO.
I'VE GOTTA GET SOME GOOD SUN-BLOCK.
WHAT MONTH IS NOVEMBER IN OKINAWA?
IT'S NO-VEM-BER THERE TOO.
Months are the same every-where.
SERI-OUS-LY?
CHIZU, CALM DOWN.
WHSH
HA HA HA! WHEN CAN I GET EXCITED OTHERWISE?
WHAM
WHAM
WHOA !!
WHOA !!

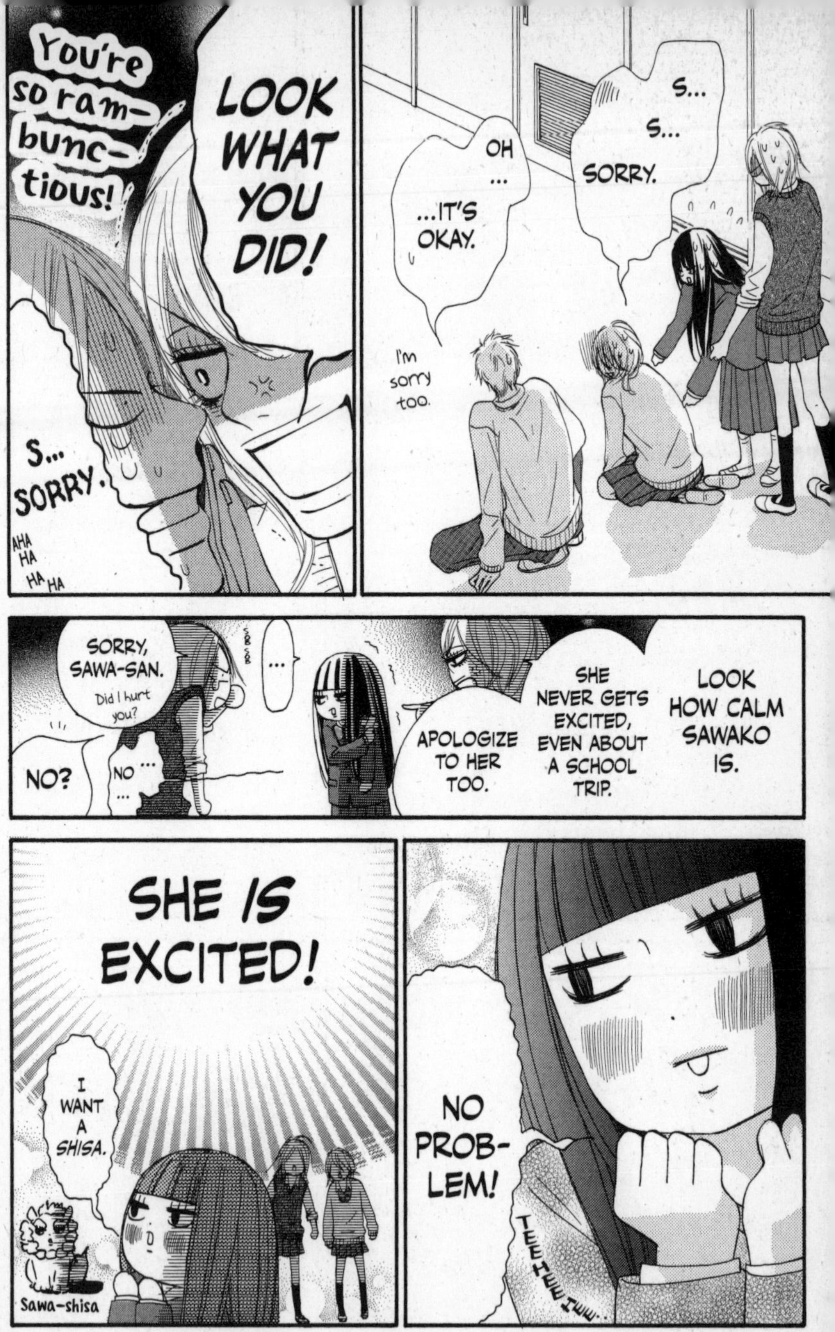
S... S... SORRY.
OH ... ...IT'S OKAY.
I'm sorry too.
LOOK WHAT YOU DID!
You're so ram-bunc-tious!
S... SORRY.
AHAHA HA HAHA
LOOK HOW CALM SAWAKO IS.
SHE NEVER GETS EXCITED, EVEN ABOUT A SCHOOL TRIP.
APOLOGIZE TO HER TOO.
...
SOB SOB
SORRY, SAWA-SAN.
Did I hurt you?
NO ... ...
NO?
NO PROB-LEM!
TEEHEEHEE...
SHE IS EXCITED!
I WANT A SHISA.
Sawa-shisa

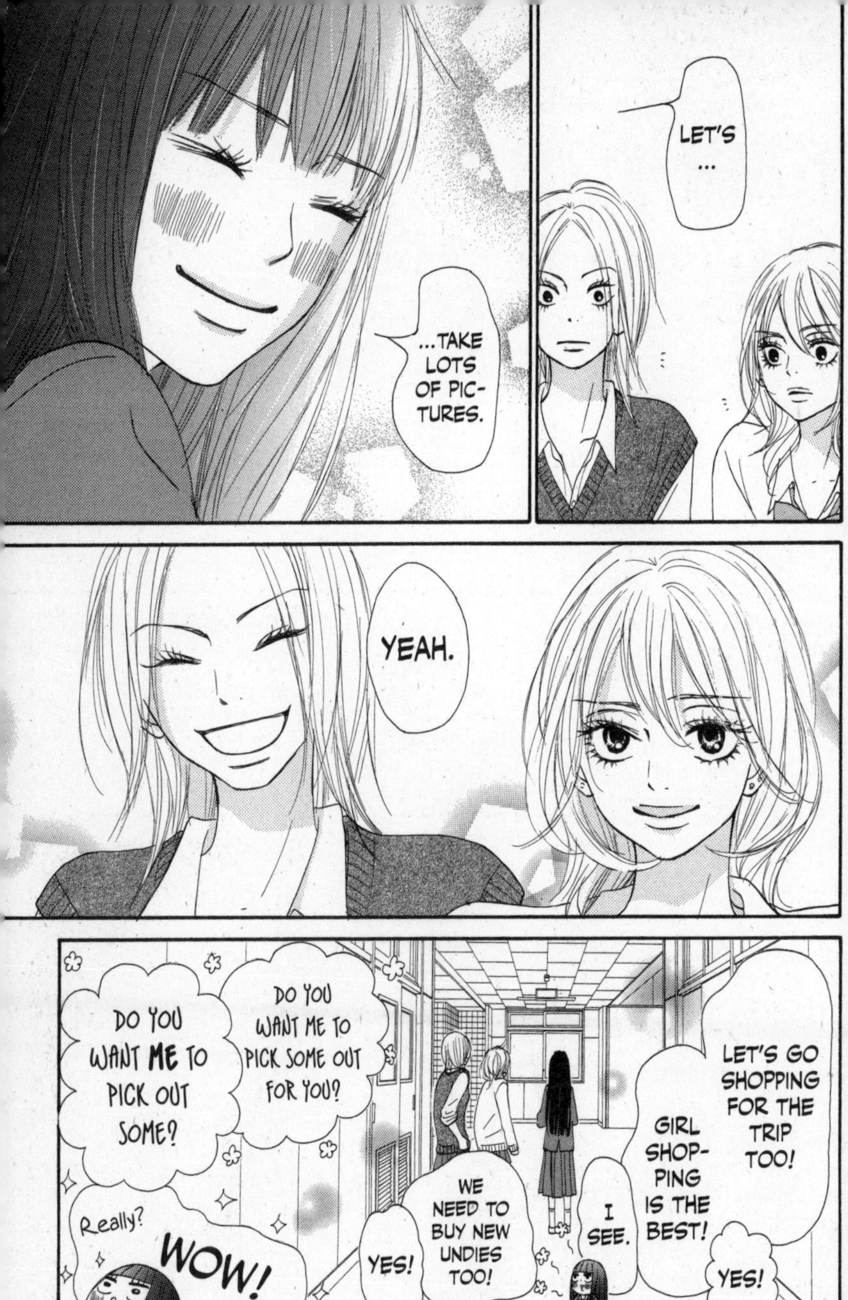
LET'S ...
...TAKE LOTS OF PIC-TURES.
YEAH.
LET'S GO SHOPPING FOR THE TRIP TOO!
YES!
GIRL SHOP-PING IS THE BEST!
I SEE.
WE NEED TO BUY NEW UNDIES TOO!
YES!
DO YOU WANT ME TO PICK SOME OUT FOR YOU?
DO YOU WANT **ME** TO PICK OUT SOME?
Really?
WOW!

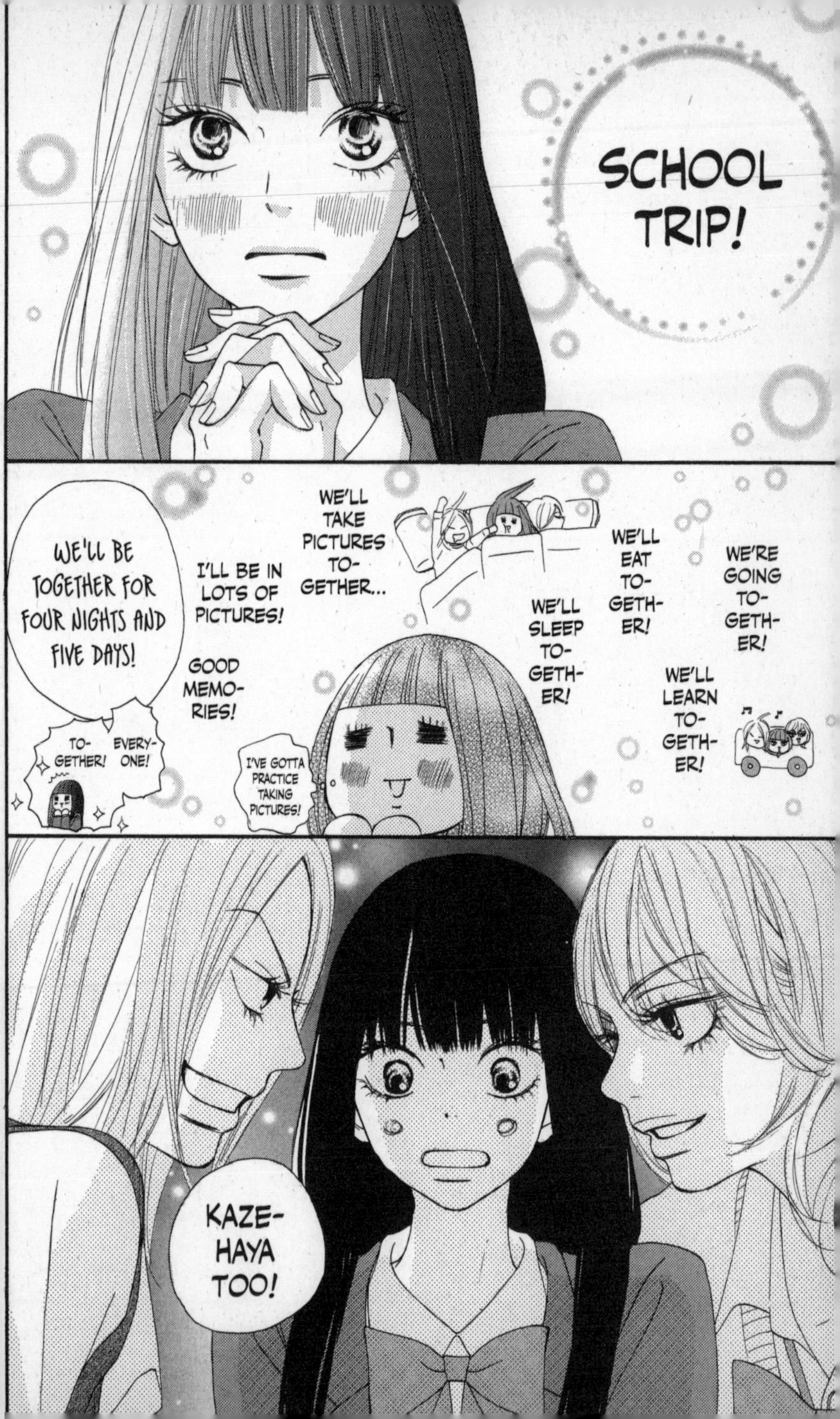
SCHOOL TRIP!
WE'RE GOING TOGETHER!
WE'LL EAT TOGETHER!
WE'LL LEARN TOGETHER!
WE'LL SLEEP TOGETHER!
WE'LL TAKE PICTURES TOGETHER...
I'VE GOTTA PRACTICE TAKING PICTURES!
I'LL BE IN LOTS OF PICTURES!
GOOD MEMORIES!
WE'LL BE TOGETHER FOR FOUR NIGHTS AND FIVE DAYS!
EVERYONE!
TOGETHER!
KAZEHAYA TOO!

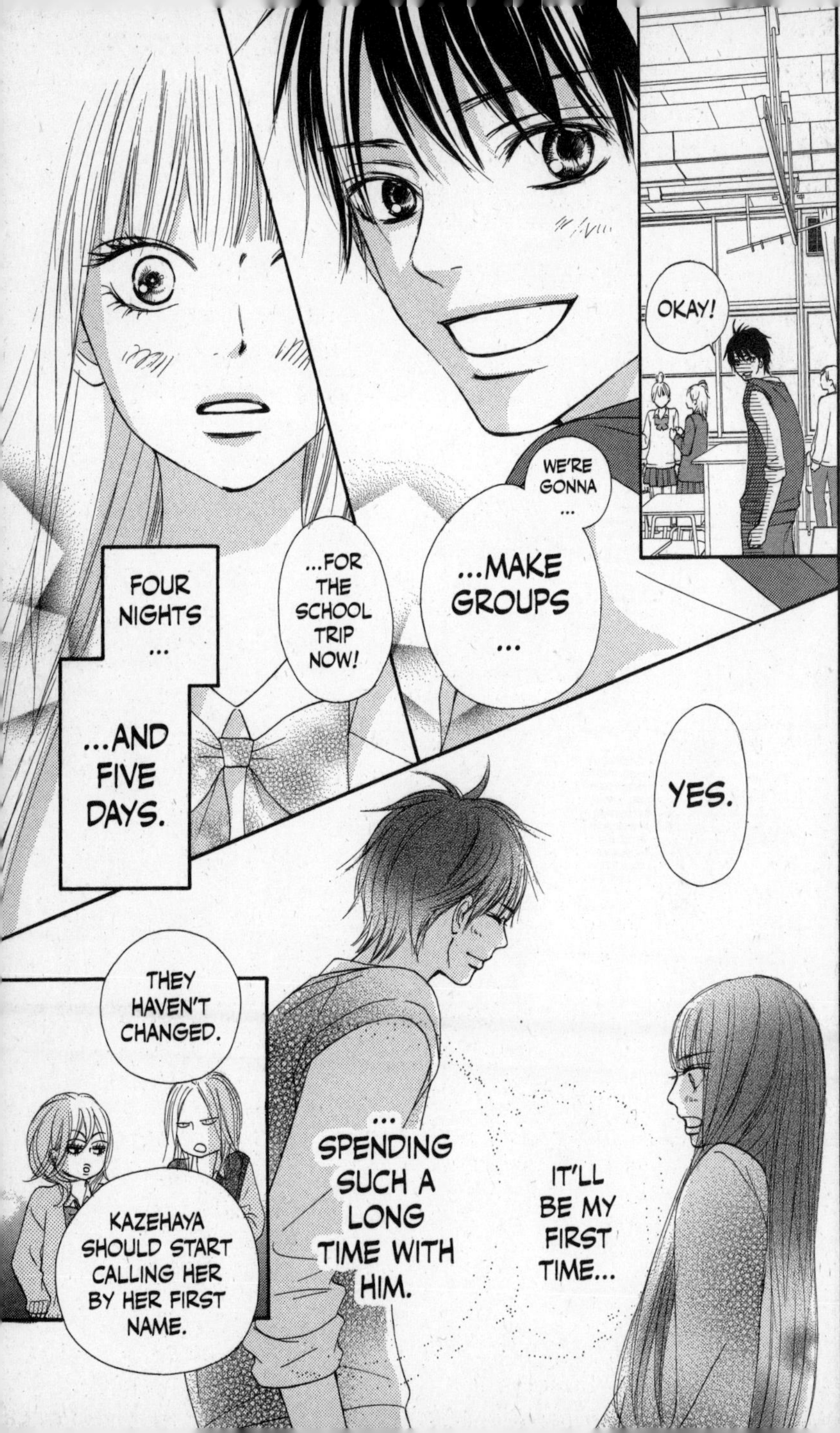
OKAY!
WE'RE GONNA ...
...MAKE GROUPS ...
...FOR THE SCHOOL TRIP NOW!
FOUR NIGHTS ...
...AND FIVE DAYS.
YES.
IT'LL BE MY FIRST TIME...
... SPENDING SUCH A LONG TIME WITH HIM.
THEY HAVEN'T CHANGED.
KAZEHAYA SHOULD START CALLING HER BY HER FIRST NAME.

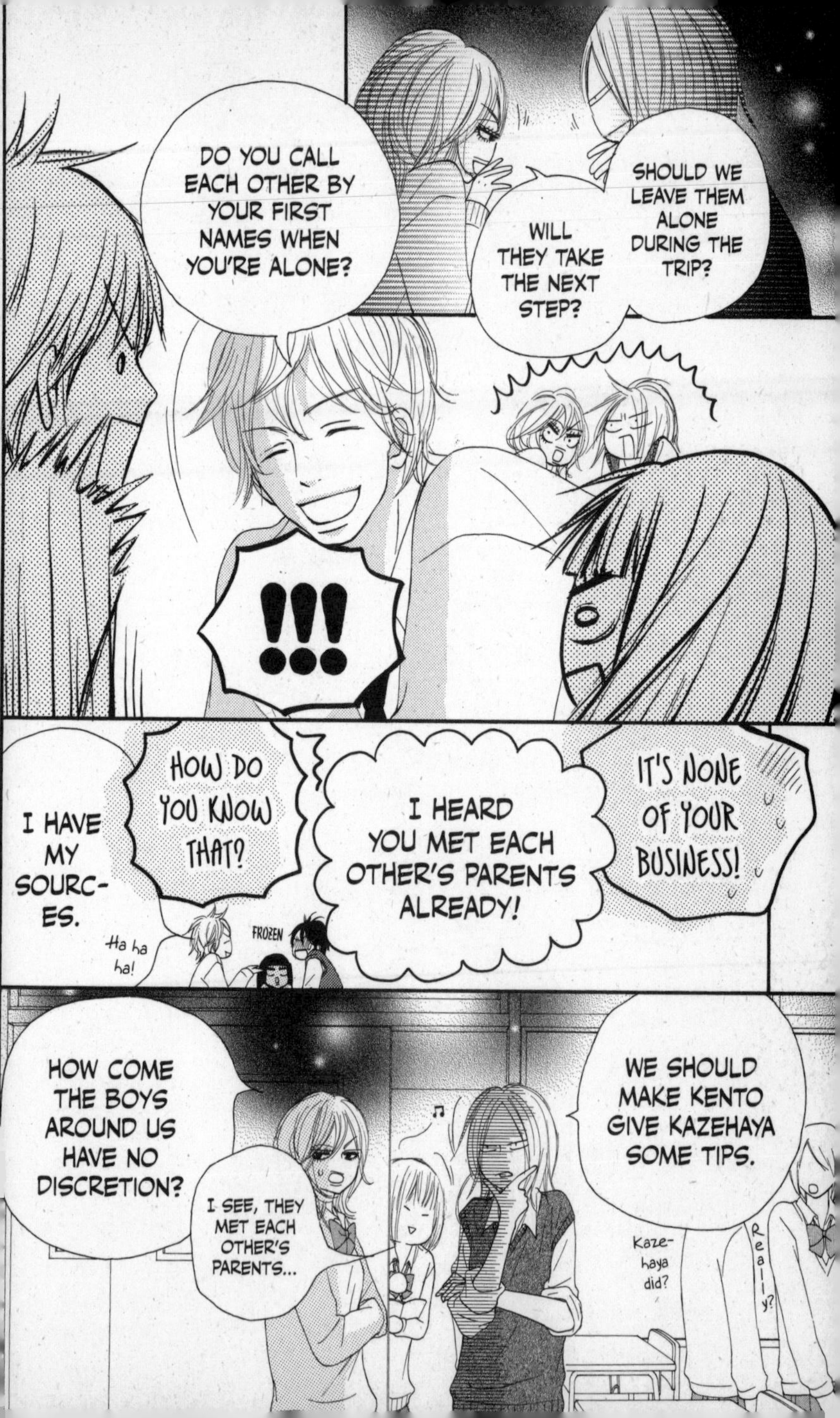
SHOULD WE LEAVE THEM ALONE DURING THE TRIP?
WILL THEY TAKE THE NEXT STEP?
DO YOU CALL EACH OTHER BY YOUR FIRST NAMES WHEN YOU'RE ALONE?
!!!
IT'S NONE OF YOUR BUSINESS!
I HEARD YOU MET EACH OTHER'S PARENTS ALREADY!
FROZEN
HOW DO YOU KNOW THAT?
I HAVE MY SOURC-ES.
Ha ha ha!
WE SHOULD MAKE KENTO GIVE KAZEHAYA SOME TIPS.
Really?
Kaze-haya did?
I SEE, THEY MET EACH OTHER'S PARENTS...
HOW COME THE BOYS AROUND US HAVE NO DISCRETION?

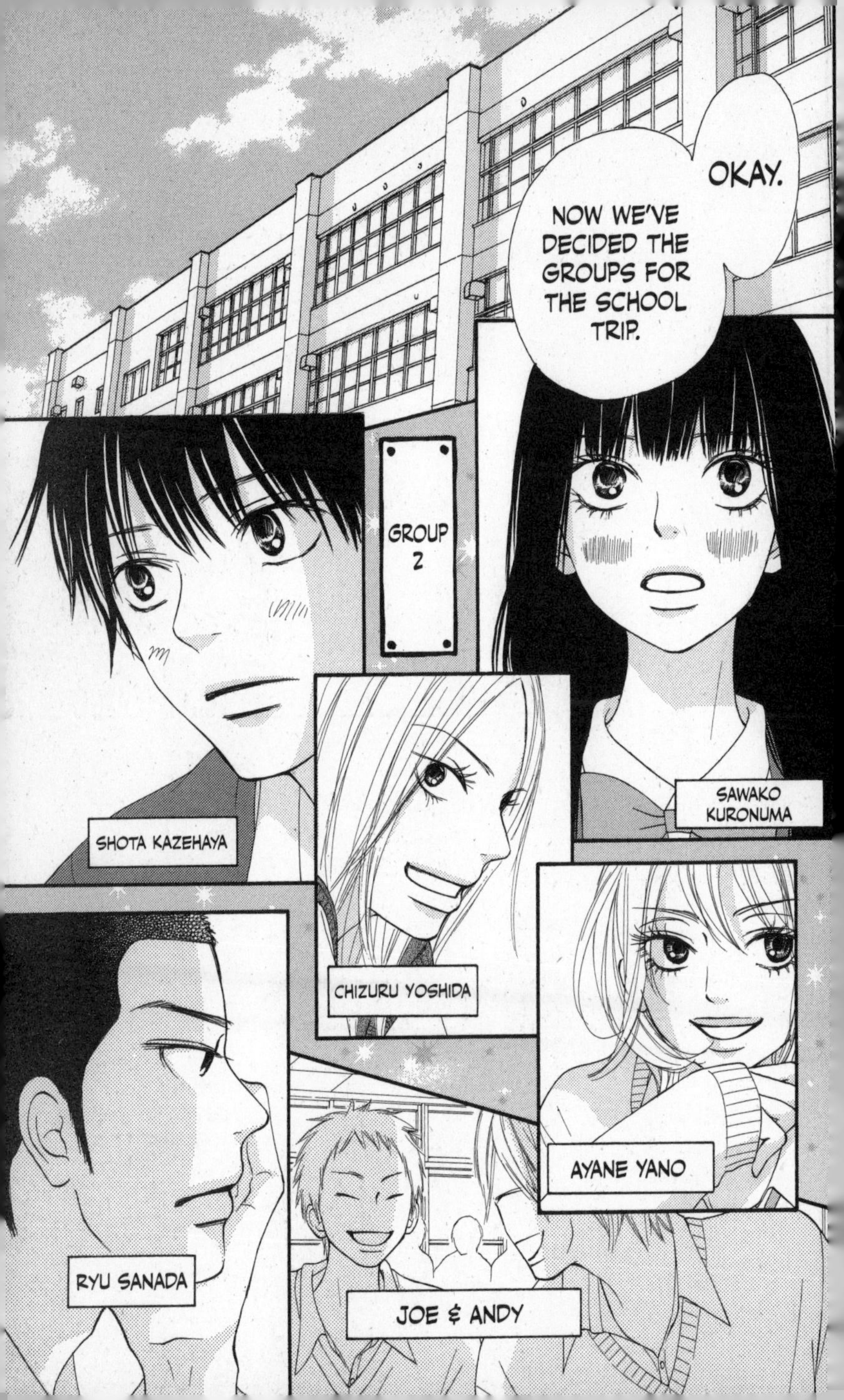
OKAY.
NOW WE'VE DECIDED THE GROUPS FOR THE SCHOOL TRIP.
GROUP 2
SAWAKO KURONUMA
SHOTA KAZEHAYA
CHIZURU YOSHIDA
AYANE YANO
RYU SANADA
JOE & ANDY

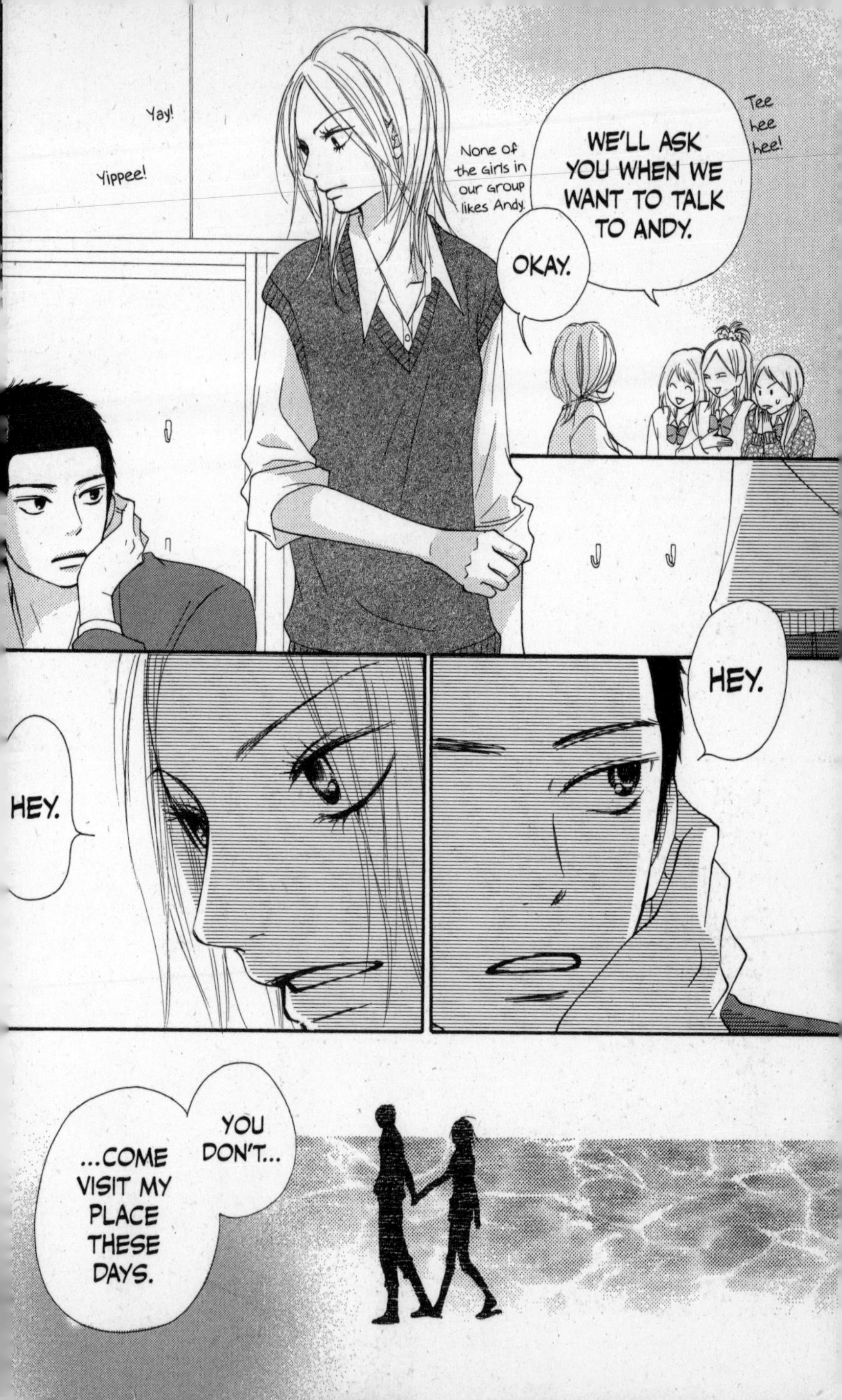
Tee hee hee!
WE'LL ASK YOU WHEN WE WANT TO TALK TO ANDY.
None of the girls in our group likes Andy.
OKAY.
Yay!
Yippee!
HEY.
HEY.
YOU DON'T...
...COME VISIT MY PLACE THESE DAYS.

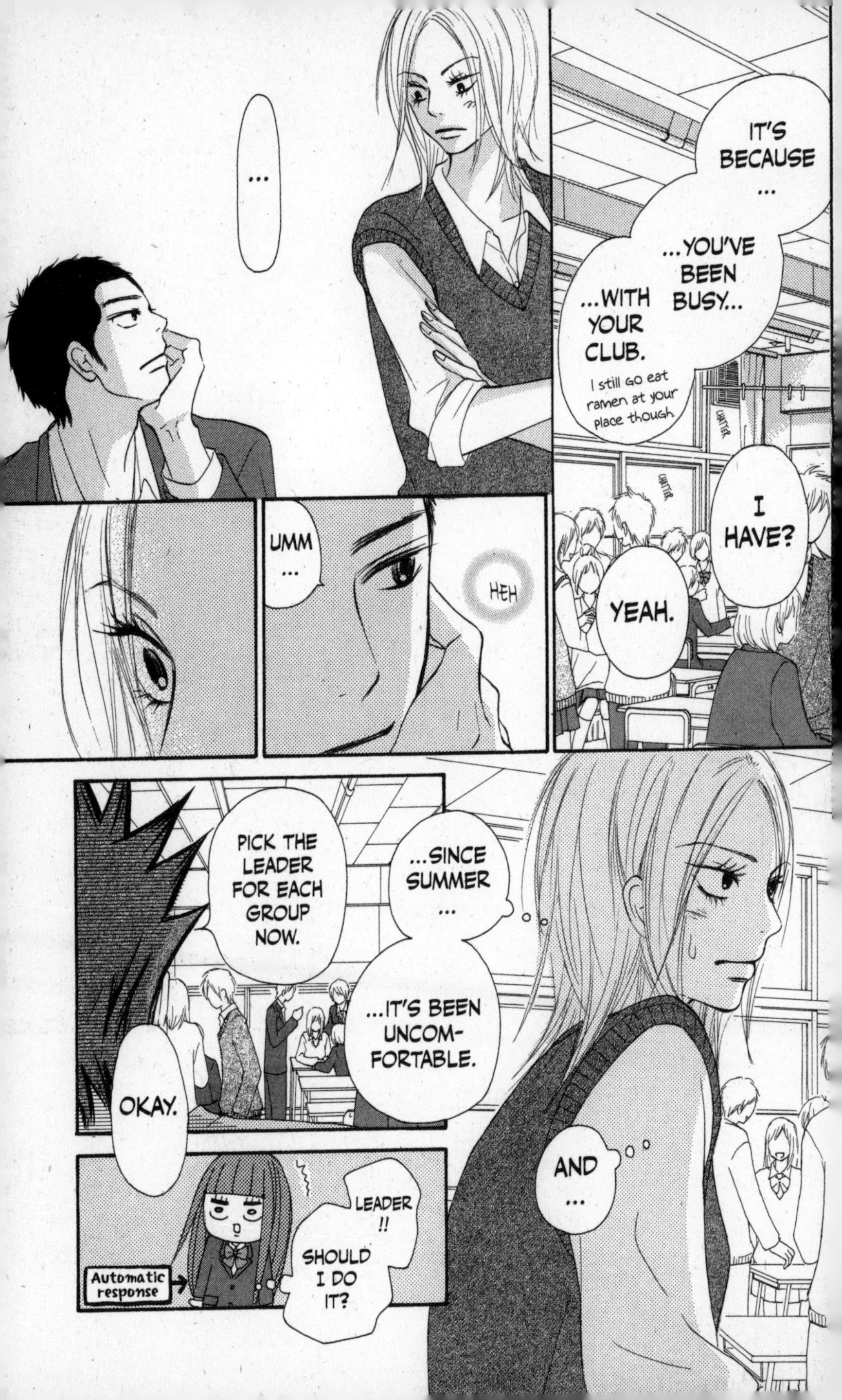
IT'S BECAUSE ...
...YOU'VE BEEN BUSY...
...WITH YOUR CLUB.
I still go eat ramen at your place though.
CHATTER
CHATTER
...
I HAVE?
YEAH.
HEH
UMM ...
...SINCE SUMMER ...
...IT'S BEEN UNCOM-FORTABLE.
AND ...
PICK THE LEADER FOR EACH GROUP NOW.
OKAY.
LEADER !!
SHOULD I DO IT?
Automatic response

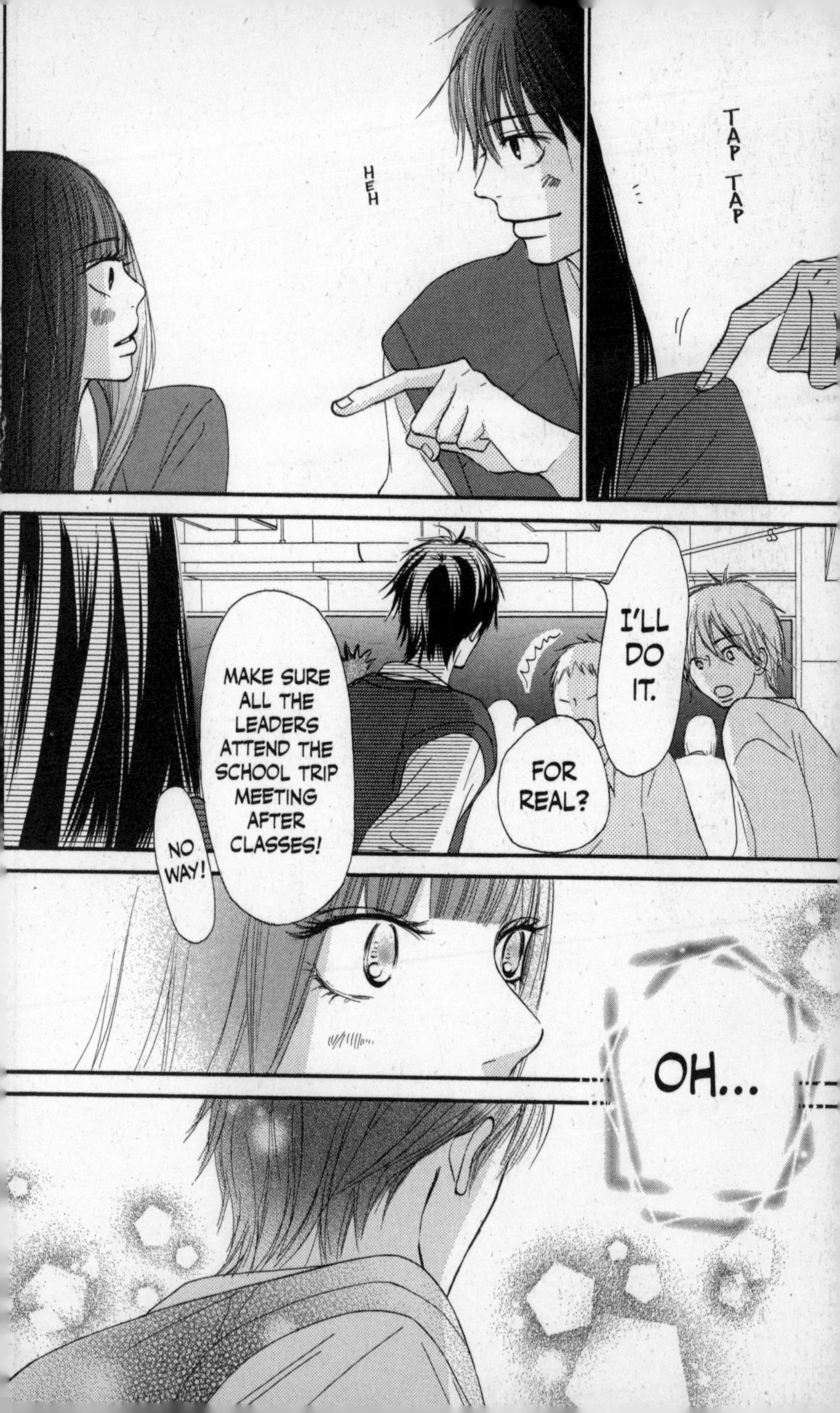
TAP TAP
HEH
I'LL DO IT.
FOR REAL?
MAKE SURE ALL THE LEADERS ATTEND THE SCHOOL TRIP MEETING AFTER CLASSES!
NO WAY!
OH...

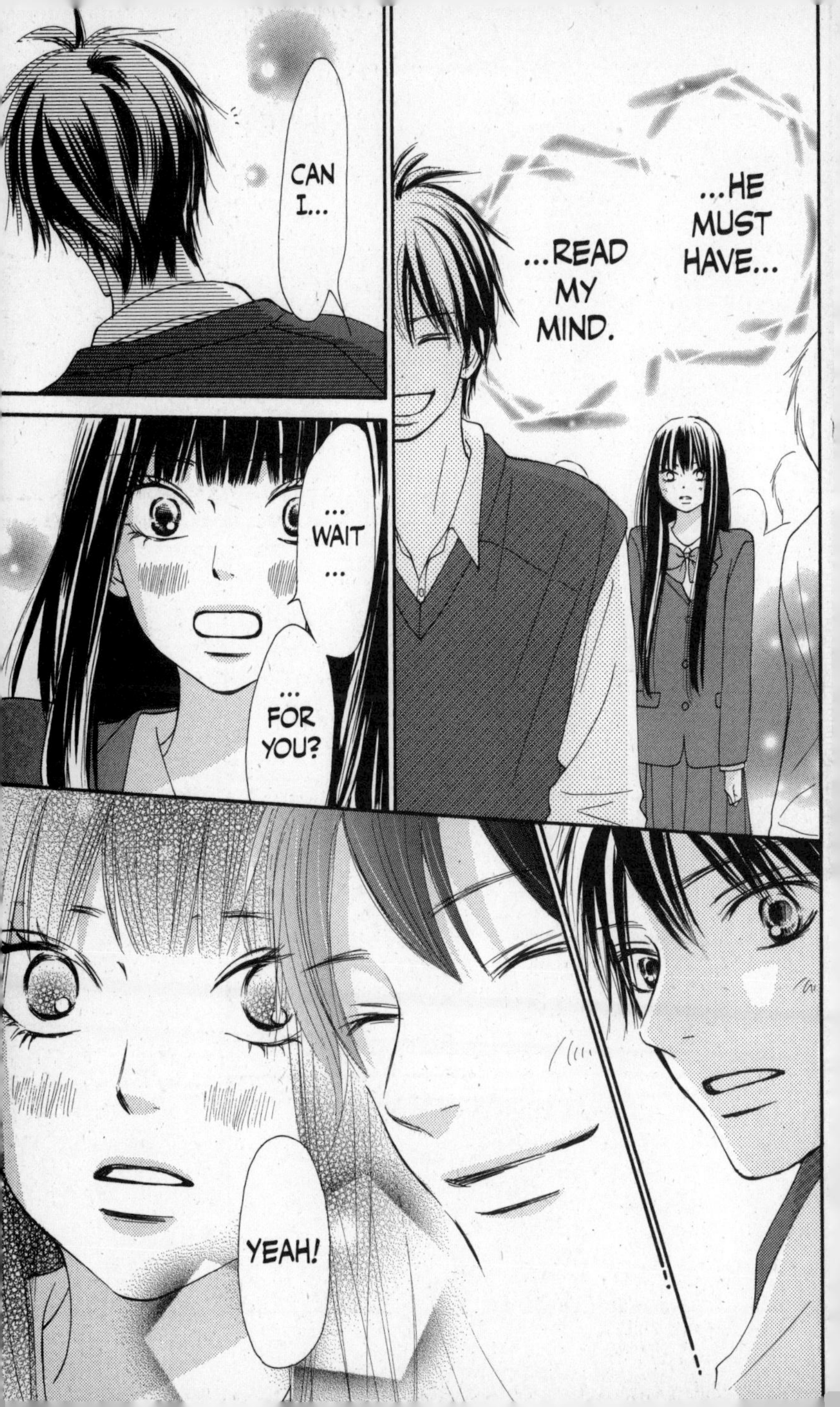
...HE MUST HAVE...
...READ MY MIND.
CAN I...
... WAIT ...
... FOR YOU?
YEAH!

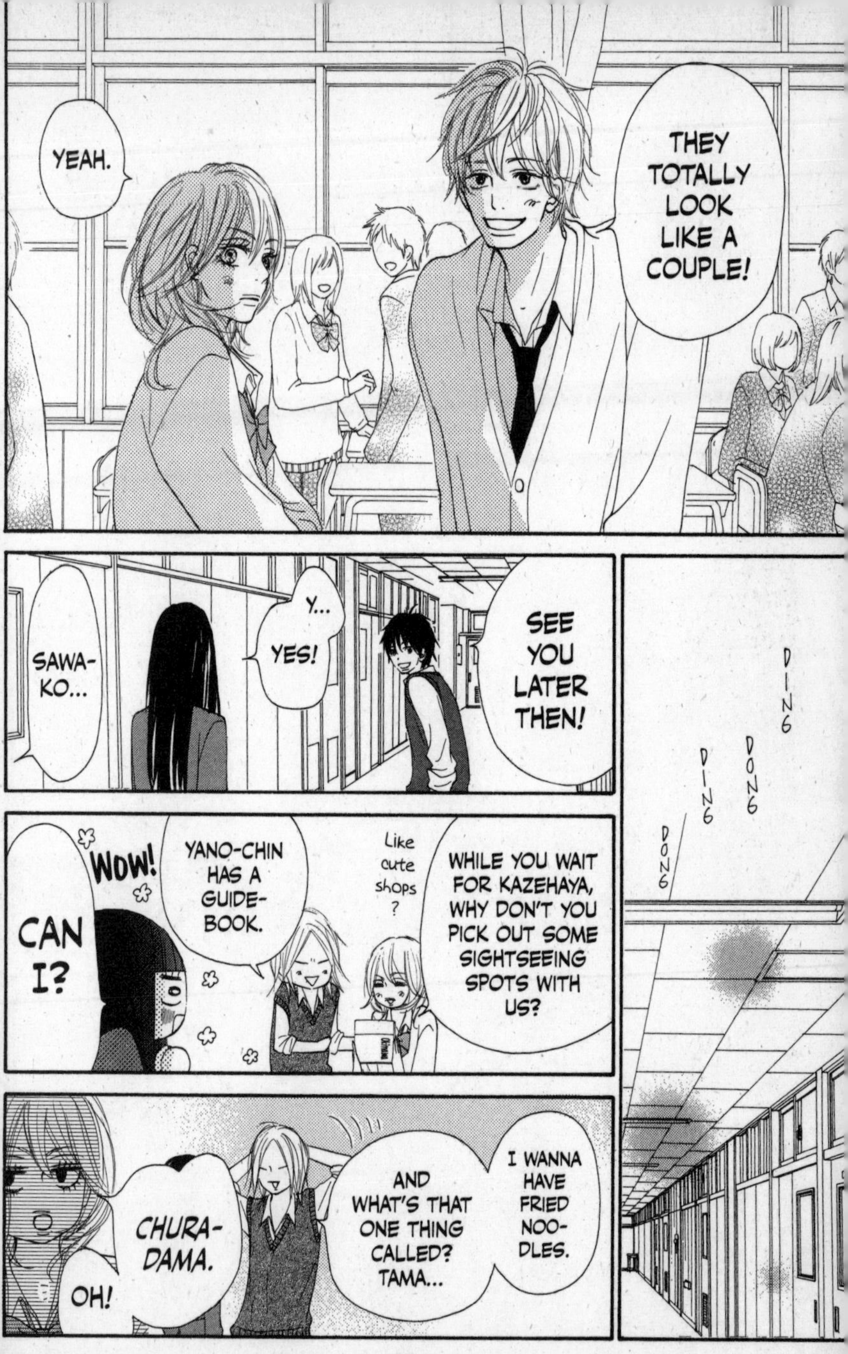
THEY TOTALLY LOOK LIKE A COUPLE!
YEAH.
DING
DONG
DING
DONG
SEE YOU LATER THEN!
Y... YES!
SAWAKO...
WHILE YOU WAIT FOR KAZEHAYA, WHY DON'T YOU PICK OUT SOME SIGHTSEEING SPOTS WITH US?
Like cute shops?
YANO-CHIN HAS A GUIDEBOOK.
WOW!
CAN I?
I WANNA HAVE FRIED NOODLES.
AND WHAT'S THAT ONE THING CALLED? TAMA...
CHURA-DAMA.
OH!

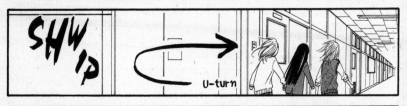

SHW IP

U-turn

...YUI-CHAN AND ANDY!

TMp TMp TMp TMp TMp

IT WAS...

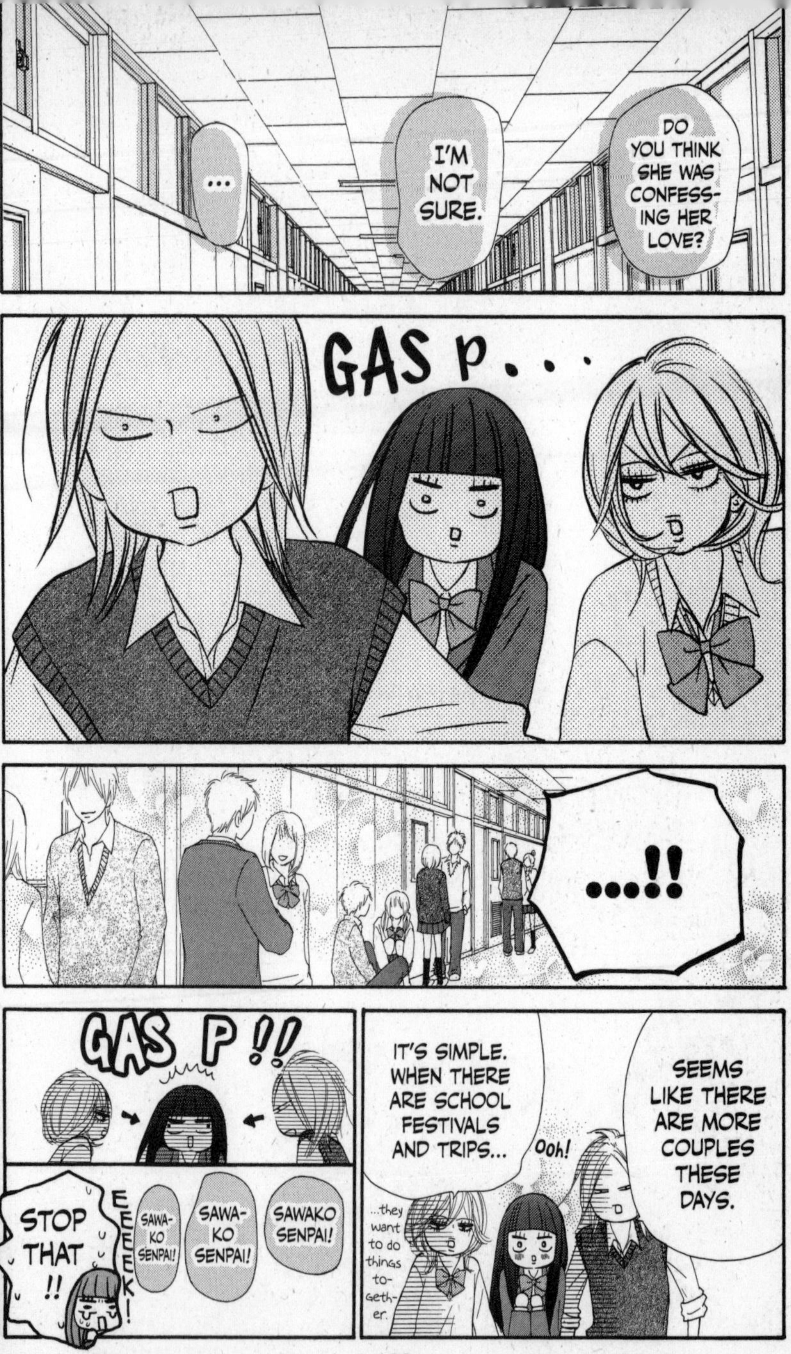
DO YOU THINK SHE WAS CONFESS-ING HER LOVE?
I'M NOT SURE.
...
GASP...
...!!
SEEMS LIKE THERE ARE MORE COUPLES THESE DAYS.
Ooh!
IT'S SIMPLE. WHEN THERE ARE SCHOOL FESTIVALS AND TRIPS...
...they want to do things to-geth-er.
GASP!!
SAWAKO SENPAI!
SAWA-KO SENPAI!
SAWA-KO SENPAI!
EEEEEK!
STOP THAT!!

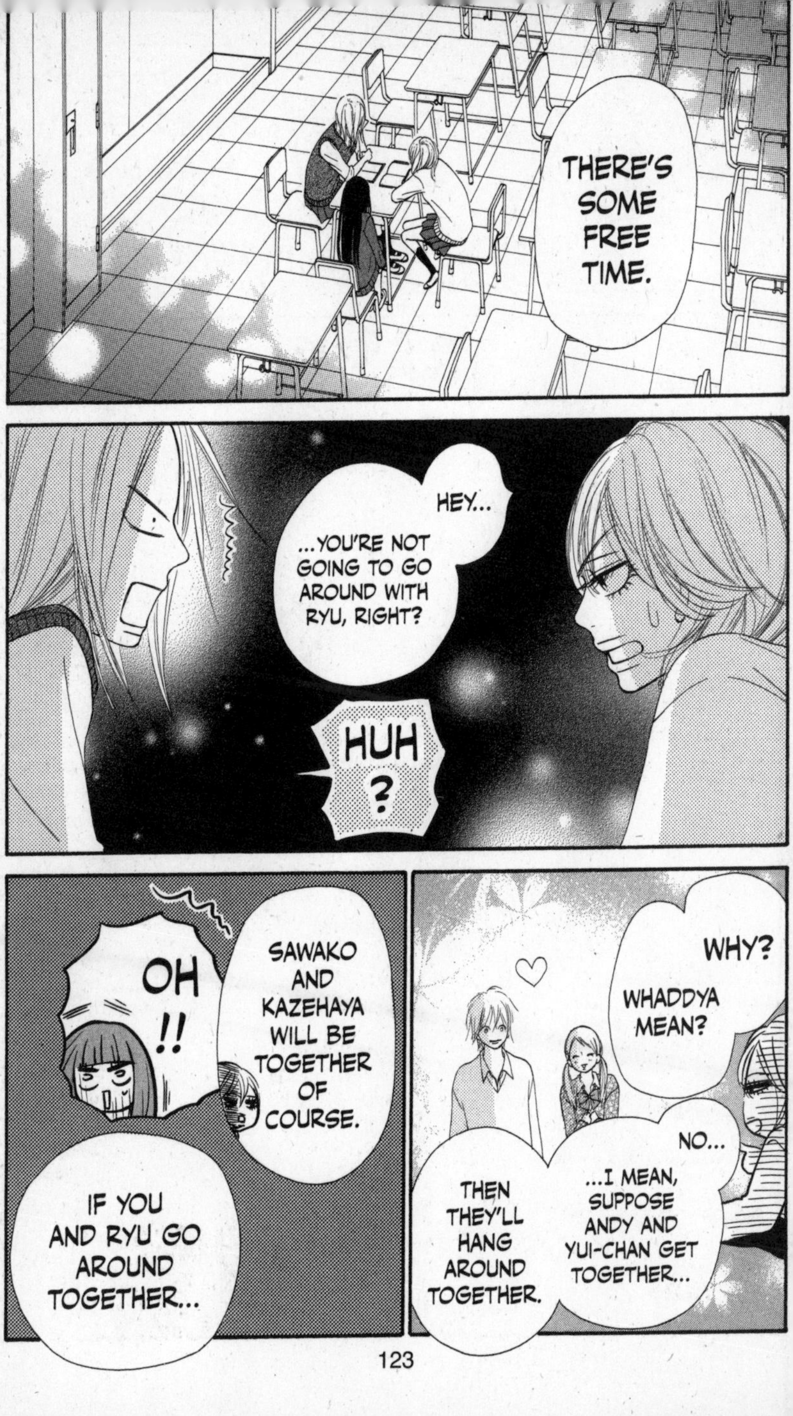
THERE'S SOME FREE TIME.
HEY...
...YOU'RE NOT GOING TO GO AROUND WITH RYU, RIGHT?
HUH?
WHY?
WHADDYA MEAN?
NO...
...I MEAN, SUPPOSE ANDY AND YUI-CHAN GET TOGETHER...
THEN THEY'LL HANG AROUND TOGETHER.
SAWAKO AND KAZEHAYA WILL BE TOGETHER OF COURSE.
OH!!
IF YOU AND RYU GO AROUND TOGETHER...

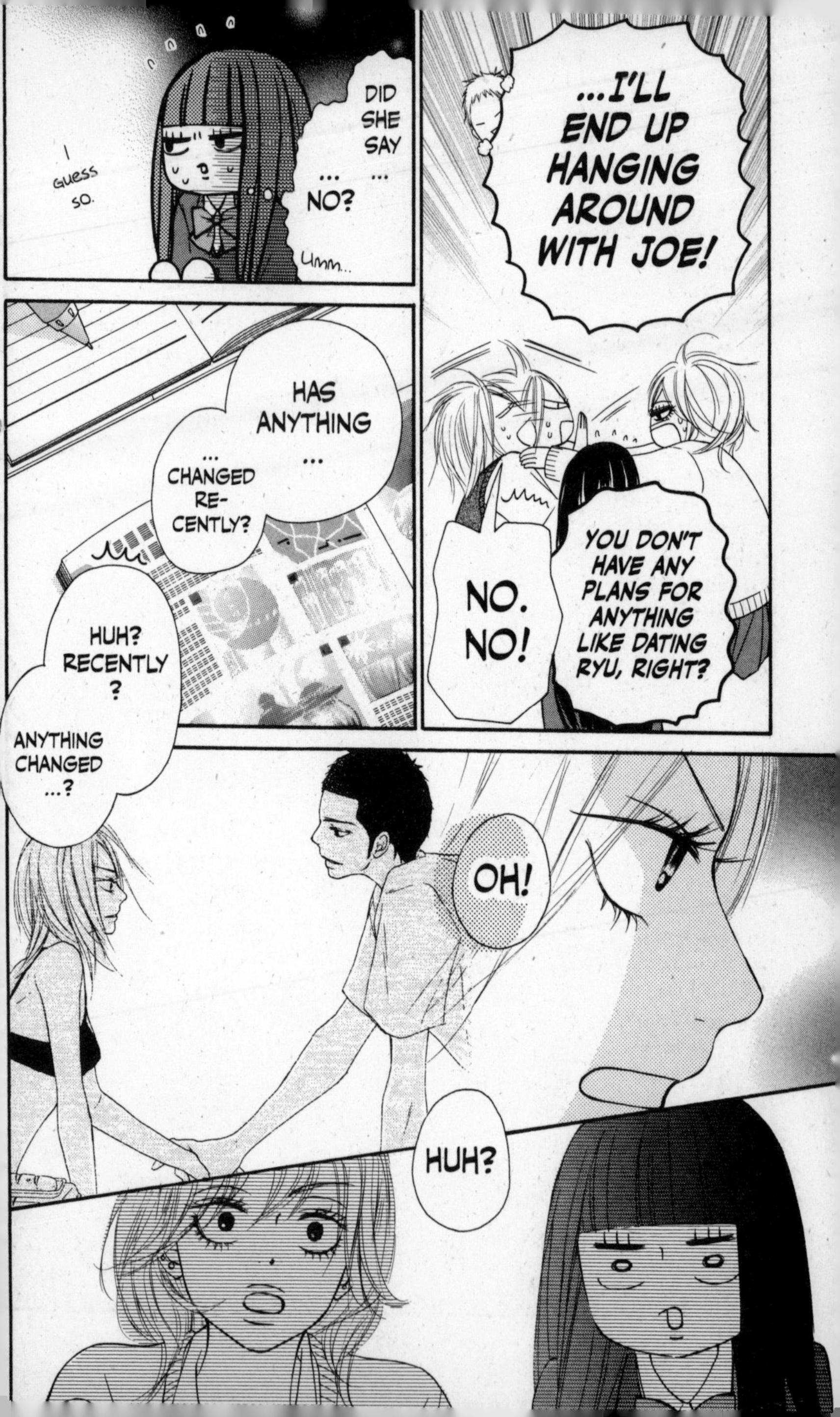
...I'LL END UP HANGING AROUND WITH JOE!
YOU DON'T HAVE ANY PLANS FOR ANYTHING LIKE DATING RYU, RIGHT?
NO. NO!
DID SHE SAY ... ... NO?
I GUESS SO.
Umm...
HAS ANYTHING ... ... CHANGED RE-CENTLY?
HUH? RECENTLY?
ANYTHING CHANGED ...?
OH!
HUH?

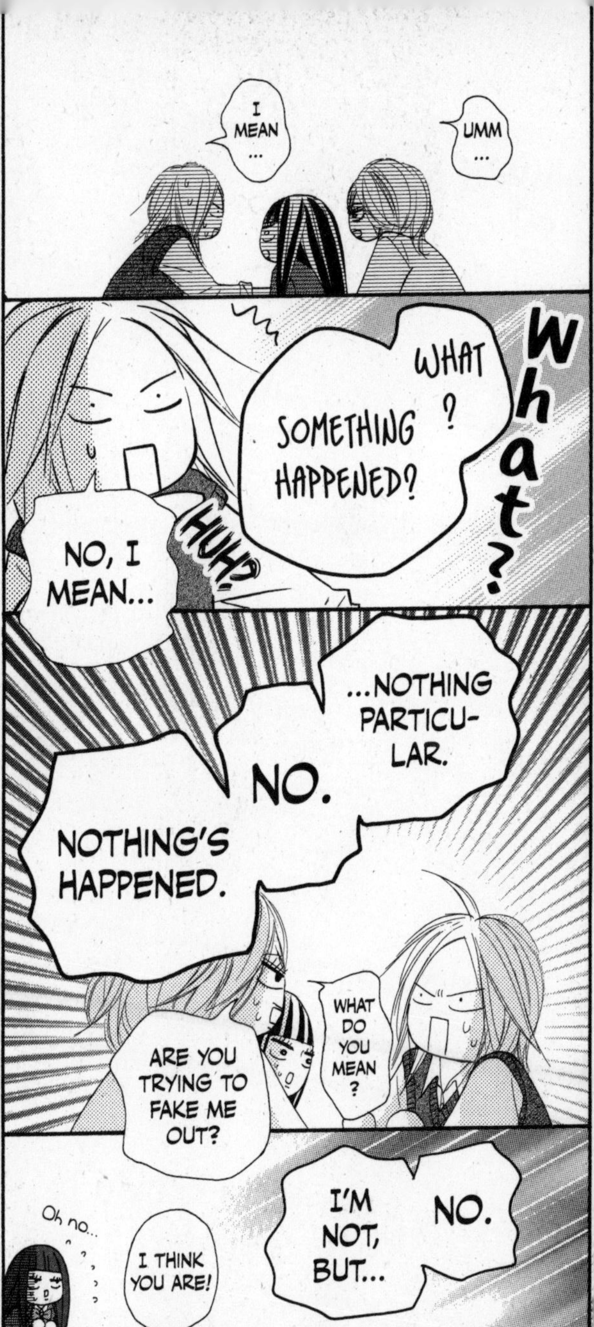
UMM ...
I MEAN ...
What?
WHAT? SOMETHING HAPPENED?
HUH?
NO, I MEAN...
...NOTHING PARTICU-LAR.
NO.
NOTHING'S HAPPENED.
WHAT DO YOU MEAN?
ARE YOU TRYING TO FAKE ME OUT?
NO.
I'M NOT, BUT...
I THINK YOU ARE!
Oh no...

KARUPIN on JAPAN 5

One more thing I'm looking forward to is observing the dubbing of the anime! By the time this volume comes out, it'll be done. I hope I can visit Tokyo without any trouble. I'm taking my daughter, so hopefully she won't cause trouble or get sick or anything.

How many years has it been since the last time I visited Tokyo?

I hope I won't do anything to ruin the trip...

I hope I won't do anything to ruin the trip...

I'm looking forward to seeing the cast perform live.

Before I go to Tokyo...

I must remove all the lint from my coat and clothes...!

I only have old shoes, but I try not to think about them.

Since I'm going with my daughter...

...I'm thinking about having her ride...

...the Cat Bus!

I hope she enjoys it!

Continued in sidebar 6 →

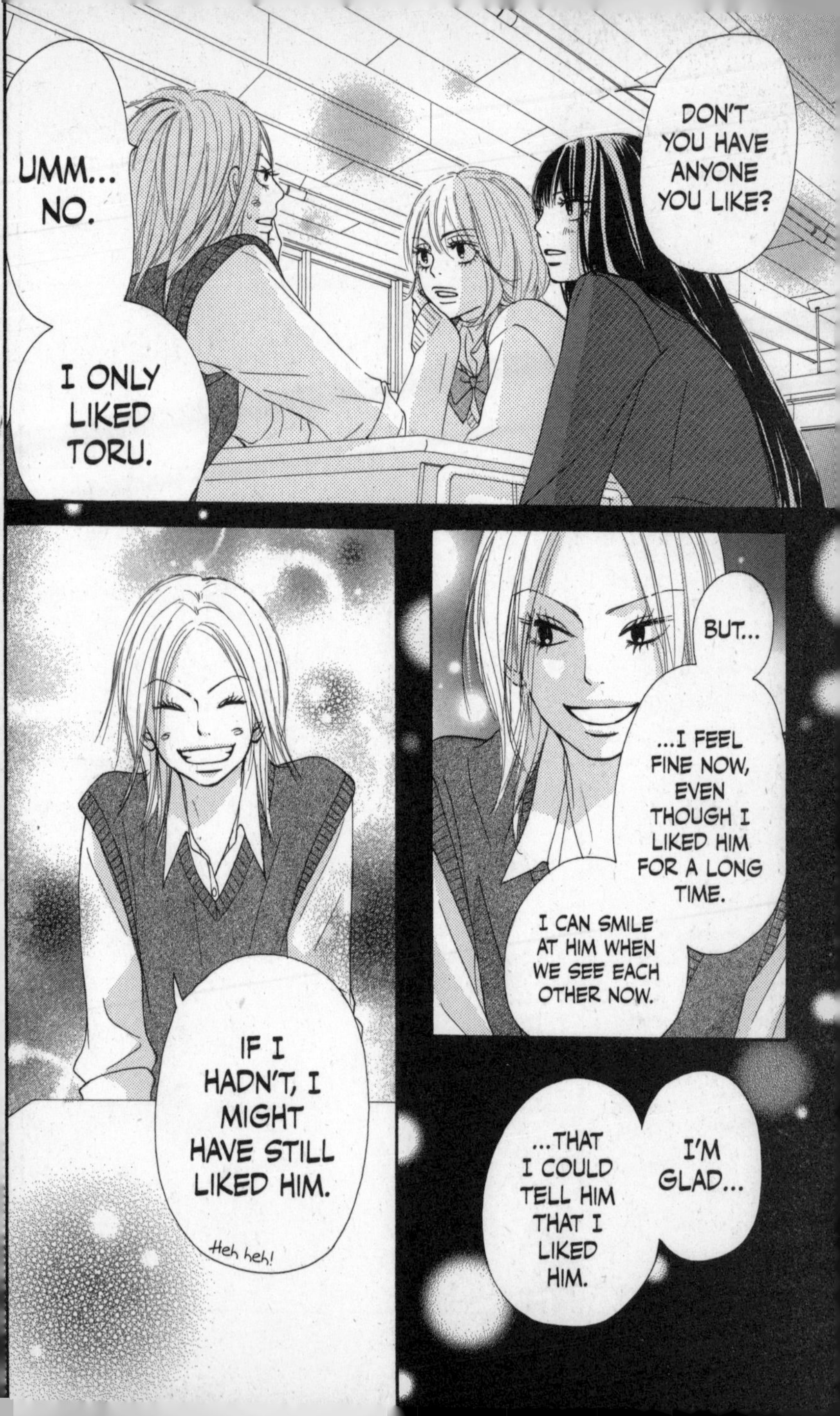
DON'T YOU HAVE ANYONE YOU LIKE?
UMM... NO.
I ONLY LIKED TORU.
BUT...
...I FEEL FINE NOW, EVEN THOUGH I LIKED HIM FOR A LONG TIME.
I CAN SMILE AT HIM WHEN WE SEE EACH OTHER NOW.
I'M GLAD...
...THAT I COULD TELL HIM THAT I LIKED HIM.
IF I HADN'T, I MIGHT HAVE STILL LIKED HIM.
Heh heh!

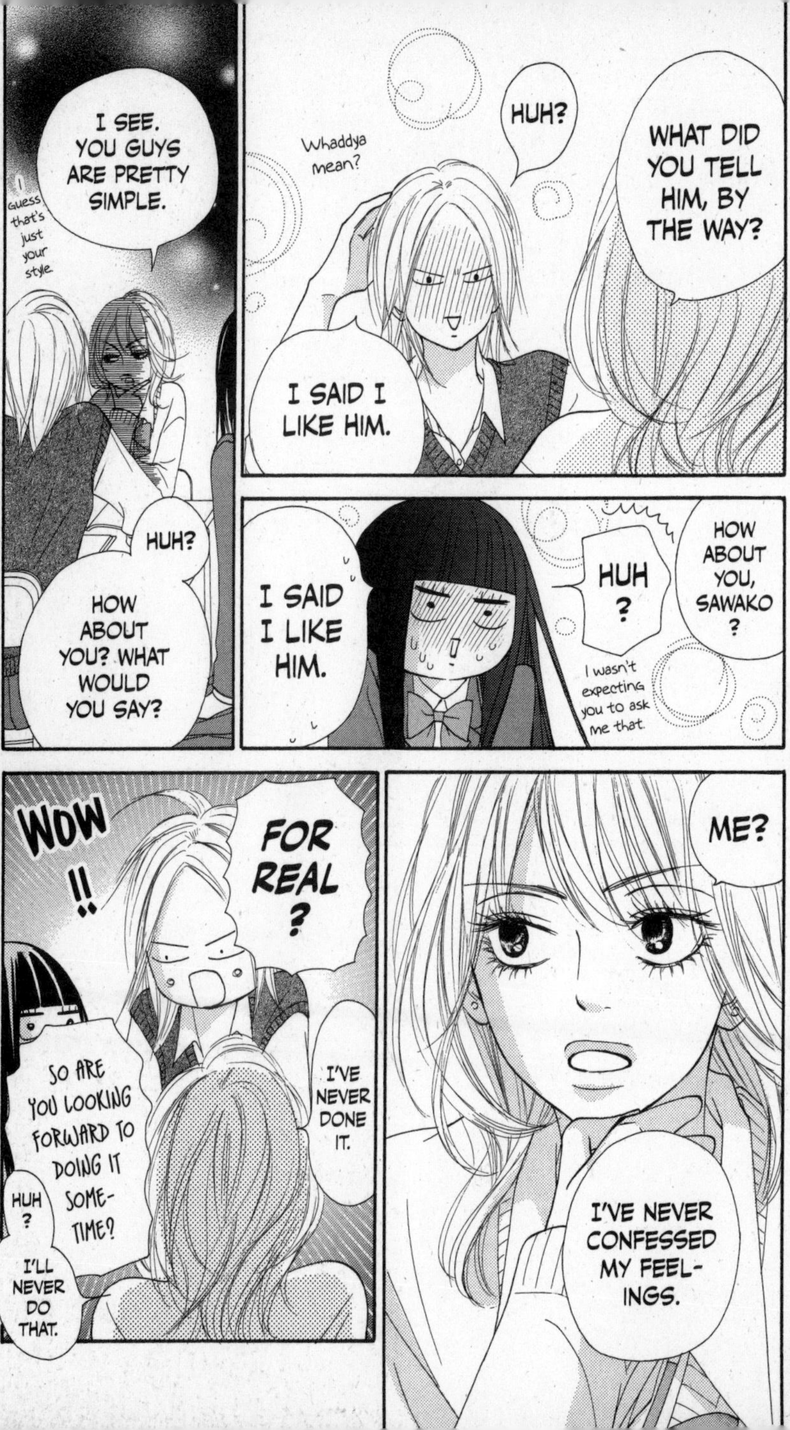
WHAT DID YOU TELL HIM, BY THE WAY?
HUH?
Whaddya mean?
I SAID I LIKE HIM.
HOW ABOUT YOU, SAWAKO?
HUH?
I wasn't expecting you to ask me that.
I SAID I LIKE HIM.
I SEE. YOU GUYS ARE PRETTY SIMPLE.
I guess that's just your style.
HUH?
HOW ABOUT YOU? WHAT WOULD YOU SAY?
ME?
I'VE NEVER CONFESSED MY FEEL-INGS.
FOR REAL?
WOW!!
I'VE NEVER DONE IT.
SO ARE YOU LOOKING FORWARD TO DOING IT SOME-TIME?
HUH?
I'LL NEVER DO THAT.

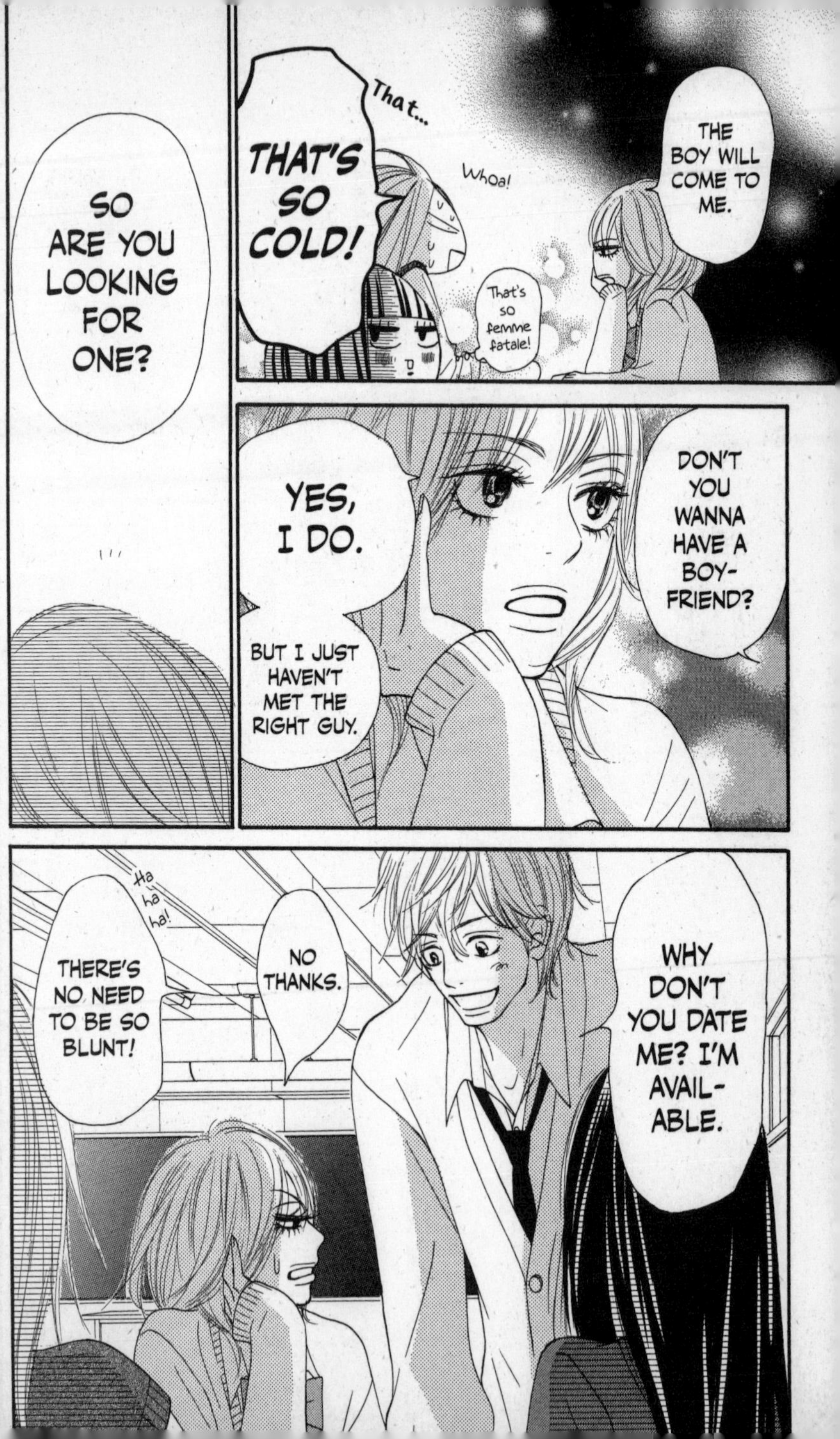
THE BOY WILL COME TO ME.
That...
Whoa!
THAT'S SO COLD!
That's so femme fatale!
DON'T YOU WANNA HAVE A BOY-FRIEND?
YES, I DO.
BUT I JUST HAVEN'T MET THE RIGHT GUY.
SO ARE YOU LOOKING FOR ONE?
WHY DON'T YOU DATE ME? I'M AVAIL-ABLE.
NO THANKS.
Ha ha ha!
THERE'S NO NEED TO BE SO BLUNT!

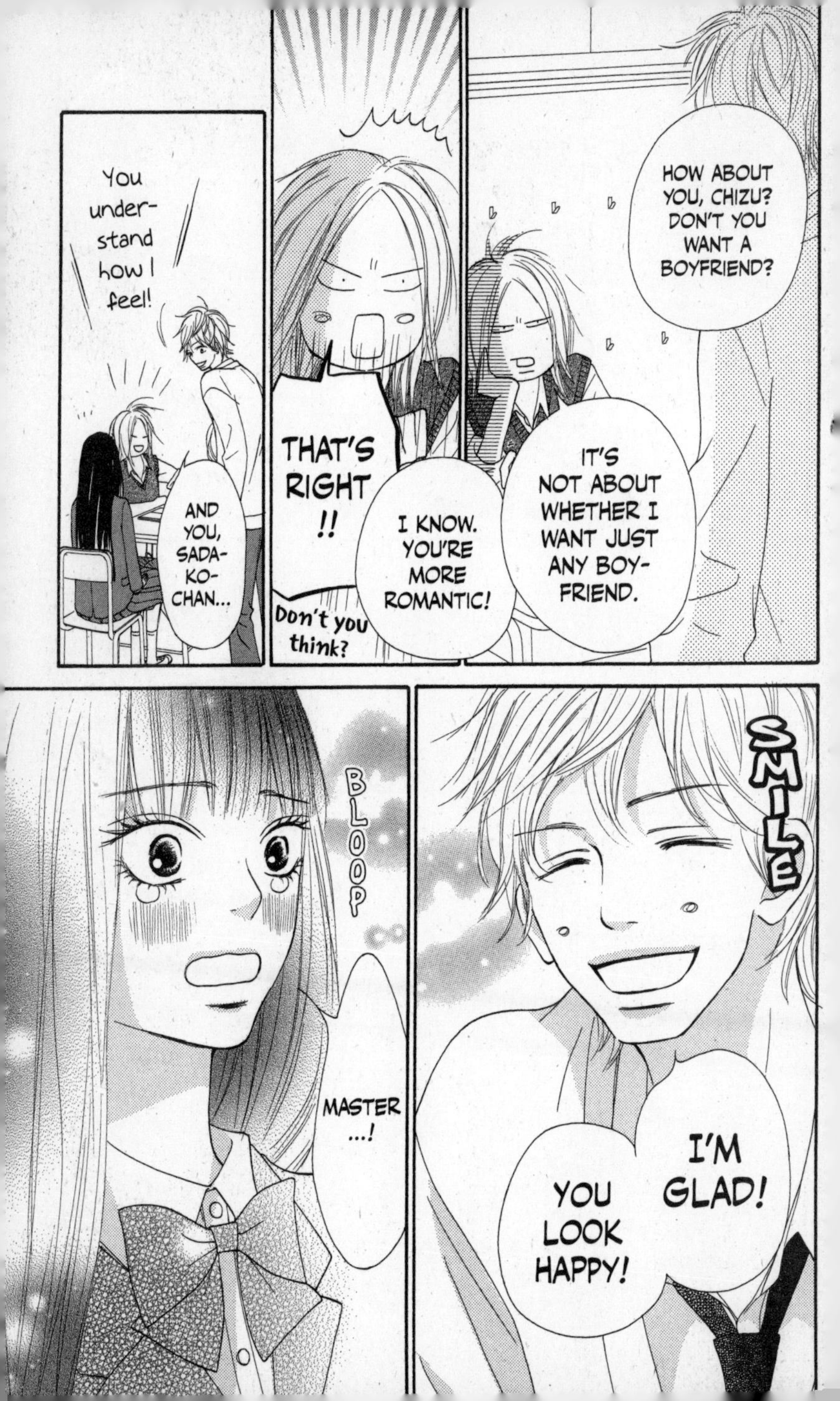
HOW ABOUT YOU, CHIZU? DON'T YOU WANT A BOYFRIEND?
IT'S NOT ABOUT WHETHER I WANT JUST ANY BOY-FRIEND.
I KNOW. YOU'RE MORE ROMANTIC!
THAT'S RIGHT !!
Don't you think?
AND YOU, SADA-KO-CHAN...
You under-stand how I feel!
SMILE
I'M GLAD!
YOU LOOK HAPPY!
BLOOP
MASTER ...!

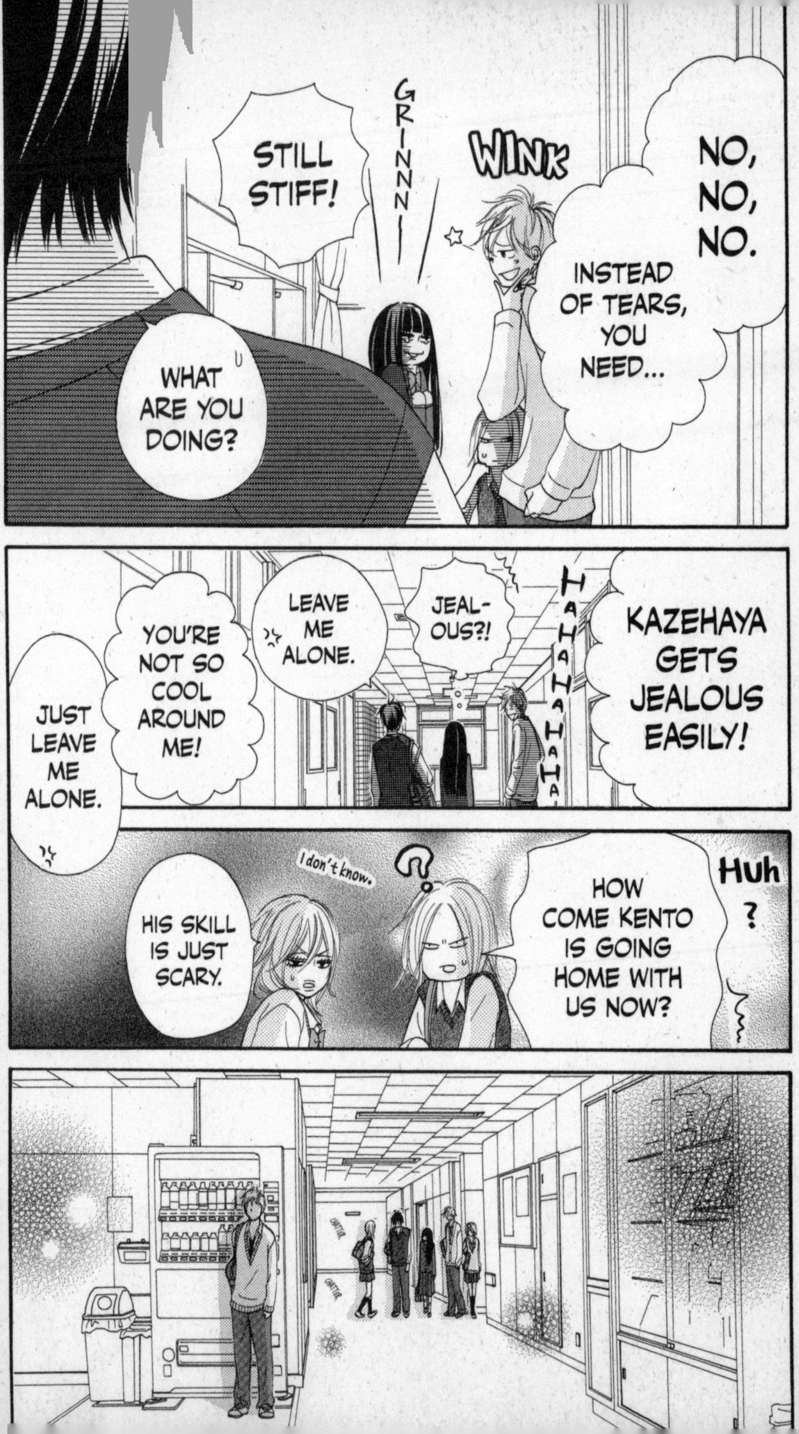
NO, NO, NO.
INSTEAD OF TEARS, YOU NEED...
WINK
GRINNN
STILL STIFF!
WHAT ARE YOU DOING?
KAZEHAYA GETS JEALOUS EASILY!
HAHAHAHAHAHA
JEAL-OUS?!
LEAVE ME ALONE.
YOU'RE NOT SO COOL AROUND ME!
JUST LEAVE ME ALONE.
Huh?
HOW COME KENTO IS GOING HOME WITH US NOW?
I don't know.
HIS SKILL IS JUST SCARY.

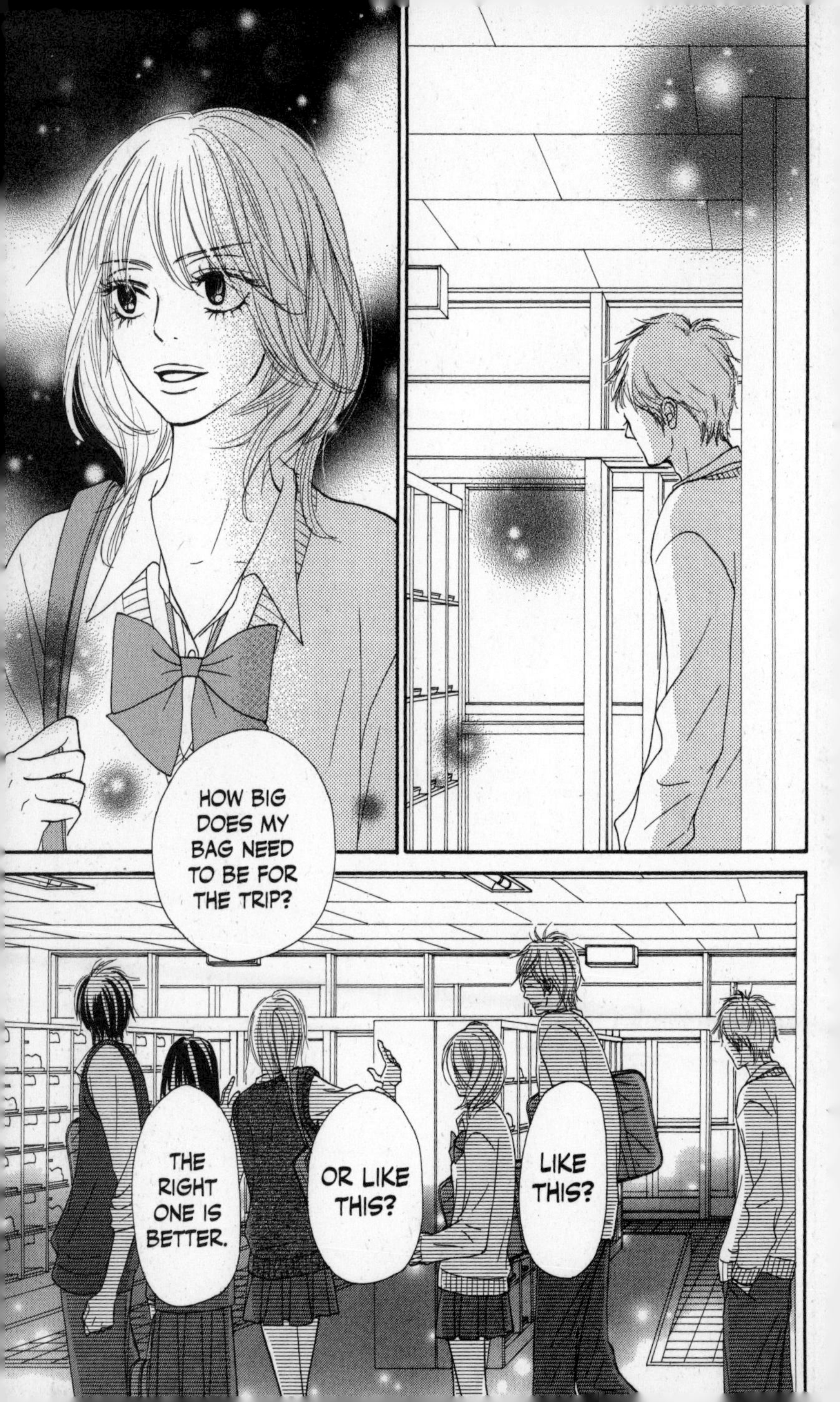
HOW BIG DOES MY BAG NEED TO BE FOR THE TRIP?
LIKE THIS?
OR LIKE THIS?
THE RIGHT ONE IS BETTER.

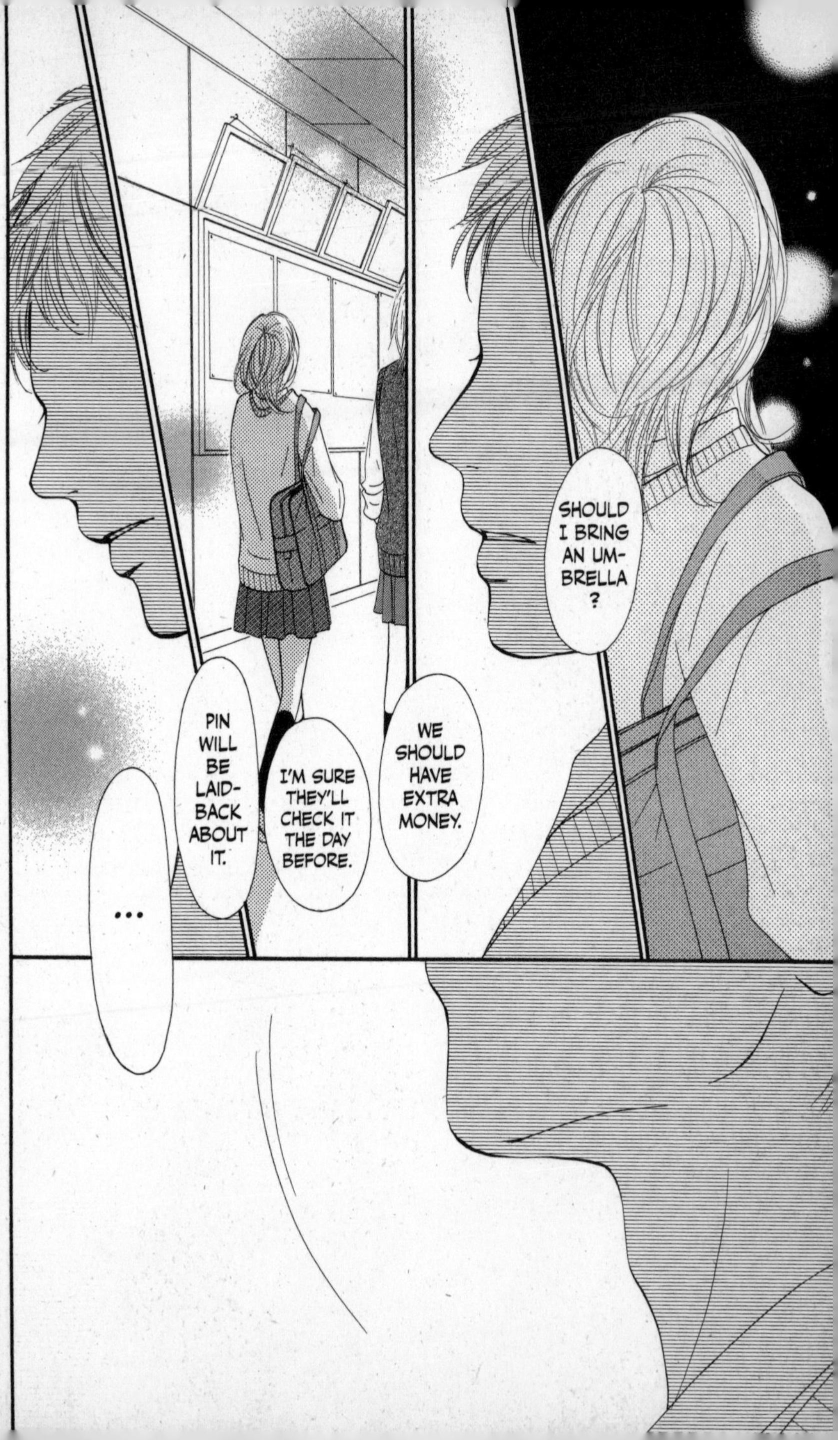
SHOULD I BRING AN UMBRELLA?
WE SHOULD HAVE EXTRA MONEY.
I'M SURE THEY'LL CHECK IT THE DAY BEFORE.
PIN WILL BE LAID-BACK ABOUT IT.
...

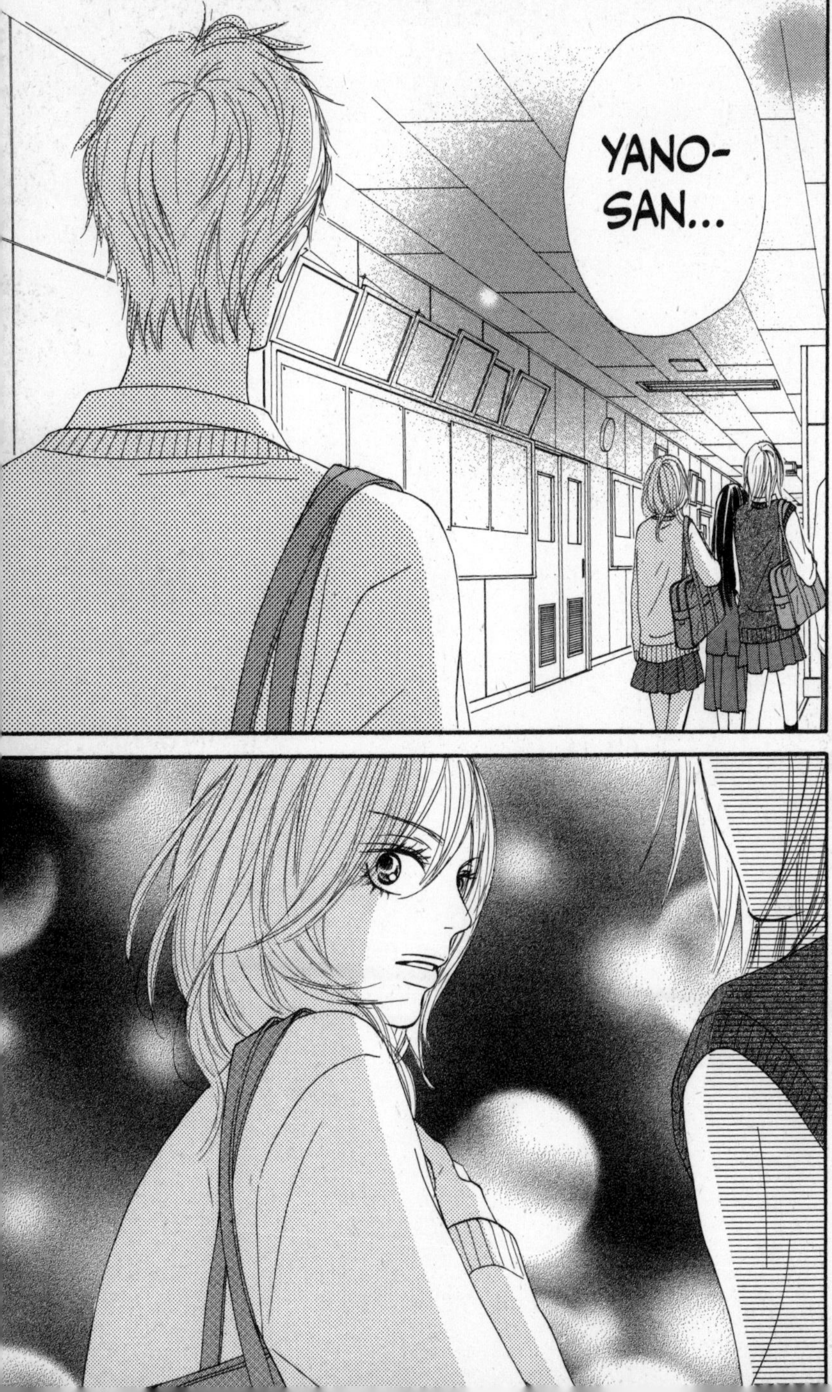
YANO-SAN...

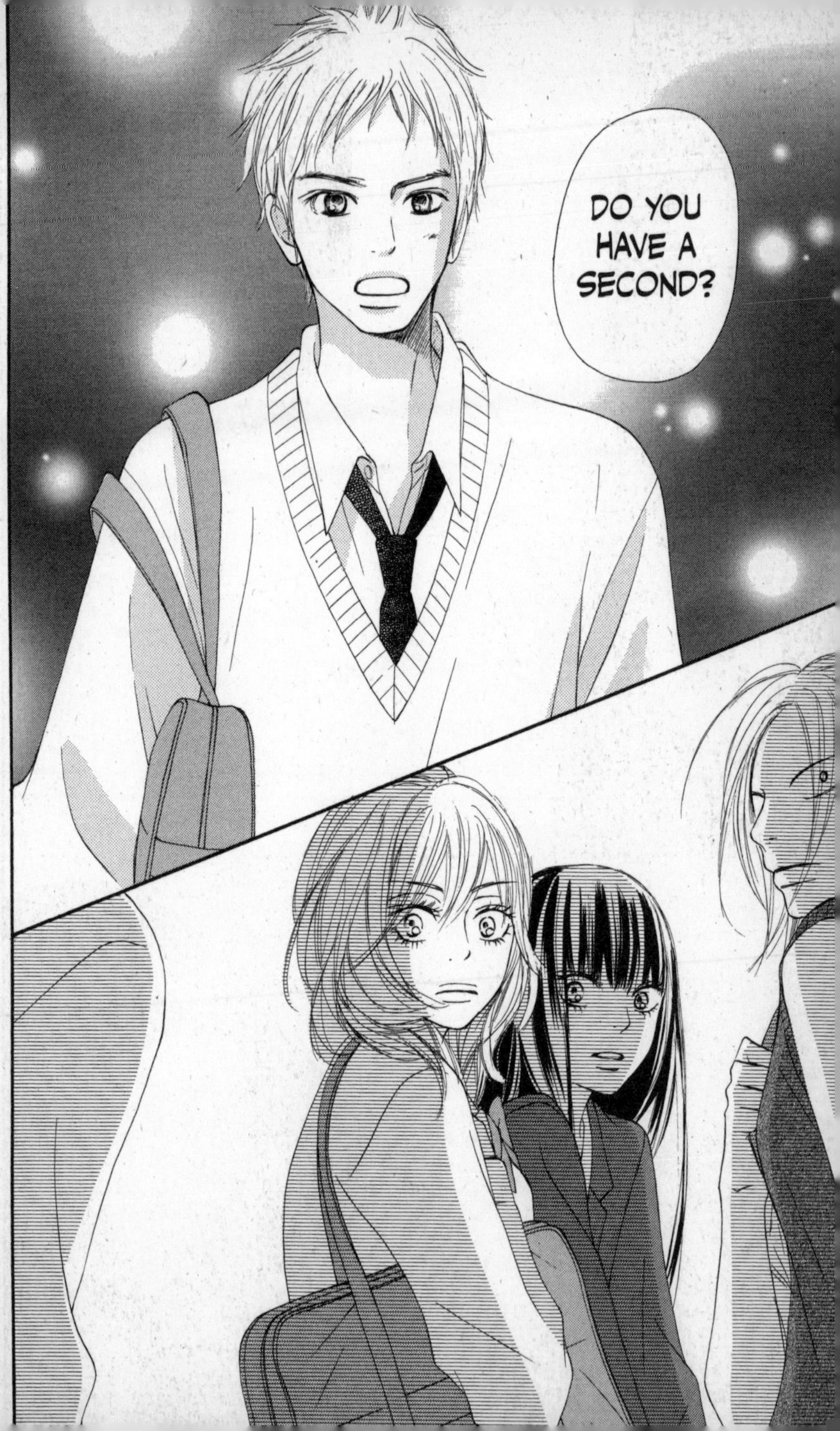
DO YOU HAVE A SECOND?

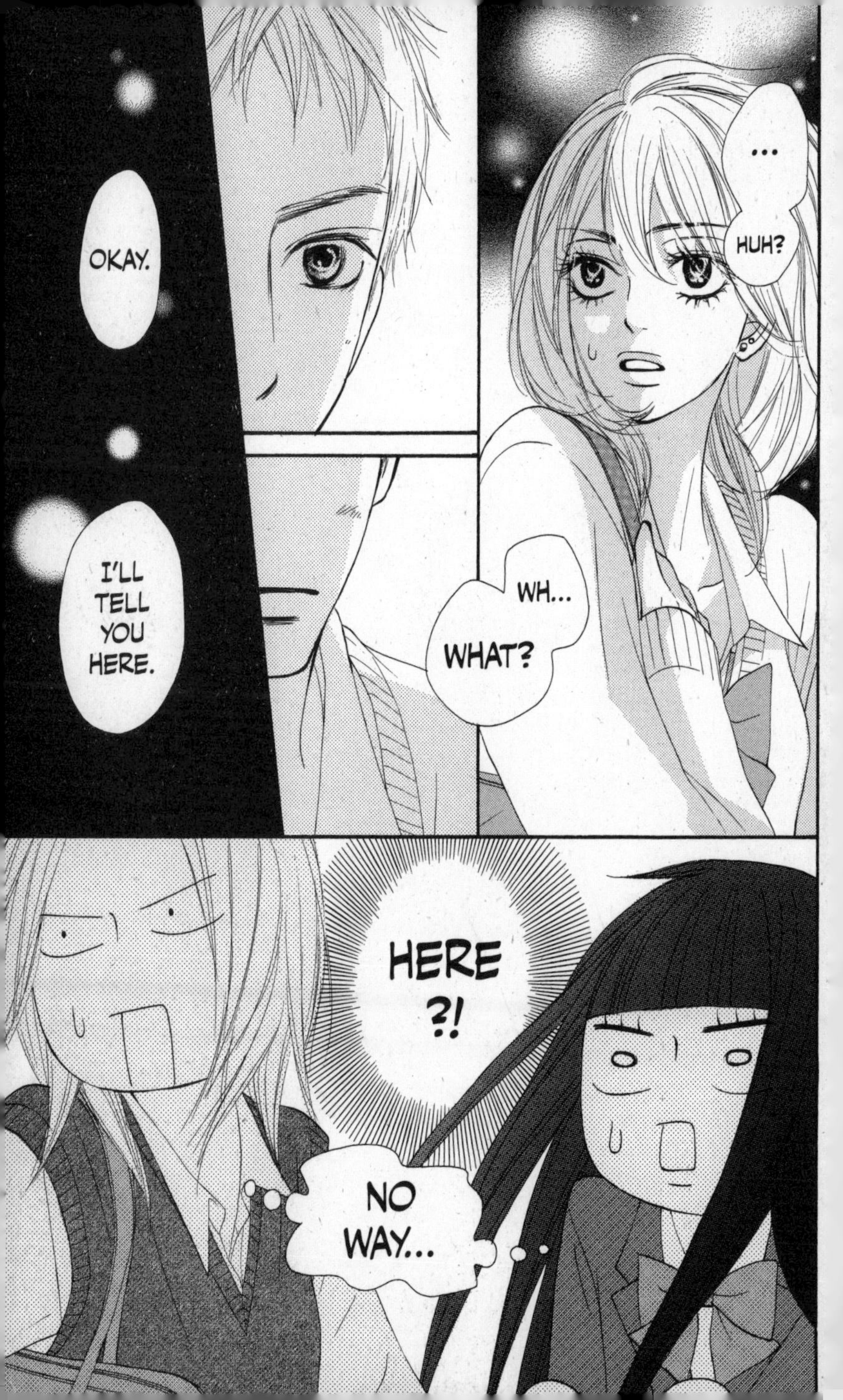
...
HUH?
WH...
WHAT?
OKAY.
I'LL TELL YOU HERE.
HERE ?!
NO WAY...

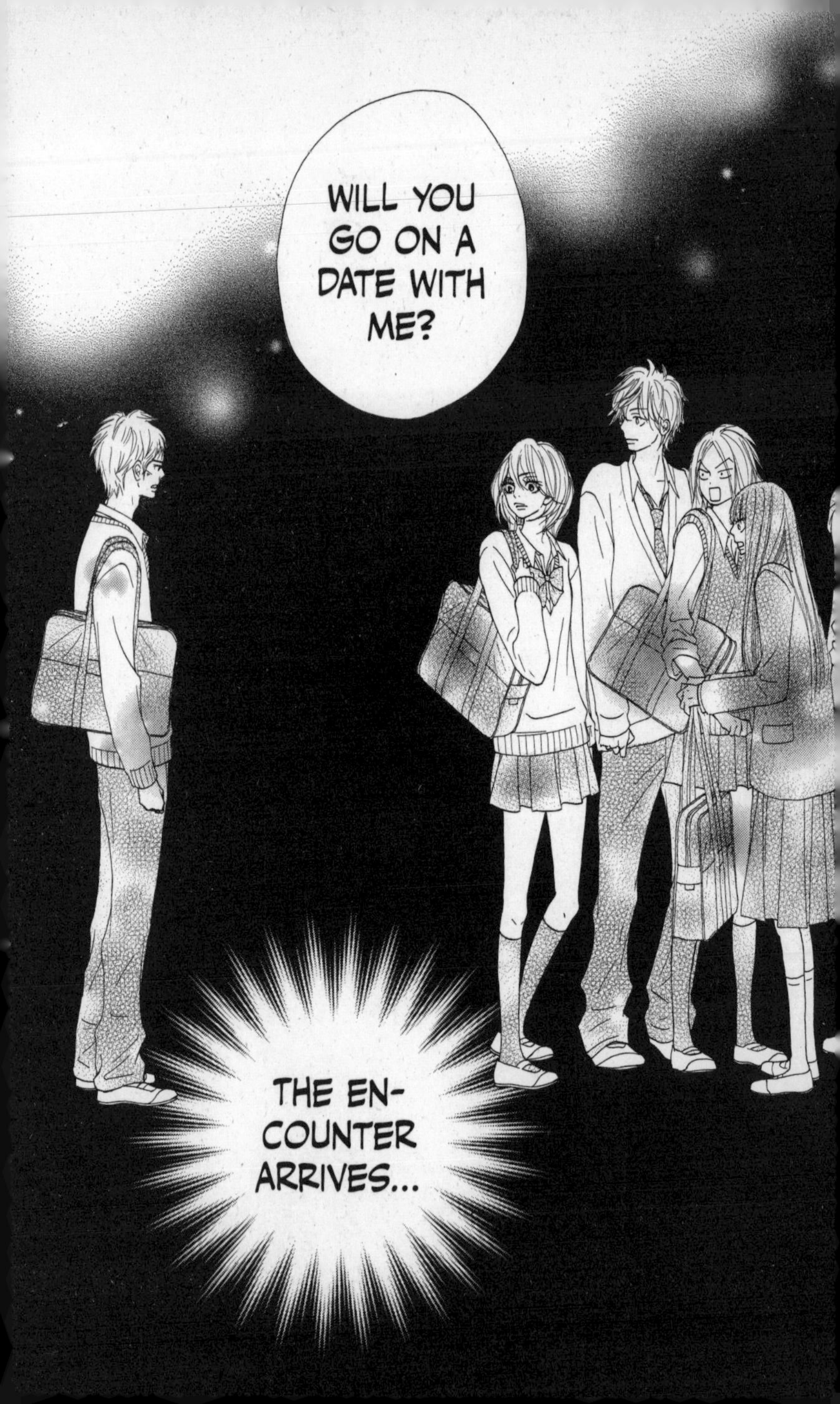
WILL YOU GO ON A DATE WITH ME?
THE EN-COUNTER ARRIVES...

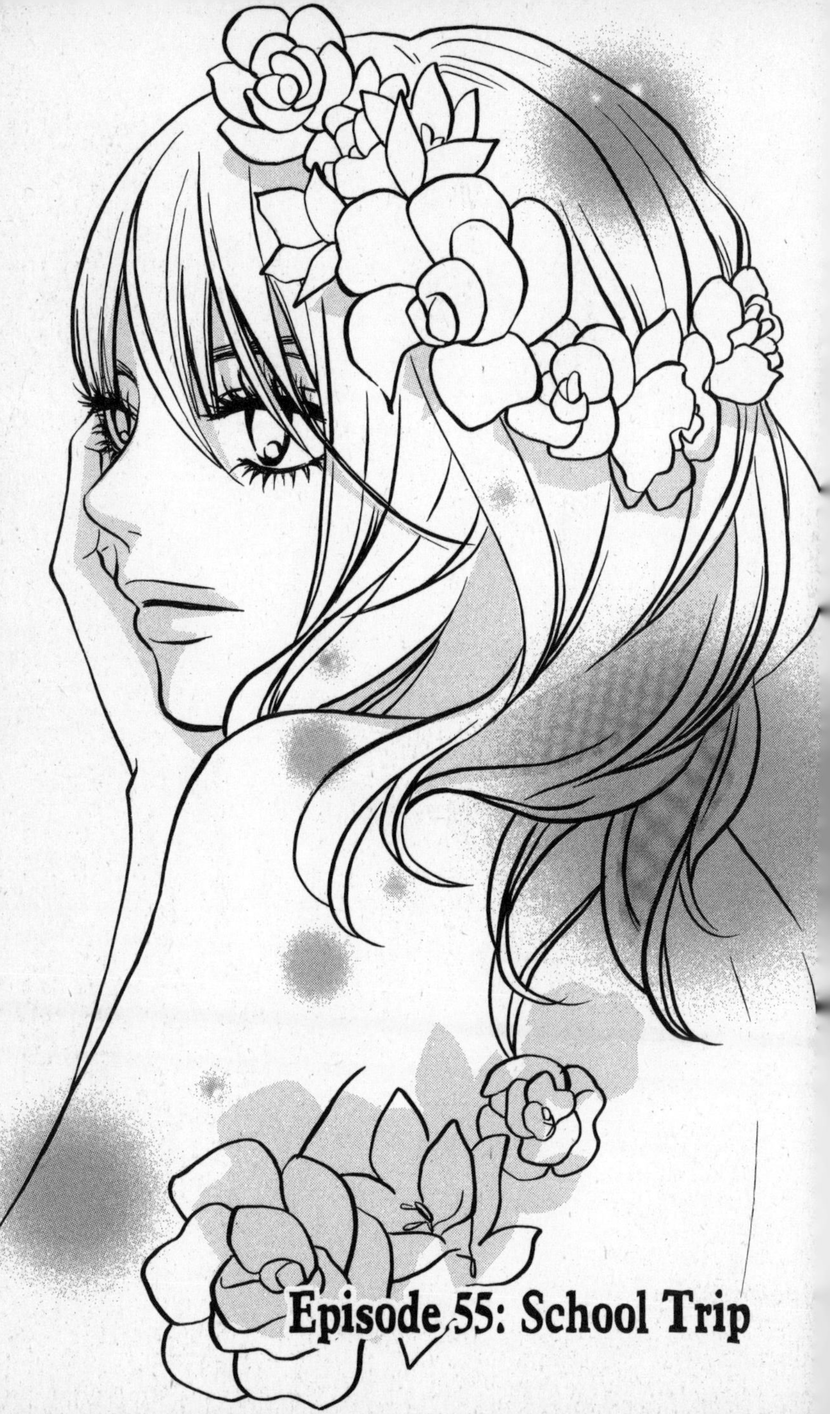

Episode 55: School Trip

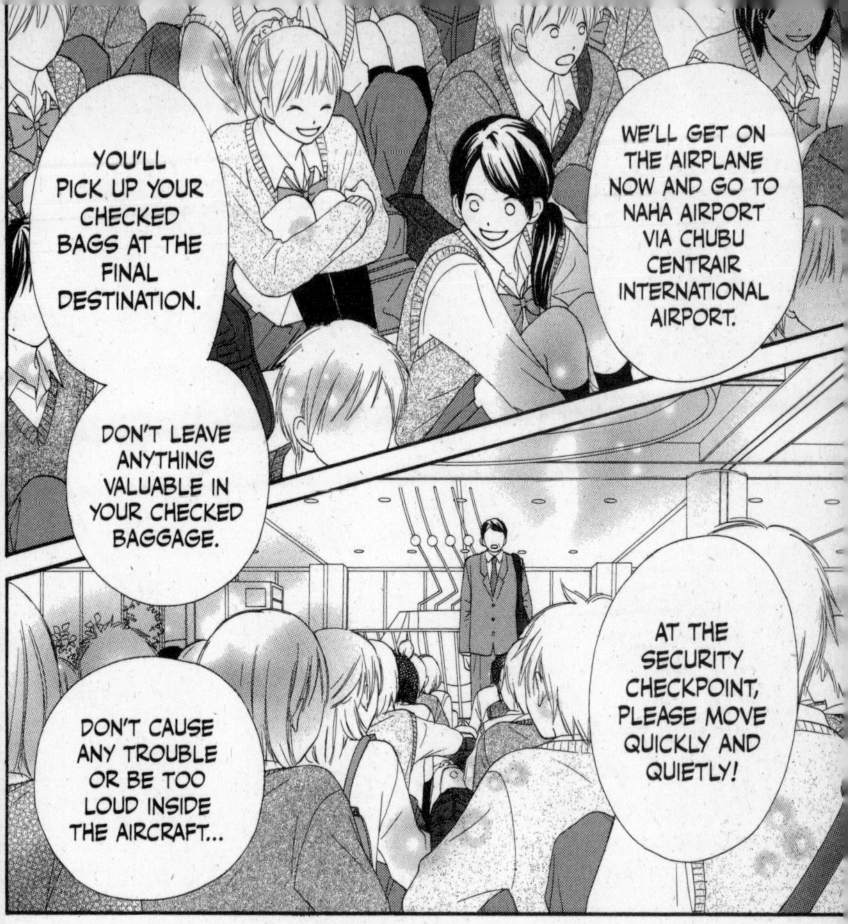
WE'LL GET ON THE AIRPLANE NOW AND GO TO NAHA AIRPORT VIA CHUBU CENTRAIR INTERNATIONAL AIRPORT.
YOU'LL PICK UP YOUR CHECKED BAGS AT THE FINAL DESTINATION.
DON'T LEAVE ANYTHING VALUABLE IN YOUR CHECKED BAGGAGE.
AT THE SECURITY CHECKPOINT, PLEASE MOVE QUICKLY AND QUIETLY!
DON'T CAUSE ANY TROUBLE OR BE TOO LOUD INSIDE THE AIRCRAFT...

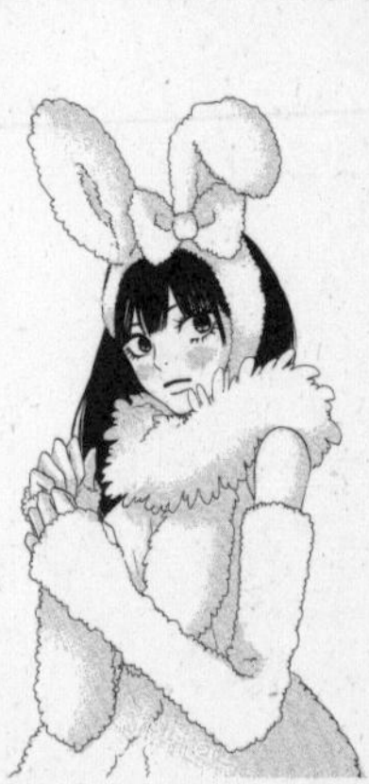

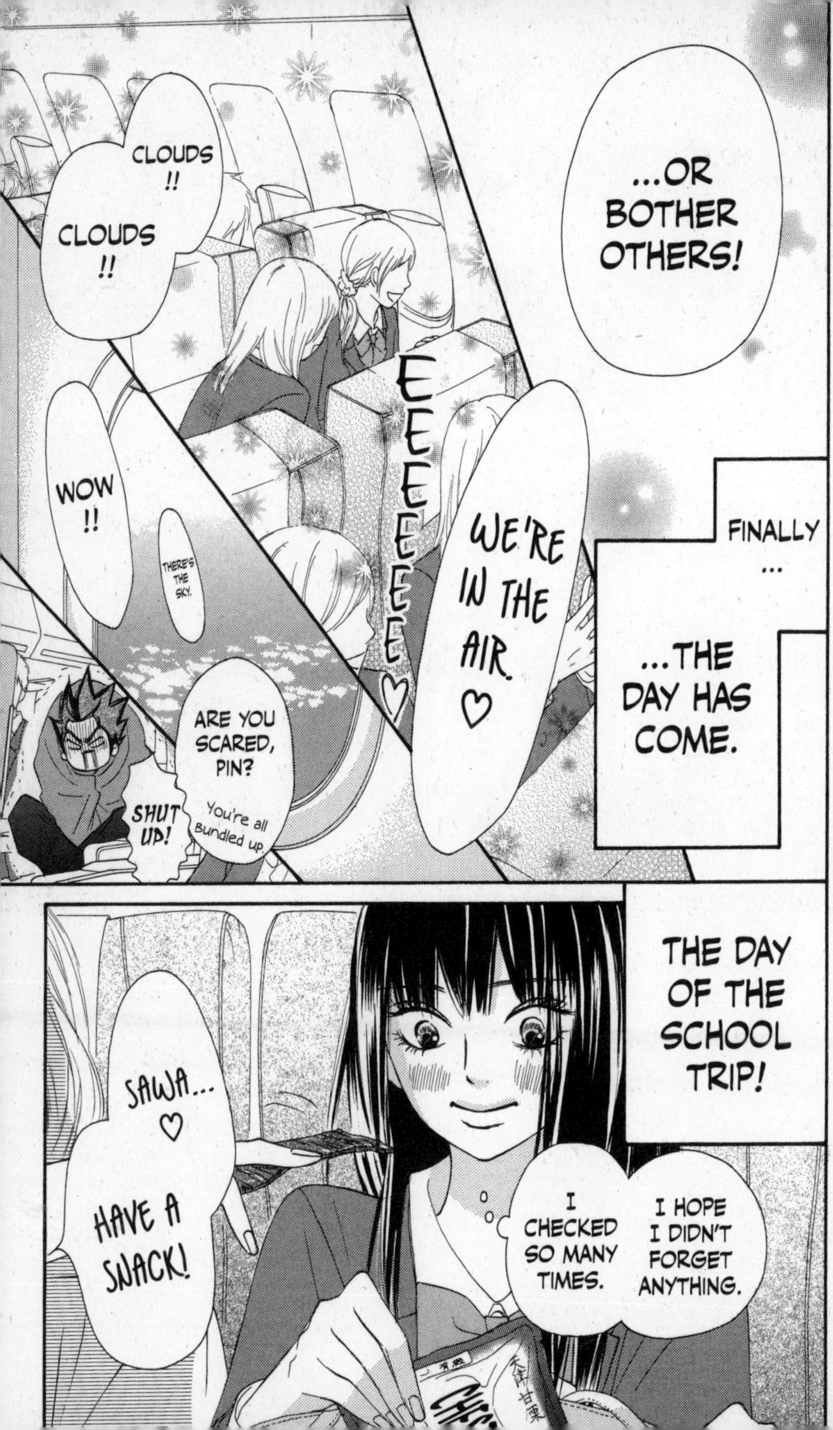
...OR BOTHER OTHERS!
FINALLY...
...THE DAY HAS COME.
WE'RE IN THE AIR ♡
EEEEEEE ♡
CLOUDS!!
CLOUDS!!
WOW!!
THERE'S THE SKY.
ARE YOU SCARED, PIN?
You're all bundled up.
SHUT UP!
THE DAY OF THE SCHOOL TRIP!
I HOPE I DIDN'T FORGET ANYTHING.
I CHECKED SO MANY TIMES.
SAWA... ♡
HAVE A SNACK!

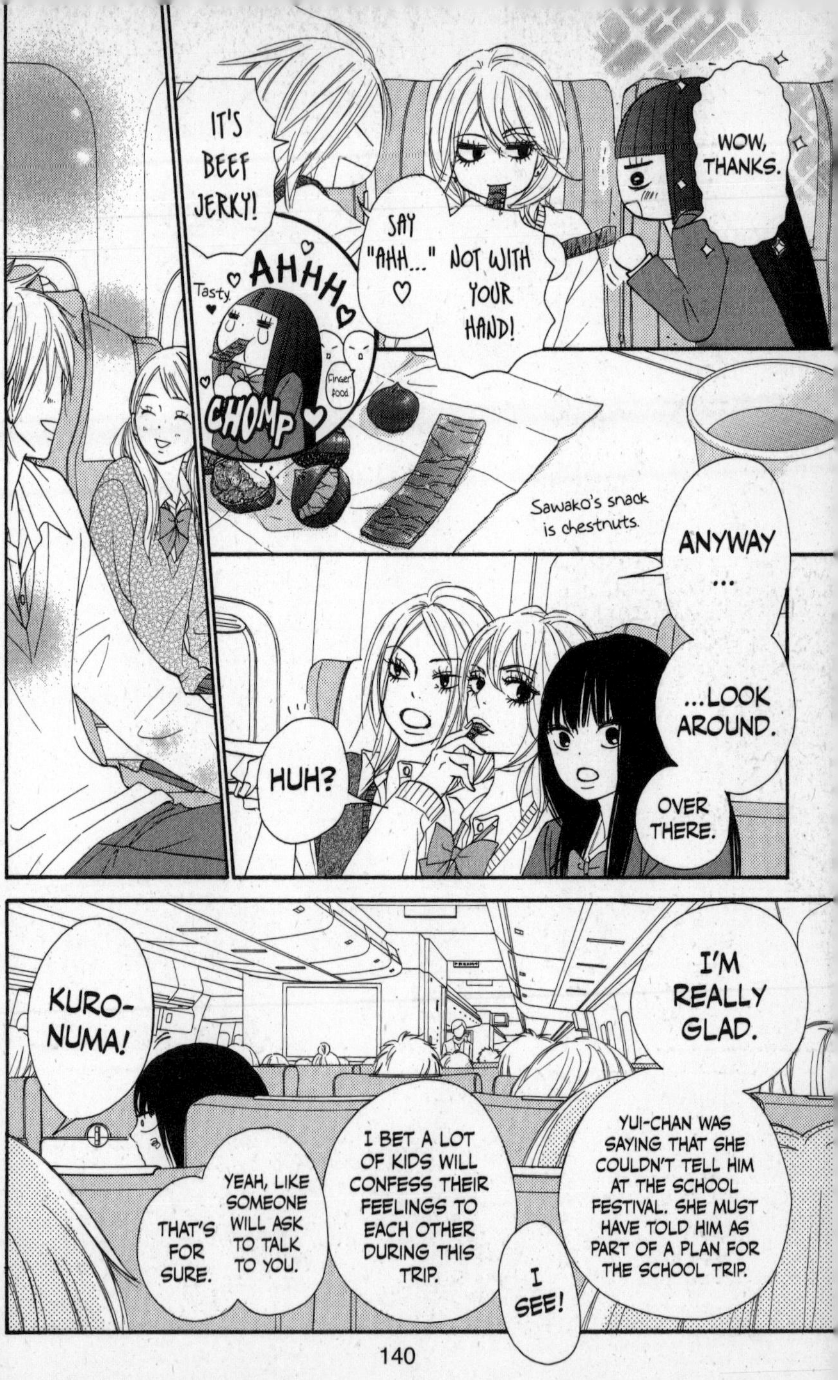
WOW, THANKS.
SAY "AHH..." ♡
NOT WITH YOUR HAND!
AHHH
Tasty.
CHOMP
Finger food.
Sawako's snack is chestnuts.
ANYWAY...
...LOOK AROUND.
OVER THERE.
HUH?
IT'S BEEF JERKY!
I'M REALLY GLAD.
YUI-CHAN WAS SAYING THAT SHE COULDN'T TELL HIM AT THE SCHOOL FESTIVAL. SHE MUST HAVE TOLD HIM AS PART OF A PLAN FOR THE SCHOOL TRIP.
I SEE!
I BET A LOT OF KIDS WILL CONFESS THEIR FEELINGS TO EACH OTHER DURING THIS TRIP.
YEAH, LIKE SOMEONE WILL ASK TO TALK TO YOU.
THAT'S FOR SURE.
KURO-NUMA!

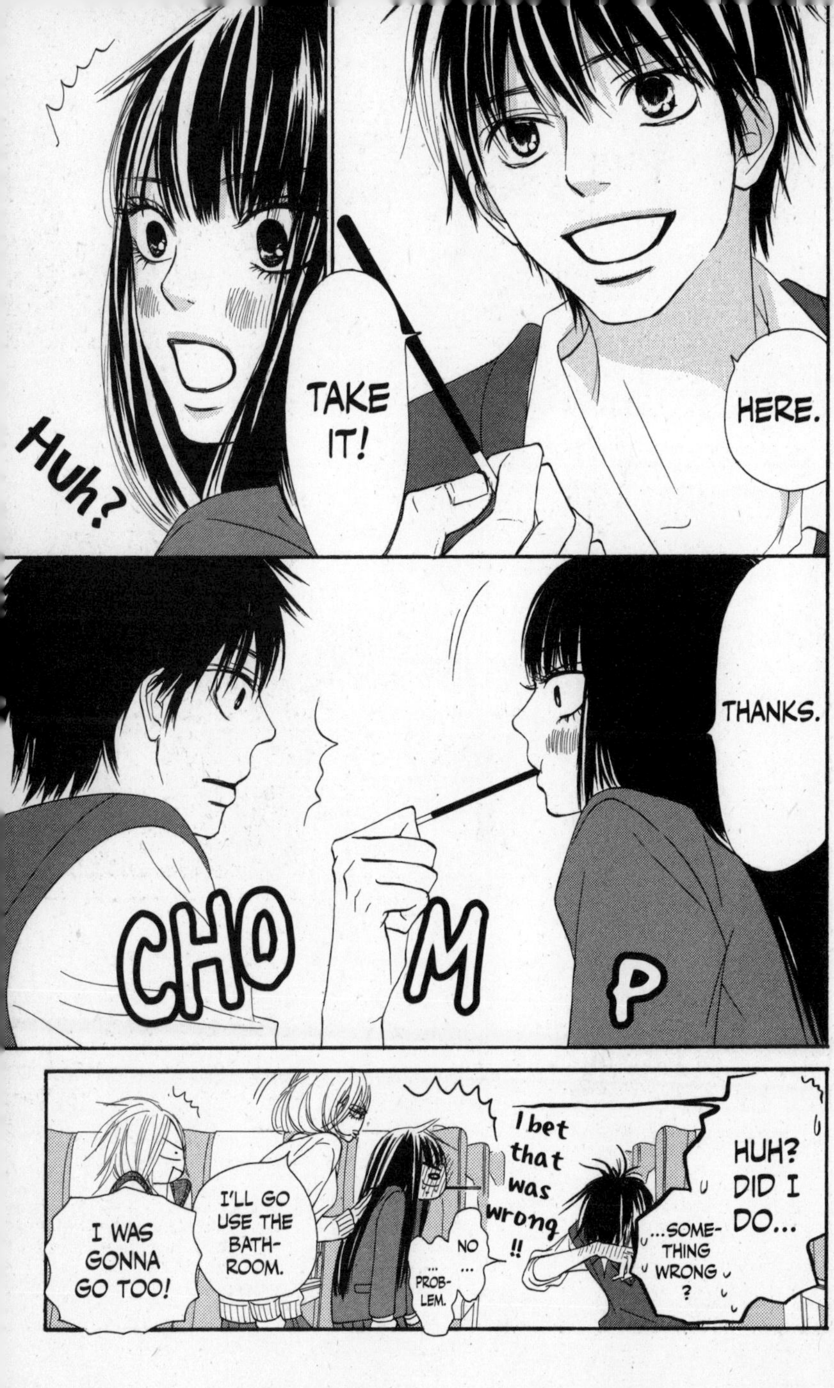
HERE.
TAKE IT!
Huh?
THANKS.
CHOMP
HUH? DID I DO...
...SOME-THING WRONG?
I bet that was wrong!!
NO...
...PROB-LEM.
I'LL GO USE THE BATH-ROOM.
I WAS GONNA GO TOO!

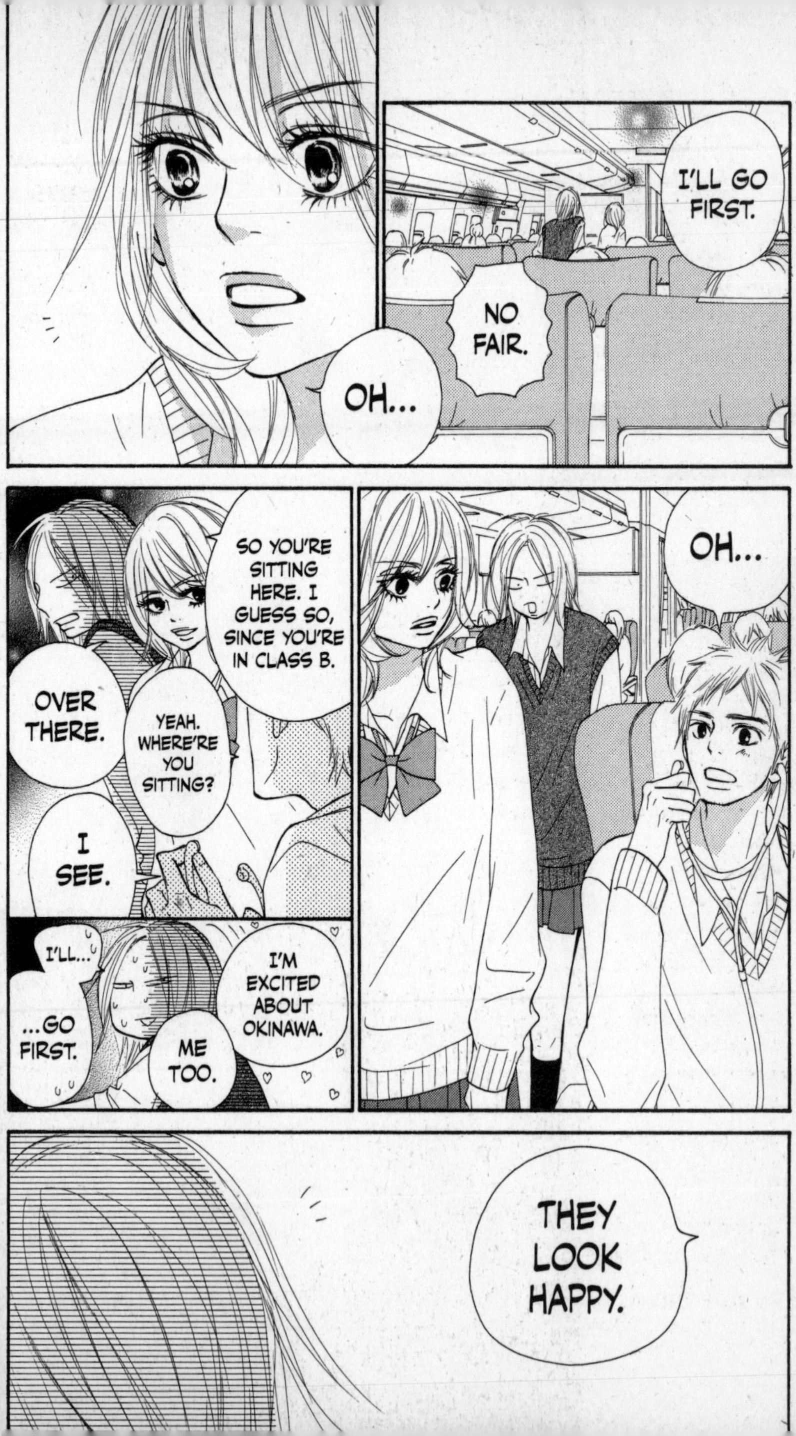
I'LL GO FIRST.
NO FAIR.
OH...
OH...
SO YOU'RE SITTING HERE. I GUESS SO, SINCE YOU'RE IN CLASS B.
YEAH. WHERE'RE YOU SITTING?
OVER THERE.
I SEE.
I'M EXCITED ABOUT OKINAWA.
ME TOO.
I'LL...
...GO FIRST.
THEY LOOK HAPPY.

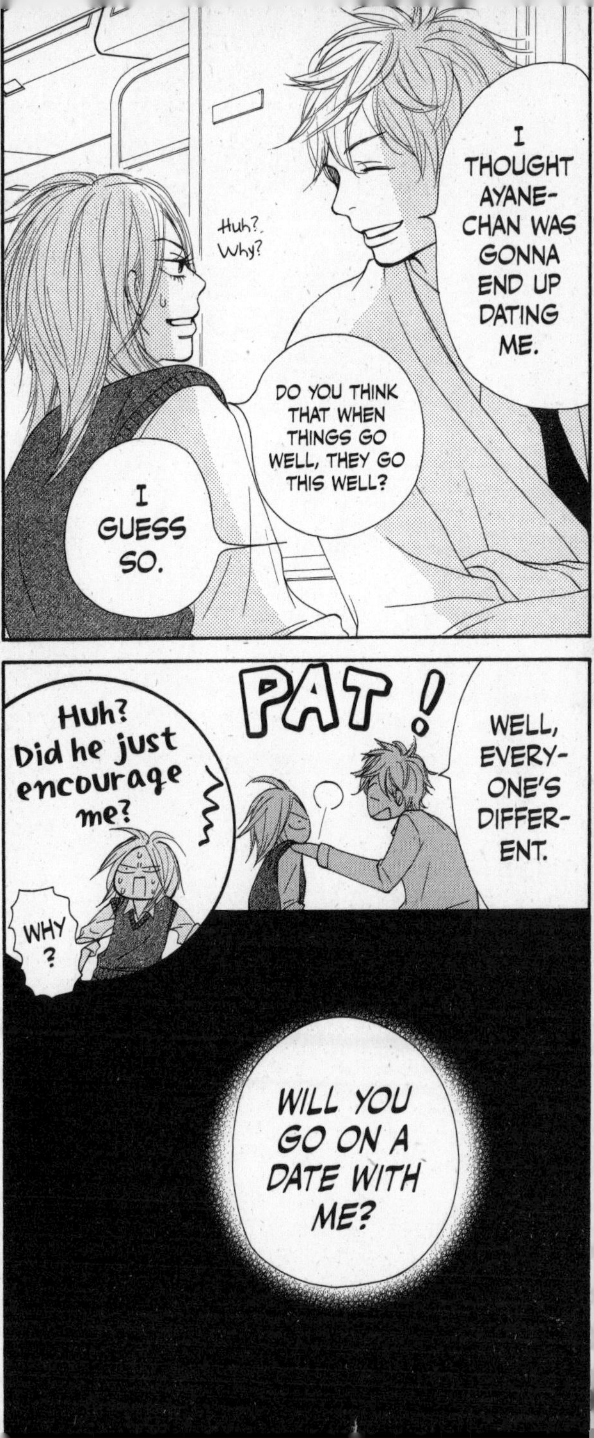
I THOUGHT AYANE-CHAN WAS GONNA END UP DATING ME.
Huh? Why?
DO YOU THINK THAT WHEN THINGS GO WELL, THEY GO THIS WELL?
I GUESS SO.
WELL, EVERY-ONE'S DIFFER-ENT.
PAT!
Huh? Did he just encourage me?
WHY?
WILL YOU GO ON A DATE WITH ME?

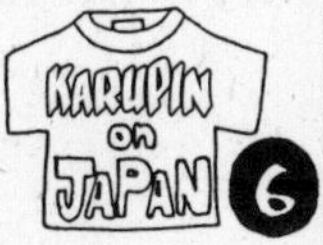
KARUPIN on JAPAN 6

My daughter is 2 now. She's started talking a lot and can say no to things.

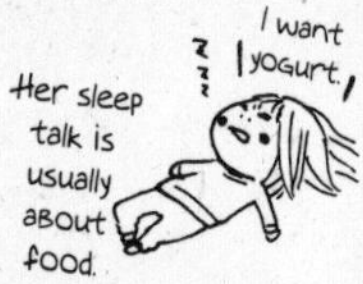
I want yogurt.
Her sleep talk is usually about food.

She talks a lot, but she hasn't forgotten "burira, burira."

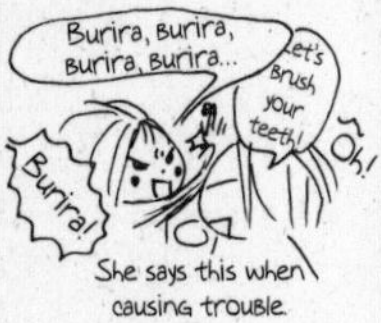
Burira, burira, burira, burira...
Let's brush your teeth!
Oh!
Burira!
She says this when causing trouble.

What does "burira" mean to you?
She says it so fast.
Anyway, after New Year's Eve and the beginning of the new year, February and March came. Time passed so quickly.
Seriously!
April and May will go past like that. Let time fly!
That's a bummer...
See you in volume 14!

✿ Karuho Shiina ✿

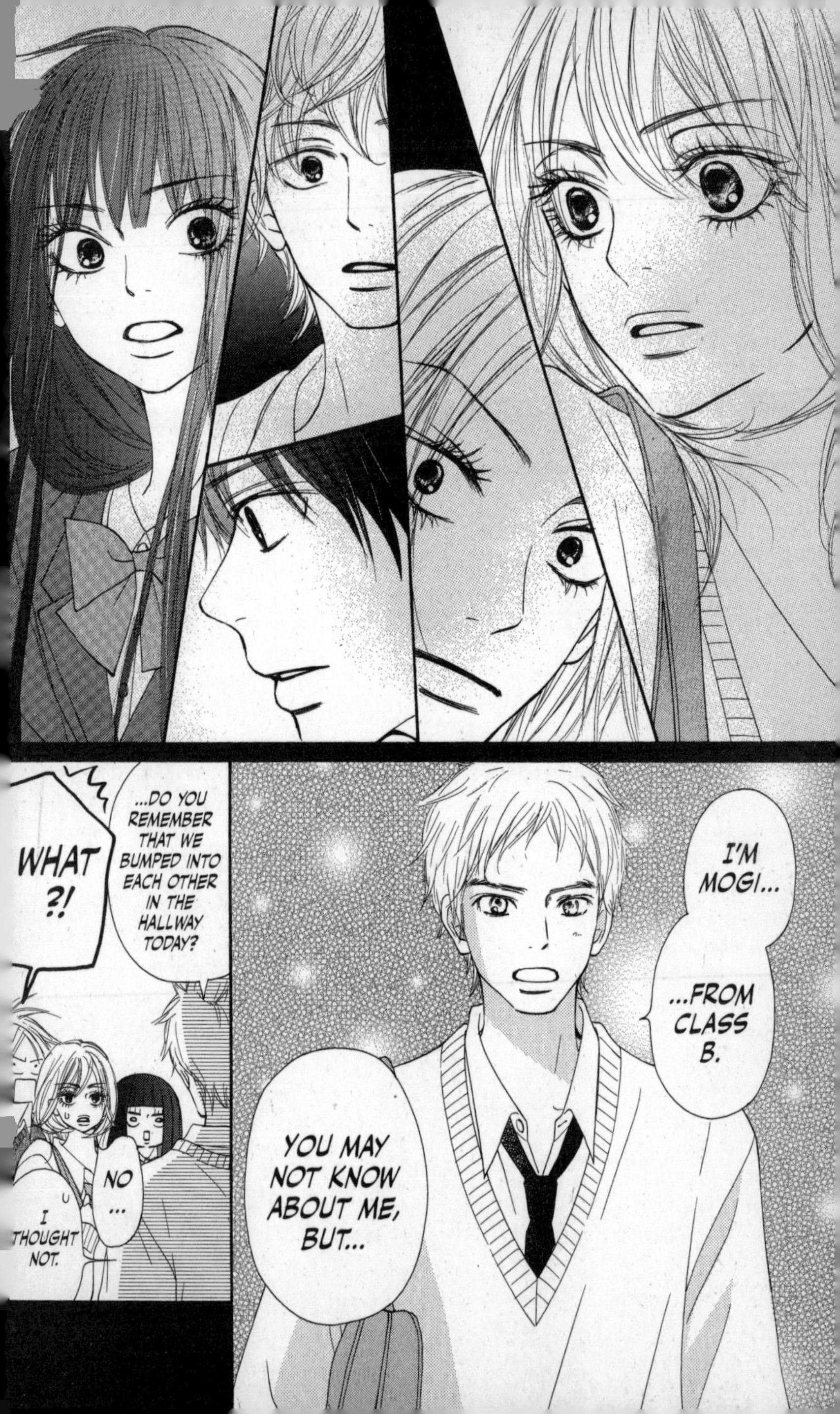
I'M MOGI...
...FROM CLASS B.
YOU MAY NOT KNOW ABOUT ME, BUT...
...DO YOU REMEMBER THAT WE BUMPED INTO EACH OTHER IN THE HALLWAY TODAY?
WHAT?!
NO...
I THOUGHT NOT.

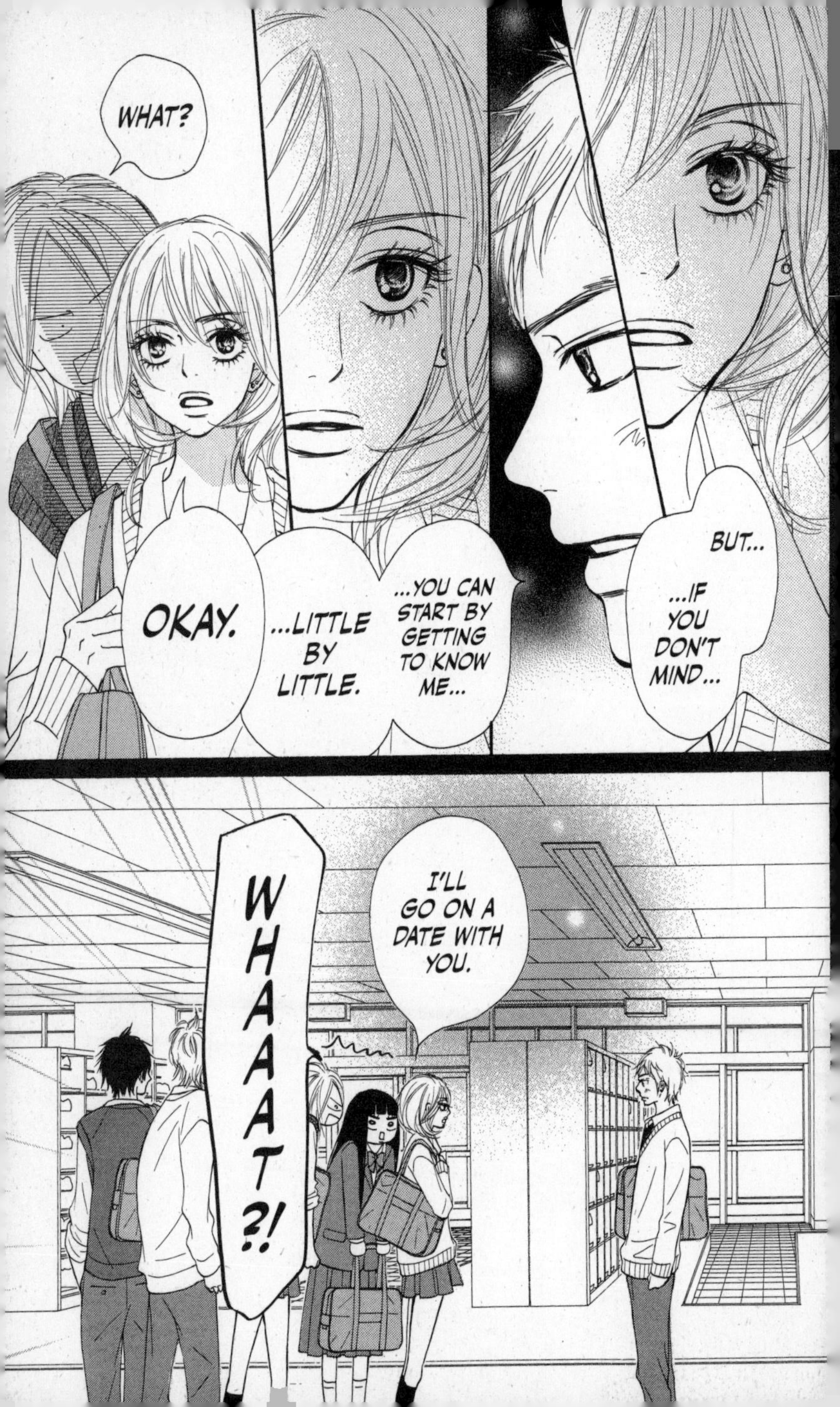
BUT...
...IF YOU DON'T MIND...
...YOU CAN START BY GETTING TO KNOW ME...
...LITTLE BY LITTLE.
WHAT?
OKAY.
I'LL GO ON A DATE WITH YOU.
WHAAAAT?!

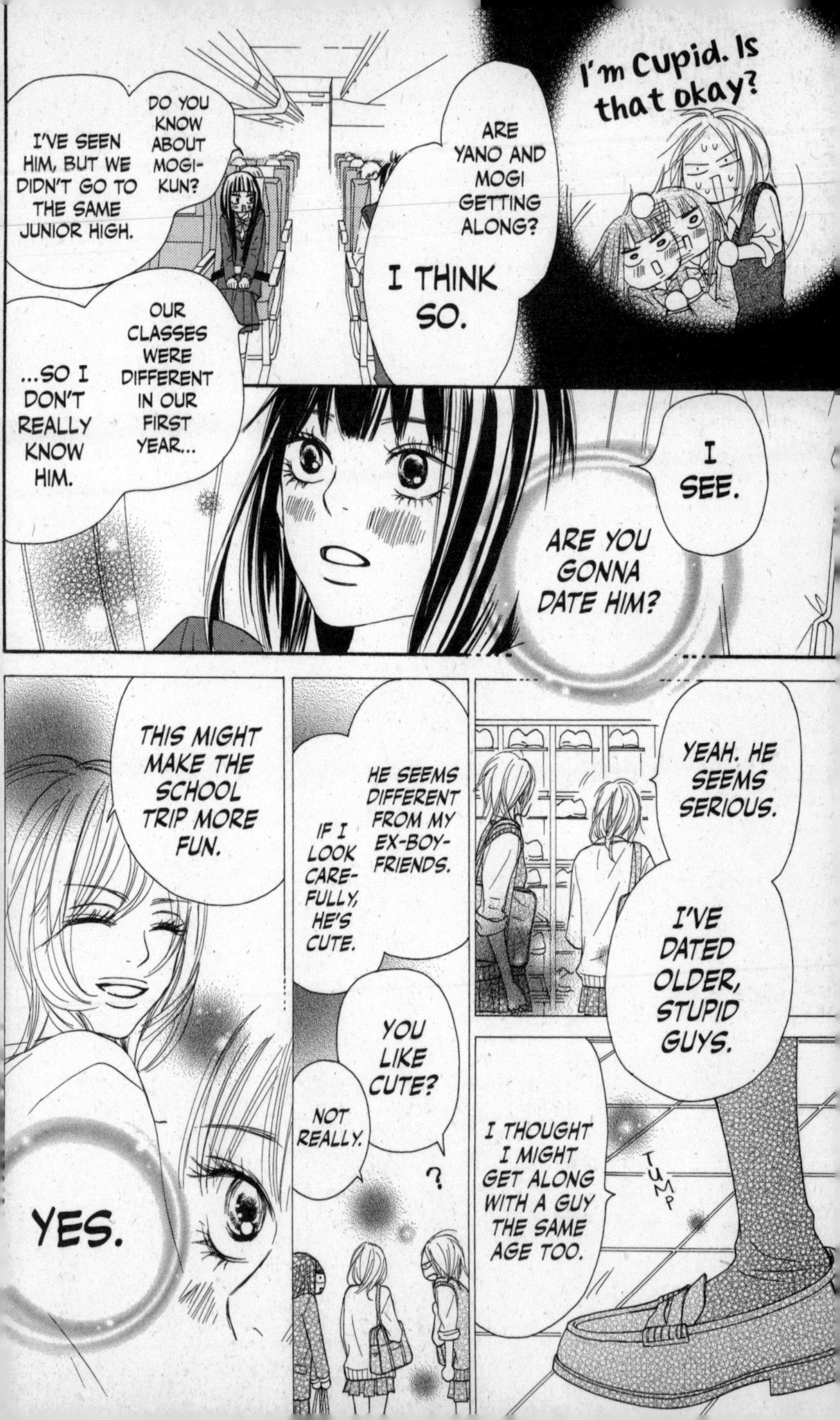

I'm Cupid. Is that okay?
ARE YANO AND MOGI GETTING ALONG?
I THINK SO.
DO YOU KNOW ABOUT MOGI-KUN?
I'VE SEEN HIM, BUT WE DIDN'T GO TO THE SAME JUNIOR HIGH.
OUR CLASSES WERE DIFFERENT IN OUR FIRST YEAR...
...SO I DON'T REALLY KNOW HIM.
I SEE.
ARE YOU GONNA DATE HIM?
YEAH. HE SEEMS SERIOUS.
I'VE DATED OLDER, STUPID GUYS.
I THOUGHT I MIGHT GET ALONG WITH A GUY THE SAME AGE TOO.
TUMP
HE SEEMS DIFFERENT FROM MY EX-BOY-FRIENDS.
IF I LOOK CARE-FULLY, HE'S CUTE.
YOU LIKE CUTE?
NOT REALLY.
?
THIS MIGHT MAKE THE SCHOOL TRIP MORE FUN.
YES.

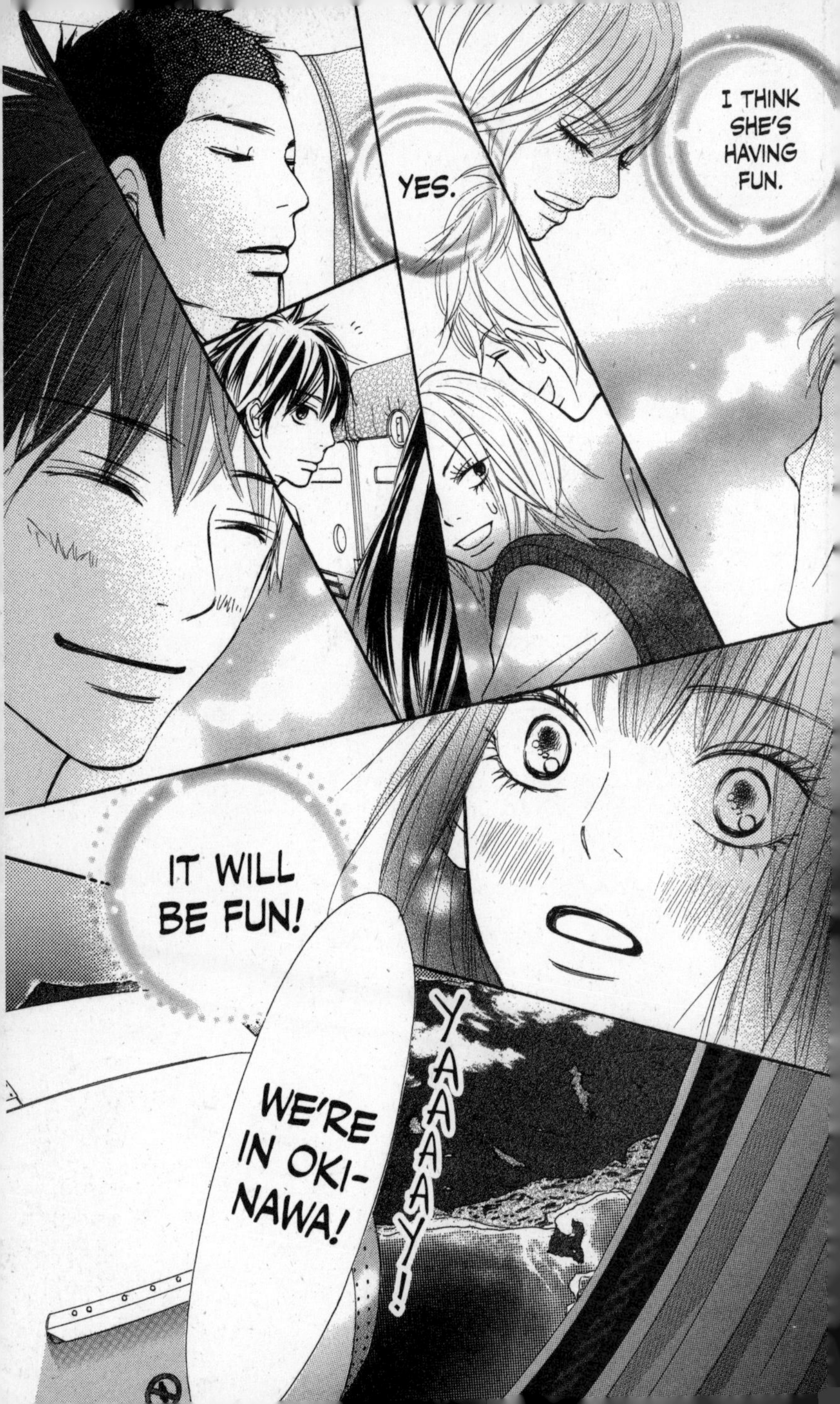
I THINK SHE'S HAVING FUN.
YES.
IT WILL BE FUN!
YAAAAAY!
WE'RE IN OKI-NAWA!

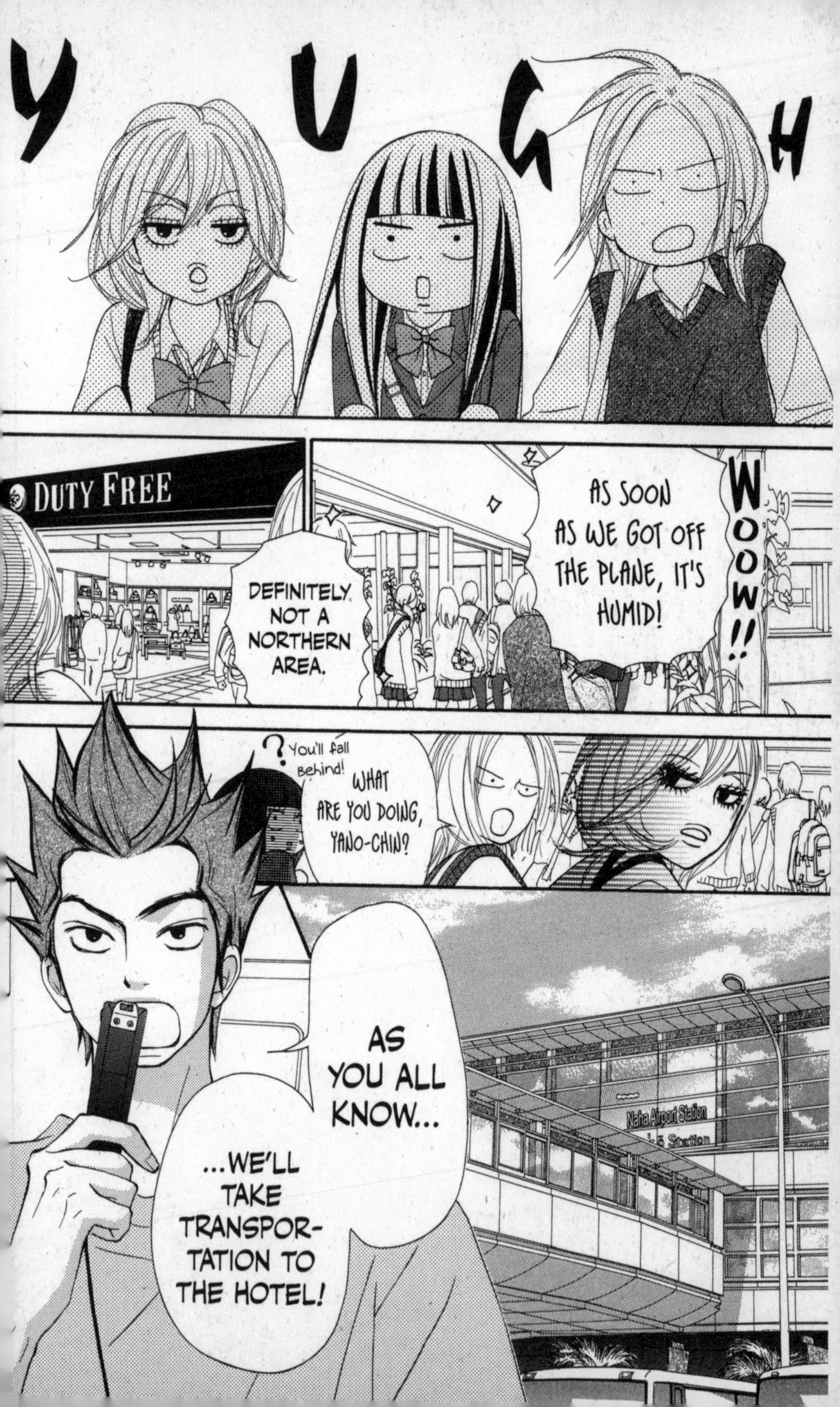
YUGH
WOOW!!
AS SOON AS WE GOT OFF THE PLANE, IT'S HUMID!
DEFINITELY NOT A NORTHERN AREA.
DUTY FREE
WHAT ARE YOU DOING, YANO-CHIN?
You'll fall Behind!
AS YOU ALL KNOW...
...WE'LL TAKE TRANSPORTATION TO THE HOTEL!
Naha Airport Station

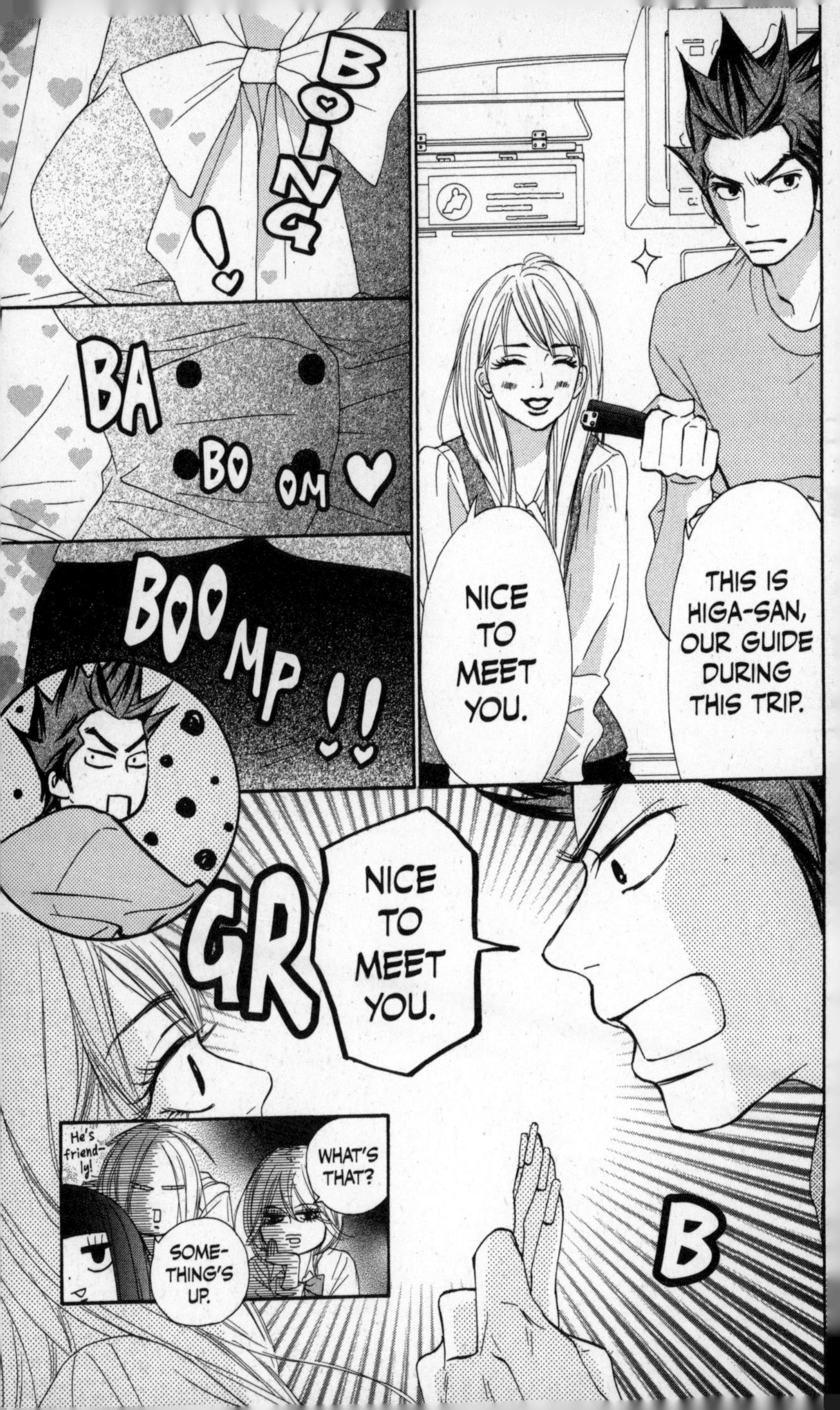
THIS IS HIGA-SAN, OUR GUIDE DURING THIS TRIP.
NICE TO MEET YOU.
BOING!
BA BO OM
BOOMP!!
NICE TO MEET YOU.
GR
B
WHAT'S THAT?
He's friendly!
SOME-THING'S UP.

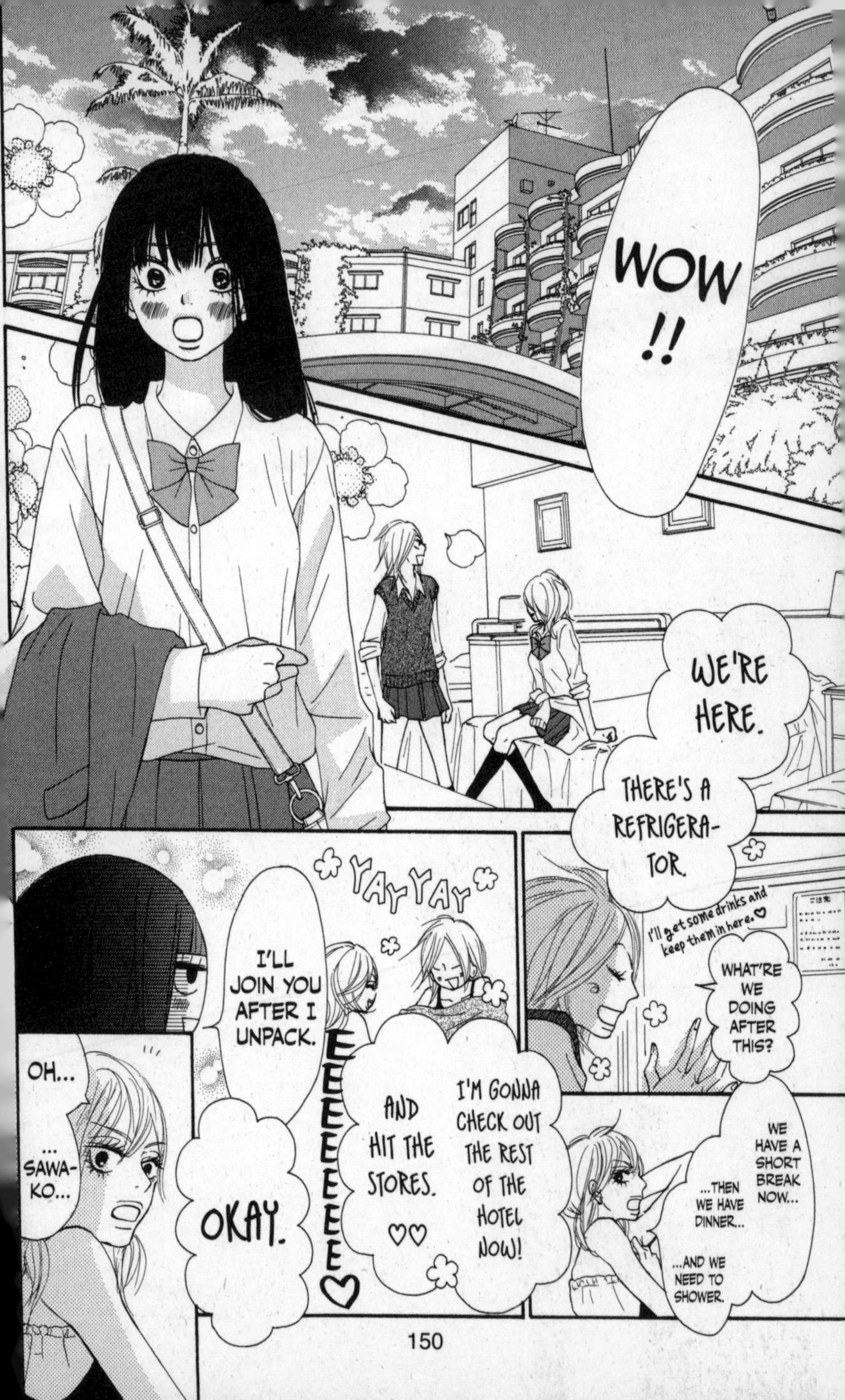
WOW!!
WE'RE HERE.
THERE'S A REFRIGERA-TOR.
I'll get some drinks and keep them in here.♡
WHAT'RE WE DOING AFTER THIS?
YAY YAY
I'LL JOIN YOU AFTER I UNPACK.
WE HAVE A SHORT BREAK NOW...
...THEN WE HAVE DINNER...
...AND WE NEED TO SHOWER.
I'M GONNA CHECK OUT THE REST OF THE HOTEL NOW!
AND HIT THE STORES. ♡♡
EEEEEEEEEE♡
OKAY.
OH...
...SAWAKO...

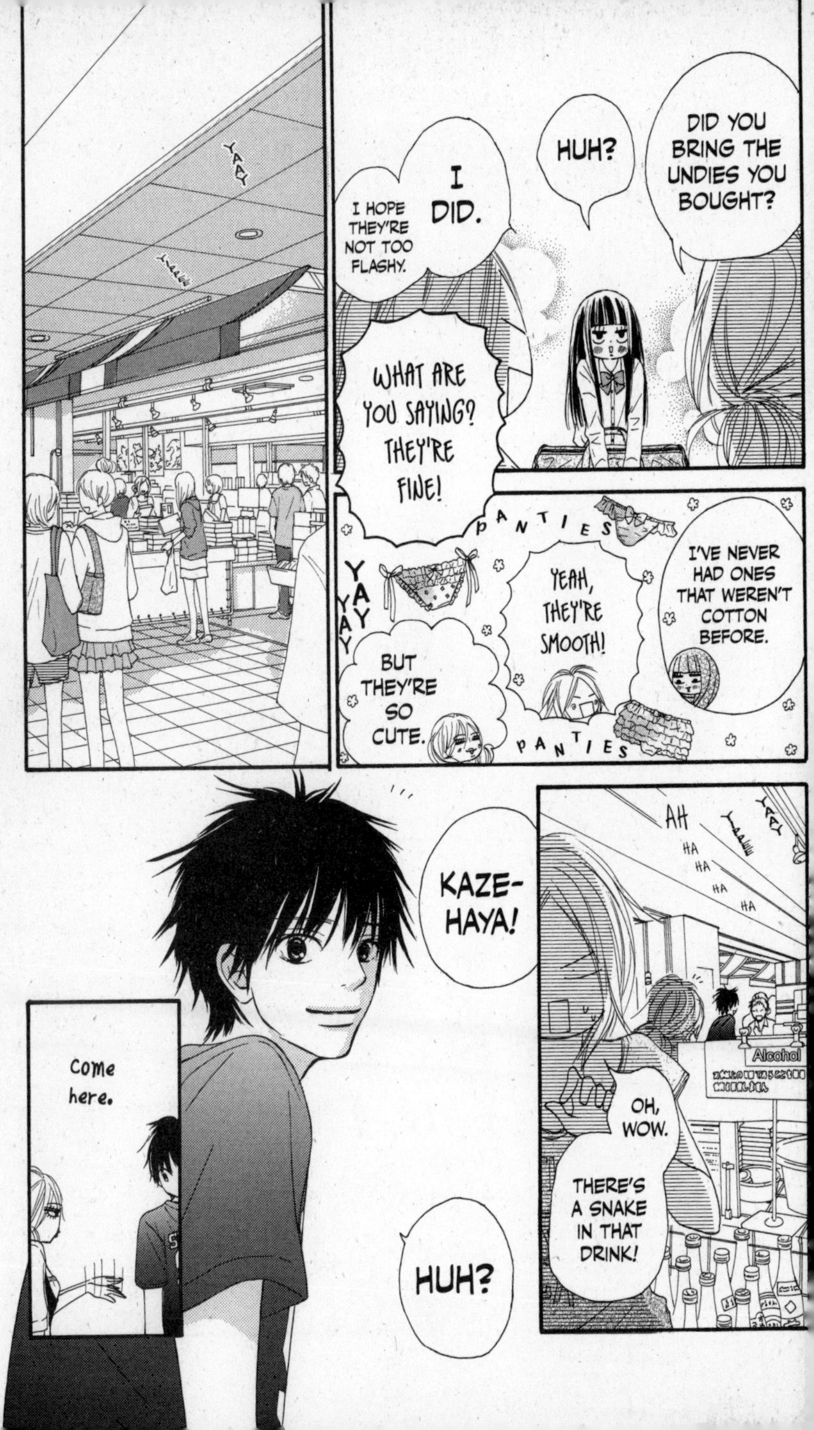
DID YOU BRING THE UNDIES YOU BOUGHT?
HUH?
I DID.
I HOPE THEY'RE NOT TOO FLASHY.
WHAT ARE YOU SAYING? THEY'RE FINE!
I'VE NEVER HAD ONES THAT WEREN'T COTTON BEFORE.
PANTIES
YEAH, THEY'RE SMOOTH!
PANTIES
BUT THEY'RE SO CUTE.
YAY YAY
YAAY
YAAAY
YAAY
YAAAY
AH HA HA HA HA
Alcohol
OH, WOW.
THERE'S A SNAKE IN THAT DRINK!
KAZE-HAYA!
HUH?
Come here.

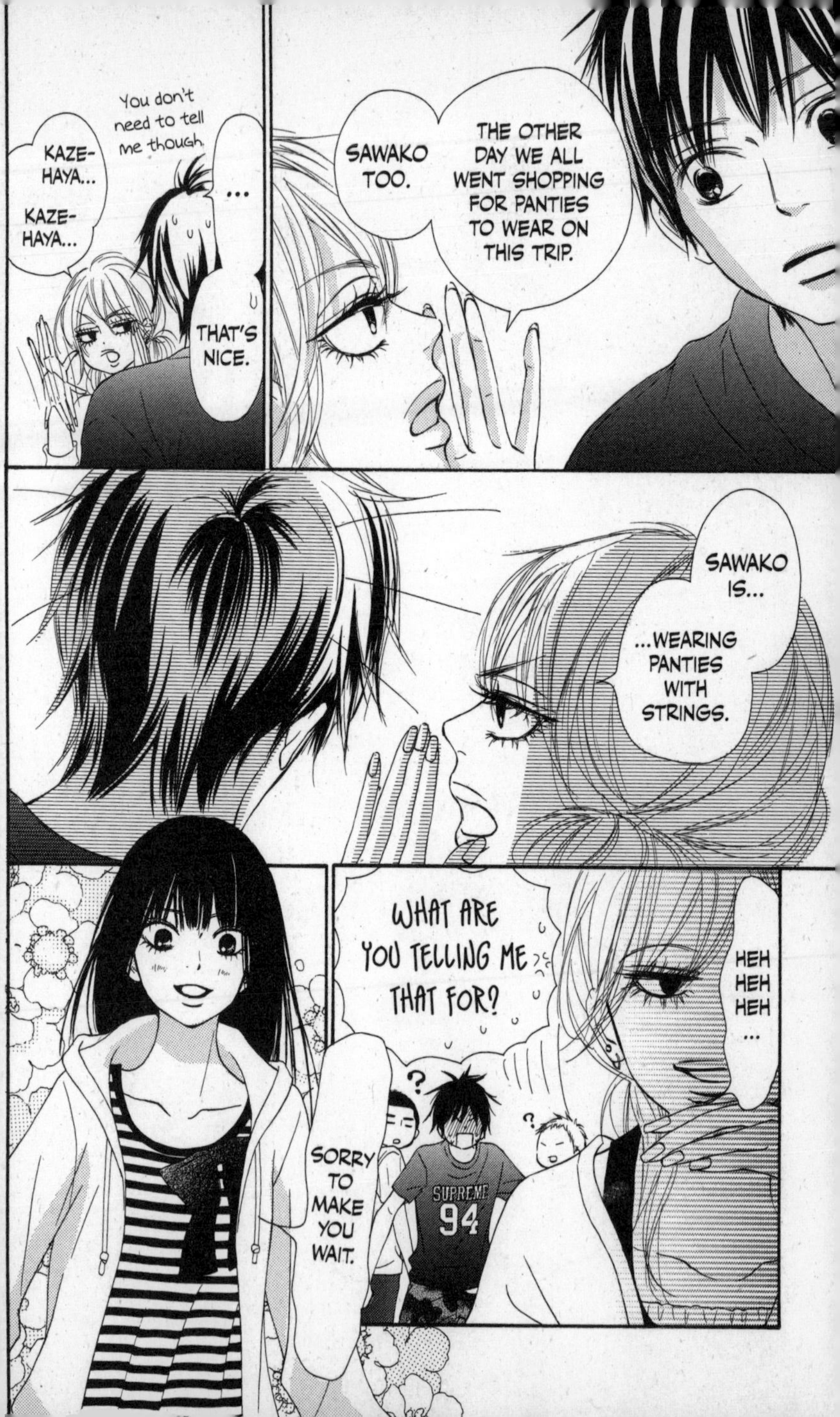
SAWAKO TOO.
THE OTHER DAY WE ALL WENT SHOPPING FOR PANTIES TO WEAR ON THIS TRIP.
...
THAT'S NICE.
You don't need to tell me though.
KAZE-HAYA...
KAZE-HAYA...
SAWAKO IS...
...WEARING PANTIES WITH STRINGS.
HEH HEH HEH ...
WHAT ARE YOU TELLING ME THAT FOR?
SUPREME 94
SORRY TO MAKE YOU WAIT.

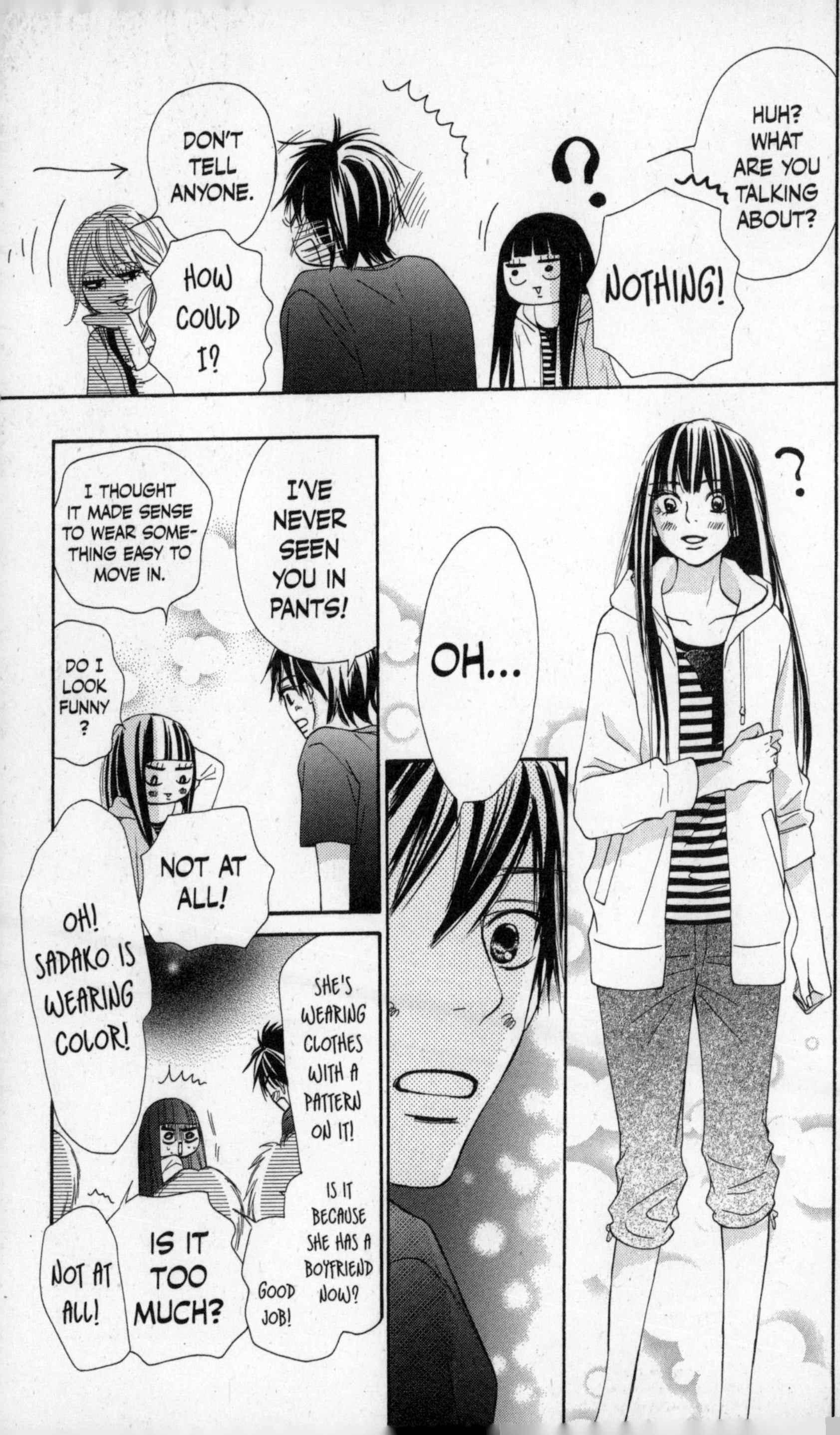
HUH? WHAT ARE YOU TALKING ABOUT?
NOTHING!
DON'T TELL ANYONE.
HOW COULD I?
?
OH...
I'VE NEVER SEEN YOU IN PANTS!
I THOUGHT IT MADE SENSE TO WEAR SOME-THING EASY TO MOVE IN.
DO I LOOK FUNNY?
NOT AT ALL!
OH! SADAKO IS WEARING COLOR!
SHE'S WEARING CLOTHES WITH A PATTERN ON IT!
IS IT BECAUSE SHE HAS A BOYFRIEND NOW?
GOOD JOB!
IS IT TOO MUCH?
NOT AT ALL!

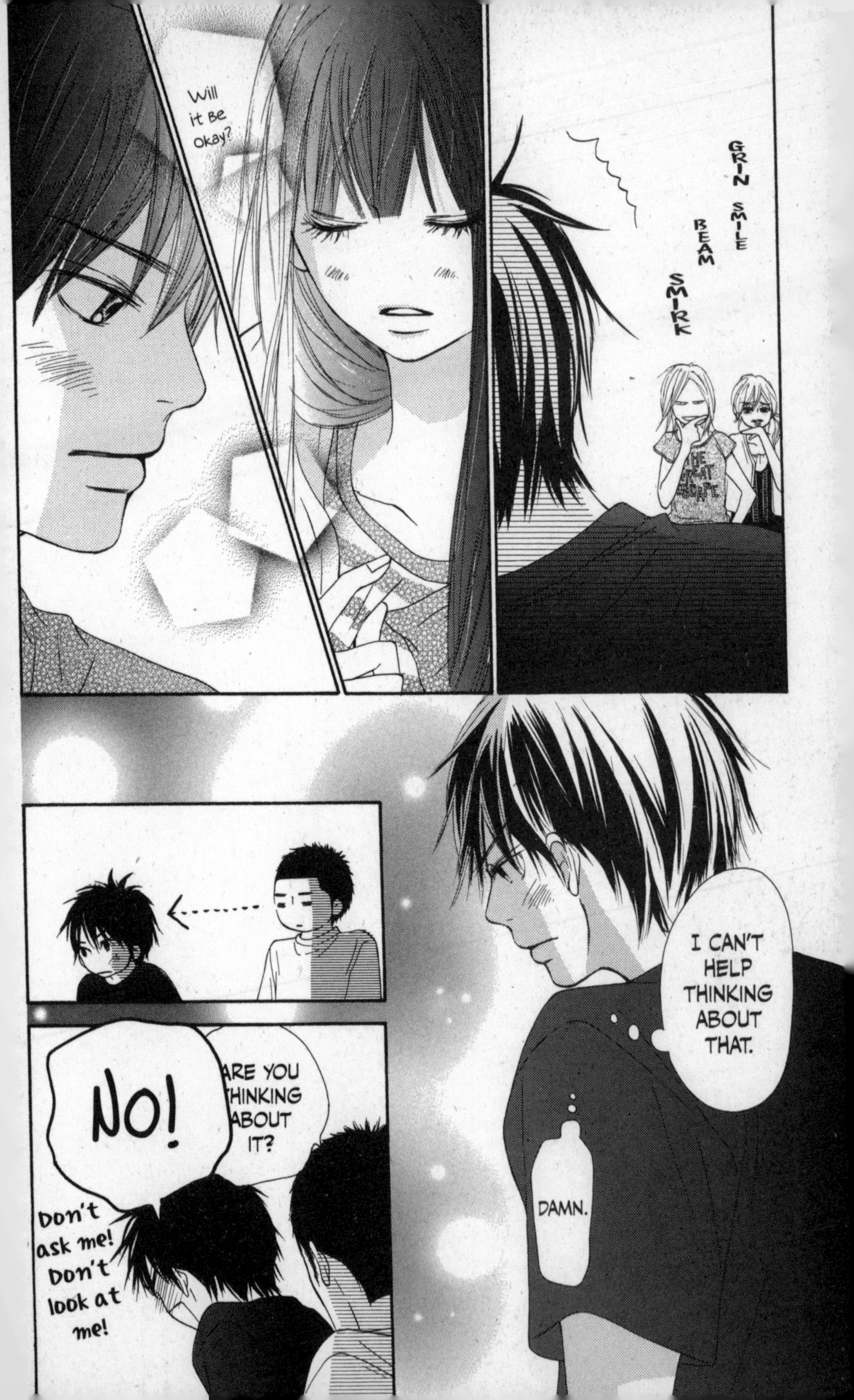
GRIN SMILE
BEAM
SMIRK
Will it be okay?
I CAN'T HELP THINKING ABOUT THAT.
DAMN.
ARE YOU THINKING ABOUT IT?
NO!
Don't ask me! Don't look at me!

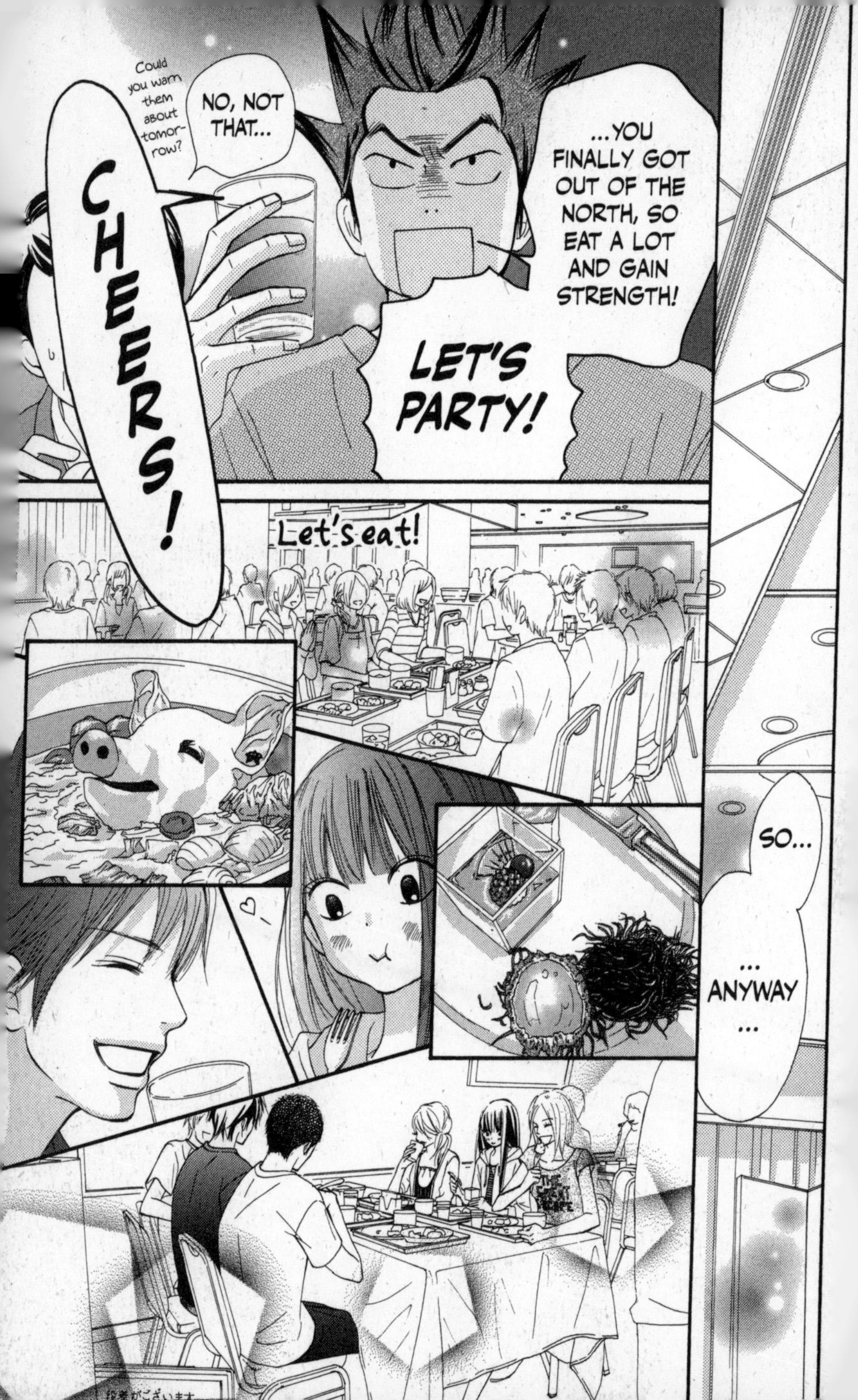
...YOU FINALLY GOT OUT OF THE NORTH, SO EAT A LOT AND GAIN STRENGTH!
LET'S PARTY!
NO, NOT THAT...
Could you warn them about tomorrow?
CHEERS!
Let's eat!
SO...
... ANYWAY ...

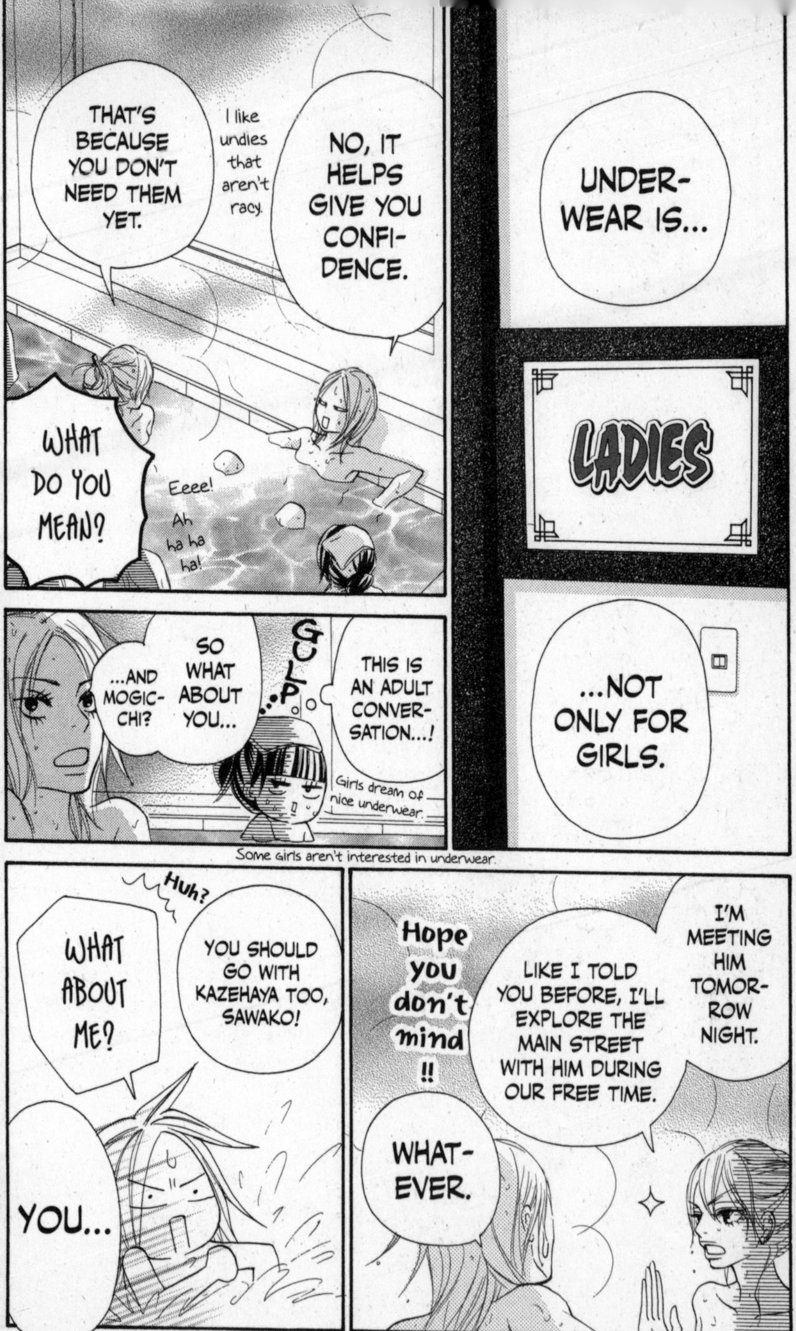
UNDERWEAR IS...
LADIES
...NOT ONLY FOR GIRLS.
NO, IT HELPS GIVE YOU CONFIDENCE.
I like undies that aren't racy.
THAT'S BECAUSE YOU DON'T NEED THEM YET.
WHAT DO YOU MEAN?
Eeee!
Ah ha ha ha!
THIS IS AN ADULT CONVERSATION...!
Girls dream of nice underwear.
GULP
SO WHAT ABOUT YOU...
...AND MOGIC-CHI?
Some girls aren't interested in underwear.
I'M MEETING HIM TOMORROW NIGHT.
LIKE I TOLD YOU BEFORE, I'LL EXPLORE THE MAIN STREET WITH HIM DURING OUR FREE TIME.
Hope you don't mind!!
WHATEVER.
YOU SHOULD GO WITH KAZEHAYA TOO, SAWAKO!
Huh?
WHAT ABOUT ME?
YOU...

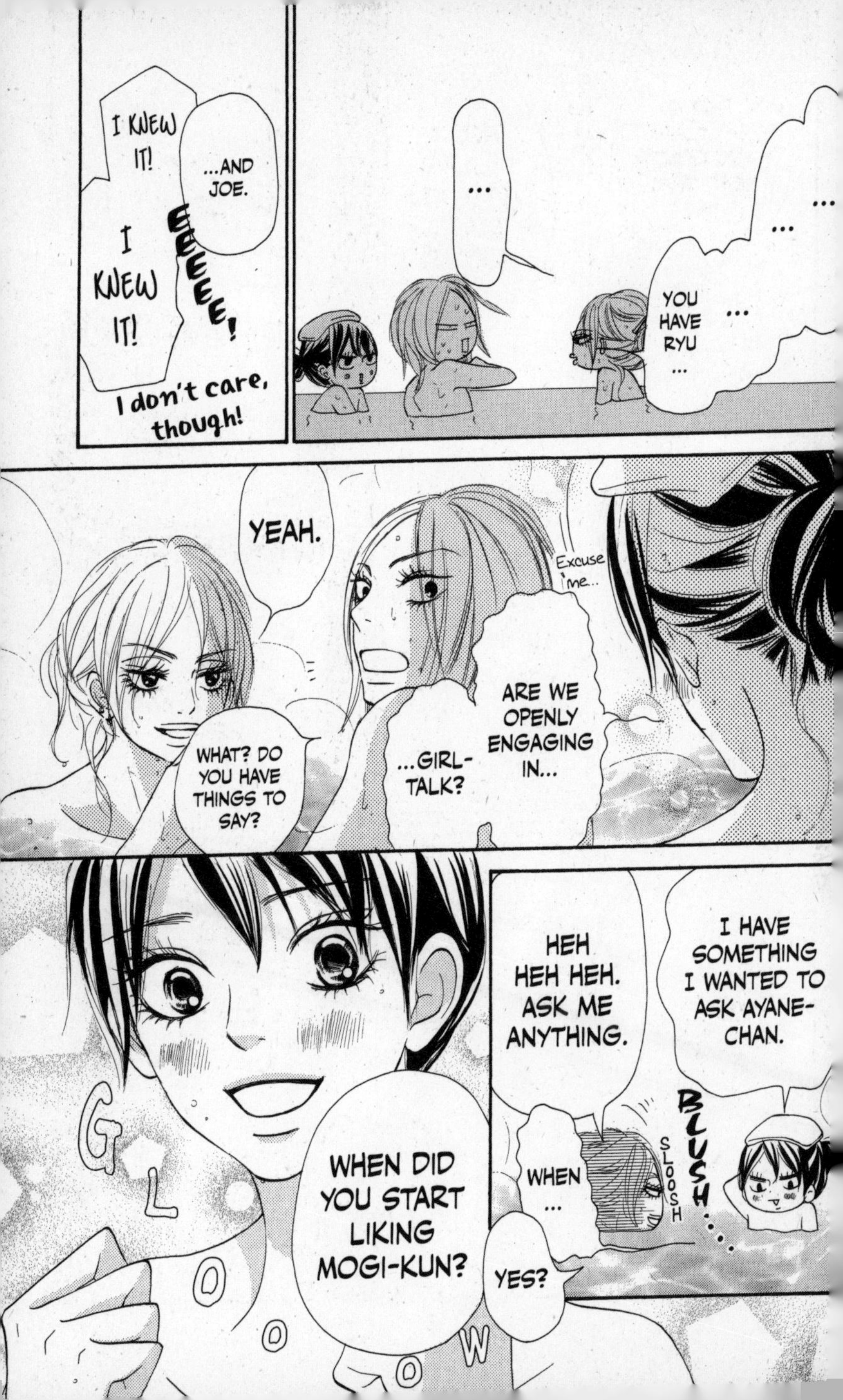
...
...
...
YOU HAVE RYU ...
...
...AND JOE.
I KNEW IT!
I KNEW IT!
EEEEE!
I don't care, though!
Excuse me...
ARE WE OPENLY ENGAGING IN...
...GIRL-TALK?
YEAH.
WHAT? DO YOU HAVE THINGS TO SAY?
I HAVE SOMETHING I WANTED TO ASK AYANE-CHAN.
BLUSH...
HEH HEH HEH. ASK ME ANYTHING.
SLOOSH
WHEN ...
YES?
WHEN DID YOU START LIKING MOGI-KUN?
GLOOOOW

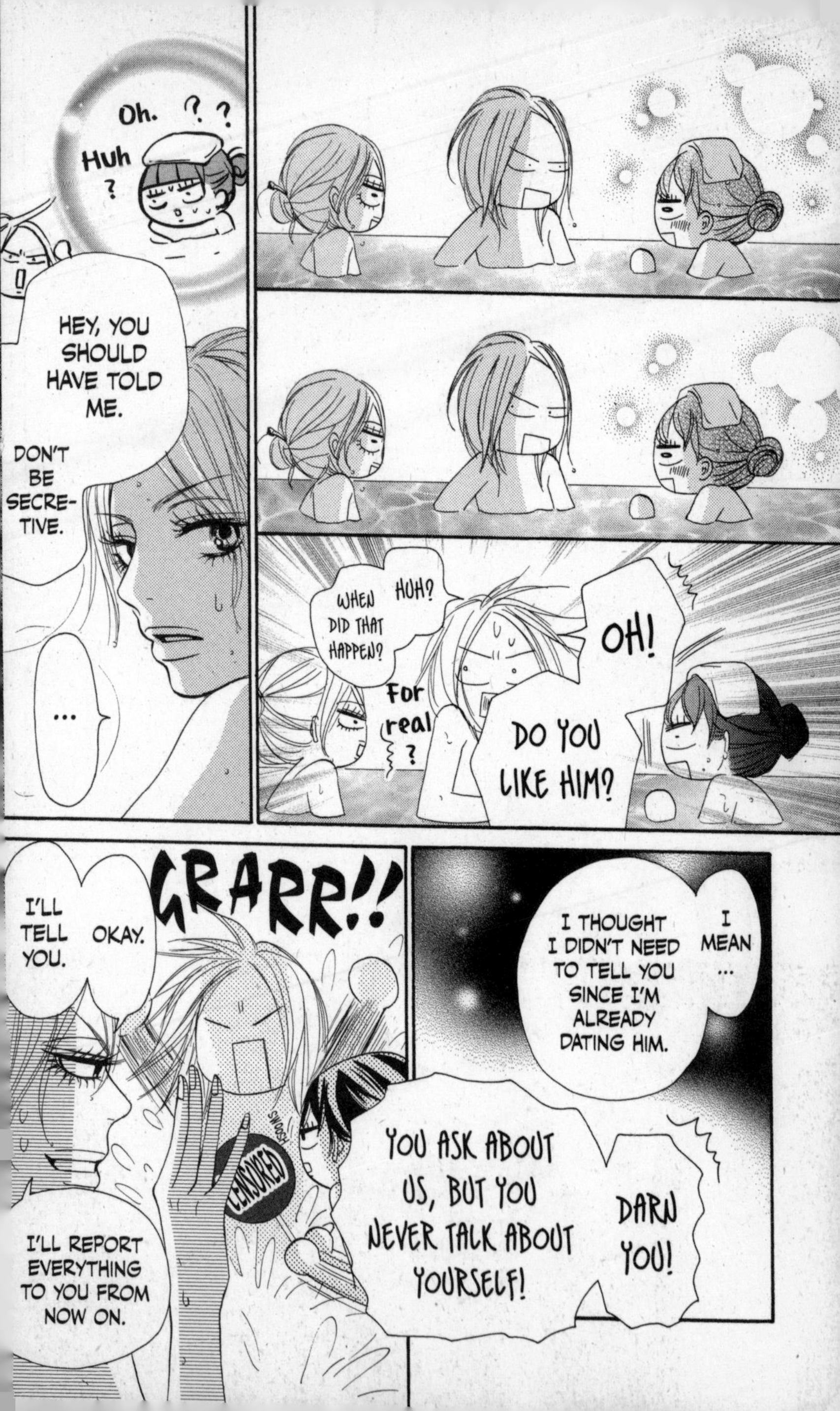
OH!
DO YOU LIKE HIM?
HUH?
WHEN DID THAT HAPPEN?
For real?
Oh. ? ?
Huh ?
HEY, YOU SHOULD HAVE TOLD ME.
DON'T BE SECRETIVE.
...
I MEAN...
I THOUGHT I DIDN'T NEED TO TELL YOU SINCE I'M ALREADY DATING HIM.
GRARR!!
DARN YOU!
YOU ASK ABOUT US, BUT YOU NEVER TALK ABOUT YOURSELF!
SWOOSH
CENSORED
OKAY.
I'LL TELL YOU.
I'LL REPORT EVERYTHING TO YOU FROM NOW ON.

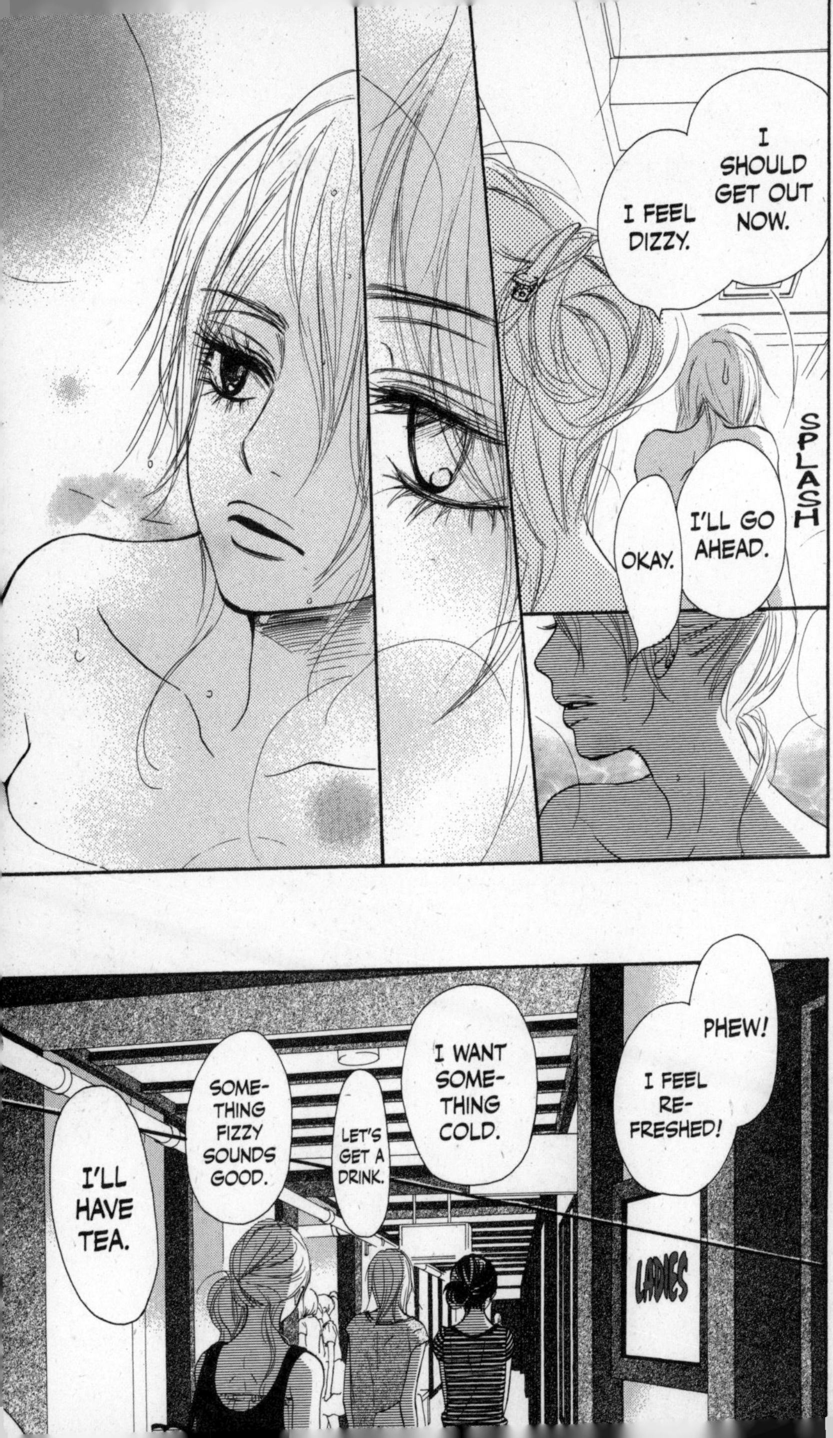
I SHOULD GET OUT NOW.
I FEEL DIZZY.
SPLASH
I'LL GO AHEAD.
OKAY.
PHEW!
I FEEL RE-FRESHED!
I WANT SOME-THING COLD.
LET'S GET A DRINK.
SOME-THING FIZZY SOUNDS GOOD.
I'LL HAVE TEA.
LADIES

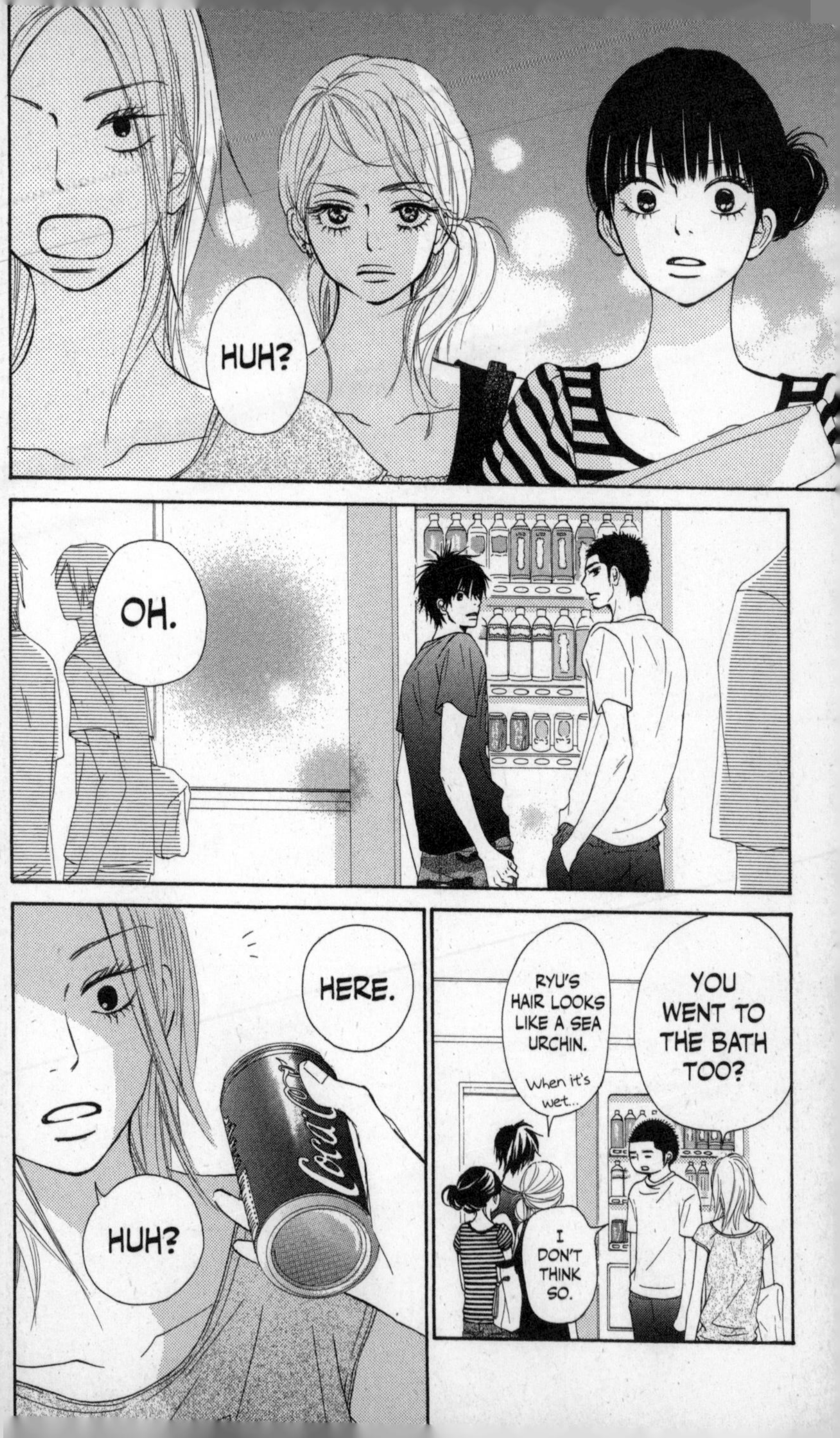
HUH?
OH.
YOU WENT TO THE BATH TOO?
RYU'S HAIR LOOKS LIKE A SEA URCHIN.
When it's wet...
I DON'T THINK SO.
HERE.
HUH?

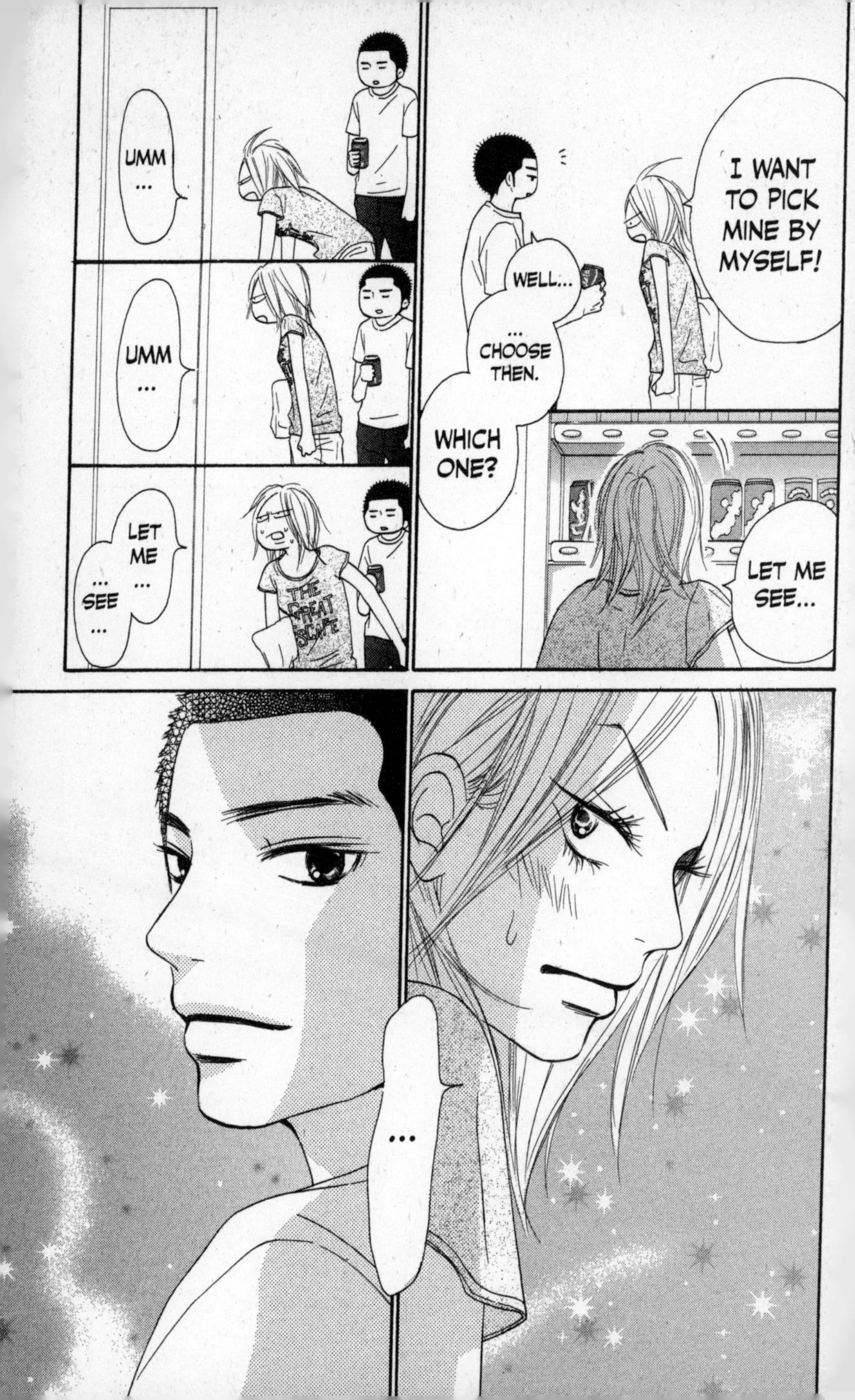
I WANT TO PICK MINE BY MYSELF!
WELL...
... CHOOSE THEN.
WHICH ONE?
LET ME SEE...
UMM ...
UMM ...
LET ME ... ... SEE ...
...

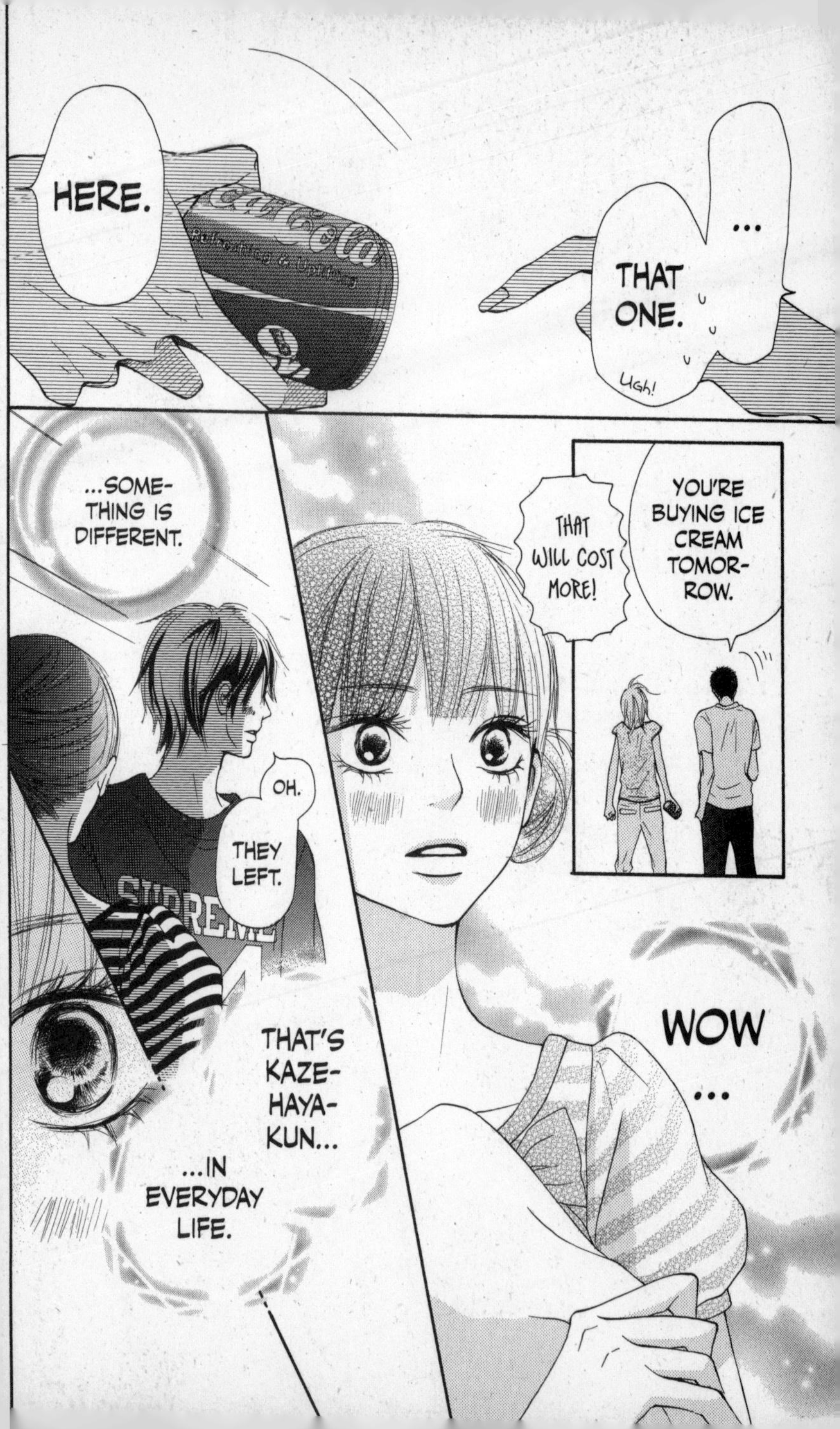
... THAT ONE.
Ugh!
HERE.
YOU'RE BUYING ICE CREAM TOMORROW.
THAT WILL COST MORE!
WOW ...
...SOMETHING IS DIFFERENT.
OH.
THEY LEFT.
THAT'S KAZEHAYA-KUN...
...IN EVERYDAY LIFE.

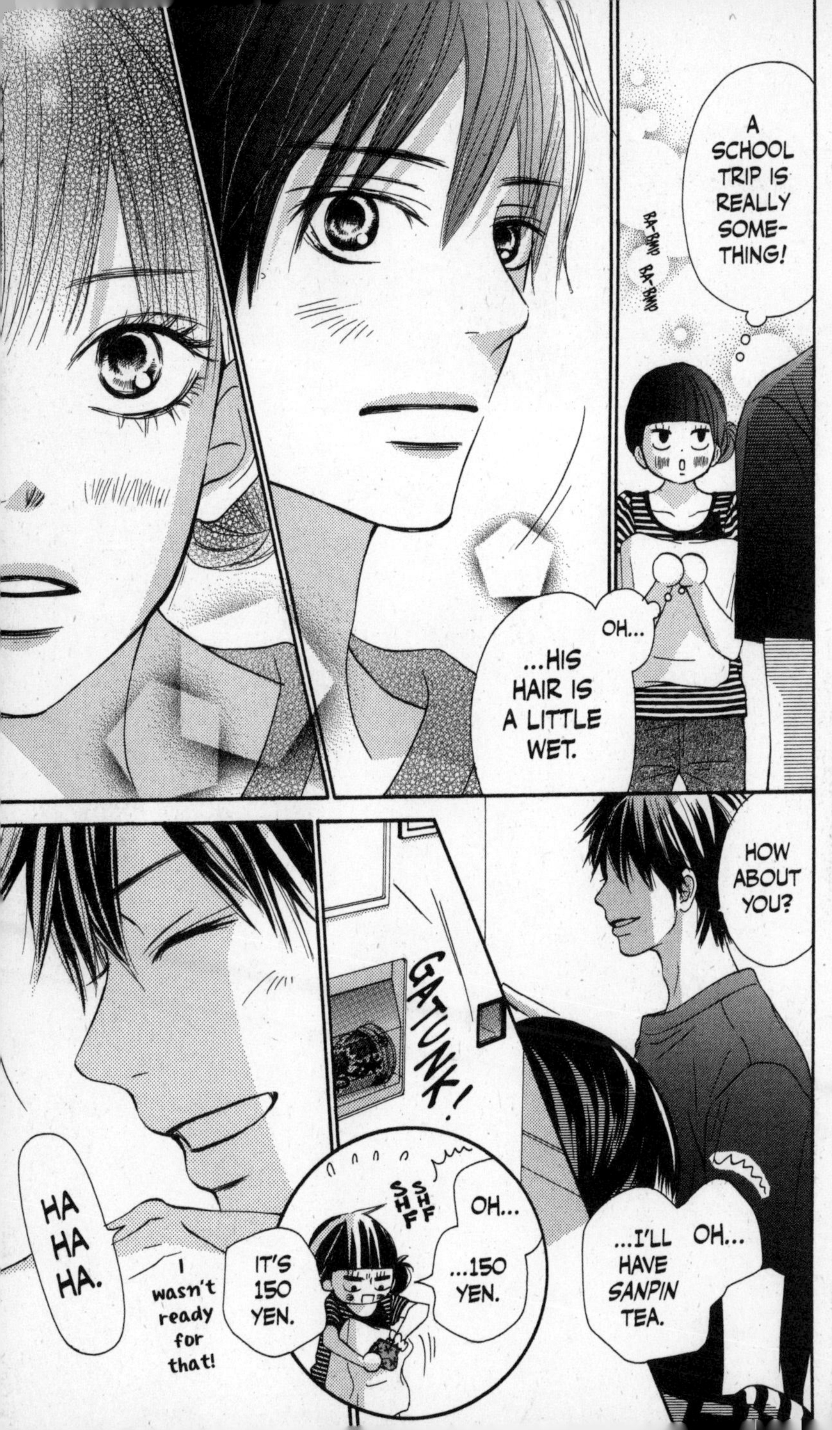
A SCHOOL TRIP IS REALLY SOMETHING!
BA-BMP BA-BMP
OH... ...HIS HAIR IS A LITTLE WET.
HOW ABOUT YOU?
OH... ...I'LL HAVE SANPIN TEA.
GATUNK!
OH... ...150 YEN.
SHF SHF
IT'S 150 YEN.
HA HA HA.
I wasn't ready for that!

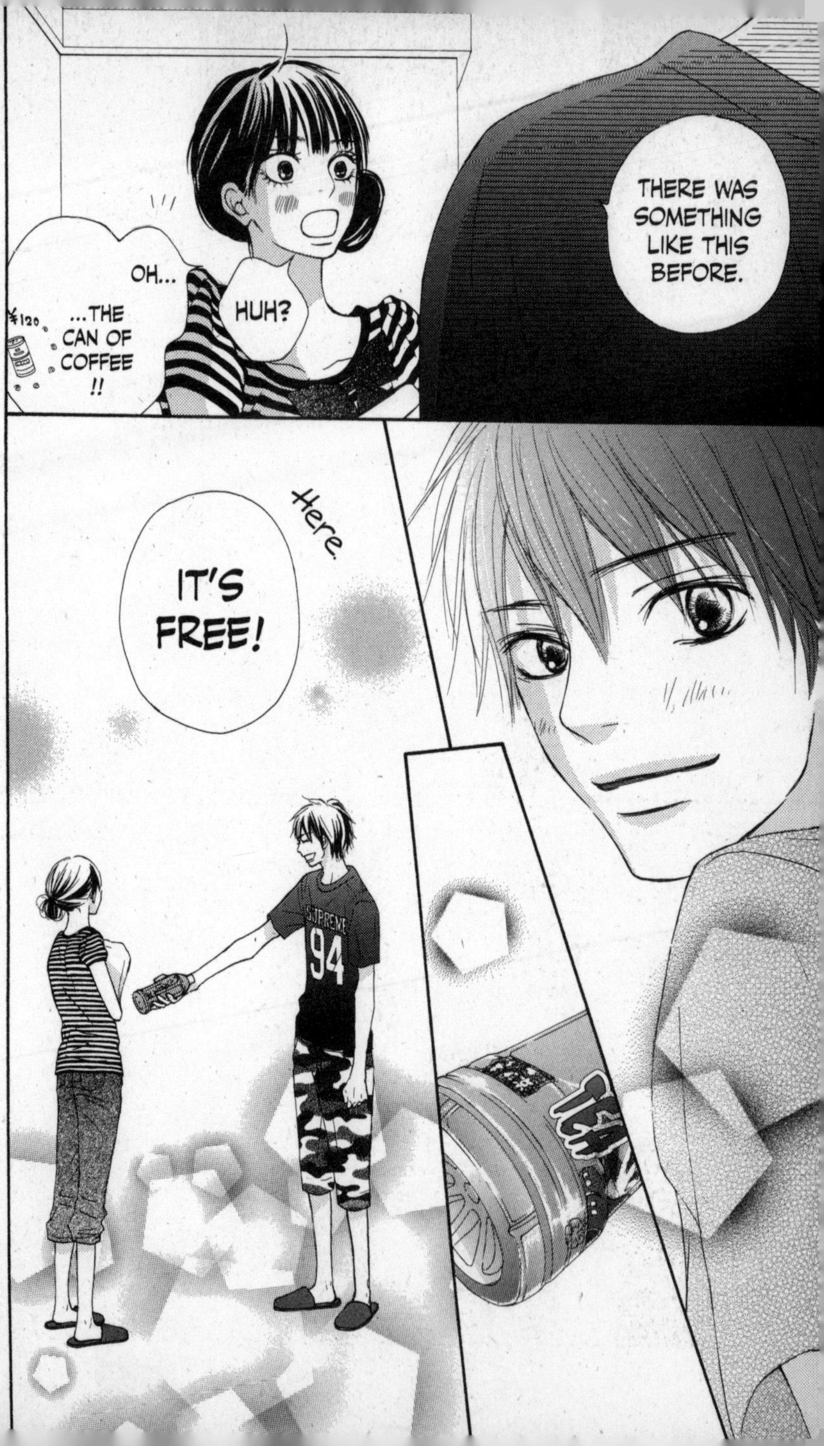
THERE WAS SOMETHING LIKE THIS BEFORE.
HUH?
OH...
...THE CAN OF COFFEE !!
¥120
Here.
IT'S FREE!

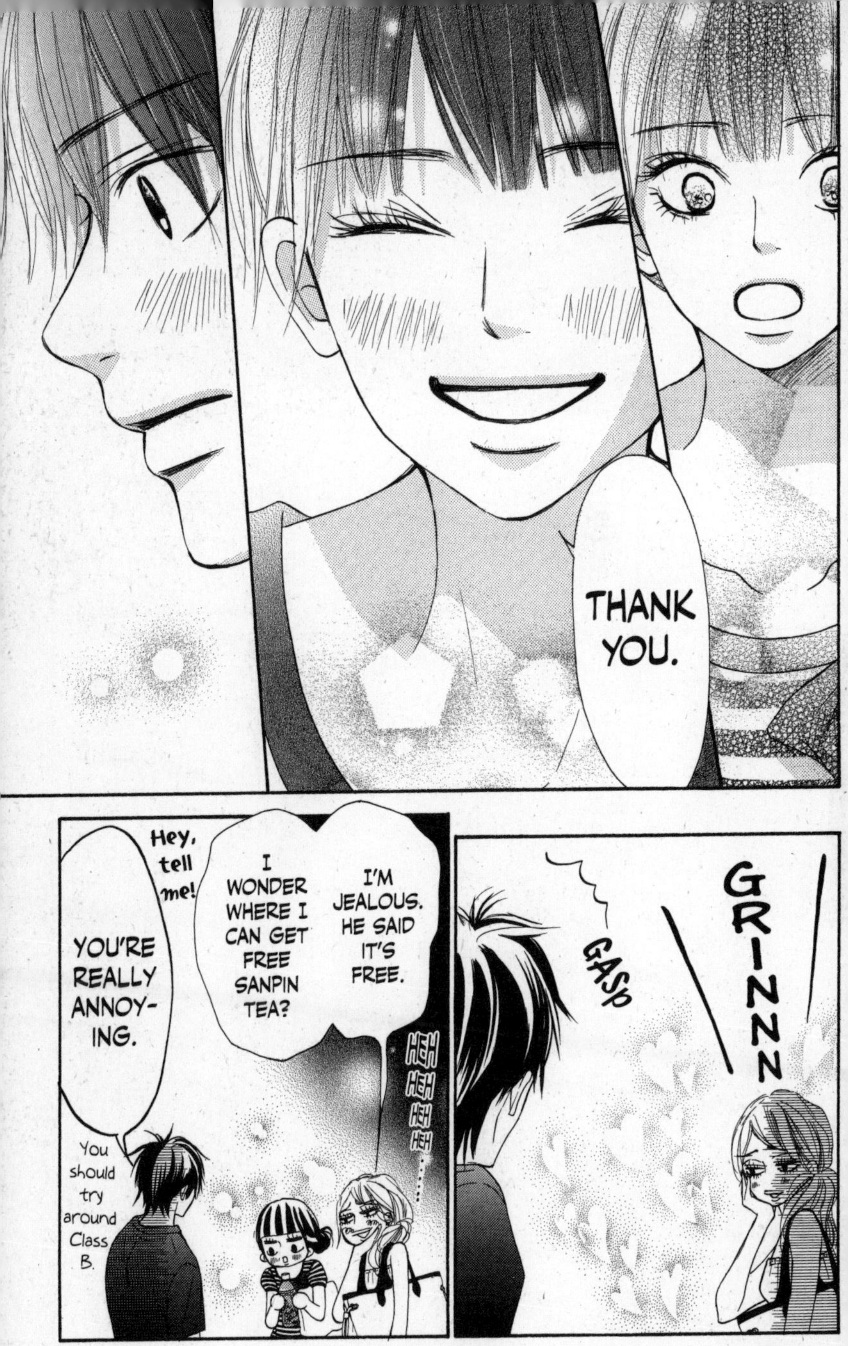
THANK YOU.
GRINNN
GASP
I'M JEALOUS. HE SAID IT'S FREE.
I WONDER WHERE I CAN GET FREE SANPIN TEA?
HEH HEH HEH HEH...
Hey, tell me!
YOU'RE REALLY ANNOY-ING.
You should try around Class B.

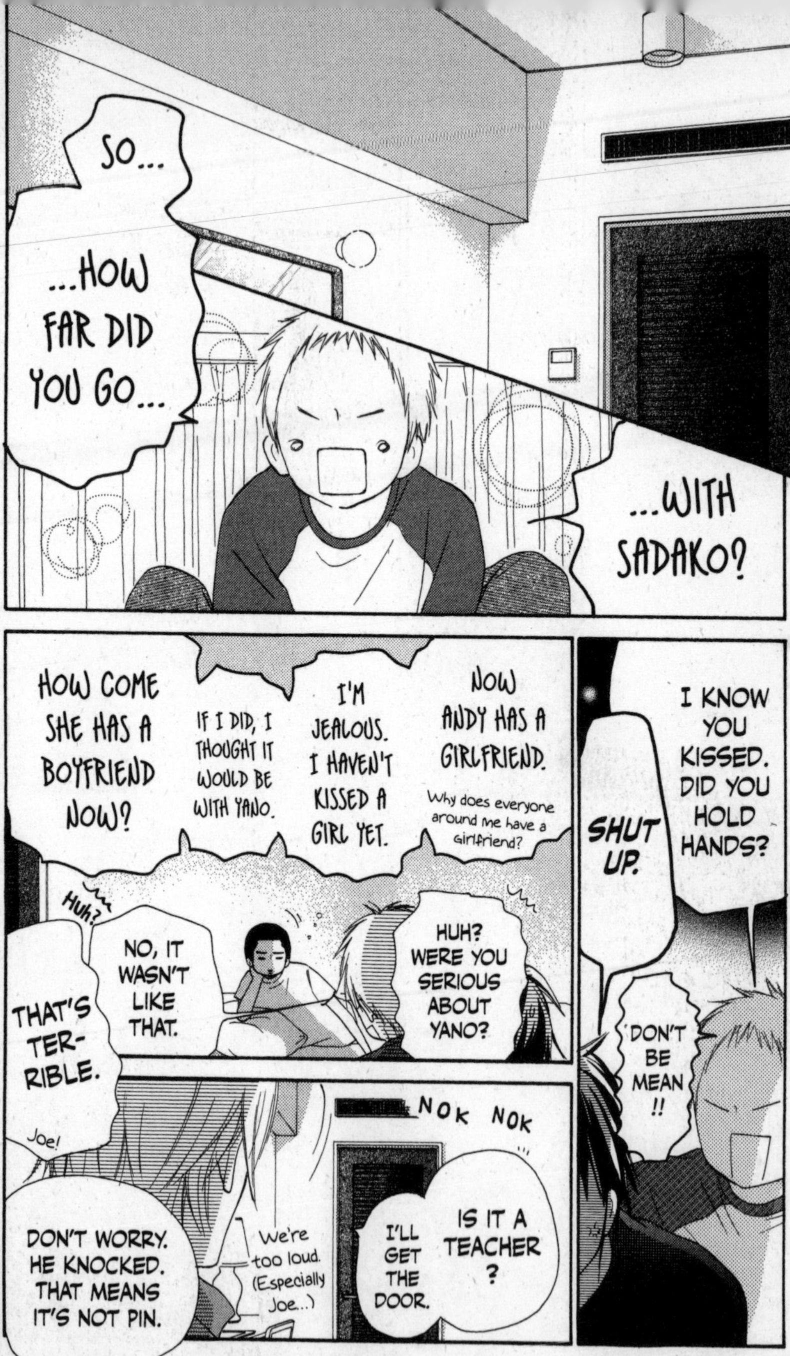
SO...
...HOW FAR DID YOU GO...
...WITH SADAKO?
I KNOW YOU KISSED. DID YOU HOLD HANDS?
SHUT UP.
DON'T BE MEAN!!
NOW ANDY HAS A GIRLFRIEND.
Why does everyone around me have a girlfriend?
I'M JEALOUS. I HAVEN'T KISSED A GIRL YET.
IF I DID, I THOUGHT IT WOULD BE WITH YANO.
HOW COME SHE HAS A BOYFRIEND NOW?
HUH? WERE YOU SERIOUS ABOUT YANO?
Huh?
NO, IT WASN'T LIKE THAT.
THAT'S TER-RIBLE.
NOK NOK
IS IT A TEACHER?
I'LL GET THE DOOR.
We're too loud. (Especially Joe...)
Joe!
DON'T WORRY. HE KNOCKED. THAT MEANS IT'S NOT PIN.

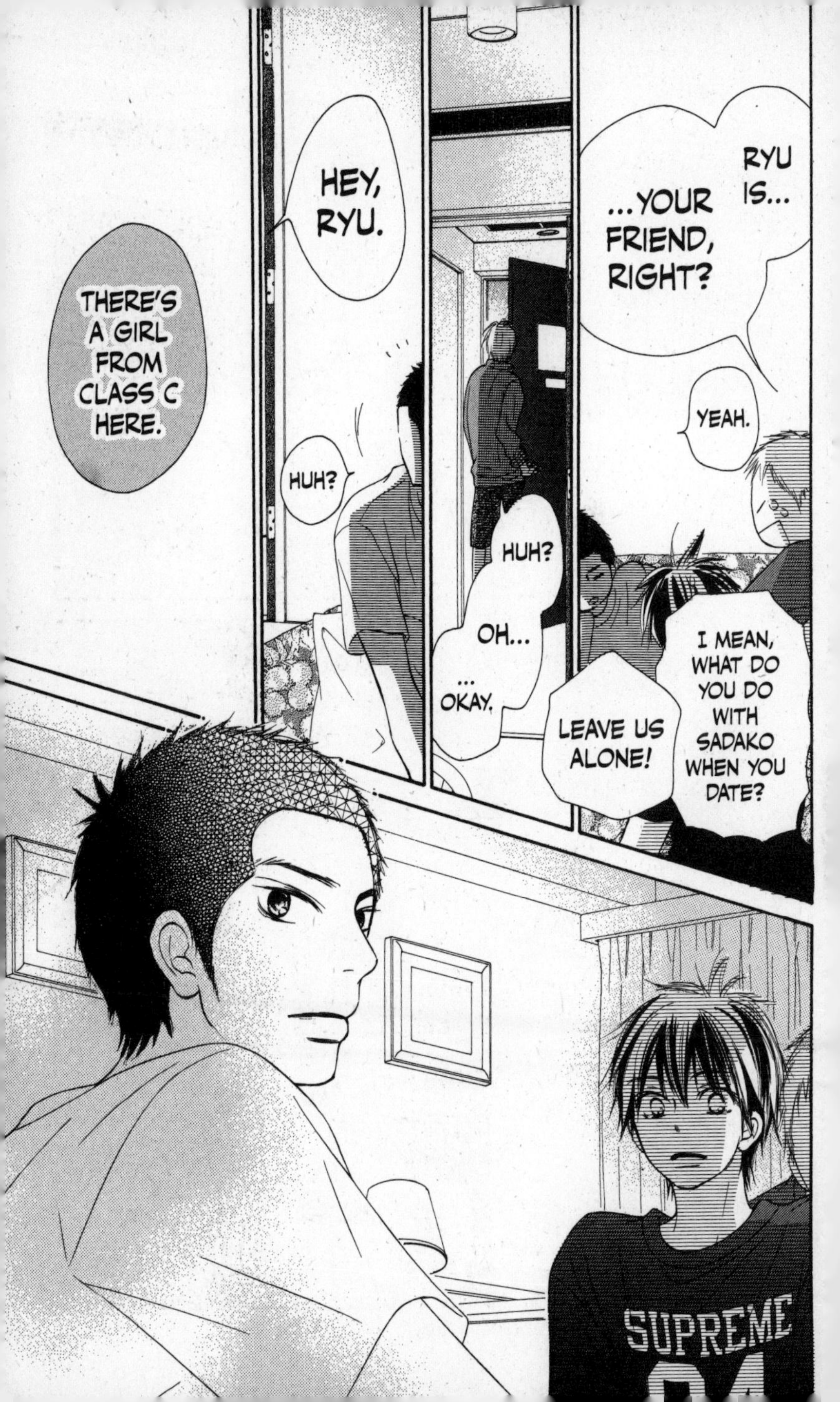
RYU IS... ...YOUR FRIEND, RIGHT?
YEAH.
I MEAN, WHAT DO YOU DO WITH SADAKO WHEN YOU DATE?
LEAVE US ALONE!
HUH?
OH...
... OKAY.
HEY, RYU.
HUH?
THERE'S A GIRL FROM CLASS C HERE.
SUPREME

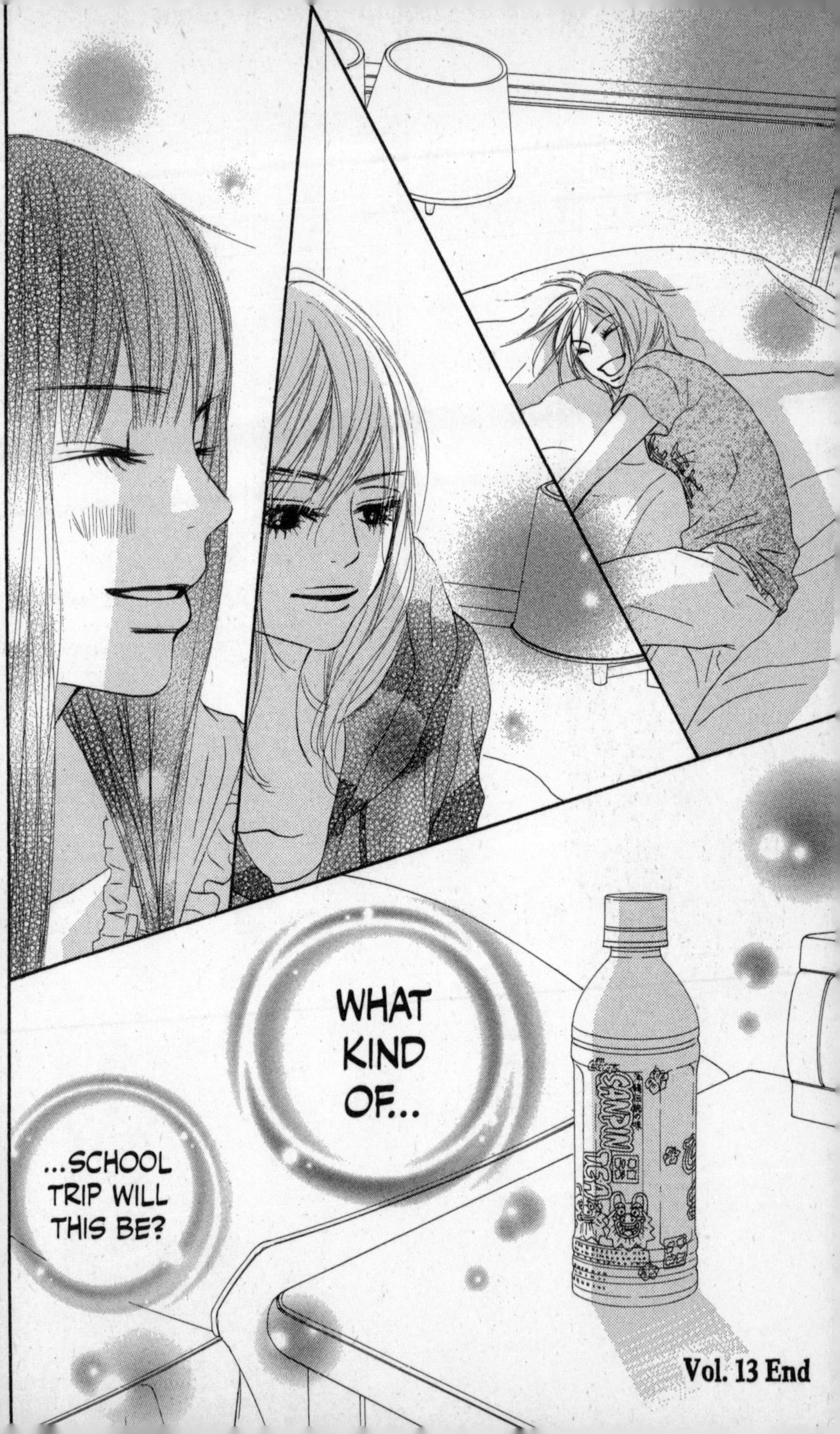
WHAT KIND OF...
...SCHOOL TRIP WILL THIS BE?
SANPIN TEA
Vol. 13 End

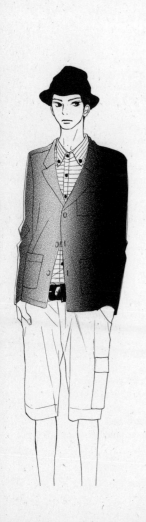

From me (the editor) to you (the reader).

Here are some Japanese culture explanations that will help you better understand the references in the *Kimi ni Todoke* world.

Honorifics:
When saying someone's name in Japanese, a suffix is often attached to indicate how familiar the speaker is with the person. Some are more polite and respectful, while others are endearing. Calling someone by just their first name is the most informal.
-kun is used for young men or boys, usually someone you are familiar with.
-chan is used for young women, girls or young children and can be used as a term of endearment.
-san is used for someone you respect or are not close to, or to be polite.

Page 23, Sapporo, Hokkaido:
Hokkaido is the northernmost and second-largest of the Japanese islands; Sapporo is the capital.

Page 31, oden:
Various foods stewed in a soy-based broth.

Page 51, Obon:
A summer Buddhist festival to honor one's ancestors.

Page 58, bending 90 degrees:
A 90-degree bow shows deep humility and respect.

Page 60, yokan:
A thick, jellied dessert made of red bean paste, agar and sugar, usually eaten in slices.

Page 67, bed:
Sawako notices that Kazehaya has a bed rather than a futon.

Page 101, ice manju:
Manju are sweets that come in many types, often with a red bean paste filling. Ice manju has ice cream inside.

Page 109, Okinawa:
An island chain in Japan's southernmost prefecture with a subtropical climate.

Page 110, shisa:
A popular type of statue in Okinawa used to ward off evil spirits; it looks like a cross between a dog and a lion.

Page 120, churadama:
Jewel-like balls often used for jewelry and trinkets in Okinawa.

Page 122, senpai:
An honorific used to address someone older or more experienced.

Page 125, Cat Bus:
An attraction at the Ghibli Museum, modeled after the character in Hayao Miyazaki's *My Neighbor Totoro*.

Page 163, sanpin tea:
A form of jasmine green tea popular in Okinawa.

Since the last cover was the Kuronuma family, I thought I would draw the Kazehaya family this time. But I thought the new characters should make their first appearance within the pages of the story, so I decided to show Shota as an older brother with his younger brother. The front cover is all about boys! It's fun to draw in full color, but also to do a picture in just one color. Yesterday, I finished drawing the cover illustration, so now I'm looking forward to seeing how many colors it will have!

--Karuho Shiina

Karuho Shiina was born and raised in Hokkaido, Japan. Though *Kimi ni Todoke* is only her second series following many one-shot stories, it has already racked up accolades from various "Best Manga of the Year" lists. Winner of the 2008 Kodansha Manga Award for the shojo category, *Kimi ni Todoke* also placed fifth in the first-ever Manga Taisho (Cartoon Grand Prize) contest in 2008. In Japan, an animated TV series debuted in October 2009, and a live-action film was released in 2010.

Kimi ni Todoke
VOL. 13

Shojo Beat Edition

STORY AND ART BY
KARUHO SHIINA

Translation/Ari Yasuda, HC Language Solutions, Inc.
Touch-up Art & Lettering/Vanessa Satone
Design/Nozomi Akashi
Editor/Carrie Shepherd

KIMI NI TODOKE © 2005 by Karuho Shiina.
All rights reserved. First published in Japan in 2005 by SHUEISHA Inc.,
Tokyo. English translation rights arranged by SHUEISHA Inc.

Printed in Canada

Published by VIZ Media, LLC
P.O. Box 77010
San Francisco, CA 94107

10 9 8 7 6 5 4 3 2 1
First printing, March 2012

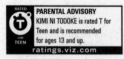

PARENTAL ADVISORY
KIMI NI TODOKE is rated T for
Teen and is recommended
for ages 13 and up.
ratings.viz.com

www.viz.com

www.shojobeat.com

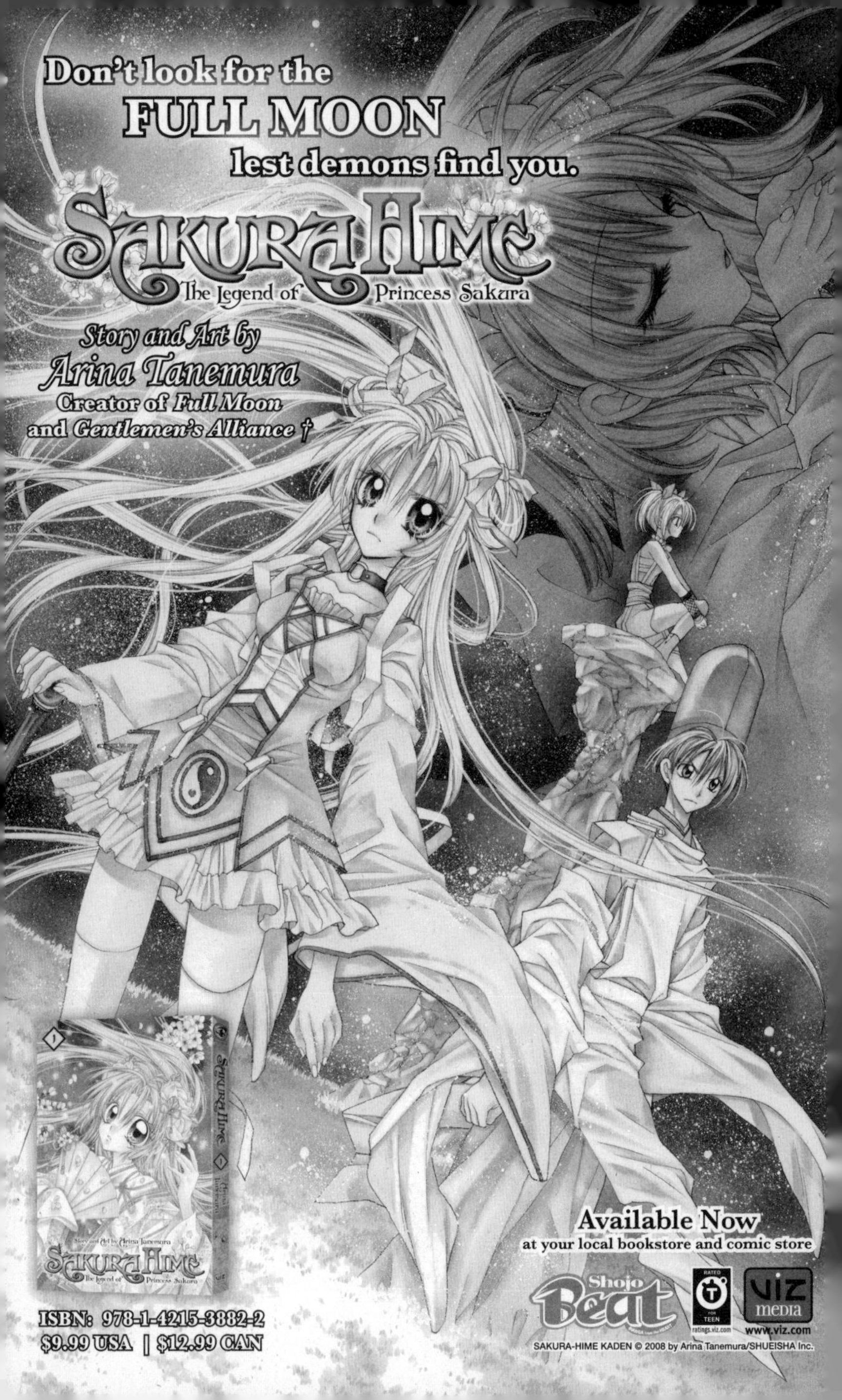
Don't look for the
FULL MOON
lest demons find you.
SAKURA HIME
The Legend of Princess Sakura
Story and Art by
Arina Tanemura
Creator of Full Moon
and Gentlemen's Alliance †
Available Now
at your local bookstore and comic store
ISBN: 978-1-4215-3882-2
$9.99 USA | $12.99 CAN
Shojo Beat
RATED T FOR TEEN
ratings.viz.com
VIZ media
www.viz.com
SAKURA-HIME KADEN © 2008 by Arina Tanemura/SHUEISHA Inc.

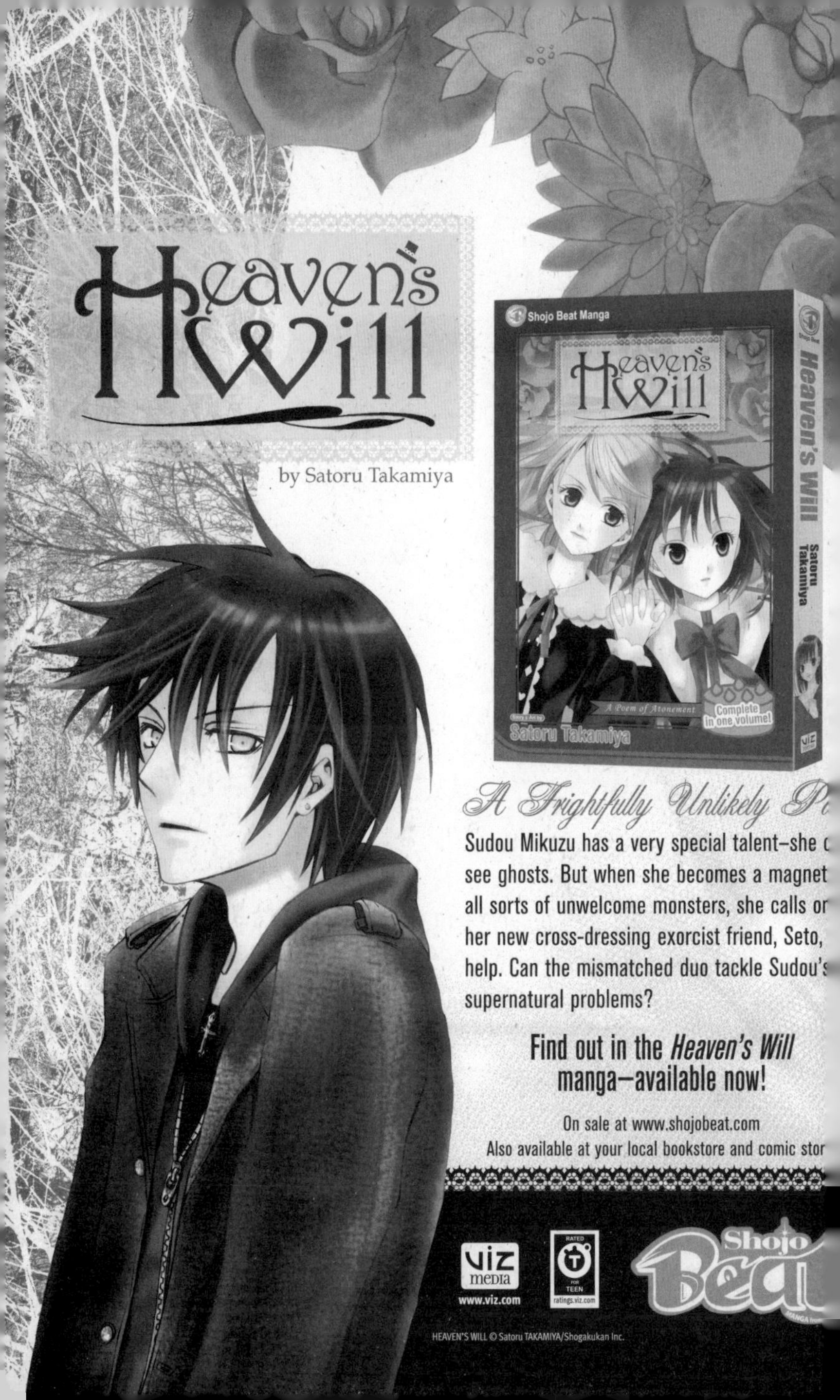
Heaven's Will
by Satoru Takamiya
Shojo Beat Manga
Heaven's Will
A Poem of Atonement
Complete in one volume!
Story & Art by Satoru Takamiya
Heaven's Will Satoru Takamiya
A Frightfully Unlikely Pa
Sudou Mikuzu has a very special talent—she c
see ghosts. But when she becomes a magnet
all sorts of unwelcome monsters, she calls or
her new cross-dressing exorcist friend, Seto,
help. Can the mismatched duo tackle Sudou's
supernatural problems?
Find out in the Heaven's Will manga—available now!
On sale at www.shojobeat.com
Also available at your local bookstore and comic stor
VIZ media
www.viz.com
RATED T FOR TEEN
ratings.viz.com
Shojo Beat
HEAVEN'S WILL © Satoru TAKAMIYA/Shogakukan Inc.

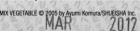